THIS BOOK BELONGS TO:-
LLOYD KNECHTEL

THE DEFENSE
NEVER RESTS

60 YEARS IN CANADA
19 33
19 93
HarperCollins

THE DEFENSE
NEVER RESTS

Bruce Dowbiggin

HarperCollins*Publishers*Ltd

"Lest We Forget" by George Gross, printed
with permission from the author.

Endsheets photograph courtesy of Don Newlands.

First Edition

Canadian Cataloguing in Publication Data

Dowbiggin, Bruce
The defense never rests

Includes bibliography and index.
ISBN 0-00-255065-2

1. Toronto Maple Leafs (Hockey team) — History.
2. Hockey — Defense.
3. Hockey players — Canada — Biography.
I. Title.

GV848.T6D69 1993   796.962'64'09713541   C93-093692-2

93 94 95 96 97 98 99 ❖ EB 10 9 8 7 6 5 4 3 2 1

To Meredith, Evan, Rhys and Clare—
the home-ice advantage

CONTENTS

ACKNOWLEDGMENTS

Every time I review my notes for this book, I'm struck by what wonderful interview subjects hockey people make. In comparison with the athletes in other sports, hockey folk are civility incarnate. I don't have any particular explanation for this phenomenon; some might make the leap of faith and call it a Canadian quality, but I have interviewed enough Canadians in other fields to know this is not so. I can only thank the nature of the game that it has produced people such as Susan Foster and Carl Brewer, Allan Stanley, Bob Baun and Lori Horton, who shared so generously of their memories and their struggles for this book. They always had a steamer trunk or a photo album or a phone number to share when it was most needed. They enriched my life; I hope I have done justice to their stories.

Legends take time to root sometimes, so to Rich Winter, who with Sue and Carl kept a light burning in the darkness, I hope the future brings you the good things you have earned. Thanks to Eddie and Norma Shack, Andy Bathgate, Colleen and Gordie Howe, and Bobby Hull, who stood up when others fell back—and to the men and women who supported them with time and money.

And this book would have been much diminished without the friendship and expertise of Lorraine Mahoney and her fine staff at Allan Smart Services in Toronto. Also to the many, many others in hockey—the players, the fans, the agents, the managers—who took the time to search their good and bad memories for the book. Hockey is a repository of a million good stories and, thanks to people such as Ron Joyce, Eddie Litzenberger and Harry Neale, I was privy to some of the best.

I would also like to thank Mark Zigler, Ed Ferren, George Donaldson, Bill Dermody, Danny Henry and Gordon Black for steering me through the intricacies of pension law and the judicial process. Likewise to Bob Goodenow, Ed Garvey, Marvin Miller, the staff at the Ontario Archives and Michael Levine for their guidance and support in realizing this project amidst my many conflicting duties.

Let me not forget my friend and the inspiration for my best work: Russ Conway, who blazed the trails and always had time to talk and share; and to Alison Griffiths and David Cruise, whose generosity, courage and advice allowed me to build upon the base they'd started in *Net Worth*.

On another front, I am grateful for the cooperation of my employers at the CBC, who have allowed me to pursue a complicated and seemingly endless project. A special thanks to Bill Kendrick for his friendship and counsel in the production of some of this material for CBC Toronto. Enjoy the island.

Very kind thanks as well to the folks at HarperCollins in Toronto; Iris Skeoch, who believed in the project; Phyllis Bruce, my patient editor; Tom Best, for his many good ideas and encouragements; and everyone else in the editorial and sales staff who helped a first author survive the process.

Enduring thanks and love to my patient family, Meredith and Evan, Rhys and Clare, who allowed me space and time to work on this project in the midst of their lives. As well, thanks to my parents and the entire far-flung Dowbiggin clan for not sawing off my branch of the family tree when things got stressful. (Now you'll all want copies, I suppose.) Family is where all good things began for me, and this book is an extension of that support and love of learning I received from a young age.

You cannot ask for a better ride on a first book than I received.

Bruce Dowbiggin,
September 1993

1

ACER SACCHARINUM

"Some cheered him home, but not as crowds cheer Goal.
Only a solemn man who brought him fruits
Thanked him; and then inquired about his soul."

—Wilfred Owen

Frankly, I grew up hating the Toronto Maple Leafs. I blame this pathological loathing on Colin Campbell, the schoolyard ferret who believed that Punch Imlach should be venerated, that captain George Armstrong ought to be invested as Governor General and that Toronto was hockey's Mecca. Campbell, who reminded me daily of the Leafs' achievements—which were many in my school days. Campbell, who symbolized the hijacking of the Stanley Cup by unworthies. Campbell, the only Leafs fan on the West Island of Montreal.

The Leafs had boring uniforms, I explained to Campbell, while dropping him headfirst into a snowbank. They had a bald coach who looked more like a funeral director than a hockey genius. And Maple Leaf Gardens—where ladies wore mink and men never threw toe-rubbers on the ice—the Gardens had all the appeal of a fallout shelter.

In my little-boy hockey world, I loathed everything about the Maple Leafs, but nothing more than their success.

At night, when the greatest players in the world would skate through my bedroom in Montreal, I willed the Leafs to lose. Under my spell, Johnny Bower couldn't stop a basketball, Carl Brewer and Bob Baun skated as if their laces had been tied together, Dave Keon shot only blanks. The universe was pure and perfect then, and the view was as crystal clear as the ice at the Forum on Saturday night where *Les Canadiens* always scored a late goal to win.

Reality was something altogether different. The Maple Leafs cut a swath through my childhood, winning four Stanley Cups at a time when such things were a matter of life and death in the schoolyard the next day. They dominated the turbulent decade of the 1960s that saw this nation emerge from its self-imposed torpor. In the midst of the sound and the fury, the FLQ and Expo 67, the Leafs seemed a great blue reminder of where we had been, not where we were going.

In Montreal, where the fortunes of *Les Glorieux* are both sacred and profane, where winning supersedes everything, including politics ... even in Montreal, the most colorful, artistic team could not surpass the Leafs' record of Stanley Cups in the '60s.

Chicago, led by the glorious Bobby Hull and teammates like Stan Mikita and Glenn Hall, saw the top prize only once. Bobby Orr, hockey's Picasso, led Boston to only one Cup. And the Detroit Red Wings of Gordie Howe, the Ulysses of the sport, ended the decade without once winning and thereby satisfying me, their greatest fan.

At the zenith of the pre-expansion NHL, in the days of the "Original Six," stood this team without sex appeal, this team with a flair only for winning. There was something blue-collar about the Leafs. Poets were remarkably unmoved by "Punch Imlach at the Gate;" songwriters were stymied by the possibilities of a ballad to Dave Keon. The biggest fan of the team was comedian Johnny Wayne, who fell several leagues short of John "The Duke" Wayne in importance.

Peter Gzowski summed up the Maple Leafs of the era in an article in a 1964 *Maclean's* magazine. "Most of the Leaf players simply don't *appear* to enjoy the game quite as much as the other teams in the league," he wrote. "There's a doggedness about their play; they forecheck ferociously; they knock a lot of people down at the blue line, and they grab and hold a lot more people in front of the goalmouth. They seem to be a group of men getting a job done."

This lack of the heroic did not discourage my schoolyard nemesis, Colin Campbell, however. He continued to replay the salient moments of recent Toronto history in the high-pitched, nasal bark of play-by-play man Bill Hewitt—the homer's homer to enemies of the Leafs: "There's the bell and the game is OVER!" Someone always silenced the Campbell/Hewitt monologues with a snowball, ending, however briefly, the annoyance. But if we could silence Campbell in the schoolyard, then why couldn't the other teams in the NHL squash this team of grinders and muckers and bottle-washers on the ice?

While the Montreal Forum was decorated like a shrine, Maple Leaf Gardens looked like an oversized Canadian Legion Hall, with its portrait of the Queen, its Union Jacks and its rows of fans fed on roast beef and Yorkshire pudding. Hockey at the Forum was High Mass while games at the Gardens in the '50s and '60s seemed more like Vespers attended by the faithful. Even after we got color TV, the Gardens seemed black-and-white.

Such color as the team had was injected by its crusty patriarch, Major Conn Smythe, a man who viewed hockey as a muzzle and players as bullets to be properly loaded and expended. Games were not entertainment but battles to be won in hand-to-hand combat by young men from mining towns in the north and farm hamlets on the Prairies. Smythe loved a good scrap in everything but labor negotiations, where he always insisted on holding the upper hand.

In Montreal, the flashier a player, the better he was loved. The masked marvel, Jacques Plante, who revolutionized the art of goaltending with his wandering and his thespian turns, was the darling of the galleries in the '50s and '60s as he led the Habs to five Stanley Cups. But Plante's reviews in no-nonsense Toronto were less than glowing. "Highly overrated," sniffed radio man Joe Morgan of CKFH (which called itself "radio for grown-ups") as Plante rose slowly from a big save. "He milks every second of it, getting up on one knee, then the other, always looking terribly pained ... as if he'd been riddled with a mess of buckshot, while the Forum crowd yell their heads off, either in sympathy or perhaps because they think it's the reincarnation of one of Sarah Bernhardt's great death scenes."

In the Montreal of my youth, there was a sense of place, of exuberance, the promise of Expo 67 in the Paris of North America. Montreal was slightly dangerous and more than a little risqué. The music scene was daring on Crescent Street or over at Rockheads for jazz. People went to Montreal on holidays.

Toronto was "Leave It To Beaver" at 7:00 p.m. on channel 9, followed by "Sing Along With Mitch" and then "Peter Gunn." A wild night consisted of dinner at the Stoodleigh Restaurant ("famous for roast beef and apple pie") and then a cocktail at the Ports of Call. You could catch a show headed for Broadway at the O'Keefe Centre, but jazz was cautious—"Hawk Swings, Rollins—Ugh," pronounced *The Toronto Star*'s cutting-edge critic in 1964.

In the opinion of Montrealers who gazed from 350 miles away down Highway 401, Toronto was a nice place to live, but you wouldn't want to visit there.

And yet, somehow Toronto and the Maple Leafs crawled into the modern age, becoming the last great hockey team—hell, the last *team* of any description—that the Baby Boomers of southern Ontario would call their own. Imagine music ending with the Beatles, architecture terminating with the Toronto-Dominion Centre, fashion with Lester Pearson and his bow tie, politics with "the Chief," John Diefenbaker.

That is the legacy of the Leafs of the '60s to a vast generation of young men and women. When Torontonians in their thirties and forties mention their favorite Leafs players, they speak of men who haven't laced up a boot in twenty-five years. The great ones like Dave Keon, Frank Mahovlich, Johnny Bower ... the characters like Eddie "The Entertainer" Shack ... even the journeymen like Larry Hillman and Don Simmons are still better recognized than the legion of men who have worn the blue and white since.

Today, when the greying veterans of the teams of the '60s gather to sign autographs or play golf for charity, they remain a group locked in a time capsule, captives of that day in April 1967 when they spilled over the boards to celebrate their upset win over the Montreal Canadiens and their last Stanley Cup. They are a period piece, like sensible shoes that never go out of fashion.

The intervening seasons since 1967 have witnessed a procession of teams too terrible to document, too inept for description, too colorless for concern. "There's only been one superstar in the past twenty-five years," says Carl Brewer. "It's not Darryl Sittler or Lanny McDonald. It's Harold Ballard. He had to make himself bigger than the players."

Ballard gained control of the Maple Leafs shortly after their last Stanley Cup, and he held them in a death grip for a quarter-century. There were two constants in Ballard's administration of the team: losing and controversy. "The press and the public vie with each other in attacking him," noted Ken Dryden in his book *The Game*, written at the height of Ballard's power, "...then pause to praise his charitable generosity or his devotion to his late wife (maybe we've got him all wrong?); then, like a wrestling villain who touches an audience to make his next villainy seem worse, he does something or says something to start up the cycle again."

The cycle continued till the last moment Ballard drew breath on this earth, and it trampled many people, not the least of whom were the players who'd worn the blue and white with distinction in the 1960s. For years they were ignored or shunned by "the Baron of Bluster," unwelcome guests rather than returning heroes when they came to Maple Leaf Gardens. With the disappearance of household names like Keon and Stanley and Baun, a large part of hockey interest followed into hockey limbo, waiting for Ballard's demise to break the spell.

"You were forgotten, especially in Toronto," remembers Norma Shack, wife of Eddie Shack. "They didn't care; you were gone, expendable."

As a result, a generation who grew up on the shores of Lakes Ontario and Erie have become baseball fans, filling the SkyDome to watch their beloved Blue Jays—their rented Americans and Dominicans and Puerto Ricans.

Unlike the Maple Leafs of the 1960s, who lived and worked year-round in the community, the Blue Jays have little pride of place and history, nor do they care to acquire any. As Toronto celebrated the Jays' World Series triumph in 1992, some star players were already on their way to the airport before the end of the rally thrown for them by adoring fans. Blue Jays players hole up in the SkyDome Hotel or rented apartments, rarely emerging to walk among their fans. On any given day in the 1950s or '60s, however, you might actually catch a glimpse of your favorite hockey players on the streets of Toronto or in the places they worked in the off-season. The Maple Leafs were of and about the city of Toronto.

If the Leafs teams of the 1960s had a core, a central nervous system, then it was made up of the men who formed the defense, men like Bob Baun, Carl Brewer, Allan Stanley and the late Tim Horton. The quartet—Horton paired with Stanley and Baun matched with Brewer—stayed intact for an astounding seven seasons and was fundamental to the success of the team under Punch Imlach.

"That group of four defensemen was the best defense combo you'll ever see in two pairs," asserts Baun. "The Canadiens of the '50s and '70s had three great players on defense, but not four. That group of four defensemen had all your hockey abilities."

"Year in, year out, they were the best four defensemen in the League," remarks Eddie Litzenberger, who played against and with the Leafs' defense dynasty.

They were the pride of the Maple Leafs for almost a decade, the bane of opposing forwards, whom they alternately mugged or mesmerized. They played through pain and disappointment and the personal problems that afflict us all. They played under labor conditions that bordered on the sweatshop. And they did it all with dignity. When they had finally outlived their usefulness to the Toronto Maple Leafs, they drifted away or were traded. The press found new heroes to extol; the fans discovered fresh faces to carry their hopes.

But the stories of these four men were merely in mid-sentence, a half-developed thought, when hockey ended and real life began. Ironically, the stoic, dutiful Leafs of my boyhood became something entirely different in retirement. Led by Baun, Brewer and Stanley, the men forged by the iron will of Conn Smythe, my boyhood antagonists, rebelled against the system that created them. With Gordie Howe, Bobby Hull, Eddie Shack, Andy Bathgate and Leo Reise, they tried to create a collective consciousness that was denied them when they played.

"It's good [the players] are standing up for their rights," says Howe. "If we had the guts and know-how back then, we should have done the same darn thing, but we didn't. Many of us were uneducated. We didn't realize how little we were making. You'd go in and ask for a raise and they would tell you that four guys could replace you."

Through their lawsuit against the NHL over mishandling of pension funds and their challenging of former NHL Players' Association executive director Alan Eagleson, they lustily bit the hand that so thoroughly held them down for years. And they warned the younger generations: never again. "As I say to the young guys today, they're in virtually the same box we were twenty years ago," says Baun. "The guys are still brainwashed by the owners. They can't say anything, they're afraid ... if we don't find out what's wrong, well, geez, we've got a problem."

"These guys couldn't care what the salaries are," says Stanley. "They're not interested in improving the pension ... they're in the same position as I was. They're going to understand this thing in twenty or thirty years."

The story of these regenerated Leafs is not always a romantic, happily-ever-after saga. When they took off their costumes and once again became mere mortals, they were men with mortgages and creaky joints and bad marriages. Perhaps for that reason their story has gone largely untold.

The Defense Never Rests is a story of retribution and self-revelation, the private exorcism of these very public men. Most had to be pushed a considerable distance before they would tell their problems to the world. Complaining was not in their nature. But neither was turning away from a fight. For that, at least, they can thank Conn Smythe.

So here they are, in all their glory and their ignominy. Colin Campbell might not recognize them now. Men, their wives, their children, who spent a lifetime in the eye of the sports storm, and who won the battle against the NHL by defeating a more formidable foe first ... themselves.

2

THE DECIDING GAME

"One of the things that I'm particularly proud of is that hockey players, including stars, are usually at the bargaining table. They are making sacrifices in the present for the future. That's the legacy they are passing on because it may be nine or ten years before all the fruits are realized and their careers will be over. But these young men love hockey."

—NHL president John A. Ziegler, Jr.,
April 6, 1989

The Ontario Provincial Courthouse sits like Parnassus at the midpoint of University Avenue in Toronto. Along University's broad expanse lie grand hospitals, sleek hotels and gleaming business towers. At the head of the tree-lined boulevard sits the Victorian elegance of Queen's Park, the Ontario Legislature. The U.S. Consulate is also on University, a Jack Webb, just-the-facts-ma'am edifice right across from the courthouse. The professionals and business people who work on University are a very serious crowd.

This is Toronto as Toronto wishes to see itself: imposing, serious, wealthy. In truth, the real Toronto is a city unsure of its place in the world, a town wrapped in a big city. A town that believes a big stadium, a big tower, will make it "world class." If Toronto were bald, it would wear a wig. No ... it would get plugs! University Avenue at least gives Toronto a hairline.

On the sunny morning of June 9, 1992, the friends of Croatia toted banners and shouted slogans at the cold, grey walls of the consulate.

"Remember Serbian Genocide," the signs implored. "CBC Ignores Struggle of Croatian People," read another. The protesters were preoccupied with events in Split and Sarajevo, not with the goings-on across University Avenue at the courthouse, where the burglars, bad-cheque artists and homicidal maniacs were taking second billing for a change.

A collection of middle-aged gentlemen in sport coats and suits—their faces worn, their hair greying—lined the halls of the Ontario Provincial Courthouse that late-spring morning. Salesmen and travel agents and accountants and retirees with their wives, they constituted a thoroughly unremarkable group in all respects but one: their unspoken bond in the past.

For those unassuming gentlemen were once hockey talents so gifted, so extraordinary, that most Canadians cannot think of their national sport without conjuring up at least a few of their names. At one time, crowds twenty deep flooded into the streets to celebrate their Stanley Cup triumphs. Once—when life and circumstance were simpler—their deeds transcended sport and became myth in this country.

Frank Mahovlich, Red Kelly, Andy Bathgate, Carl Brewer, Ted Lindsay, Allan Stanley—they made the stroll from University Avenue to Courtroom C-8 on the second floor as if it were the well-worn trek from the dressing rooms to the ice surface at Maple Leaf Gardens. In the glory days, hockey fans from coast to coast cheered them as they stepped on the ice in their uniforms with the maple leaf of Toronto, the winged wheel of Detroit, the bold tricolor of Montreal displayed on their chests. They were the stars of Saturday night to a generation raised on TV. Twenty-five years later, dressed in the uniform of middle age, the only sound to be heard was the echo of their steps on the marble floor. The residue of their once-considerable fame was modest.

Two autograph hounds hovered on the periphery, brandishing player cards printed long before they were born. The taller one wore a brand-new Ottawa Senators jersey. His long-haired sidekick wore a Mickey Mouse cartoon T-shirt and shifted anxiously from foot to foot. "Is that the Big M? Is Gordie coming today?" he asked his partner.

The lucre of collectibles, not the lustre of accomplishment, had drawn these rink rats to the courthouse. A signed rookie card of Frank Mahovlich might be worth serious money at the card shows. If these entrepreneurs thought of hockey at all it was of Pat Burns, the newly signed coach of the Maple Leafs, or Mario Lemieux, who had led the Pittsburgh Penguins to their second consecutive Stanley Cup just days before. For the most part, these old guys at the courthouse were just names on a checklist.

The souvenir hounds had not even been born in the sensational season of 1960-61 when "the Big M" scored forty-eight goals and "Boom Boom" Geoffrion hit the magic fifty. They had no way of knowing the grace of eight-time All-Star Red Kelly in his prime, the speed and skill of the young Carl Brewer, the ferocious drive of "Terrible" Ted Lindsay as he burst in on goal with Gordie Howe on his wing.

In the days of the NHL's "Original Six," men like Kelly and Brewer and Lindsay and Howe scored, skated, slashed, hacked, punched and kicked their way to fame. In doing so, they made the NHL extremely rich and very powerful. The NHL remained rich and powerful on this June morning, but the fame the players had purchased with their blood and muscle wasn't cutting much slack with their bank managers or credit officers when mortgages matured. And riches? The lasting debt the NHL owed to them for their courage and skill was now overdue at compound interest.

These legendary stars were on the final leg of an odyssey, headed for a showdown with their former employers, the National Hockey League. This time, they would play without cheering crowds or television cameras. But the stakes had never been higher. The players were looking for almost $50 million from the League, coincidentally the going rate for a new NHL franchise like the Ottawa Senators or Tampa Bay Lightning. Fifty million dollars may be chump change in the world of big-time sports of the 1990s, but it represented a lifetime to the band of men and women filing into the benches of Courtroom C-8.

Years of friendly cajoling and earnest letter-writing to the NHL over their pension plan had produced only lip service and vague promises that led nowhere. Players once worshipped by the Canadian public couldn't get their phone calls answered after they had hung up their skates. In utter frustration, they were now turning to the courts—the iron fist in the velvet glove—to balance accounts.

For years, the players had hoped to avoid this drastic step with their old employers. "Maybe I'm too simple and from Saskatchewan," said Gordie Howe as he reflected on the chain of events, "but I say, let their men get together with our men and decide who's right or wrong ... if we're wrong, we shake their hands, say we're sorry and leave. But if they're wrong ... we'd like our money back."

It didn't work out that way. As the retired stars trooped into the courtroom, the time for handshakes was past. The NHL had dropped its gloves; the players had been challenged. A hockey player instinctively knows that there is no backing down when the gloves are dropped. If you failed to meet the challenge of Lou Fontinato or Reggie Fleming in the old days, they ran you off like a scared calf; you were out of the League before Christmas. Nothing much had changed from those days except the venue. The sheet of ice beneath their feet was now the marble floor of the courthouse.

"For over 25 years the retired NHL players have been kept in the dark about their pension fund," Carl Brewer wrote in 1990. "Those watching the fund have made it clear that they are protecting the clubs' interests, not ours. This must change."

The cause that now united them was obtaining justice from the NHL Pension Society, the organization that collected and administered the pensions of NHL hockey players. These players had trusted the NHL executives who ran the Pension Society on their behalf to do the right thing. Now they heard people describing the pension plan as "the biggest sucker play in sports," and they wanted some straight answers.

The NHL Pension Plan and Trust was the pot of gold at the end of the hockey rainbow for players who doubled as car salesmen and brewery reps and hat salesmen to make ends meet in the summers of the 1940s and '50s and '60s. It had been hailed by both former NHL president Clarence Campbell and NHL Players' Association executive director Alan Eagleson as the "best pension plan in all of sports."

"From the amount of money made available, this is financially the strongest plan I know of," John Bain, an adviser to the plan, had informed the annual meeting of the society in 1957. The truth had proved to be something less glowing.

In an era where $7,500 was a damn good annual wage for an NHL regular, and playoff bonus money bought groceries, not a second Porsche, men like Howe and Bathgate had sacrificed $900 to $1,500 a year—after taxes—on their dreams for the future. For the 120 or so men who had scrambled to the top of the hockey heap, the NHL pension plan was an investment on a par with buying a house.

Having surrendered their schooling years to a hockey apprenticeship, men like Eddie Litzenberger and Ivan Irwin and hundreds of others looked forward to a healthy pension to make up for opportunities and careers lost to hockey, and for the price exacted from their bodies by a punishing game. It seemed a fair bargain at the time.

And they believed. "Hockey players are very trusting people," remarks Bob Baun, with a tight smile.

"You always felt everything was done properly," recalls former Buffalo and Detroit player Danny Gare. "The NHL, Alan Eagleson, they were great names when you were a young player, and you felt everything was supposed to be done the right way."

"There was a lot of trust on the players' part that the right thing would be done," says Toronto investment executive Lorraine Mahoney. "It is unfortunate that the right thing was not done." The retired players had been cut adrift in the hockey ocean with no paddles, no compass and a bad map.

The NHL gave them reason to trust. It promised to sweeten the pension pot for players using money from the All-Star Game and the playoffs—two lucrative attractions. Later, millions of dollars from the players' participation in international hockey play were also supposedly plowed back into the pension plan to improve pensions. Patriotism and pensions was the line they were fed by the NHL and Alan Eagleson, the head of the NHL Players' Association.

Somehow, the payouts that emerged 20 years after the promises never equalled the sums contributed years earlier. Gordie Howe had poured almost $25,000 of his hard-earned dollars into the plan from 1947 to 1969—the equivalent of a few years' salary back in the '50s. But Howe's pension when he started to collect was just $13,000 a year. Says Eddie Shack, the former Toronto Maple Leaf: "He'd have made a lot more if he'd just put down his hockey stick and picked up a shovel."

"You were so embarrassed ... it wasn't even enough to make the car payments," says former Rangers star Andy Bathgate, shaking his head ruefully.

By their nature, hockey players are secretive about their money; they always have been reluctant to talk salaries, even with their roommates, their closest friends in the game. This fiscal conservatism stretches back to the days of King Clancy in the 1920s. "A good player was a player who'd play for peanuts," went the owners' credo. A great player, like Clancy, said he'd play for nothing—and meant it. "He was the most amateur athlete I'd ever met," marvelled a grateful Conn Smythe, owner of the Toronto Maple Leafs, who then paid Clancy accordingly.

Management sold the players on the virtues of keeping salaries strictly private, and the players, at least, kept up their end of the bargain. "That's what management preyed on when we played," says Bobby Hull, the famed "Golden Jet," who helped rescue the Chicago Black Hawks from financial collapse in the 1950s. "Don't tell anybody what you're making, don't get together, don't be a group ... an organization, keep it a secret so everyone stays apart. And it's still that way."

The story of Gordie Howe, the NHL's top attraction with the Red Wings for almost twenty years, has become symbolic of the exploitation created by the "silence-is-golden" policy preached by management. While the more independent Bobby Hull created new thresholds for player salaries with his bold $1-million jump to the World Hockey Association in 1972, Howe trusted the NHL to reward him for his service and loyalty.

Howe had been promised by Detroit management that he would be the best-paid player in the game, but in 1969 he discovered he wasn't even the top-salaried player on his team. While he made $45,000 a year, Bob Baun collected $67,000 and Carl Brewer $90,000. "I wish I had been smarter," Howe wrote in 1992. "I wouldn't have played hockey so long."

It wasn't until Wayne Gretzky's blockbuster $3-million-a-year deal in 1988 with the L.A. Kings that full salary disclosure was given to NHL players. Using the amounts comparable players were making as a guide, agents and players pushed up salaries 200 to 300 percent within a couple of years.

"There were only six teams at the time, 120 players in the League with 300 waiting to come up," recalls Lori Horton, the widow of six-time All-Star Tim Horton. "The guys were so grateful to be playing that they didn't realize they weren't being treated as well as they should've been. Tim always said his alternative would have been working in the mines in Sudbury."

"A couple of bad games and you might find yourself back in the minors," wrote eighteen-year veteran Paul Henderson in his autobiography, *Shooting For Glory*. "The competition was cut-throat.... Management used this fear as leverage to get you to do what they wanted. The front office held all the cards and ruled a player's life completely."

That included their sex lives. Back in the late 1950s, Rangers coach "Fiery" Phil Watson called in the wife of his goalie Gump Worsley for a lecture on the virtues of celibacy during a hockey season. Too much sex was sapping the energies of his number-one goalie, Watson claimed. Her amorous demands were hurting the team's playoff chances. Doreen Worsley sat in slack-jawed amazement ... she was seven months pregnant at the time.

Players also learned not to trust the team doctors, especially when the playoffs rolled around. One season, Stan Mikita, the greatest center in Chicago history, was experiencing terrific pain in his arm, but club doctors cleared him to play. It was just a case of tennis elbow, they assured him. Mikita tried to play with the pain, but finally he was forced to submit to an exam by an independent orthopedic doctor. He discovered that Mikita's tricep muscle had torn completely off the bone. Even then, he had to insist on an operation to correct the problem. Another time, a broken shoulder went undiagnosed by team doctors, even after X-rays.

Mikita was lucky enough to be a star; journeyman players like Jim Harrison didn't have choices. Harrison had had three back operations during his NHL career and could barely stand up straight by the late 1970s. He needed painkillers to play. Afraid of losing his position with Chicago, he rushed back to action just six weeks after his third operation in 1978. Hobbled by the pain, he continued bravely, but his play suffered, and the Hawks sent him to the minors.

When the pain in his back prevented him from playing altogether, Harrison suffered a final indignity: Black Hawks doctors said he'd fully recovered from his back operation, and Harrison was denied all but $10,000 of his disability insurance. Harrison's doctor later discovered he needed a spinal fusion.

Still they played, because management knew that in every player there lurked a little boy who'd play for nothing and, later, who'd submit to almost any indignity to remain in the hockey fraternity.

Bill Gadsby, who endured broken bones and over seven hundred stitches to his person in twenty NHL seasons, learned that first-hand in Detroit. After retirement, he uprooted his family from their longtime home in Edmonton and went to Detroit to coach his old club. For the entire 1968-69 season, he endured the meddling of their playboy owner, Bruce Norris, who phoned Gadsby during the game to demand that players be benched. Gadsby suffered in silence, benching players when he knew it was wrong. Then, after winning the first two games of the following season, he was fired as coach without explanation. Norris magnanimously promised to pay Gadsby in full for the season ... provided he didn't say anything to the press about his firing or the organization.

And there were the pathetic stories of stars and journeymen alike who lived from paycheque to paycheque, abandoned by hockey and living in poverty: Doug Harvey, the great defenseman of the Canadiens, an alcoholic who lived in a boxcar for a time; Turk Broda, perhaps the greatest Leafs goalie of all time, who died virtually penniless, his NHL pension barely enough for food after twelve NHL seasons; George Hayes, the Hall of Fame linesman, whose widow collected just $16.98 a month from his NHL pension. Even Hall of Fame inductees felt the slighting hand of the NHL—the greats of the game had to purchase their Hall of Fame rings themselves.

Having endured this climate of fear and suspicion of management, players took a long time to summon the nerve to challenge the League. And it took even longer to spread the word about their meagre pension levels. Gordie Howe: $13,000 after twenty-six seasons. Bobby Hull: $10,500 after sixteen seasons. Jean Béliveau: $12,000 after twenty seasons. Bobby Orr: $8,400 after twelve seasons. They talked about the injustice of it while golfing or over beers. Angry words were spoken, resolutions discussed, action contemplated. And nothing was ever done.

The reasons are tribal in nature. As Bob Baun learned when he tried to organize retired players in 1981, hockey players remain intensely suspicious of even the worthiest causes pushed by former colleagues—unless the big names are involved. Says Larry Regan, director of the National Hockey Alumni in Ottawa, one of several bodies that seek to represent retired players, "You have to get the superstars to get anything done in hockey." Years of being outspent and outwitted by management had taught the players of the NHL's "Original Six" the harsh reality of trying to organize against the owners, even with the marquee players onside. And Howe, Hull, Orr and Gretzky—the four names that can inspire awe and action—have been very careful about backing the wrong horse in a race with owners.

If the grievances about the pension plan had dragged on for many years, and the confidence of the NHL and the Pension Society grew bolder by the day, it was also because management knew that its best ally in controlling the players were the players themselves. For generations, owners and general managers had slept comfortably, confident that the players would never trouble them as long as they had old scores and jealousies to settle amongst themselves.

"Bob Pulford's an asshole, and you can print that," says Bobby Baun of his former teammate and friend, who is now part of NHL management with Chicago. "Bert Olmstead was a prick then, and he's a prick now," sneers Carl Brewer of his teammate with the Leafs in the '50s and '60s. Ted Lindsay's intense rivalry with Montreal's legendary "Rocket" Richard, for instance, still leaves the two Hall of Famers shifting uncomfortably when they have to appear together today. "There was a certain amount of hatred there," remembers Howe. "And when the Rocket finally shook Lindsay's hand in public, Stan Mikita said, 'I'm not ready for this' and left the room."

There was much healing to be done, and in some contrary fashion, the NHL pension plan finally gave the retired players the common ground on which to start this cathartic healing process, exorcising at last the demons of years past. "That love/hate relationship," says former Leaf Jim Dorey. "You know, Montreal doesn't talk to Toronto, and Toronto doesn't talk to Montreal?... Now we're comparing notes, talking about our stab wounds as well as our hockey wounds. We're finding out about each other finally."

Carl Brewer remembers visiting Bill Gadsby's home in Michigan for breakfast as the court date neared in 1991. Towards the end of the meal, Gadsby wandered away from the table to gaze out the window. Gadsby's wife, Edna, called to him, "Is anything wrong?" Gadsby looked back to the table and smiled. "If someone had told me twenty years ago that Carl Brewer would ever be having breakfast in my home, I'd have said they were crazy."

The story of the pension plan remained buried as well because the media were uneasy with the issue of retired players on welfare, living in poverty. Such a disturbing concept didn't fit comfortably in eight hundred words or a minute-thirty's air time, and it played hell with the nostalgia market that demands retired players be equal measures of lovable Wilford Brimley and irascible Gabby Hayes. It required moving the margins, jeopardizing contacts in the quote factory that propels modern sports reporting, sacrificing years of material for that one piece. It required looking away from the middle of the road to the soft shoulder, peering into the murky water in the ditch. And the disapproving look or tone from NHL president John Ziegler or Chicago owner Bill Wirtz that froze young hockey players had a similar debilitating effect on reporters who probed too close to a nerve.

Ken Dryden—who stoked the media machine from the other side as a player—found the sorry lot of retired players to be self-evident, a tale too simple for telling. "It is in no way a remarkable story, though the celebrity of the names involved makes us think it is," Dryden wrote in *The Game*, perhaps the best book ever written by an athlete about the athlete's life. "Rather it is simply the universal story of having something before you can appreciate it, then having it go away when you can ... it's an easy story. Like nursing-home abuses for an investigative reporter, it's one that's always there, you only have to decide to find it."

Except no one bothered to find it. Perhaps following Dryden's world-weary observation, most journalists took the story for granted, a resource so obvious, so wide and deep that it would always do in a pinch when a rainy-day column or weekend piece was needed. All it took was a phone call or two ... a story that wrote itself. Yet the pension plan became a piece always half-written, a report never aired. And it fell to the players to fight the battle and write the history at the same time.

There was optimism in the days leading up to the trial. "Will we win the lawsuit?" asked Ken Dryden, the Cornell-educated goaltending legend for Montreal in the 1970s. "That's up to the judge. Do we deserve to win? Absolutely!"

But, as the retired players sat in Courtroom C-8, the physical distance between them mirrored the philosophical differences among the seven members who put their names to the lawsuit—Gordie Howe, Bobby Hull, Eddie Shack, Carl Brewer, Andy Bathgate, Allan Stanley and Leo Reise. Bathgate, the Hall of Famer who played for the Rangers, Red Wings and Maple Leafs, headed a group seated by the room's south wall. Moderates, they preferred to keep the rhetoric to a minimum, avoiding public confrontations with NHL president John Ziegler or former NHL Players' Association executive director Alan Eagleson. They wanted nothing to distract from their focus on winning the pension lawsuit.

In Bathgate's camp were former Ranger, Black Hawk and Red Wing Leo Reise, Allan Stanley and Eddie "The Entertainer" Shack.

The seventy-year-old Reise, who is now an accountant, sat quietly in the benches on the right of Bathgate, peering out from behind his thick glasses. Reise is the only applicant in the lawsuit to have actively served on the board of directors of the Pension Society back in the 1950s.

Bathgate, who runs a golf center in Toronto, was flanked by his wife, Merle. A modest, self-effacing man who once won the Hart Trophy as the League's top player with one of its worst teams, the Rangers, Bathgate paid more than $15,000 out of his own pocket to the Pension Society in his sixteen-year career. He received $866 a month in benefits in 1992.

Allan Stanley, in an open-necked shirt, looked for all the world like a gentleman farmer contemplating corn futures as he waited for the trial to begin. Stanley played an astounding twenty-one seasons in the NHL as a defenseman. His pension in 1991 was $12,000 a year.

On this beautiful June day, Eddie Shack was golfing. Despite being one of the highest money-earners on most of the teams he played for, Shack receives just $9,000 a year for the seventeen seasons he played in Toronto, New York, Buffalo, Boston, Los Angeles and Pittsburgh. His wife, Norma, whose work raised much of the estimated $300,000 needed to pay the legal bills of the group, represented him in the courtroom.

Gordie Howe and Bobby Hull, the two great players who dominated the "Original Six" for a generation, fall somewhere in the middle of the two camps in the lawsuit. They are outspoken about the money they feel was taken from them, but they remain attached to the fans and the traditions they helped to foster. Of all the players involved in the lawsuit, they stand to lose the most by pulling the NHL's considerable tail. Hull and Howe are the only two members of the suit not to have directly contributed to the legal fees.

On this first day in court, Howe is on a previously booked promotional appearance on a hockey cruise in the Caribbean with his wife and adviser, Colleen. Hull is making a promotional appearance at a golf tournament in Hamilton for Algonquin, the beer company he represents.

The man who started the lawsuit and the firebrand of the applicants, Carl Brewer, sits by the north wall, his bald head gleaming under the courtroom lights. His companion, Susan Foster, without whom the suit would still be a dream, is beside him. Brewer's powerful frame bulges beneath his summer suit. He looks not unlike a bouncer at a posh gambling casino, ready to take on trouble at a moment's notice. Foster is dwarfed.

Brewer's temperament is adversarial, but Foster has softened his standard operating procedure somewhat. Brewer now would rather litigate you to death than put you through the end boards with a hipcheck. He envisioned the pension lawsuit as simply the first step to cleaning up the NHL's hockey business and removing its power brokers, John Ziegler and Alan Eagleson.

It would be accurate to say that the players involved in the suit were barely on speaking terms by the time the trial began. Old divisions thought buried had arisen once more in the months leading up to the trial. Disagreements over tactics and legal bills had fractured their solidarity, although not enough to scuttle the suit. The culmination of the legal action would free them from this enforced conviviality. None of the applicants in the suit looked as if he was regretting the prospect.

Besides, "the Big M" was there to add his support. Frank Mahovlich sat with his wife, Marie. As he watched the proceedings, his manner was reminiscent of his playing style: somewhat bemused, his powerful figure leaning slightly forward in concentration. When Mahovlich arrived, there was a cluck of pleasure from everyone involved: "The Big M's here. That's great, that's the support we need."

To Mahovlich's left sat Red Kelly and his wife, Andra. Kelly, now a successful businessman in the aircraft industry, still has traces of his trademark red hair and the fresh, earnest expression of a man you'd buy a horse from without a moment's hesitation. He leans forward, his head turned slightly, ready to catch every syllable of the arcane discourse of pension law. The soft-spoken Kelly knows that, despite the passage of thirty-three years, some former NHLers still blame him for the failure of the first Players' Association in 1957. His presence in the court seemed a pact with the past.

Kelly's old Red Wing teammate Ted Lindsay was another pleasant surprise on opening day. A man whose face looks like a masterpiece of the tanner's art, Lindsay tried to start a players' association back in the '50s, only to see it crushed when Detroit's general manager Jack Adams intimidated his Red Wing teammates, like Kelly and Howe, into backing out. Lindsay was a tiger on the ice, and he held his sixty-year-old frame ramrod straight on the hard wooden benches, seemingly as ready to scrap now as then. Lindsay—who has done well in business—looked a lone, forbidding figure, staring icily at NHL counsel Earl Cherniak, a scrapper in his own right.

While there were other retired players in attendance—men such as Sid Smith, Ivan Irwin and Pete Conacher—the turnout was somewhat disappointing considering the many millions at stake for the former players. "Hockey players are dumb," Lindsay was heard to whisper to another player.

In the back row of Courtroom C-8 sat Norma Shack and Lori Horton. There was a quiet dignity in their manner. Hockey wives, after all, are often the strongest, most decent people in the business. Norma has been an energetic figure behind the scenes with the lawsuit, but on this day she seemed happy to be a spectator in the drama.

"Had I known how much work was involved when Carl first came to our house," she says, "I don't know if I'd have said yes to all the work."

All eyes were fastened on the front of the courtroom where Justice George W. Adams, Q.C., of the Ontario Court of Justice General Division, a dapper, handsome man, sat surrounded by the thousands of pages of submissions and documents assembled for the case. A Harvard Law School graduate and former chairman of the Ontario Labour Relations Board, the forty-seven-year-old Adams wrote ceaselessly in the margins of the documents, his head reclining ever so gently on his left hand. Occasionally, he shot a glance over the top of his glasses at the lawyers, then just as quickly returned to the volumes before him.

Before Adams stood thirty-seven-year-old Mark Zigler, the lawyer representing the players in the lawsuit. Despite his dark beard, his robes and the austere trappings of his profession, Zigler gave the impression of a high school math teacher about to broach algebra for the first time with his class. Zigler's specialty is employee benefit law and labor relations; he is a man who specializes in representing employees in pension matters. His fingers danced across the binders and documents perched before him, choreographing a story he'd first heard two years ago from Carl Brewer in the Toronto office of Koskie and Minsky, where he is a partner.

Zigler, who had watched the hockey players perform all his life, was about to have them watch him in action. "I don't know what athletes go through," he says, "but there's anticipation ... and adrenaline and preparation involved in presenting a case like this. You can't be nervous. This is what you do for a living, and you've got to be prepared to make your pitch."

Next to Zigler sat lawyer Ron Davis, who had assisted him in preparing the case. Behind them sat Paul Saunders, the actuary responsible for much of the research in the players' eighty-six-page complaint. Saunders, who works for the Toronto firm of G. B. Buck, is usually found on the management side in cases that involve insurance and pension matters. Circumstances had him playing for the other team this time.

Across the aisle from Zigler sat the NHL's counsel, Earl Cherniak, a senior partner of Lerner and Associates, waiting for his colleague to begin. A man with an eagle profile and deliberate manner, Cherniak has a deserved reputation for competence in the field of personal-injury law. He is a legal hired-gun, his practice restricted to trial and appellate work. The courtroom is his home.

Cherniak had produced a 162-page response to the players' complaint. He and associate Kirk Stevens would present the NHL's side of the case when Zigler wrapped up in two days. Behind Cherniak and Stevens sat representatives of Manufacturers Life, the insurance company from whom the NHL Pension Society had purchased retirement annuities on the players' behalf.

In the sparring between the sides before the trial began, the players had won a minor victory. As they requested, the trial would have no live testimony, no riveting moments of cross-examination, no spontaneous outbursts from surprise witnesses, no orders to clear the courtroom from the judge. The evidence that Judge Adams was reviewing had been assembled in affidavits and cross-examination and discovery before the trial. For five days in court, the lawyers presented what were in effect closing arguments, summing up the points of their case.

More retired players arrived during the next few days to watch the proceedings—Normie Ullman, Jean-Guy Talbot, Dollard St. Laurent and others among them—but even the most committed to the cause found an excuse to slip out of the courtroom from time to time. Courthouse staff—who were in awe of their celebrated visitors—whipped up popcorn for them and shoved scraps of paper forward to collect autographs.

As seminal as the trial was to those players and their wives and friends who'd struggled to bring it about, it would never match the passions that had inspired it. To understand this improbable moment, with stars of the game—united for once—confronting a league that they had known and feared for most of its seventy-five years, one has to go back to the days of the "Original Six" to find the source of the owners' power and influence, the root of the players' insecurity.

For that, there is no better place to look than to the Toronto Maple Leafs, the personal domain of Conn Smythe for forty years and the hockey showpiece of English Canada—an organization that prided itself on an unflinching dedication to success through hard work and loyalty.

3

THE
MAJOR

To appreciate the forge that molded Bob Baun, Carl Brewer, Allan Stanley and Tim Horton, the fires that shaped them as players and men, one must first appreciate the hockey furnace known as the Toronto Maple Leafs. Not the Maple Leafs of the past twenty-five years—the long-running Harold Ballard carny sideshow—but the team as it was before it collapsed into ineptitude in 1970: the venerated national institution built by Major Conn Smythe.

The Maple Leafs before Harold Ballard were a tribute to God, King and Country. To succeeding generations of Torontonians they embodied the British virtues of thrift, hard work, loyalty and duty. An oversized portrait of King George (and later Queen Elizabeth) regally surveyed players from on high at Maple Leaf Gardens. So did the Major. Woe betide any Toronto player who missed the significance of their fearful symmetry.

The style of Smythe's Maple Leafs—if they had one—was best summed up in 1964 in *Maclean's* by a young Peter Gzowski. "The Leafs, as a team, are more mechanics than artists," he observed. "Defeat, as the famous sign in their dressing room says, does not rest lightly on their shoulders, and neither does anything else. They are very serious fellows."

For forty years, these very serious fellows and their mechanical efficiency were immortalized across the nation on radio and later TV by broadcaster Foster Hewitt. Maple Leafs players gave no quarter, expected none in return and offered blood, sweat and tears, not excuses. They were a hockey team the way Eaton's was a store and the CPR was a railway.

No player embodied the Maple Leafs values cherished by Smythe and immortalized by Hewitt better than Syl Apps, the captain of three Stanley Cup winners in the 1940s. Apps played eleven seasons with Toronto, served in World War II, represented Canada at the Olympics, was a five-time All-Star, a teetotaller and later a cabinet minister in the Ontario provincial government. In short, he was nigh on perfect.

Billy Harris, who later played with the Leafs, vividly remembers a speech Apps delivered to his peewee hockey team in 1948. "He was more interested in trying to explain to us what was necessary in order to be successful, not just in sports, but in life," recalls Harris. "The speech was inspirational. From that day on, I not only wanted to be a hockey player like Syl Apps, I wanted to be a person like Syl Apps."

As a result of proselytizing by Apps, Hewitt and others, Maple Leaf Gardens—the altar of Leafdom—became an icon for every young man born in English Canada after the Depression. Skating across the frozen stillness of the Gardens' ice took on mythic proportions for the young men privileged to do so. A teenage George "Punch" Imlach (later the coach and general manager of the team) echoed the feelings of most young men of his day after his first practice at the Maple Leaf Gardens in the '30s. He simply called it "the most important day of my life up until then."

Most crucial of all, Conn Smythe's Maple Leafs were—with rare exceptions—extremely successful on and off the ice. From 1932 to 1967 the team won eleven Stanley Cups and finished first or second fifteen times. The stars of the team were perennial NHL All-Stars and won the League's top trophies. They were in demand for advertisements and personal appearances. And when they went away to war—many Leafs players enlisted in World War II—they won there, too.

The only place Toronto players regularly lost was at the pay window: the Maple Leafs were among the poorest-paid players in the NHL. Maple Leaf Gardens remained the most profitable NHL club each year, however, and Smythe himself was paid $501,687.83 as director of the Leafs from 1931 to 1957.

In short, the team was everything held dear by its founder, Conn Smythe, the pre-eminent Toronto sportsman of this century. They were profitable, they were loyal, and they were winners—which might just as well have been the epitaph Smythe set out to write when he came into the world. Leading with jut-jawed determination, he dominated everything connected with professional hockey north of the Great Lakes and west of the Ottawa River from 1927 to 1965. In an era when NHL owners like Big Jim Norris of Chicago operated like maharajahs, Smythe acted more like the upright Protestant owner of a modest shoe factory.

The five-foot, six-inch Smythe was by turns benevolent and tyrannical, heroic and without scruples. In keeping with the sensibilities of the era, he was suspicious of "New York Jews" and "Frogs" who dodged military service. He was a patriot and a soldier whose clear blue eyes seared an indelible mark on the hide of every man who ever laced up his skates for the Toronto Maple Leafs.

Even when Smythe knew he was dying, he remained as pugnacious as ever. Bob Baun, who played eleven years in Toronto, remembers meeting Smythe at the Gardens just a few months before his death in 1981. Baun approached Smythe in the back of his limousine. "Hi, Mr. Smythe," said Baun gently, extending his hand through the lowered window. "It's Bob Baun."

Smythe's blue eyes blazed. "I know who the fuck you are," he hissed, firmly returning Baun's handshake.

Constantine Falkland Cary Smythe was a true product of turn-of-the-century Toronto, a quiet community whose flashpoint was the rivalry between the Protestant Establishment and the Catholic proletariat. Toronto was still Canada's second most important city at the time, ranked behind Montreal, but already it was a banking and manufacturing center eager to escape its roots as "Muddy York." Music in the Toronto of Conn Smythe's boyhood was played by military bands, and art was "The Thin Red Line" or "The Charge of the Scots Greys."

Smythe was born to modest means a few blocks from the site where he later built his temple, Maple Leaf Gardens (a fact he never let anyone forget). The product of Ulster Protestantism and having to grow up fast and tough, he was a survivor. Unlike many of the prominent men he would later come to know and dominate, Conn Smythe did not enjoy a pampered, sheltered childhood.

Smythe's creed became "If you can't beat 'em in the alley, you can't beat 'em on the ice." In stark contrast to this truculent pose stood his pacifist father, A. E. S. "Alfred" Smythe, a theosophist and a vegetarian from Belfast who once gently urged his boisterous son to read the *Bhagavad Gita*. While Conn would later be sceptical of journalists, he proudly noted that his father wrote for a number of the top publications at the time, including *The Toronto World*.

Smythe's mother, Polly—who had met his father on the ship coming to Canada from England—was unlike her husband in every way, a fun-loving alcoholic who disappeared from the family home for extended periods during Conn's boyhood. He appears to have been torn in his feelings for her, embarrassed by her eccentric appearance but compelled by a son's love. Once he told schoolfriends who saw her approaching that she was his housekeeper, a remark he later felt great remorse for. In spite of his shame, Smythe claimed he very much loved the plump, pretty, carefree Polly, and he attributed what little sense of fun he had to her.

The marriage of his parents was a turbulent, unhappy one. In his autobiography *If You Can't Beat 'Em In The Alley* ..., Smythe admitted that in today's society his parents likely would have divorced. Instead, his mother stayed away from the family home for extended periods, leaving Smythe and his sister Mary alone with their father, who struggled to earn a living from his writing.

Mary died in a Toronto hospital in 1903 at the age of twelve while her mother was away in England. Smythe attributed her death to a goitre caused by drinking unpasteurized milk, a practice he avoided. No doubt it was an early sign to Smythe of his destiny that he be spared while his sister died. Three years later, his mother died in the same hospital from the effects of alcoholism. She was only thirty-eight. With her death, all the diminutive, determined eleven-year-old Conn had left in the world was his father.

The lack of stability had its effect on Smythe, who later countenanced very little liberality in his own life or from his employees. For instance, when one of his players in the '40s got his girlfriend pregnant, Smythe sent him to the minors and then traded him. "With all the turmoil, I figured he couldn't keep his mind on hockey," rationalized Smythe.

While his relationship with his gentle father was a loving one, Smythe was not prepared to adopt his father's philosophy of pacifism. He readily brawled with the Catholic boys in his neighborhood (later he disapproved of his son Stafford marrying a Catholic), and he was a feisty football and hockey player, in spite of his scrawny 120-pound frame.

For a time, Smythe attended the prestigious Upper Canada College, but he disliked the snobbery of the place and soon left. While formal education did not excite Smythe, he was passionate about sports and competition. Like many of the young men of the era, Smythe played a number of sports. The actor Raymond Massey remembered Smythe as one of the stars of the 1914 University of Toronto football team, although Smythe admitted, "I always prefer to be promoted when it's the truth. At Varsity that year I was never better than third string."

Smythe's first sporting love was hockey. He was, among other things, the captain of the University of Toronto Varsity Juniors, who played for the Ontario Hockey Association title in 1914. Despite his small size, he scored thirty-three goals in fifteen games for Varsity, and later reflected on the accomplishment with some pride. "I was beginning to make my first mark, in hockey," he noted in his journal.

As it did for many young men of the day, World War I interrupted the games, and the patriotic Smythe quickly heeded the call of King and Country, spoiling for a fight. He enlisted as a gunner in the 25th Field Battery, an artillery brigade, and was shipped overseas with the 40th Field Battery of the Canadian Army in 1915.

In the charnel house of the trenches during the Great War, Smythe was witness to the slaughter of many Toronto friends and colleagues. A number of those who did survive were emotionally scarred for life by the experience. Rather than breaking Smythe's spirit and character, however, the carnage around him stiffened his resolve to make something of himself if—and when—he returned home. With each succeeding brush with death, he came to see himself as cut out for a special destiny.

On the killing fields of the Somme and Vimy Ridge, Smythe began to formulate his ideal of the sportsman who never alibis, who plays with pain, who follows orders and gets the job done right. Individual liberty, according to Smythe, could be won only through unquestioning obedience to great leaders, who earned loyalty through their bravery and vision. In mankind's worst hours, Smythe was typically using himself upon which to build an idealized model to judge men and hockey players for the next half-century. Had he possessed a gift with words, he might have said that he did not break faith; he took the torch from failing hands and held it high.

Smythe saw action in the worst battles of the war for British troops: the Somme, Ypres and Vimy Ridge. Several times he barely escaped death, and he was awarded the Military Cross at Vimy. He led a scouting party behind German lines, carrying only a pistol for protection. After shooting several Germans, he ran out of ammunition halfway through the mission, a fact he discovered only upon reaching the safety of his own trenches.

The headstrong Smythe was never one to brook the rigidity and mediocrity he encountered in the British and Canadian armies. Fed up with the officers he served under in the artillery, he transferred to the Flying Corps as a gunner in 1917. The Flying Corps was just emerging as an important weapon in combat, but Smythe's career as a flyer didn't last long. He was shot down and wounded at Passchendaele in 1917, and the Germans took him prisoner. At first he was reported as missing in action by the Toronto newspapers, who found space among the many casualty reports to mourn the loss of a sporting gentleman of Smythe's temperament.

Smythe was quickly located in a POW camp, where he cooled his heels for the rest of the war in a pair of riding boots given to him by a fellow prisoner, a Russian (whom he later hired to work at Maple Leaf Gardens). He even undertook a few failed escape attempts. As he chafed in the camp, waiting to return to Canada, Smythe came to believe his survival meant that he was cut out for better stuff back home.

Upon his return to Toronto in 1919, Smythe set about realizing his personal Manifest Destiny. In short order, he completed his education, married his sweetheart, Irene Sands, and set up the Smythe Sand and Gravel Company, which he was to direct until the 1960s. With more practical matters taken care of, he then set out to create a legacy that would make his name synonymous with sport in North America.

Throwing himself headlong into the hockey scene in Toronto, he was soon managing and coaching at the amateur and university levels around Toronto. Smythe worked all day at the sand and gravel business, then at night he would coach one of the several teams he was involved with. His greatest achievement was managing the Varsity Grads, who won the Olympic gold medal for hockey in 1928. His keen eye for talent and his organizational skills soon drew the attention of hockey people and landed him the job he was looking for.

Smythe's first stab at managing a pro hockey team came in 1926 when Boston Bruins owner Charles Adams recommended him to Colonel John Hammond, the owner of the newly founded New York

Rangers. Hammond was looking for someone to quickly provide him with a winner for the New York fans. The resourceful Smythe seemed the ideal man.

Soon after being hired, Smythe embarked on a rapid tour of North America, assembling a wonderful young team from all over Canada and the United States, including Frank Boucher, Bill and Bun Cook, Ching Johnson, Taffy Abel and Lorne Chabot (all of them future Hall of Fame members), for a meagre $32,000.

His introduction to big-time hockey didn't last, however. Smythe was cashiered by the Rangers just a few months after taking over the job as manager. Typically, he had quarrelled with Colonel Hammond over whether to sign Babe Dye, a star player who the fastidious Smythe felt was a little too fun-loving for his new club. Smythe was looking for a new job before the team he'd built had played a single game. The Rangers team he assembled, however, went on to win two Stanley Cups, a fact he was quick to point out in succeeding years.

Undaunted, Smythe returned to Toronto to exploit the series of business and sporting contacts that would make him a legend. His first order of business was to use the $7,500 severance he'd received from the Rangers to buy the ailing Toronto St. Patricks in 1927. He then changed their name to the more patriotic Maple Leafs, changed the team colors from green and white to blue and white, and began plans for a palace of sports to house his team.

Smythe was a bundle of contradictions during his life. Because of his mother's tragic example, he frowned on alcohol (champagne from the Stanley Cup was his cocktail of choice), and, publicly at least, he disapproved of sexual liberality. When he married his wife, Irene, in 1921, he noted proudly, they were "both still virgins. I never noticed that it hurt our marriage." Yet Smythe saw nothing wrong with gambling, whether on horses or his financial future. "I never had anything against gamblers," he said. "They are straighter than a lot of people ... I welcomed gamblers [to the Gardens] as long as they didn't get into trouble with the law and indirectly bring bad publicity to the Gardens."

In fact, his first great player acquisition for the Leafs was underwritten by the profits from a bet. By 1930, Smythe had begun to assemble the racing stable that would later win him more stakes races in Canada than anyone but E. P. Taylor. Horses bearing the blue-and-white silks with the maple leaf twice won the Queen's Plate. One of his earliest horses was a two-year-old filly named Rare Jewel, a none-too-promising candidate for the Coronation Futurity that year.

A more promising talent, however, was playing hockey that fall in Ottawa. Twenty-seven-year-old Frank "King" Clancy of the Senators was a colorful All-Star defenseman in the early days of the NHL who delighted in taking "a reef out of those hard-headed Protestants" on the Maple Leafs. The Senators were suffering financially, however, and Smythe learned Clancy could be had for the sum of $35,000, an onerous price tag in the Depression. The most Smythe could lay his hands on was perhaps $25,000.

Smythe was determined to buy Clancy, however, and Rare Jewel was the unlikely device to obtain him. On race day, she was the longest shot in the Futurity; nonetheless, an excited Smythe placed a $40 bet on Rare Jewel with bookies at the King Edward Hotel, and at the track he put down $60 across the board on the filly. Despite a rough ride from jockey Duke Foden, Rare Jewel won the race and paid the biggest pari-mutuel price in Canada that year. Smythe collected between $11,000 and $12,000 on his bets, plus the purse of over $3,500.

Smythe then used the money to purchase Clancy, and the diminutive defenseman was the Maple Leafs' first great star. But having a great product, Smythe also felt he needed a great showplace for his hockey team, an arena where spectators could dress up in their best bib and tucker.

The story of how Smythe built the Gardens at the height of the Depression has achieved legendary status in the intervening years. According to the accepted history, Smythe gambled control of the team he'd painstakingly built up, turning Maple Leaf Gardens Ltd. into a public company to raise money for the Gardens. With financing so perilous, goes the story, the project came close to foundering several times. The turning point came when Smythe's assistant, Frank Selke, arranged to have the workmen on the site agree to accept stock in the company instead of money to finish the work. Selke, a member of the Electricians Union himself, set an example by mortgaging his house to buy stock.

The truth is somewhat less dramatic, of course. As part of Maple Leaf Gardens going public, Smythe and the original investors traded their interests in the hockey club—with its limited revenues—for controlling interest in Maple Leaf Gardens Ltd., where the real profits lay. And having the workmen and unions accept stock allowed Smythe to save on cash flow for the construction, and then later snap up the stock at bargain prices when the workmen sold their shares to make ends meet in the Depression. While Smythe complained in his autobiography of the cash shortages and hardships involved, he and his partners had enough cash lying around in 1930 to buy up three credit notes owed to the Dominion Bank by Thomson Brothers, the contractors on the project, who were in danger of going bankrupt. And there was enough for Smythe to take a handsome five-figure salary by 1932.

Finally, the Gardens turned a $40,535 profit in 1931, the year the building opened, mostly on the strength of advance ticket sales. But that was his genius. Conn Smythe talked the buttons off businessmen who should have known better, and he could get the media to write the story his way.

None of this financial maneuvering mattered on November 12, 1931, when the Chicago Black Hawks and the Maple Leafs faced off before a capacity crowd of 13,542 in the first game ever at the Gardens. The twenty-two directors of Maple Leaf Gardens, including Smythe, arrived in evening dress, and the bands of the Royal Grenadiers and the 48th Highlanders played "Happy Days Are Here Again." Only a 2-1 win by Chicago ruined the script.

The hockey world had never seen anything quite like Maple Leaf Gardens before and would not see anything like it for a while after its completion. Jutting out below the oversized portrait of the King on the south wall was a bandshell to house the military bands Smythe favored. There was an enormous Wurlitzer organ, later propelled with Mephistophelian zeal by a gentleman named Horace Lapp, its pipes seemingly carved into the south wall. Perhaps greatest of all achievements, there wasn't an obstructed seat for hockey in the house—pillars were nowhere to be found in the House of Smythe.

"It was a period piece—elegant colonial Toronto," wrote Ken Dryden years later, "... perfectly, shamelessly preserved from a time before glitter and spectacle came to the city; and came to sports." And as befits an institution, there was a dress code. Until he left the Gardens for good in 1965, Smythe insisted that season ticket holders in the top seats wear a jacket and tie during games—or else lose their coveted ducats for good. Few, if any, defied the ban.

All this new hockey palace needed was an oracle, and Foster Hewitt soon became the chronicler of the exploits of Connie Smythe's hockey team with his patented "Hello, Canada and hockey fans in the United States and Newfoundland, and a special hello to our men overseas."

Conn Smythe was a man who made his own breaks, but the marriage of hockey and radio was the sort of fortunate coincidence that also marked his career. It would be impossible to calculate the impact of Hewitt's weekly broadcasts from the gondola high above the ice surface at the Gardens. The tradition of Saturday night hockey in Canada remains to this day, with "Hockey Night in Canada" the highest-rated television program in this country. And the names of the Maple Leafs stars Hewitt called out in his clipped, high-pitched delivery—Clancy, Apps, Kennedy, Conacher, Mahovlich—became synonymous with hockey in the minds of every fan across the land. Smythe couldn't have bought better publicity for his fledgling team.

"Foster Hewitt did just as much for hockey as anybody who ever participated on the ice," says Allan Stanley, who listened to Hewitt on the radio in the northern Ontario mining town of Timmins. "He made every bad game sound good, and he made you want to be at the Gardens all the time ... even for the bad games."

"Those of us who grew up on the Prairies listening to his voice will never forget his coming over the airwaves and greeting us," wrote Trent Frayne upon Hewitt's death in 1985. "And then he'd tell us, the millions of us spread right across the country, brought together in living rooms and kitchens and bathtubs and cars and on lonely dark farms and in small snow-packed towns and in brightly lit cities from one ocean to the other, all of us in our mind's eye watching the matchless giants on the ice below."

Billy Harris remembers the impact of Foster Hewitt's broadcasts on creating new fans and bringing new players to the Maple Leafs. Harris recalls listening to Hewitt's call of the game on radio the night the 1942 Leafs won the Stanley Cup from Detroit, the only team on record to recover from a 3-0 deficit in games. After hearing Hewitt describe "Sweeney" Schriner's goal that iced the Cup in a 3-1 win, Harris recalled, "I don't have to tell you what the script was for a very tired six-year-old, but when I went to bed that night I tried to orchestrate a dream in which I would some day play for the Toronto Maple Leafs and we would win the Stanley Cup, and I would score the winner in Game Seven."

While Harris never scored a Cup-winning goal, he did play for three Maple Leafs Cup winners; his was the dream of millions of little boys across Canada who could barely skate. And they rewarded their fantasies with loyalty to Conn Smythe's Leafs.

In Smythe's frugal fashion, he received all this publicity for free. The savings realized by clubs who got their publicity for free on radio and later TV (or were paid to do it) were among the hidden resources that sports teams never explained to players when they negotiated contracts. And it set a standard for sports promotion in Toronto that didn't change until the baseball Blue Jays came to town in 1977.

Foster Hewitt did not become a rich man by being a pawn for Smythe. He used his enormous celebrity and his influence with the sponsors of "Hockey Night in Canada" to pick off a few plums for himself. Hewitt bought a radio station, changed its call letters to CKFH ("Foster Hewitt's Station in Toronto," beamed the ads), and had his station broadcast the team's games for many years. Hewitt also had a deal whereby he received a healthy percentage of many promotions and commercials done by Maple Leafs players. Toronto players often discovered that Hewitt's take from a promotion doubled or tripled their share.

By the time Billy Harris heard Hewitt describe Schriner's goal in 1942, Smythe was leaving hockey behind, embarking on his most demanding project: raising an artillery battery made up of Toronto sportsmen to fight for the Canadian Army in World War II. Among the men who enlisted with Smythe's "Sportsmen's Battery" were sportswriters Ted Reeve and Ralph Allen, golfer Jim Boeckh and Don "Shanty" McKenzie, later the building supervisor at the Gardens.

Smythe took refresher courses in flying and artillery and drove himself to get in shape to meet the demands of leading a group of fighting men. But the Canadian Army was less than enthusiastic about allowing a forty-three-year-old businessman to gallop into the front lines against the Wehrmacht, even if he did run the Toronto Maple Leafs.

Smythe was determined, however, and offered his rationale for serving twenty-five years after his first military stint in World War I. In January 1942 he told radio interviewer Wes McKnight, "I'm the kind of fellow who, when the King and Queen came out to Canada a couple of years ago, every time I saw them I got a tingling sensation in my spine. I started out in life as a barefoot boy, and friendly advice and generous help given me by many people have put me where I am today. If I wouldn't fight for my country, who would?"

Smythe urged every employee of the Gardens and player on the team to enlist or sign up for reserve duty, at the very least. An impressive number—including his son Stafford, who enlisted in the Navy—did just that. And Smythe, like many in English Canada, publicly noted the high percentage of deferrals among the Montreal Canadiens' players and staff.

Having called in enough favors with his powerful friends, Smythe and his "Sportsmen's Battery" were finally sent overseas in 1943, leaving the running of the Maple Leafs and the Gardens to his able lieutenants, Frank Selke and Hap Day. Day would also continue to run the sand and gravel business in Smythe's absence.

Having arrived overseas, the dashing Major Smythe was forced to wait—along with everyone from Stalin to Shanty McKenzie—for a Western Front to open in Europe. The 30th Artillery Battery remained in England for over a year, awaiting its first action. Smythe fought the boredom by drilling his men rigorously, and he kept up with the team and the Gardens through his correspondence with Day and Selke (whom he felt was siding with members of the board of directors who wanted Smythe ousted). And he followed Stafford's progress in the Navy as well.

In 1944, the "Sportsmen's Battery" was finally sent into action in northern France after D-Day, taking an active role in the field near the front lines. But Smythe's patriotic adventure didn't last long. Soon after being deployed near Caen, Smythe's war was ended by a German artillery shell that hit a nearby munitions dump. He was critically wounded in the back and side by shrapnel from the explosion, which killed several men. His bowels and urinary tract were ripped apart, and there was nerve damage to his leg.

In fact, Smythe was perilously close to death for a time and needed an extended convalescence to recover from the injury. The nerve damage caused his toes to pull under his foot, and he was unable to walk without a limp again. The effects of the other wounds nagged him the rest of his life as well.

Typically, Smythe amused himself during the long, painful recuperation process by challenging the Canadian war effort. From his hospital bed, he claimed that Canadian soldiers were dying needlessly for want of experienced replacement troops. He urged Parliament to draft a tough conscription law, and he railed on at hockey clubs like the Canadiens who helped most of their top stars avoid the war by giving them civilian jobs deemed necessary to the war effort. Years later, when Canadian tax officials hit him with a large bill for disallowed exemptions, Smythe claimed it was just the Liberal Party mandarins in Ottawa exacting revenge on him for his criticism of the government's war effort.

While Smythe recovered from his injuries at home (he didn't resume full-time work at the Gardens until 1947), the club continued to flourish on the ice. In part, this was because he had the knack of surrounding himself with excellent hockey people. In the early days, he hired the wily Frank Selke from Kitchener; together they produced the fine hockey clubs of the 1930s that finished first four times in seven years.

Later, Hap Day was his right-hand man; Day either played for, coached or managed every Stanley Cup winner before 1962. King Clancy was also a loyal Smythe soldier for many years after retiring as a player. And Conn was there to pass the baton to Punch Imlach in 1958 for the last great Leafs dynasty.

But from the earliest days, Smythe was frustrated when his employees didn't meet the exacting standards he set for himself. Frank Selke, who later assembled the great Montreal teams of the 1950s, was found lacking in loyalty, despite his considerable efforts in building both the team and the Gardens. Selke finally quit in 1946 when Smythe upbraided him for leaving the Gardens one lunch hour without permission. Selke left a note: "Lincoln freed the slaves. Goodbye. I quit."

"Because of his hockey knowledge, hard work and sobriety, he [Selke] was a good man up to a point, but then he was a minor leaguer, as far as I was concerned," Smythe wrote later. The Canadiens, who won six Cups and finished first eight times under Selke, apparently found his loyalty to winning a better yardstick.

And Hap Day was publicly humiliated after years of work for Smythe at both the Gardens and at Smythe Sand and Gravel. At a press conference in 1957, Smythe claimed complete responsibility for the Maple Leafs' awful performance that year. In the next breath, he intimated that Day might be responsible for the collapse of the Leafs, asking publicly if the man who'd been his right-hand man for thirty years "would be available to carry on" the next year. Day quit the next day, saying, "My legs have been cut out from under me."

The ultimate individualist, Smythe ironically wanted his players to subvert their individuality to the team. He demanded that the Leafs he managed be bruising, unforgiving platoons of team men, sportsmen who played through pain and adversity. It was a trademark that characterized his teams into the era of Baun and Brewer and Stanley and Horton. "You see, professional hockey is total war," he wrote. "On and off the ice, everywhere you go it's war."

He had little use for flamboyant scorers like Charlie Conacher and Harvey "Busher" Jackson—"they were too busy driving their new cars and chasing women" to get in shape, he sneered. And the old sobersides never could fathom the juvenile pranks and mischief that keep athletes loose and united during the rigors of a long, often boring season. "I never knew what was so funny about cutting a teammate's tie in half or bashing in his new hat," he confessed without a trace of humor.

Smythe's kind of player was Red Horner, his team captain, who led the NHL in penalties eight years in a row. "I approved of that," Smythe recalled. "He was the first policeman we had, and he won many a game for us by other teams ganging up on him and taking more penalties than Red would get."

In fact, Smythe was the first to realize that a strategy of controlled mayhem on the ice could help a team win. Until that time, the NHL saw plenty of blood spilled, but almost all of it randomly. Smythe—with his "can't beat 'em in the alley, can't beat 'em on the ice" philosophy—institutionalized a policy of controlled violence through players like Horner, Gus Mortson and "Wild" Bill Ezinicki that dominated hockey thinking in Canada until the Soviets demonstrated unequivocally that you can't win games from the penalty box against skilled players. (To get a sense of how pervasive this theory remains to this day, hockey sages like Don Cherry still promote Smythe's tried-and-true philosophy that you win championships with killer instinct and knuckles, despite the clear example of the Soviet teams.)

The noted Toronto newspaperman Ted Reeve—who served in Smythe's "Sportsmen's Battery" during World War II—captured the fiery Smythe managerial style in a newspaper column: "That white, white fedora with the ruddy face and flaming blue eyes underneath it, sailing around the Gardens' aisles and corridors like the white plume of Navarre, action every step of the way and gathering uproar as it went."

Though Smythe always cut a refined figure in his spats, his tailored suits and his hats, he led by example when it came to the rough stuff. In the 1938 playoffs, he himself exchanged punches with Bill Stewart, the coach of Chicago, in the hallway of the Gardens before the first game of the championships. The two men were at odds over the choice of a substitute goalie for the Hawks, who had lost their regular man, Mike Karakas. It took six men to break up the scuffle.

And several times, Smythe went toe-to-toe with Art Ross of the Bruins over turf matters of League business or simple pride. (He once sent an impressed Ross a congratulatory wreath with a Latin inscription. Ross was less impressed when he found that the Latin urged him to perform an anatomically-challenged act.)

Smythe was a hands-on manager, never content to stand still. He felt he had held on too long to Joe Primeau and Jackson and Conacher, the stars of his Stanley Cup winners of 1932, and he vowed never to repeat the error. And so most players, great and not-so-great, were gone from the Gardens by their early thirties. Smythe's trick, at least until the 1950s, was having a new young star to replace them with and to placate the fans.

And while Smythe never stood behind the bench to coach the club, his presence loomed large over the shoulders of his coaches like Dick Irvin and the faithful Hap Day, who coached or managed all seven Cup winners before the '60s. Smythe sat in his perch in the green seats at the Gardens on game night (not-so-fondly dubbed "Berchtesgarden" by Day) relaying strategies to his coaches via sons Stafford or Hugh or an ailing player. When the messenger system broke down, Smythe installed a phone next to the team bench to relay instructions directly to his coach. When his coaches began to ignore the flashing light, Smythe hooked up a ring to be worn by the coach that would deliver a mild electric shock whenever the phone was ringing. And Smythe's personal box was armed with devices of his own invention as well. For instance, there were twenty separate clocks to chart the playing time of each and every player in a Leafs uniform that night.

Often, Smythe came to the Leafs dressing room between periods for a little bombast. "Hap knew what I could do in a dressing room. I was good at touching the raw spots, even with people I trusted. I'd give them as much as I knew they could take, send them out hating me, and they'd go and destroy the enemy just to show me up."

Occasionally, Smythe's idea of how much a player could take differed radically from the player's estimate of how far he'd be pushed. But with just six teams in the NHL and the real possibility of being blackballed out of hockey, those players kept their humiliation to themselves, and Smythe continued to see himself as an inspirational genius.

Even the Junior A Marlboros felt his wrath. "Once a year he'd come into the dressing room and give us shit," remembered Harry Neale, who played for the Marlies in the 1950s. "Our coach Turk Broda would say we need a little shaking up, he'd come in. You'd be looking down at the floor. All you could see was the spats. He was like a dictator ... and he had the same effect on the Leafs."

Players great and ordinary experienced the Smythe motivational touch first-hand. Cal Gardner, for instance, was hauled on the carpet in the wake of a great moment, Bill Barilko's Cup-winning goal in overtime in 1951. Smythe told Gardner he was being fined the staggering sum of $1,000 because Barilko, not Gardner (who had also been on the ice), had scored on the play.

"He showed me the film and said, 'Now why didn't *you* put the puck in the net?'" Gardner told Dick Irvin for his book *The Habs*. A shocked Gardner mustered his reasons for letting Barilko take the shot. It took two or three viewings of the game film before Smythe finally relented. "But that was Smythe," says Gardner. "No nonsense with him."

The fun-loving Babe Pratt experienced Smythe's razor tongue as well. The Maple Leafs had just lost to Detroit in overtime. The winning goal came when the forward shot the puck between Pratt's legs as he furiously skated backward. The shot eluded Broda in goal. Afterwards, in a hushed and despondent dressing room, Smythe paused in front of Pratt's locker. Babe hesitated, not knowing quite what to say. "Major," he finally said, "I guess I should've kept my legs together."

Smythe paused for five seconds and hissed, "No, your mother should've," and walked away.

A Smythe tradition copied by everyone in hockey was his organization of a farm system to feed his club with young talent. In the Leafs' system—overseen by his son Stafford—Catholic boys were usually funnelled through St. Michael's College in Toronto, while Protestant boys came up through the Marlboro junior team. "Put the dogans in the Micks' school and the Protestants in with the Marlboros," Smythe noted with his typical sensitivity. Exceptional or borderline, they played it Connie's way or they didn't play, at least not in Toronto. Many times, the Maple Leafs would sponsor a team, an entire league or a recreation program to capture a prize prospect—as happened when Toronto sponsored Dave Keon's team in Noranda, Quebec, or the hockey program in Shumacher, Ontario, home of the young Frank Mahovlich.

Unlike the American-based NHL teams, the Leafs also enjoyed the benefits of Foster Hewitt's salesmanship. Until the 1970s, when the Maple Leafs wanted to sign a young man from English Canada, they didn't have to sell him on the Leafs—he was already a fan. Leafs scouts had only to dangle the blue-and-white sweater (and very little money) before a prospect to get his signature on a contract.

Smythe's feeder system produced a steady stream of great players: Charlie Conacher and Harvey "Busher" Jackson, Red Horner, Ted "Teeder" Kennedy, and from the club that dominated the '60s, a flood of talent in the form of Bob Baun, Carl Brewer, Tim Horton, Bob Pulford, Dave Keon, Dick Duff, Bob Nevin, Billy Harris, Frank Mahovlich and many others.

Because of this rich pipeline, the Leafs needed to trade only when they wanted a gifted player like center Max Bentley of Chicago or Detroit's brilliant defenseman Red Kelly to complement the home-grown talent, or to punish a disloyal or wayward product of the farm system. It was a formula that brought fourteen trips to the Stanley Cup finals in thirty NHL seasons.

The Leafs team of the '60s featuring Horton, Stanley, Baun and Brewer was the fourth great squad assembled under the Smythe reign. The first, from 1930 to 1936, featured Primeau, Conacher and Jackson—"the Kid Line"—plus Clancy, Horner, Ace Bailey, Hap Day and Harold "Baldy" Cotton. Despite an impressive record, reaching the Stanley Cup finals in six years, they won only once in 1931-32 and became known as a team that peaked too early in the regular season.

The next golden era of the Leafs began in 1941 and ran through the war years until 1947. These were the teams of Syl Apps, Frankie McCool, Gus Bodnar and the Metz brothers, Nick and Don, that won three Stanley Cups. This group was immediately succeeded by the third dream team, led by Ted Kennedy, Howie Meeker, Bill Barilko, Max Bentley and Turk Broda. This group hung on until 1951.

The teams led by Apps and Kennedy rarely finished first but conserved their energies for the big prize, the Stanley Cup playoffs.

Those wonderful teams combined to bring the Stanley Cup to Toronto on six occasions in eleven seasons.

When Bob Baun, Carl Brewer, Allan Stanley and Tim Horton suited up together with the Maple Leafs for the first time in September 1958, it had been a long time since the Cup had called Toronto home—at least by Maple Leafs' standards. The Leafs had been out of the playoffs as often as not in the seven years since Bill Barilko's overtime goal won them the Cup in 1951. That overtime goal against Montreal on April 21, 1951, was in Barilko's last game as a Maple Leaf. The bruising defenseman would disappear shortly thereafter when his plane went down on a fishing trip in northern Ontario. With him, the tradition of great Leafs hockey seemingly disappeared, too. Barilko's body would not be found for eleven years, until the summer of 1962, the next time the Leafs won the Cup.

As the final golden era of hockey dawned in Toronto, Conn Smythe had partially removed himself from the daily running of the Gardens, preferring to spend his time with his racing stable or at the famed Breakers Hotel in Palm Beach, Florida, to avoid the discomforts brought on by his war wounds. Smythe very much wanted the Maple Leafs passed down as a family enterprise to his son Stafford and then his grandson Tommy, and so he began preparing his exit in 1956 by stepping down as manager of the team. Management of the club was handed to Stafford and the "Silver Seven," the group of businessmen who formed the steering committee for the club. Broadsides in the press and public appearances guaranteed Smythe's continuity into a fourth decade, but he was turning day-to-day matters over to a younger generation.

Like a true soldier, however, he could never entirely stop fighting. And he had one last "good fight" left in him: crushing a players' union.

4

IF YOU CAN'T BEAT 'EM ON THE ICE, THEN ORGANIZE

The disintegration of the Maple Leafs championship machine during the 1950s left Conn Smythe befuddled and curiously ambivalent about how to rectify his club's laughable ineptitude. His usually sure assessments of talent failed him. More and more he turned to his horse-racing stable for fulfillment and reassurance. In fact, he might have left the hockey business altogether had it not been for the Players' Association formed in 1957.

Crushing organized labor was the final sacred mission of Conn Smythe's hockey career. With his team dead last in the League, he found purpose in the holy task of cleansing hockey of its union sympathizers.

As the quintessential self-made man, Conn Smythe believed passionately in the social Darwinism of his turbulent childhood and military experience. "He isn't a union-hater," wrote Scott Young in *The Globe and Mail*, "but he is a man who hates the way unions sometimes interfere with the only 'ism' he really respects—individualism."

A man who had escaped poverty, then dodged death and dismemberment in two wars, the Major judged men on their reactions to the fight. A man who stood tall in the face of the odds, who did not flinch when the fists or the bullets flew and who never took a backward step, was the kind of man Smythe wanted for his hockey club. King Clancy, Red Horner, Syl Apps, Teeder Kennedy—these were the men Smythe wanted wearing the blue and white. They were tough, and they gave no quarter. They also had another characteristic that endeared them to Smythe. Off the ice, they duly deferred to "the Maj," as he fancied himself. They observed a respect for rank as if they were enlisted men in his "Sportsmen's Battery."

"I recall the first day I was with the Leafs and had to go to [Smythe's] office," recalled Cal Gardner, who came over from the Rangers in the late '40s. "When we met I called him 'Conny,' like a cocky kid, I guess. Ten minutes later I was leaving the office and it was 'Yes, Mr. Smythe, no, Mr. Smythe, that's right, Mr. Smythe.'"

A Smythe directive could take many forms, as Howie Meeker discovered. Meeker had been the Rookie of the Year with the Leafs in 1947, and for all the world appeared to be just a kid from Kitchener who wanted to play hockey. But folks in Meeker's home town of New Hamburg decided he was just the man to represent them in Parliament as a Progressive Conservative. Though he didn't have a political bone in his body, Meeker was actively pursued by none other than George Drew, the party leader.

Drew finally caught up to a reluctant Meeker at a campgrounds in Quebec. He demanded to know Meeker's objection to running for the Tories. "I don't have a chance of winning, and I can make more playing hockey for Toronto than I can in Ottawa," Meeker informed him, wishing he could get on with his fishing trip. But, instead, the persistent Drew swept Meeker into his limousine and proceeded to the nearest telephone, where he was connected with Smythe in Toronto. Loyal Tory that he was, Smythe thought Meeker's candidacy a capital idea and said he'd guarantee the difference in salary and would give him the time off in the unlikely event Meeker won. Coming from Smythe, that constituted an order.

Thus, Howie Meeker put his name up for election and—against all odds—was elected for a term as a member of the House of Commons, though the Tories themselves did not win.

For all his approbation of pluck and independence from his players in public, Smythe could never tolerate those qualities of an employee in private. When it came to a battle between Smythe and the men who worked for him, as hockey players or as laborers at his sand and gravel business, Smythe had no stomach for a fair fight. He had not only to possess the whip hand but to employ it as well when it came to suppressing dissent.

When the employees of the Sand and Gravel Company announced their intention to form a union, Smythe gave them a day to think it over. The next day, the men confirmed their plans to proceed, and Smythe acted swiftly. "He told them, that's fine, we're shut down," remembers Bobby Baun. "He put everything in mothballs. Stafford and Des James—he was the superintendent at the Gardens—had just finished buying twenty tractor trailers worth $600,000 or $700,000. Conn sprayed everything with oil and left it. Put them all out of business."

At times, of course, Smythe could be remarkably philanthropic. His efforts with the Easter Seals charity in setting up the Variety Village complex were Smythe at his benevolent best, working long and hard to provide a facility for crippled children in Ontario.

And he could be generous with his players, too, when it suited him. After one particularly ugly brawl with Stan Mikita and Reggie Fleming of Chicago, Bobby Baun was fined a whopping $2,800 by the NHL for his part in the fighting. "He never paid the fine for me," remembers Baun, "but that Christmas he sent a nice cheque to my wife for $2,800 with a very nice letter."

Carl Brewer saw both sides of the Smythe legend. "In my first year, I was second in the Calder voting, and Milt Dunnell wrote in *The Star* that I should be expecting a $1,000 bonus," remembers Brewer. "Now, if Milt wrote it, you know it was coming from Conn Smythe. Come the end of the season, I didn't get the bonus, so I went in to see the old man ... he treated me gruffly, like he always did. But a few weeks later, I got a cheque from Smythe for $1,000. He said, 'Here, Carl, give it to your favorite charity.'"

But when Ted Lindsay of the Red Wings, Doug Harvey of the Canadiens, and Leafs captain Jimmy Thompson announced their intention to form a players' union in February 1957, the largesse was replaced with a vicious counterattack from Major Conn.

In this final battle of wills at the Gardens, Conn Smythe would fix his private proletariat* in its true place in the hockey firmament, a notch ahead of the rink attendants but several pegs below the office staff. As the unchallenged authority with the Maple Leafs, and with the NHL's Board of Governors as well, he would lay down the law to

---

* In Smythe's personal papers are detailed definitions of the word "communism" and "proletariat." The definition for proletariat reads "the poorest and lowest classes."

the hockey prima donnas. The watchword of the day in hockey was enlightened despotism, and Conn Smythe was the biggest despot in the hockey world.

The formation of the Players' Association had been an idea in the making for a considerable time. As players returned from wartime service, they began to reject the dewy-eyed idealism of Smythe's prototypical "amateur" hockey player who plays for pride and glory alone. Players wanted more control of their careers, which were often short and not very lucrative. Eddie Shack remembers that his biggest paydays in hockey came not from the game itself but from selling his home each time he was traded to a new city. Players like Bill Gadsby realized—too late—that they had greater negotiating power after they'd retired. When Gadsby finally quit Detroit after twenty NHL seasons, the struggling Red Wings offered him $50,000 to make a comeback. One year earlier, however, Gadsby had had to battle just to get $30,000 from the club.

A new determination was evolving among players, and one of its first manifestations emerged in 1946. In that year, a number of Detroit Red Wings began a process to set up a players' pension fund. Through Detroit insurance agent C. Jean Caspar, the Detroit players announced plans to create a pension fund for players—a nest egg for when they retired. They began to collect seed money to start the fund; the owners of the Red Wings themselves kicked in $2,500 to help the project.

But they hadn't bargained with Smythe, who saw a pension fund run by players as an attempt to subvert the discipline and control the NHL held over its players. At his insistence, the NHL owners took over the project in 1947, forced Caspar to send his money to them and entrusted the freshly minted NHL Pension Society to their newly installed president, Clarence S. Campbell.

Campbell—who had once been an NHL referee—proved a valuable servant to the owners over the years as front man for causes good and bad. In a moment of candor, Stafford Smythe offered this assessment of Campbell's value to the League: "Where would we find another Rhodes Scholar, graduate lawyer, decorated war hero and former prosecutor at Nuremberg who'll do what he's told?" Campbell's deft handling of the players over their pension fund in 1947 was a testament to his loyalty to the owners.

"Clarence often said the pension fund was his proudest achievement," says his widow, Phyllis, "although people don't seem to be quite so sure these days." If starting the pension plan was Campbell's finest public moment, hijacking it from the players ranked up there with Smythe's most clever covert actions.

In the NHL's scheme for the Pension Society, the players put up most of the money to fund the purchase of annuity contracts (often contributing as much as 20 to 25 percent of their after-tax salary), while the owners made the decisions on when and where the funds were to be invested. Because the annuity contracts were guaranteed by the government (and later the company) that sold them, there was no risk to the owners. Further, the players could not hold the owners liable if the plan failed at a future date.

Most of the NHL's contributions to the plan before 1957 came from the profits of the playoffs and All-Star Game, in which the players participated for free. In effect, the players subsidized their pension both directly (their own contributions ranged from $900 to $1,500 a year) and indirectly (via the All-Star Game). No wonder that when the NHL Club Pension Plan and Trust came into being, Campbell, in a burst of effusive praise, called it "the best in all of sport." For the owners, it certainly was the best of all worlds.

With owners gaining financial and administrative control over the pension plan without much struggle, a contented Smythe turned his attention elsewhere, confident that the germs of player disaffection had been sufficiently quarantined. But players had been accorded two of the five positions on the board of directors of the Pension Society, and several of them—including Ted Lindsay, Doug Harvey and Leo Reise of the Red Wings—had no intention of meekly rubber-stamping decisions made by the owners. Throughout the 1950s, they peppered Campbell and the League representatives on the board with questions about how the money was invested, what interest it was making and why an independent trustee didn't control the fund. The players were also particularly concerned with reducing their considerable share of the contributions.

"In New York in 1958, I made $7,500, and for that I had to check guys like Howe and Litzenberger every night," says Shack. "Of that money, $900 went to the pension plan. Living in New York on that money, I had to sell hats, whatever I could do to make ends meet."

The players' concern about how the NHL handled their pension was reflected by Lindsay at the ninth annual meeting of the Pension Society in Montreal in October 1956. Speaking to Campbell about the president's annual visits to the clubs, he noted: "I think that when you talk to the players, they don't understand what the pension means to them, and they would have difficulty explaining the benefits to their wives.

"And I think if possible, you should do something to educate us ... I have talked to the fellows on my club and a lot of them don't understand it five minutes after you leave the room."

The answers Lindsay and the players received to their requests about their pensions were often evasive, with issues referred to the NHL Board of Governors for further study or left ignored. The fiery Red Wings left-winger began to make plans of his own.

It was no secret that even the greatest players lived in fear of the NHL's cavalier approach to labor relations. Facing a monopoly and with no players' association to fight for them, players came to dread a demotion (or worse) after a bad game. "In those days, we'd take a lot of crap," says Larry Regan, who played for Boston and Toronto. "You were never comfortable."

"Everything was so secretive," recalls Andy Bathgate, who played for eighteen NHL seasons. "You didn't dare ask a question of management ... you'd likely have your head taken off."

"Hockey's a very unforgiving sport," adds Carl Brewer. "And management at that time didn't mind publicly questioning the level of intelligence a player had."

For every player of the time, there is a story of a life uprooted, a career crushed, a personal snub. "When our first child was born," recalls Gordie Howe, "the general manager, Jack Adams, called the hospital and told the doctor to keep Colleen and little Marty in the hospital, because they didn't want anything affecting my game." Another time, Howe tore cartilage in his ribcage during a game in Boston. A doubled-over Howe had to hail a cab himself to take him to hospital.

Howe's long-time boss was "Jolly" Jack Adams, a former NHL player who matched Conn Smythe's zeal when it came to union-busting. Adams was nicknamed "Jolly" under the blanket proviso that all fat people are happy. "Jolly" Jack, however, was a specialist in fear and manipulation. He liked to stroll through the Red Wings dressing room with two train tickets to Detroit's farm team in Omaha jutting from the breast pocket of his jacket, and he is frequently mentioned as a central character in players' horror stories.

Eddie Litzenberger's tale is typical. Playing on a line with Howe and Alex Delvecchio, he had scored six goals in his first five games with Adams' Red Wings in 1961. Howe had just one goal, however, and Delvecchio none. Adams called Eddie aside at a practice one day and said, "You know, Eddie, there's no such a thing as being too unselfish on the ice." In other words, pass the puck more to Howe and Delvecchio.

Litzenberger digested the message and replied, "Mr. Adams, I was always taught to do the intelligent thing as early as possible and let the puck do the work." The next day Litzenberger was traded to Toronto.

And there was always the unspoken pressure to return as early as possible from injuries. Boom Boom Geoffrion once hacked the cast off his broken leg with a kitchen knife so he could play in the semifinals against Chicago. When the painkillers wore off, "I cried like a baby," Geoffrion recalled. These personal nicks and cuts, married to a long list of grievances ranging from training-camp expenses to moving allowances to life insurance, helped Lindsay convince like-minded players like Doug Harvey of Montreal, Tod Sloan of Toronto and Bill Gadsby of New York that the time was ripe for an association to represent the interests of players. Even mild-mannered players such as defenseman Allan Stanley (then with Boston) recognized the time had come. "It was just time for the players to have an association," he says. "After all, the players in the other sports were organizing, too."

By 1956, the only thing that Lindsay and the organizers needed to realize their project was a catalyst, a flashpoint to convert long-held emotions into actions. In the summer of that year, the spark was supplied during a chance conversation Lindsay had with star pitcher Bob Feller of the Cleveland Indians, a founding member of the baseball players' association. Feller told Lindsay about the two men who had helped the ballplayers negotiate a precedent-setting contract with baseball owners: lawyers Norman J. Lewis and Milton Mound of New York. Feller said that Lewis and Mound had arranged to have a percentage of the TV contract from the World Series directed to players' pensions.

At his own expense, Lindsay decided to seek out Lewis and Mound, and their assessment of the state of hockey shook Lindsay, perhaps the most sophisticated businessman among the NHL players at the time. Compared to the other team sports, they told him, hockey was locked in the Dark Ages. Owners controlled the revenue, the players, and the facts about both. Whatever Lindsay knew about the NHL was what the NHL wanted him to know.

Lindsay, who had come expecting to hear a more muted message, was flabbergasted. Despite a truculent nature that made him the most feared left-winger in the game, Lindsay was still very apprehensive about what to do with the information Mound and Lewis had supplied him with. Like every hockey player before him and most after him, he could not quite steel himself to the implications of a union. Would it mean the players decided who played and who didn't? Would the union negotiate for the players collectively? Would fans think that union solidarity would kill competition? These doubts plagued even the self-assured Lindsay (and would be ruthlessly exploited by the owners later).

Lindsay's misgivings were common to athletes in other sports, too. A decade later, Marvin Miller built the baseball players' union into the most powerful and effective union in pro sports. Yet he remembers that his hardest task was to force baseball players to see beyond the banal and trivial, and recognize themselves as men doing a job, rather than actors in some boyhood fantasy, responsible for perpetuating the American Dream. Miller discovered that most baseball players were more concerned with splinters on the benches in the dugouts than with arbitration procedures and collective bargaining. In his autobiography, *A Whole Different Ball Game*, Miller recalled the effect of strike talk on the players in the '60s: "It was the owners' worst nightmare. And most (not all) players felt the same way." Said Pittsburgh pitcher Bob Friend: "It would destroy baseball if fans were exposed to the spectacle of someone like Stan Musial picketing a ballpark." "A union would be bad for us," chimed in Nellie Fox of Chicago. "I don't see how conditions can be improved."

In such a climate, Lindsay moved cautiously to recruit player representatives from the other clubs. It meant breaking down not only prejudices against organized labor, but prejudices born of a thousand elbows to the head, sticks to the ankle and punches to the nose. Some of the men Lindsay worked with most closely in organizing the Players' Association—Jimmy Thompson, Fern Flaman, Maurice Richard—were men who hated every fibre of his wiry 160-pound frame on the ice.

Such was the appeal of his message, however, that the new Players' Association secretly signed up all but one player in the NHL at the time—Ted Kennedy of the Leafs, who was retiring at the end of the season anyway. When he announced the formation of the Association at a press conference on February 12, 1957, Lindsay was hoping the organization—with the help of Milton Mound in New York—would effect change, not revolution, in hockey. They soft-pedalled the union aspect. In fact, from the mild comments of the executives of the Players' Association, you might have wondered why they organized at all.

"Actually, we don't have any grievances," advanced Lindsay. "We just felt we should have an organization of this kind."

"We're not out to make trouble," said one player. "We get along fine with [the owners]," said another. If this was a threat to anyone, it was a mild one.

Milton Mound, too, soft-pedalled the cause when he held his first meetings with the League. "Mr. Mound was at pains to make the conversation friendly," Smythe was told by his trusted *consigliori*, Ian S. Johnston. "And he pointed out that the players were very anxious to do nothing to hurt the game of hockey."

But Smythe saw the union as treason, nothing less. The soldier in him no doubt wanted to get a brick wall and a firing squad and settle accounts that way. After all, he reasoned, hadn't he been fair with the players all along, giving them a good wage, a place to play and moral guidance? "The Maple Leaf Hockey Club has never allowed drink in the dressing room or in the team car when travelling on the road. It will never be said that our team was in any way involved in starting any of these young fellows on a drinking career," he declared in his best Jimmy Swaggart voice.

The 1931 prospectus to buyers of Maple Leaf Gardens stock epitomized Smythe's sentiments towards the lads who carried his team's colors. "We consider them pals rather than business associates," he wrote, "and do not care to place a price on their hockey ability." But the formation of the Players' Association—with his own captain, Jimmy Thompson, as the first secretary—sent the mercurial Smythe into a fury of revenge. At a press conference in March 1957, he threw down the gauntlet.

"I find it very difficult to feel that there is time during a hockey season for the captain of my club to go around and influence young players to join an association, which has—as far as I can find out—no specific plans or ideas of how to benefit hockey. I also feel that anything spawned in secrecy as this Association was, certainly has to have some odor to it."

Smythe went on to suggest that if the players wanted to do something really worthwhile, they should lobby the government for tax breaks, not undermine the fragile underpinnings of his empire. "The record of the Association in nearly a year is that they are causing a good deal of trouble," Smythe blustered at the 1957 annual meeting of Maple Leaf Gardens shareholders, "and that no one can point out one thing that has been done which is helpful for hockey ..."

With Johnston as his hired gun, Smythe then set out to rid his team of the players who wished to subvert his control. And if it meant rendering his club uncompetitive for twenty years, the price would be paid. He was determined to purge the union sympathizers immediately.

While the principle of the union offended Smythe's sensibilities, a few of the specific demands by the players—a portion of the League's TV revenues (by the 1960s Toronto was making almost $1 million a year from its TV contracts) and greater control of the pension plan—sent him into a shallow orbit. Armed with this assault on his hockey sovereignty, Smythe convinced the other NHL owners to create a special fund to fight the ratification of the Players' Association. The fund was publicly advertised as a scheme to help out the Chicago franchise, but its benefits came in the form of players, not cash, when the Black Hawks received the lion's share of the union organizers banished from their old clubs.

The captain of Chicago, Eddie Litzenberger, was the Black Hawks' representative in 1957. By the next season, he saw he suddenly had familiar company. "Tod Sloan, Jimmy Thompson, Dolly St. Laurent, Eddie Sandford ... they'd all been involved with the Players' Association and they'd all been traded to Chicago."

Using an inside informant on the Maple Leafs recruited by Johnston, Smythe was able to determine the agenda and the tactics of the Association. "The 'pipe line' tells me that Mound was told to stay away from the meeting and he appeared against the wishes of the players," Johnston wrote to Smythe in one letter. "My informant tells me that Sloane [sic] dislikes Mound, wants nothing more to do with him and says the Association is finished ..."

Smythe also employed his general manager, Howie Meeker, to quiz the players on their feelings about the union. In a letter to Smythe in

September 1957, Meeker outlined the modest demands of the players for training camp allowances, moving expenses and compensation lost in summer jobs when a player was injured. "Most of them are convinced the above-mentioned demands could be obtained from the owners without a Players' Union and everyone I have talked to has expressed marked dissatisfaction with the demands presented to the NHL owners."

"Smythe tore a strip off me for not knowing about the union when it started," says Meeker today. "But if hockey needed anything at that time, it was a players' union. I was not a fan of Mr. Smythe's."

Smythe kept other rabid anti-union figures like Jack Adams and NHL president Clarence Campbell well supplied with information on the players' actions. They developed a strategy to separate the ring-leaders and then wait them out. "Acknowledge the correspondence but don't recognize the correspondent" became a watchword in the NHL executive offices for dealing with Lindsay and the Players' Association.

The League's stalling tactics eventually diffused the momentum of the Association. The time they won by delaying allowed Smythe and Adams to inculcate the notion that Mound was an interloper and for-eigner who wanted to submit the players to draconian socialism. "I have been in hockey practically all my life, and he has never crossed my path," Smythe proclaimed of Mound. "So I think I am safe in say-ing he has absolutely no knowledge of hockey whatsoever." Players began worrying that there would be a standard wage for all of them, and that they'd soon be better off in Stalin's Russia.

Having sown dissent, Smythe, Campbell and Adams launched the second front in their war against the Players' Association during the summer of 1957. It was a brutal but effective exile of the union lead-ers. "I traded Jimmy Thompson to Chicago, bang," bragged Smythe later. "Ted Lindsay, the Association's first president, was traded to Chicago as well. In a sense, we thus isolated the Association and it was nearly ten years before it became effective."

But the Association didn't disappear as quietly as Smythe reported. Despite the banishment of Thompson and Lindsay and Sloan, the players remained adamant in requesting that their Associ-ation be named their negotiating agent. An embattled Mound applied in all the NHL cities for certification of the Association as the bar-gaining agent for the players.

Along the way, the players scored some symbolic victories as they battled for legitimacy. The chairman of the Ontario Labour Relations Board, Jacob Finkelman, infuriated Smythe when he opined that the NHL was a business, not a sport. That prompted Smythe to write lawyer John Robinson, "I suppose if they rule we are a business, we will read of the games we win in the Births columns, and of the games we lose in the Deaths." Robinson replied, "I do not agree with this, nor with any other of the views expressed by him [Finkelman]. The only belief we share is that the Jewish race produced the Messiah, but I do not agree that he was J. Finkelman."

When guerilla tactics such as loyalty oaths, individual interviews and harassment failed to break the solidarity of the players (some, like Frank Mahovlich, were given a breakdown of how much money the Leafs had spent on their development), the Major reverted to a full frontal assault. With approval of the Association as the players' legal bargaining unit to be heard by the Labour Relations Board two weeks later, Smythe, son Stafford, lawyer Johnston and NHL president Campbell pulled a surprise attack on the Leafs dressing room on November 4, 1957.

Players had learned through bitter experience that a visit by Smythe to the dressing room was the prelude to a tirade. "I remember that when he got mad, he had eyes like the Rocket," recalls Howie Meeker. "He had that wild look, and his cheeks were as red as apples." "You knew when he got real mad," adds Bob Baun. "His eyes got further back in his head, and they'd go a real deep blue."

For two hours Smythe's eyes were as blue as indigo as he and his associates harangued the players about the intrusion of New York lawyers and "Jews" into the purity of the hockey business. At one point, Smythe, transported by demons and infidels of his own making, hurled a chair skyward, where it lodged firmly in the ceiling of the room. Fearing for their lives if they moved, the players stared up at the dangling chair for the rest of the meeting.

After further rhetoric on loyalty and fair play from Campbell, Stafford Smythe and Johnston, Smythe demanded an immediate vote by the players on whether to reject the Association as their bargaining unit. In a moment that epitomized the end of Conn Smythe's control over his players better than any other single event, his beloved Maple Leafs failed to give in to his demands. They subsequently voted in favor of the Association as their legal bargaining unit.

With Smythe's failure to crush the rebels, it fell to Jack Adams, the Red Wings' general manager, to issue the killer blow to the Association days later. He called in loyal press sources, who dutifully wrote that Lindsay had been traded to Chicago because he was a "cancer" and "only out for himself." Lindsay was portrayed as a dupe for Milton Mound, who was dreaming of leading players into some socialist utopia.

Similar sermons to the players in the Detroit dressing room finally broke the will of the intimidated Red Wings. Hoping to find a safe middle ground between Mound and the NHL, Red Kelly, Marcel Pronovost and Gordie Howe turned against their former teammate Lindsay. In the misguided notion that they might "negotiate" as gentlemen with the owners without using strikes or bargaining units, the Red Wings quit the Players' Association on November 13, 1957.

The Red Wings were vilified for abandoning their colleagues. "As you should know from hockey," wrote Jerry Hartford, a Canadian United Automobile Workers official, to Red Kelly, "gutless guys always get their comeuppance ... I wouldn't go across the road to see a bunch of company lovers do anything—even if it was free."

The Detroit players were similarly hazed by players still loyal to the Association on other teams. Jack Adams wrote to Campbell requesting support for his team after they had been called "scabs" and "brainwashed" by the Chicago players. Citing the "considerable courage" it took for the Red Wings to scuttle the union, Campbell vaguely promised action. "Keep your chin up," he told Adams, although it wasn't clear which of the rotund Adams's chins he was referring to.

Sabotaged from without and within, the Players' Association lasted only six more months. It was replaced by an Owner/Player Council, a punchless platform given to the players as a reward for dropping their anti-trust and unfair-labor demands. Of fourteen items brought up by players at the Owner/Player Council meeting of 1974, for instance, three (including prompt payment of bonuses) were accepted, six (including no Sunday afternoon games following a Saturday night game) were denied and the remaining five were sent to discussion-stage limbo.

But for Conn Smythe, the giant-killer, the satisfaction was muted. The Players' Association had been smashed in Detroit, not in Toronto, and by someone other than Conn Smythe. His "pals" on the Maple Leafs had voted to find new allies in hockey, although it would take another ten years for Alan Eagleson to once again harness their discontent.

The Toronto players of the day remain surprisingly understanding of Smythe's role in the affair. "It's all the time element," says Baun. "When he grew up, he thought he was fair to people. Maybe he was."

"If you're going to hold him responsible, you've got to look at all the rest of them, too," says Stanley. "They did the same thing. It was a sign of the times."

Only Brewer remains critical. "Conn Smythe was a mean, vindictive man. It would be hard for me to say something nice about him, even when he tried to buy me off for $1,000. He has to answer to someone other than me."

The newspaper accounts of the day also were curiously muted in their coverage of the events. Scott Young in *The Globe and Mail* acknowledged the absence of Tod Sloan from the Leafs after his trade, albeit in muted tones. "That was a personal thing," he wrote at the time. "Conn Smythe versus Tod Sloan. Leafs have never tried to say it wasn't—but they didn't want Sloan on the team because of his connection with the Players' Association."

But little was said about how Smythe had stripped the club of several of its finest players—in effect conceding defeat—in his attempts to decide if "the Maple Leaf team and its individual players would be better under the direction of the Players' Association, or the management of the Leafs. I didn't want anyone telling us what to do."

His best energies spent on delaying the NHL's inevitable day of reckoning with its players, Smythe effected one last legacy on the Leafs. With Tim Horton on the Leafs' defense, Allan Stanley en route via trade from Boston and Carl Brewer and Bob Baun graduated from the junior Marlies, Smythe and his son hired an outsider to run the hockey affairs of the team along with coach Billy Reay. In temperament and will to win, Smythe couldn't have chosen a more natural successor to himself.

The new man was a balding, forty-year-old Torontonian who had managed Jean Béliveau and the Quebec Aces to titles in the Eastern Professional League, and most recently had worked for Eddie Shore with the Springfield Indians. They called George Imlach "Punch," and he would preside over the most successful and most turbulent decade in Maple Leafs' history.

Imlach's hiring and the revolt of the Leafs players marked the end of Smythe's day-to-day influence on the team. By 1961, with Imlach firmly in control of the hockey product, Smythe sold controlling interest in the Leafs to Stafford and Ballard and their investment group. He still maintained an office at the Gardens and, as anyone who continued to feel his wrath knew, Conn Smythe would never disappear completely from the hockey scene he had fostered for forty years.

With Conn away from the everyday operations, however, conditions changed in the old building at Carlton and Church Streets. The military bandstand was removed by Harold Ballard to make way for more seats. The portrait of the Queen was moved, then removed to storage. The capacity of the building was increased by adding new seats and making other seats smaller.

Entertainment acts like the Beatles and the Dave Clark Five played the Gardens on nights when the team was away. Outside of a few public harrumphs, Conn kept his displeasure about such goings-on largely to himself.

The final, symbolic straw for the patriotic Smythe occurred in 1966 when Ballard arranged to stage a heavyweight boxing title fight featuring the young Cassius Clay at the Gardens. Clay was fighting induction into the U.S. military at the time on the basis of his acceptance of the Black Muslim religion. He would soon be known as Muhammad Ali.

The idea of a "draft dodger" taking center stage at the house of Smythe, who had served his country twice in war, proved to be the exit cue for Conn Smythe. In disgust, he unloaded his remaining stock on Stafford and his partners and devoted himself to his work with crippled children and to his racing stable.

Smythe, the man who had defined hockey in Toronto for almost a half-century, was effectively through with the club at the zenith of its popularity.

5

PUNCH

Punch Imlach was having a beer prior to boarding the train that would take his Maple Leafs back to Toronto to face the Montreal Canadiens for the Stanley Cup in 1960. The scene was a decrepit bar on Detroit's unfortunate side. Imlach was savoring the Maple Leafs' triumph over the Red Wings in the semifinals along with his brew, a win that would send his team against the mighty Habs, winners of four straight Stanley Cups. One might have said Imlach was letting his hair down, but Imlach's hairline had long since retreated over the horizon of his skull.

A Montreal fan approached Imlach, pushing four fingers under Punch's nose.

"What's that mean?" growled Imlach.

"Four straight," crowed the Habs fan. "For Montreal. Just how do you think you're going to stop Montreal?"

Imlach fixed his antagonist with a steely stare. "That isn't the question at all," he responded. "How is Montreal going to stop ME?"

Conn Smythe couldn't have produced a better surrogate hockey son than George "Punch" Imlach. Imlach preserved and perpetuated Smythe's Maple Leafs myth. "Punch grew up in the armed services under Smythe," says Bob Baun. "He knew Conn from the old days, knew how he operated." That meant operating in the black and from a point of strength.

Ironically, Imlach's zeal in continuing that legacy precipitated the very things both he and Smythe feared most: player unions, lawsuits and the end of the NHL's hegemony over the minds and souls of their players.

The only child of Scottish parents raised in Toronto's working class Riverdale neighborhood (which later produced Billy Harris and Carl Brewer), the slightly built Imlach came from a sports background. His father wanted "wee George" to make his mark in soccer. When he was twelve, Imlach was the ball boy on a successful soccer team his father coached in east-end Toronto. That team included two Ulster boys, Sammy and Bobby McNabney, whose nephew would later play a major part in Imlach's life with the Maple Leafs and Sabres of the NHL. Their nephew's name was Alan Eagleson.

But like many products of immigrant parents, Imlach left his old sport behind. His passion was hockey, and he was weaned on the rough-and-tumble style employed by Conn Smythe and made legend by Foster Hewitt on "Hockey Night in Canada." Even his nickname, "Punch," bespoke a two-fisted approach to the game (although he got the name not from delivering a punch but from being knocked "punchy" by a bodycheck during his playing days).

"Aggressiveness is the most important thing on any team," he wrote in his first autobiography, *Hockey Is A Battle*. "As a coach, I have stood behind benches at hockey games everywhere from Chicoutimi to Los Angeles for more than 20 years ... I see what other people see, but I also think a coach has a chance to see a little deeper, right into the soul of the game. And what I see as the soul of a hockey game is a tough man who never backs up."

Perhaps that unyielding philosophy was shaped by growing up a small man in a harsh, unforgiving game like hockey. Imlach's own career was hampered by his inability to bulk up his wiry frame much past 140 pounds. On several occasions, unimpressed coaches sent the skinny kid home, only to find the persistent Imlach back again the next day, lacing up his battered skates, ready to try again. He knew he'd finally made it when a local coach presented him with a set of barbells. His successful—if undistinguished—playing career was more a tribute to his pluck than to any natural gift.

By the time he arrived in Toronto to coach the Maple Leafs, Imlach had thoroughly tested his theories on toughness. When World War II broke out, he'd left behind his job at a bank to join the army and become a drill instructor. For two years, he put recruits through basic training in Cornwall, Ontario. He thrived in the role of the doughty drillmaster. Starting as a corporal, he was promoted to lieutenant without ever seeing active duty. Much as it had done for Smythe,

Imlach's experience preparing men for war made him a believer in regimen and discipline. And so he drove his troops to win in every company competition.

Once, he had his platoon out for a three-mile march in full pack. Under Imlach, it became a three-mile run. A former Ottawa policeman in the platoon looked over to Imlach. "Jesus Christ," he puffed, "*we* don't have to get in shape for hockey, do we?"

Imlach growled back, "I don't want the Germans catching you running either way." There was never any arguing with Punch.

Imlach received his first coaching experience in the army, leading the camp teams. Once out of the service, Punch refined his ideas while coaching hockey teams like the Quebec Aces and Springfield Indians. (Strategy was always considered a poor cousin in hockey coaching before the Soviets belied that notion.) He became a minor legend in Quebec, where he coached the young Jean Béliveau on a powerhouse semi-pro team that filled the Quebec Colisée to the rafters. People joked that Béliveau—who was an idol in Quebec— would have to take a pay cut to join the Montreal Canadiens.

A small hockey-crazy city like Quebec in the 1950s was the perfect time and place for Imlach to hone his craft; in the dog-eat-dog atmosphere that prevailed during the six-team NHL, players on the Aces were in no position to resist the whims of an autocratic coach. Twenty years later, Imlach still marvelled at the courage and devotion of his semi-pro players on the Aces. The headstrong young stars of the Toronto Maple Leafs would prove to be a tougher nut to crack.

But the showdowns and recriminations with his talented team lay far in the future on the sunny summer day of August 1, 1958, as the forty-year-old Imlach first sat down at his desk at Maple Leaf Gardens, opposite Billy Reay.

Typically, Conn Smythe had been unimpressed with Imlach during contract negotiations until the Boston Bruins (for whom Imlach worked in Springfield) asked him to back off. "They said Lynn Patrick, their general manager, was ill and they might need Imlach badly," he recalled. "Hmm, I thought. Is he that good?" Boston's interest piqued Smythe's desire to acquire Imlach.

Negotiations were threatening to break down over Imlach's insistence on getting the general manager's job in Toronto. Stafford Smythe was offering the assistant GM job instead. Conn Smythe got right to the point with Imlach. "What's the matter? You want to stay in the minors forever? Are you afraid to take a chance?"

In one brief exchange, Smythe had instinctively hit all the right buttons on Punch, who'd paid his dues coaching in the army and the minors. Imlach, his pride challenged, agreed to share the assistant GM job with King Clancy until he'd proved himself worthy of the top job. Then he set about doing just that.

Everyone knew Imlach had coached Béliveau in Quebec for several years, but he remained very much an unknown quantity to his players, to the press and to the men who'd hired him as that first season dawned. The anonymity disappeared faster than you could say "Frank Mahovlich."

"He is one of the most keep-punching types I've ever met," marvelled Scott Young at the time. "His shoved-back brown fedora, open gabardine coat, hands-in-pockets stance and aggressive, quizzical look I think will soon be known in every rink in the land."

The team got off to a slow start in 1958, winning just five of their first sixteen games. So Imlach did the inevitable: he fired Billy Reay as coach and took over himself on a "temporary basis" that was to stretch eleven seasons.

Noted Rex McLeod in *The Globe and Mail*: "The Leafs have won five of their first sixteen games, so in a sweeping move, have promoted George Imlach to be [coach and] General Manager. So meteoric has been the rise of this young hockey executive that it is conceivable he might make it to President if they lose a few more games."

The hockey team Imlach inherited at Maple Leaf Gardens was a mess, but by no means was it unsalvageable. The club had finished fifth in 1957 (a year torn apart by the Players' Association squabble) and last in 1958, the first time a Leafs team had done so since Smythe took over the team in 1927. There was no luck involved. The clubs earned their ignominy.

Yet the farm system, which had fallen into disrepair after Smythe's banishment of Frank Selke to Montreal (where he was to win six more Stanley Cups in twenty years), was again overflowing with talent. The Toronto Marlboros Junior A team in the Ontario Hockey League, run by Stafford Smythe and Harold Ballard and coached by old Leafs stalwart Turk Broda, had won back-to-back Memorial Cups in 1955-56.

The roster of those Marlies teams of the '50s reads like a who's who of hockey for the next decade. Bobby Baun, Billy Harris, Bob Pulford,

Bob Nevin, Al McNeil, Ron Stewart, Gary Aldcorn and Carl Brewer, among others, played for the Marlies under the watchful eye of the younger Smythe and his hockey advisers, Bob Davidson, Buck Houle and Broda.

Uptown at St. Michael's College, the line of talent produced for the Leafs was no less impressive. Frank Mahovlich, Dave Keon, Dick Duff and Tim Horton all played for the Buzzers. Others went on to star with other NHL clubs. In all, seventeen products of the Marlies or St. Mike's played on the Leafs Stanley Cup winners of the '60s.

Some of the Leafs' prospects were two-sport stars before Bo Jackson ever saw the light of day. "I remember going one Saturday to see Gerry James play in the Grey Cup game for the Winnipeg Blue Bombers," recalls former Marlies defenseman Harry Neale. "He gained a hundred yards at running back ... the next day, he's sitting beside me on the Marlboros bench. Turk [Broda] said we won't play you much today. Of course, he played about thirty minutes." James later split his time between the Leafs and Winnipeg until an injury ended his career.

"Imlach's timing couldn't have been better," notes Baun. "Here was a team loaded with young talent and probably the best old talent, too."

Ah, yes, the old talent. There were additions to the Maple Leafs at the other end of the experience scale, too, in the summer and fall of 1958. The Maple Leafs introduced the first of their "geriatric" ward to the roster. Players like thirty-three-year-old goalie Johnny Bower, thirty-four-year-old defenseman Allan Stanley and thirty-two-year-old forward Bert Olmstead arrived in Imlach's custody, discards from other teams that felt the players had outlived their usefulness.

Imlach's genius was in recognizing that players could have useful careers past the age of thirty if mixed in with young players. "That was his whole thing," said Allan Stanley. "Youth and experience. He could put talent together to make talent. When I first came to the Leafs, he had me and Baun playing together, and Brewer with Horton.

"I thought Boomer and I played pretty well together, but he didn't like it. He made one move, Carl with Baun and me with Horton. We played like that for most of ten seasons."

Stanley and Bower remained with the Leafs for four Stanley Cups. They were later joined by Red Kelly, Eddie Litzenberger, Dickie Moore, Terry Sawchuk, Andy Bathgate, Don McKenney and Marcel

Pronovost as "Golden Oldies" on the roster who helped bring the Maple Leafs a Stanley Cup.

Bert Olmstead might have remained part of that group, too, had Conn Smythe not mentioned in passing that he might make a fine coach someday. "Olmstead had the ear of the owners, they liked him," remembers Stanley. "Somebody said, 'they're looking at management down the line, they're grooming him for Punch's job.' Well, Punch is no dummy. He got rid of him right after we won the Stanley Cup in 1962."

Olmstead was dealt to New York for future considerations, but he retired rather than report to the Rangers. Imlach, meanwhile, preserved his job for another six seasons.

Imlach also added journeymen like Larry Regan and Gerry Ehman to the club in 1958 to solidify the roster, giving up very little in return. Finally, he ended the laissez-faire atmosphere around the Gardens by stressing conditioning and two-a-day practices during training camp. Under Imlach, the Maple Leafs led the NHL—if not the world—in practise time. (All right, he was tied with Anatoli Tarasov in the USSR!)

"Punch was like a corporal," remembers Eddie Shack. "He worked the hell out of you. In practice, you'd be so tired, you couldn't always bounce back for games."

Dave Keon was one of Imlach's best players in his Toronto years and a favorite of the coach. A frustrated Carl Brewer noticed a correlation between the two facts. "Everyone talks about how the hard work in practice made us winners," he says. "But Davey rarely had to practise, and he played so well and lasted so long. Doesn't that tell you something?"

Of course, with the Players' Association crushed the year before he took over in Toronto, Imlach had total control when it came to manipulating his players. Fines and demotions were still the order of the day, and a player's only recourse when he felt exploited was to retire. As Jimmy Thompson learned after his run-in with Conn Smythe over the Players' Association, even an All-Star and club captain can be blackballed by the six teams in the NHL and out of hockey very quickly.

Imlach, like Smythe, believed that a tough man never backed down to pain. They both held that a high pain threshold made for a great player. "One thing I learned," Punch remembered, "was how much the human body can take as long as the mind in that body won't give up."

Among Imlach's most valiant warriors was defenseman Bobby Baun. The saga of Baun scoring the Stanley Cup-winning goal against Detroit on a broken leg in 1964 has now passed into the realm of legend, so much so that Baun winces when the tale is revived by a reporter or fan.

On another less-celebrated occasion in New York, Baun was sliding along the ice when Camille Henry's skate blade pierced Baun's throat just under his chin. Baun was taken to the clinic at Madison Square Garden where Dr. Kazuo Yanigasawa, the Rangers' team doctor, did a quick suture job on the wound and sent Baun out to finish the game. By game's end, Baun was experiencing severe pain in the area of the hemstitching and had difficulty breathing. On the bus to the airport following the game, he suddenly collapsed at the feet of his teammates. Apparently, Dr. Yanigasawa had failed to detect internal bleeding and Baun had begun to hemorrhage.

Tim Horton carried Baun off the bus to a nearby hospital, where he was refused treatment because the staff thought the rough-looking Baun had been injured in a knife fight. Baun was finally treated at another hospital and travelled home with the team. He never missed a game due to the wound.

Even greater were the many torments of goalie Johnny Bower, who endured a string of painful injuries to become the greatest goaltender in Maple Leafs history. On one bloody but typical night, Bower was steamrollered by Detroit's boisterous defenseman Howie Young. The collision removed one of the few teeth extant in Bower's mouth. Worse, his left leg was doubled back under him, severely wrenching the quadriceps and hamstring muscles. Bower arose, barely able to put weight on his left leg.

Most mere mortals would have called it a night, if not a career. But after having his battered mouth attended to, Bower limped back into the net to face the Red Wings once more. Supporting himself by leaning on the crossbar with his left arm, Bower still shut out Detroit the rest of the way to preserve a win.

The hemorrhaging in his leg after the game was such that Bower spent the next few days in hospital and missed the next five weeks of the season.

"Talk about guts," marvelled Imlach. "Nobody ever, anywhere in sports had more. He was the greatest athlete I've ever seen."

"Punch would always say how great Bower was," says Shack, "but he wouldn't pay him that way."

Bower had plenty of company in that regard on the Leafs. In a way that endeared him to Conn Smythe, Imlach spent money as if his pockets had been welded shut at birth. As the assistant general manager and later the general manager and coach, Imlach guarded the Maple Leafs' millions as if they were his own.

According to Billy Harris, who languished in Imlach's doghouse for much of his career in Toronto, Imlach's frugal nature created problems with the players. "After Punch in his role as general manager had denigrated us all and signed everyone as cheaply as possible to keep within his budget, he then as coach had to convince us we were good hockey players and a great team and could beat all our opponents."

"I remember Ed getting very upset after negotiating with Punch," says Norma Shack. "He'd tell me all the things Punch had said about him. And I said, 'If he's saying all those terrible things, why does he even want to sign you?'" What probably saved Imlach was that the same process was being repeated in every dressing room around the six-team NHL.

In the early days of Imlach's career with the Leafs, his abrasive style behind the bench and at the contract table kept the players on a short leash. Among the devices Imlach employed to intimidate his players was refusing to meet with a player's agent or lawyer at contract time.

"It's bad for a player to negotiate for himself," says Norma Shack. "They start cutting you down, you don't think rationally to come back with things you should say ... you just want to whack them one."

Contract time had been much different in the days of Hap Day, who told a young Billy Harris, "Son, this is the big leagues. We don't deal in hundreds, we deal in thousands." Imlach scrabbled for every nickel at contract time.

Had Maple Leaf Gardens been a money-losing operation, this might have been understandable. But the Gardens had long since been clear of its debts. In addition to paying dividends of $2,577,906 to shareholders in the twenty-five years between 1932 and 1957, it was declaring healthy after-tax profits even as the team wallowed in the NHL basement.

Perhaps most perplexing to the players was the discrepancy between what Imlach pegged their value to and what they saw as their value on the open market. In 1962, for instance, Chicago owner Jim Norris offered Harold Ballard $1 million for Frank Mahovlich at a raucous party at Toronto's Royal York Hotel. Ballard eagerly agreed to the sale, and it cost an angry Stafford Smythe considerable prestige and time to wriggle out of the deal. A disgruntled Mahovlich watched in amazement as he saw his contract valued at $1 million while Imlach battled him tooth and nail for a $500 bonus in his contract. He never had another great season in a Leafs uniform after the aborted sale. (The bitterness intensified seven years later when Stafford Smythe and Harold Ballard were charged with skimming hundreds of thousands of dollars from Maple Leaf Gardens money for their personal use while the players were denied even the money from the use of their pictures on Beehive Corn Syrup cards.)

Imlach and Smythe also agreed that when it came to continuing education, players "could not serve two masters," in the words of the Major. As part of his mania for control, Imlach particularly disliked the fact that several of his players, including Brewer, Pulford, Harris and Dick Duff, were actively pursuing a university education at the same time as they played for the Leafs.

The players were aware of his prejudice against academics and took the opportunity to jab back at Imlach. In an article for the Maple Leafs' program in 1964, players were asked for their advice to youngsters regarding a hockey career. Mixed in among the exhortations to skate till your ankles bleed and shoot the puck without ceasing are these nuggets from Pulford: "Get your schooling. Don't quit school. If you're good enough to make the NHL, you'll make it whether you're going to school or not."

Pulford's roommate, Harris, was no less direct: "Remember that you're gambling against very heavy odds when you attempt to make the NHL. Very few make the grade, and it's wise to keep up your education and have something to fall back on." One can only imagine Smythe and Imlach turning shades of crimson while reading that sage advice from their supposedly single-minded employees.

Some of Imlach's gambits were a little more frivolous. Perhaps because of his own shortcomings in the hair department, he abhorred mustaches and sideburns. And the longest sideburns on the Leafs in the late 1960s belonged to goalie Bruce Gamble. Imlach had bet a newspaper reporter two dollars that he could get Gamble to shave his sideburns. Confronting Gamble in the dressing room, he demanded in front of the team that the offending hair be razed.

To the astonishment of the team, Gamble acquiesced the next day. Afterwards, Imlach quietly shared the two-dollar payoff with Gamble, who had already agreed with Imlach before camp started to shave off the sideburns. He was rewarded with a dollar for his part in Imlach's little charade.

Imlach's other techniques were to have his charges walk home to the hotel from the arena in Peterborough during training camp while he and King Clancy took a cab (a few actually made the trek). Or isolating his team from their friends and family at playoff time.

Eventually, Imlach began working on a system that allowed him to control a player's career both coming and going. If a player needed a little seasoning or discipline, Imlach could send him to the Leafs' farm club in Rochester (part of the American Hockey League) or Vancouver (part of the Western Hockey League). The catch was that Imlach, along with his loyal assistant and sometime coach Joe Crozier, owned parts of both teams. In effect, Imlach the Maple Leafs' GM could help out Imlach the club owner from time to time with a few warm bodies at a price that was nice. And he could effectively control the player's contract until he was dispatched to another system.

The sale of the Leafs' farm clubs by Stafford Smythe was one of the sources of friction that led to Imlach finally leaving the Maple Leafs in 1968. It caused a great deal of enmity between Imlach and Smythe, who, along with Harold Ballard and John Bassett, Sr., controlled the Leafs from 1957 to 1969.

In his first book, *Hockey Is A Battle*, Imlach was ingenuous about the deal. It was "a lousy deal," he wrote. "It was okay for Stafford and the owners, they got the money. But I'd built up the farm system ... I was the guy who had to find players to win hockey games." Imlach eventually owned up to his investment in the farm clubs in his second book of memoirs, *Heaven and Hell In the NHL*.

Another attitude that Imlach shared with Smythe was his intolerance for organized labor interfering with how he ran his hockey club. Imlach had an ego as big as Maple Leaf Gardens (Punch claimed that Stafford Smythe was jealous of him because the Leafs were "his team, not Smythe's"), and there wasn't enough room in the NHL for both Punch and Alan Eagleson. Unlike Smythe and his fellow owners in 1957, however, Imlach met with considerably less success in eradicating the Players' Association.

Alan Eagleson was part lawyer, part politician, part back-alley hustler who rose to power during—and some say because of—Punch Imlach's reign at Maple Leaf Gardens. A relentless deal-maker, by 1967 he had parlayed a friendship with Bob Pulford into the job as first executive director of the NHL Players' Association (NHLPA). He and Imlach were bookends for over a decade, scrumming over contracts and players' rights. Ironically, the eventual diminution of Imlach's power as a manager came more from Eagleson's influence on his personal clients than from his leadership of the NHLPA, but Punch still ascribed the shift in hockey's power structure to rampant unionism. "People said the players were slaves, not getting paid," opined Imlach. "Hell, if I offered someone off the street a contract, he'd be in here to work like there was no tomorrow ... it wasn't exploitation, it was what the market would bear."

When his own players, like Pulford and Baun, recruited Eagleson to start up another Players' Association, Imlach went on the offensive, even though most of the owners in the NHL already appeared resigned to the project. His own boss, Harold Ballard, for instance, was already warming up to Eagleson. "I think Eagle's a great man for hockey," said Ballard later. "He is a good businessman, and I always try to promote him. I tell my boys who don't have lawyers to go to the Eagle."

When word of the Association was announced in 1967, Imlach—like some hockey Napoleon contemplating Elba—surrounded himself with his Old Guard. Stanley, Horton, Bower, Armstrong and Kelly were summoned to his office high above the ice surface at the Gardens for a loyalty oath. Imlach repeated his claim that the NHLPA was causing his high-strung star Frank Mahovlich grief. Imlach went so far as to blame the newfound NHLPA for causing Mahovlich's nervous collapse.

Years later, Stanley remembers the scene vividly. "I need some help," Imlach announced to the men who'd helped him to Stanley Cup glory. "I'm going to have a vote down there, and we're going to stop this Players' Association. If you vote for it you're gone." He stared hard into the faces of his trusted players.

Down in the dressing room later, Imlach repeated the threat to the entire team, except the Association's first president, Bob Pulford, who had been sent out to skate alone on the Gardens' ice. "Anybody who is for the fucking Players' Association get the hell out of the room," Imlach roared, hoping the influence of his stalwart veterans would intimidate Pulford and his upstarts.

For a few seconds, there was no movement; then Stanley and Horton, charter members of the Old Guard, got up and left the room. They were soon followed by the rest of the team. It signalled the end of Imlach's ironclad hold on his team, a hold he'd had for a decade.

It was a grip that caused players such as Brewer, Mahovlich (whom Imlach insisted on calling "Maholovitch") and Harris to chafe under the unrelenting barrage of Imlach's no-nonsense approach. Mahovlich, in particular, suffered from depression and anxiety during his days as the Leafs' one bona fide star. Twice, he was disabled by the team to allow him time to recover from clinical depression and exhaustion.

The quixotic Brewer retired twice from hockey to continue his education before officially calling it quits on the Maple Leafs for good in 1965, in part because of his love/hate relationship with Imlach.

"I was the fastest skater on the club, but I could never let up in practice," Brewer remembers. "I was the standard by which Imlach judged everybody else, and if I slowed down in practice, then he gave me shit."

Harris, meanwhile, found himself nailed to the bench for most of his career with Imlach. When he finally escaped to Detroit in July 1965, the slick playmaker's best years were behind him. "Punch was insensitive to sensitive people," recalls Harris. "I have often wondered what might have happened if Punch had handled Mahovlich and Brewer with the same compassion and personal understanding as he did Gilbert Perreault" (whom he managed with the Buffalo Sabres in the 1970s).

Mike Walton, Pete Stemkowski and Jim Pappin were other Maple Leafs who flourished when they escaped Punch's "my way or the highway" style. Even the career of the loyal Bobby Baun came to a premature end in Toronto when Imlach found out he was advising rookies on their contract negotiations with him. Imlach benched the hero of three earlier Cup triumphs during the 1967 playoffs, and Baun was drafted by Oakland in the 1967 expansion draft.

Paul Henderson—who played for Imlach during Punch's final years in Toronto—admired Imlach, but even he had to admit that Punch took some getting used to. "With a sky-high ego and an inclination to be overly superstitious, he often coached on hunches, which made it hard to agree with him a lot of the time."

King Clancy, Imlach's assistant and good-humor man, was often called upon to soothe players angry with Imlach. "Clancy used to motivate the guys," says Shack. "He'd say, 'Don't worry, goddamn it, we'll get 'er done ... we'll get 'er done.' When Clancy took over, it was such a relief, we wouldn't lose a game. You play for a prick, and then suddenly you're having fun out there again."

But for every player Imlach rubbed the wrong way in his dual roles as coach and general manager there was a Stanley, a Bower or a Horton who thrived under Punch's control. According to Horton's widow, Lori, it wasn't till Imlach took over the Leafs that Horton came into his own.

"Punch gave him a lot of self-confidence," she recalls. "There were stories in the paper about how Tim hadn't reached his potential, that sort of thing, under Bill Reay. He was very unhappy. It took Punch Imlach to give him the confidence he needed to play hockey."

Allan Stanley also flourished under Punch, even when he stood up to him over the Players' Association. "The amazing thing with Punch, you could be who you wanted to be," he says. "I never heard one word after the Players' Association thing, never any sign that he held a grudge. Punch would look at it and say, 'Hey, I gave it my best shot. Let's move on from there.'"

"The older guys got along with Imlach because they understood him," says Eddie Litzenberger, who played two years under Punch. "We were from an old regime, the old school. I knew Imlach like a book. The young guys weren't used to it, and it was real uncomfortable for them."

Despite his doctrinaire approach, Imlach did possess a sense of humor. Al Arbour, the Leafs' reserve defenseman who later became one of the NHL's greatest coaches with the Islanders, was sent out by Punch in the dying minute of a losing effort. Arbour, who hadn't taken a shift all night, skated to his own end and then, before the puck was dropped, returned to the bench and called over to Imlach: "Do you want me to just tie it up, or should I put us ahead?" asked a deadpan Arbour. Even in defeat, Imlach had to bury his face in a towel to keep from laughing.

While the dressing room was divided on Imlach, the public and media lionized the cantankerous Punch from the start for leading their downtrodden team to the Stanley Cup finals in his first year against the mighty Montreal Canadiens.

"His moods dip from sour to downright nasty," wrote an approving Red Burnett of *The Toronto Star* in 1964, "depending on whether he has just left a workout or failed to sign a player. He only smiles when someone gets knocked flat on his pants. At times, he chortles, 'I love them with murder in their hearts and larceny in their eyes.'"

Imlach's wife "Dodo" was sought out by the press for insights into her now-famous husband. "I'm sure some people must regard Punch as overconfident, even boastful, and I can understand that, because they don't know him," she confided to writer Margaret Scott in 1960. "But he has a philosophy of life. He feels you can attain anything if you want it sufficiently to make it your one goal. Right now he wants the Cup, and if a human being has the power to shape destiny, then I think my husband will fulfil his dreams."

While he battled the "Silver Seven" (the nickname for Stafford Smythe's management group that ran the Maple Leafs during his time in Toronto) on everything from trades to train schedules, Imlach cultivated the media in Toronto. Imlach used them to get his messages across, as Billy Harris discovered. One day after making a contract demand, Harris was startled to read about it in a Toronto paper: "One of the young Leaf players had the audacity to ask for a $5,000 raise," read the quote from Imlach. "Naturally, I was embarrassed," remembers Harris, "and feared that all my teammates knew who the culprit was."

"I like a lot of things about Leafs management," wrote Scott Young, the most candid of the writers on the beat at the time. "But I do think they could leave the booing to the public—and see how that works."

Though there were flashpoints between Punch and the press— writers once boycotted his practices for locking them out of the dressing room after a tough loss—Imlach was simply such irresistable copy that the media could not ignore him for long. Once in the 1959 playoffs Imlach slapped a toupee thrown to him by a Boston fan on his bald pate. And after an embarrassing 11-0 loss to Boston in 1964, Imlach threatened to fine the waiters $100 each if they put butterscotch or chocolate sauce on the ice cream of the disgraced Leafs. On another occasion, he sent a case of Guinness stout to the home of the ectomorphic Billy Harris, with orders that he consume two a day till he put on some weight.

And there were his famous predictions, beginning with his wild boast in 1959 that his first Leafs team would make the playoffs even though they appeared deader than Tutankhamen in mid-March. Of course, the team pulled a miracle comeback and the legend of Imlach was born.

It was a legend that Imlach enthusiastically embraced, and a legend that eventually wore thin with many of the players who did the playing for him. "Punch came along at the right time," says Bobby Baun. "If he'd been Toe Blake, he'd have won seven Stanley Cups, not four. His ego just got in the way."

Billy Harris took note of the liberal use of the first-person singular in the two books Imlach co-wrote with Scott Young (emphasis is added): "How the hell were Arnie Brown or Rod Seiling going to play when *I* was winning three Stanley Cups in a row, and had Stanley-Horton, Baun-Brewer?" Imlach asked in *Hockey Is A Battle.*

"After 1963, we became faceless pawns on a chessboard," recalls Harris. "If George went to his final resting place believing that he did win all those Cups by himself—so be it."

Imlach came to see himself as virtually infallible in hockey matters. "He did anything he wanted," remembers Allan Stanley. "He brought in his son Brent to play with the Leafs. And King Clancy's son Terry. And Joe Crozier who later coached for the Leafs? He brought him in to play defense, for Chrissakes."

Imlach's personal behavior—and that of other Leafs executives—also rankled. While he was married himself, it was a case of "do as I say, not as I do" when it came to women on the road. "On the road he was pretty notorious for some of the things he'd do," says one player from that era. "You just can't do that in front of young hockey players."

"He'd expect us to behave a certain way on the road," says another player. "He'd fine us for having women in our rooms. Then he'd be doing the same thing. It didn't set much of an example to the players."

The money fights and the double standards concerning behavior eroded the respect players had for Imlach. And the changing nature of society intervened as well. The advent of the 1960s, with its personal freedoms and drugs, had its effect on hockey discipline, although it took a while to sink in. The last one to receive the message was Imlach.

Persistence and resistance were the bywords of Imlach's long hockey career. He was a survivor with unique instincts about the game he dedicated his life to, instincts that helped him assemble winning teams in Toronto and Buffalo. To create one winning team may be happenstance. To do it twice, as Imlach did, signifies something more than luck.

Like his mentor, Conn Smythe, Imlach was also resistant to change or interference. As an owner, Smythe could afford to have his opinions and whims. No one would fire the owner. Imlach had no such luxury when his personal agenda conflicted with winning. That uncertainty forced his hand a number of times, causing him to sacrifice the future of the Leafs for their present, even a mediocre present. For that reason, Imlach played a battle against time at the rink, where his team grew old on him, and away from the rink, where society's changing standards of discipline and attitude overwhelmed his conservative 1950s world.

For Brewer, Stanley, Baun and the others on those great Toronto teams, Imlach's themes of persistence and resistance finally culminated in their challenge to the League's ironclad hold over their pension fund years after his death. As much as the Stanley Cups and the notoriety they brought, that is part of the Imlach legacy.

6

SAM

Allan Stanley had this nagging problem during his career. It wasn't his skating or his shooting, although Lord knows his shot couldn't break a pane of glass and his skating time was measured with a calendar. No, the problem was his first name, or rather, the fact that no one ever spelled it properly. It was always "Alan" or "Allen," not "A-L-L-A-N," as his mother had intended. Hardly the respect befitting a star hockey player.

By the time he was traded from Chicago to Boston in 1956, the quiet man from Timmins grew tired of the permutations visited on his Christian name and decided to take remedial action.

"I've got a problem," he explained to Dave O'Hara, the Associated Press bureau chief in Boston. "They're spelling my name wrong. I'd appreciate it if you spelled my name right all the time."

"Allan, that's a five-letter name ... I have trouble with five-letter words," O'Hara told Stanley. "And my boss won't let me use four-letter words."

"Well, you have to call me something," said Stanley.

"How's about I call you Sam? That has three letters."

"I can handle that," replied Stanley.

"Yeah, and on good days, I'll call you Big Sam. That's two three-letter words. That sounds good."

And from then on he was Sam. Sometimes "Silent Sam." Sometimes "Big Sam." But at least it was never "Alan" Stanley.

Of all the names that appear on the retired players' lawsuit against the NHL (they're all spelled correctly, by the way), Allan Stanley's seems the least likely to be there. Never a firebrand or a clubhouse lawyer during his twenty-one-year career, most times Stanley was downright Establishment. He was a charter member of Punch Imlach's Old Guard, the last bastion against long hair and sideburns with the Maple Leafs, and he once even ran unsuccessfully for the Progressive Conservative nomination in his home town of Timmins. But when it came time to read the roll of those willing to launch a frontal assault against the NHL in Toronto, Allan Stanley's name was on the application.

Stanley was as green as new timber when he emerged from the mining country of northern Ontario to play hockey. Timmins—along with nearby Kirkland Lake and Cochrane—was a hockey breeding ground for young men looking to escape the North and a life in the mines. "If it wasn't for hockey," says Tim Horton's widow, Lori, "Tim would've ended up in the mines around Cochrane like all his friends."

The long winters and the prospect of a life below ground sharpened the hockey skills of northern boys like Stanley and Bill Barilko and Pete Babando and Dean Prentice. Later, the mining country produced Dick Duff and Frank Mahovlich and Ralph Backstrom and George Armstrong ... the list of stars turned out in this frozen part of the country began in the last century and stretches into today.

One of the first players from the Timmins area to make it big was Stanley's uncle, Russell "Barney" Stanley. Allan's father, Bill, and his five uncles were all good players, but it was "Barney" Stanley who first put the family name on Lord Stanley's Cup in 1915 when he played for the Vancouver Millionaires. Not that many noticed, of course.

"When we won the Cup in the '60s," says Stanley, "my wife and I looked for his name on the trophy. We couldn't find him. Looked all over but no name. Then my wife looked inside the bowl. His name was scratched inside one of the little S grooves. All the other names were on the outside, but his is on the inside."

"He visited us one year. He was on a business trip. I was just a kid then, but I remember the question I asked him. 'What do hockey players drink between periods to make them play hockey better?' He said, 'We usually drink tea with honey.' And so I drank tea and honey for years after that. It seems to have helped."

Stanley learned his hockey on clubs sponsored by the Holman Drilling Company, the English firm that made diamond drills and pluggers for the mines. "We were just a bunch of kids hanging around the general store," he remembers. "The parents of one of the kids was the agent for Holman, and he wrote them asking the company to sponsor us, you know, buy the sweaters and socks. The Holman people thought it was a good idea, and so we played together as a team for three years against anybody who'd play us and then two years in the juvenile league."

Stanley and his older brother Jeffrey were among the mainstays on the Timmins team, which quickly developed a reputation for its skill. Stanley, who didn't play defense regularly until his final year of juvenile in Timmins, was often called up to play center with the older boys. He teamed up with his brother on the forward line.

"We were terrific with me at center, but I didn't play there steady. Whatever team I was playing for, the coach would drop me back to defense for a rest. I played most of the game, but I never thought much about it. That's just the way it was in those days."

In the team's fourth year together, they lost the Northern Ontario title to a team from Kirkland Lake, which featured a very young Ted Lindsay. In the fifth year, the team won the All Ontario Juvenile championship. The title game was at Maple Leaf Gardens against a team from St. Catharines, and the Holman team from Timmins won 6-5 in the sudden-death, one-game final.

"Playing in the Gardens was the biggest thing that ever happened," says Stanley. "My parents were hockey fans, and when they listened to Foster Hewitt broadcast the games from the Gardens, I listened too. I thought, boy, is this great. I just looked at all the pictures hanging on the walls ... when you go down there, you've got to look at those pictures."

Nine of the players from the Holman team, including Stanley, Barilko, Babando and Eric Prentice (Dean's brother), drew the attention of the scouts and went to pro training camps. Stanley's brother Jeffrey, however, opted to become a chiropractor and headed off to Chicago for school.

It wasn't until scout Harold "Baldy" Cotton saw the team at the Gardens that the idea of playing professional hockey entered the mind of the sixteen-year-old Stanley. Up until then, the game had been just fun with his friends, a way to while away the winter. There was no one pushing him to take his hockey career any further. Suddenly, the lure of quitting school and playing for money intervened.

"I had to make a decision, my parents had to make a decision," he recalls. "I wasn't the worst student—my brother was better—but I went to my parents and said I'd like to try it. I didn't like school, and I said I just wanted to play hockey."

The Stanleys decided to let their rangy son take a flyer on hockey with the Boston Olympics of the U.S. Eastern Hockey League. In the fall of 1941, Allan Stanley was on his way to the Boston Bruins' training camp in Quebec City with "one of those two-dollar suitcases that come out of the bush" under his arm.

Doug Quinlan was the other Timmins boy in the Bruins' camp, and he took Stanley under his wing in Quebec, sharing a flat with him and offering sage advice on the vagaries of a hockey life. The first thing Quinlan did, however, was to try to steer Stanley to play in Oshawa with him, instead of in Boston. A rather callow Stanley thought this a capital idea and went to inform the Bruins' legendary manager, Art Ross, of his decision to forgo Boston for Oshawa. Now, Art Ross was the sort of man who used his fists to solve problems, and when the young Stanley blithely told him of his plans, Ross nearly went through the roof of his office.

"Those bastards have been screwing me for years," Ross roared at Stanley. "You're going to Boston. I'll call Frank Sargeant at the Canadian Amateur Hockey Association, and he'll straighten this out. If you don't play for me, you won't play for anyone ever again."

With Ross standing a few feet away, spewing venom, Sargeant patiently spelled out Stanley's options to the young man over the phone. Faced with a possible suspension and the eternal wrath of Ross, Stanley decided to give Boston a try. "I have no regrets," he recalls today. "Oshawa won the Memorial Cup that year without me, but we won the U.S. Amateur Hockey Seniors title."

The seventeen-year-old Stanley, just a year removed from the bleak beauty of Timmins, found himself touring the United States from coast to coast with the Olympics that year. After winning the Eastern title, the team took the transcontinental train to Seattle for a week, San Diego for a week and then on to Hollywood for three weeks.

"I was seventeen, took the train across America. Saw the universe. We went to Hollywood, to Universal Studios, met the actors, saw Basil Rathbone making a Sherlock Holmes movie ... an absolutely great day. I had no regrets then about not going to Oshawa."

The Olympics were the Bruins' farm team, but despite Ross's enthusiasm for Stanley coming to Boston and the general shortage of talent brought on by enlistment in World War II, he was never recalled to play in the big time. Instead, he whiled away his hockey apprenticeship playing in the six-team Eastern American Hockey League against the Brooklyn Crescents, the New York Rovers, the Philadelphia Falcons, the New Haven Ramblers and the Baltimore Coast Guard team (you remember them, don't you?).

The Coast Guard was especially strong, containing future stars such as Frankie Brimsek, Art Coulter and Alex Modder. They played an exhausting schedule. Stanley remembers playing before a packed house at Boston Garden on Saturday night, then following with a Sunday matinee at Madison Square Garden before another sellout crowd. Sunday night they'd play again in New Haven. "We always wondered why they threw sand on the ice in New Haven," he says with a laugh. "Man, that was heavy going."

The travel didn't make it any easier. "We were always going through the New York corridor during the war. Talk about Grand Central Station ... there wasn't a seat on any of the trains. They saved us four bench seats on the train and that was it, you were on your own. So you travelled with a hard suitcase. You put it down. You sat on it in the aisle or between cars."

Stanley went into the Canadian Navy the following year, then returned to play with the Providence Reds of the American Hockey League. Boston had lent his contract to Lou Pieri's Providence team but later found itself forced to give up a player to the minor-league Reds. Boston decided to choose between selling Stanley or his team-mate Jack Shill to Providence based on a one-game trial.

"They came down to look at a game in Providence. I'd just got out of bed. I'd been in bed for a week with the flu or a virus. Pieri played me the whole damn game. After that, the Bruins sold me to Providence."

Stanley might have remained buried there, playing in obscurity for Lou Pieri, but for some providence of his own following his second season with the Reds. The New York Rangers' defense corps had been decimated when three or four players were hurt in a car accident during training camp, so the hapless Rangers purchased Stanley for the 1948-49 season.

For a man supposedly delivered into hockey heaven, Stanley greeted the move with typical nonchalance. Stanley was at a team party for Providence when informed of the deal. "You've been traded to New York," he was told by his breathless messenger.

"Is that so?" he replied. He then dove back into the party.

"I don't get excited too easily," Stanley says today as he looks out over Pigeon Lake from his home in Bobcaygeon, Ontario. "I get quiet and I get more determined." In fact, Stanley's easy manner and unhurried style on the ice were often misunderstood, and it slowed up his path to the NHL.

"Stanley was known as a guy who made the game look too easy— never a wasted stride," wrote a hockey columnist of the day. "The cynics ignored his obvious effectiveness and called him lazy."

He finally got his chance in 1948. "New York always hyped everything," he recalls. "I was suddenly the biggest deal since sliced bread ... they gave up five or six players plus $75,000 in cash to get me. It's a funny thing, but a few years ago, I was at a photo shoot and this fella came up to me. He says, 'I've been looking for you for a long, long time.' It turns out he was in the deal. He wanted to get even."

When Stanley arrived in New York in 1948, the city was the sports and entertainment capital of the world. Broadway was enjoying its golden hour as the great musicals—from *Oklahoma* to *Guys and Dolls* to *South Pacific*—drew enormous crowds to Manhattan. Frank Sinatra crooned to millions, and Hollywood had yet to claim the heart of TV production.

In baseball, the New York Giants and Brooklyn Dodgers were commencing a rivalry so bitter that it separated families, while the Yankees uptown in the Bronx carried off World Series titles by the carload. In football, the New York Giants of Charlie Connerly, Frank Gifford and Y. A. Tittle were the most dashing, sexy team in an NFL just reaching its zenith. The team filled Yankee Stadium and won two NFL championships. The New York Knickerbockers turned on a whole generation of basketball fans with their play at the Garden, and boxing was in its heyday, with the great boxing writer A. J. Liebling chronicling the feats of Rocky Marciano, Sugar Ray Robinson and Jersey Joe Walcott.

Stanley was in his element, a twenty-one-year-old from Timmins, Ontario, at the heart of Gotham. "Broadway was my beat," he recalls. "I lived at the Belvedere Hotel on 49th Street between 8th and 9th, right across from the press gate at Madison Square Garden. I saw all the fights ... Marciano, the whole crew. It was absolutely great."

The Rangers, however, were not something to write home—or A. J. Liebling—about. The 1940 Stanley Cup winners of coach Frank

Boucher and general manager Lester Patrick—Davey Kerr in net, Bryan Hextall, Babe Pratt, the Colville brothers, Ott Heller—were a distant memory, and by 1951, the current Rangers were in an annual battle with the atrocious Chicago Black Hawks to avoid the cellar.

"I was there six years," says Stanley. "I think we went through seven coaches. We ruined coaches. We went through 'em like nothing."

Of course, there was no great impetus from management for the Rangers to get better. The team was run by the affable General John Reed Kilpatrick, but it was owned by James D. Norris of Chicago, who also owned the Black Hawks and the Detroit Red Wings. The Red Wings, who finished first in the NHL seven consecutive seasons from 1949 to 1956, were Norris's pet project. The Black Hawks were a tenant for his building, the Chicago Stadium; they were little more than an afterthought.

And the Rangers were simply a sideshow for Norris's boxing interests in New York. His International Boxing Club (IBC) so effectively tied the careers of the great prizefighters of the era to Norris that the anti-trust bureau of the U.S. Department of Justice charged Norris and the IBC with racketeering to force it out of business.

The Rangers filled the calendar dates at Madison Square Garden when boxing or the circus left the building dark. So far down the list of priorities were the Rangers that several times they had their playoff games bumped to another city when the circus made its annual April visit to New York.

The team went five years without making the playoffs before sneaking in again in 1956 (in a six-team league, to boot!). New York's fans responded to the ineptitude of players like Stanley and Charlie Rayner and Edgar Laprade and Tony Leswick with vicious booing, insults and projectiles tossed from the upper deck. Stanley was a principal target.

"In New York, early in the 1952-53 season," wrote Dan Parker in *Sports Illustrated,* the fans "booed Captain Allan Stanley off the Garden ice and stayed away in such numbers that the top gallery was closed off briefly for hockey or the poor imitation thereof on display with the Rangers."

Stanley recalls those years with the woeful Rangers with a touch of incredulity, as if observing the actions of someone else. "Things got so rough down there, for me in particular. The galleries were so tough. You're playing to maybe five thousand people—half of them on free tickets—and there's nothing to cheer about.

"The old Madison Square Garden, the balcony is right up there, straight up, it's hanging there. It's quiet in there, and then the loud-mouths ... 'Eh, ya bum, Stanley!' I wasn't the first guy they picked on and I wasn't the last."

Eventually, Rangers coach Frank Boucher began benching Stanley at home when the fans booed the team's captain during the warm-ups. While it calmed Boucher's conscience, the benching changed nothing at the Garden. The Rangers still lost and the fans still booed.

"I was always on the power play," Stanley says. "So they'd play me at home on the power play. One time I get out there on the point. Paul Ronty was centering to the left of their net, and he looks back at me and gives me a nod. So I give him the nod. He gets the puck back to me ... there was nobody around me ... and just as the puck gets to me, I look up to see the hole. Well, the puck went under my stick, the other team got it and they went down and scored. You never in your life heard anything like it. The longest trip I ever made was from the blueline to the bench."

The jeering by those few fans still perverse enough to attend games grew worse. Soon after, Boucher took Stanley aside. "We got to get you out of here awhile," he said mercifully. And so Stanley was shipped off to Vancouver till things cooled down. The Rangers fans, wrote journalist Bob Zak in 1963, booed Stanley "all the way to British Columbia." (Appropriately, the night the Rangers recalled Stanley from Vancouver, he tore the ligaments in his knee and never played for New York again.)

Stanley's painful stay in New York can be summed up in one incident. His future wife, Barbara, was also in New York, living at Fifth Avenue near 59th Street, while Stanley labored for the Rangers. She was from Timmins, and her brothers had played hockey with Stanley back home. With Allan already there, Barbara had come to New York to study fashion, modelling and dance. When she wasn't in school, she often went to the Garden to watch Stanley play.

"I usually knew what seat she was in," remembers Stanley. "But this one night, they put her in different seats. Well, I didn't know it, and so I took a shot at our net during the warm-up. Chuck Rayner, our goalie, deflected the puck up into the stands. I skated away, and then one of our players, I think it was Terry Usher, comes up and says, 'Al, did you see who you hit? You hit Barbara.'

"So I look up, and the guy next to her is holding a towel to her head as they lead her out. The next day, on the front page of *The New York Times*, there's a story and a picture: 'Allan Stanley's One-In-A-Million Shot.'"

(The appearance of Stanley's name in the paper almost led to Barbara performing a little surgery on him once. One paper romantically linked singer Kaye Starr with Al Stanley. Barbara was only placated when the paper correctly identified Starr's paramour the next day as *Hal* Stanley, her manager and future husband.)

Escaping New York after five seasons did not change Stanley's luck, however. In 1954 the Rangers sent him and Nick Mickoski to the only team more futile than themselves, the Black Hawks of Chicago, hockey's Black Hole of Calcutta. The Hawks—who gave up Billy Gadsby and Pete Conacher—were last in seven of eight seasons from 1951 to 1957, and attendance at Chicago Stadium was so poor (just 140,000 paid to see the Hawks in the entire 1955-56 season) that Norris threatened to sell the club if things didn't improve.

"We usually had last place cinched by Christmastime," recalls former Chicago captain Eddie Litzenberger with a faint trace of pride.

The agony of playing for the Black Hawks didn't end with losing, either. The team played games away from Chicago to drum up support in other Midwestern U.S. cities. "One year," recalls Litzenberger, "we had a thirty-day road trip. We played in St. Paul, Minnesota—everywhere. We'd get home just long enough to get clean underwear."

Conn Smythe used the inept Black Hawks as a dumping ground, a convenient cover when he shipped off Players' Association organizers Jimmy Thompson and Tod Sloan in 1957. For public consumption, Smythe rationalized the moves as an attempt to equalize talent in the League, giving the hopeless Hawks a helping hand: "No use having a strong team in Toronto if there's no League to play in." But no one was fooled by the charade of Conn Smythe giving away anything for free.

Things improved for the Black Hawks eventually, but it had more to do with the U.S. government's prosecution of Norris than anything else. When his IBC was ruled a monopoly, Norris finally turned his full attention to building the Black Hawks. Within five seasons, a Chicago team led by Bobby Hull, Stan Mikita, Pierre Pilote and Glenn Hall won the Stanley Cup.

Not that Allan Stanley was around to witness the turnaround. The Hawks were dead last in both his years in Chicago. The only silver lining in his Chicago career occurred when he returned to Madison Square Garden for the first time and scored two goals.

"Hey, Stanley," shouted the gallery gods, "why didn't you play like that when you were here?"

"Chicago was a terrible experience, they were lost years," he says. "It's not healthy to live too long at one end of the totem pole. I don't care who the guy is, losing has to affect them in some way. I did learn one thing from it—that you shouldn't quit."

His persistence paid off. Lynn Patrick, who coached Stanley and the Rangers to a near upset win over Detroit in the 1950 playoffs, considered him his most effective player in those years. And when he became the general manager of Boston, Patrick made obtaining Stanley a priority for his new team. So in 1956 Stanley was delivered from his Chicago exile to the Boston Bruins, his first winning team in the NHL. The Bruins were then propelled by the "Uke Line" of Vic Stasiuk, Bronco Horvath and Johnny Bucyk, and they had a rough defense corps headed by Fern Flaman, Leo Boivin and Leo Labine.

During the Montreal Canadiens' string of five straight Cups, the Bruins were perhaps the second-best team of the era. They met the Habs in the finals twice, losing both times to "Rocket" Richard and Jean Béliveau and those marvellous Montreal teams.

By this point, Stanley had settled into his role as a sound journeyman defenseman. He had begun to refine the techniques of disarming puck-carriers that he would employ—and teach to Bob Baun, Tim Horton and Carl Brewer—with the Maple Leafs. His only concern was that he had reached his thirties, the unofficial age of decline in the NHL, when clubs routinely abandoned their players for younger men.

Had it not been for Punch Imlach's notions about mixing veterans like Stanley with youngsters like Baun or Brewer, he might well have ended his career in the minors rather than on a Stanley Cup winner. Stanley was thirty-three years old, heading into his twelfth season in the NHL, when the Bruins decided he had reached the end of the line.

"I was sitting in the Boston dressing room when Fernie Flaman came in with a paper that said the Bruins had traded Bob Armstrong to Toronto.

"'Do you think Bob knows about it?' Flaman asked Stanley.

"So I looked over, and Armstrong's getting dressed. He wouldn't be getting dressed if he knew about this. So I went over to show it to him. You know Bob is very pale, but geez, he went absolutely white when he saw the story."

The half-dressed Armstrong hastily threw his coat on over his equipment and stormed up to the office of Milt Schmidt, the Bruins' general manager, to have it out. A short time later, he returned, and Stanley approached him to offer a soothing word or two.

"I said, 'Gee, Bob, I'm real sorry. That's a bad deal.' And he said, 'It's not me that's been traded, it's you, Sam.'"

Stanley nonetheless practised one last time with his old teammates, some of whom still hadn't heard about the deal. When Stasiuk came roaring in on Stanley, Stanley sent him crashing into the boards with a check.

"What did you do that for?" said an enraged Stasiuk. "This is a practice."

"I'm a Maple Leaf now," Stanley said, smiling. "You better get used to it."

Stanley was traded for a younger defenseman, Jim Morrison, at the beginning of the 1958-59 season. While Morrison bounced around to three more clubs in his career, Stanley stayed ten years with the Leafs, "as honest and dependable a hockey player as a coach could hope for," according to Imlach.

The 1958-59 season was a watershed year for the Maple Leafs with the arrival of Imlach, Brewer, Bert Olmstead, Johnny Bower, Larry Regan and Stanley—the sort of life-giving impetus that comes along very rarely in the life of a sports franchise but which can propel it to greatness.

The changes clearly inspired Scott Young, who sensed something in the air around the Gardens that September of 1958. Young took considerable ribbing when he picked the Leafs—who had finished last the year before—to finish third. (They finished fourth but made it to the finals.) And in no small measure, he attributed the change to Stanley. "It's been a long time since I've seen the kind of gritty defense that Allan Stanley is giving his new employers," he wrote in the fall of 1958.

Despite Young's enthusiasm, Stanley was hardly the kind of dynamo to turn around a franchise with his laconic style and his calculated work on defense. "Imlach had to work Stanley hard," says Litzenberger, "or else he'd fall asleep."

"Al was like a Clydesdale horse, plowing away," says Eddie Shack. "He'd get Gordie [Howe] all the time. We'd just steer Gordie right toward Al every time."

Perhaps the best capsule comment on Stanley's less than overwhelming package of physical talents came from Peter Gzowski in 1964: "...Allan Stanley, who falls short of being the fastest skater in the NHL by roughly a hundred and eight players, but whose poke-check is a work of art."

Not that he disappeared altogether; despite the presence of flashier teammates like Horton and Brewer, Stanley received personal recognition, too, being selected a second-team All-Star three times.

"When he was at his best over on the left side," marvelled Imlach, "he could play forwards coming in on him as if he had them on strings.... Not many defenseman got more goals. And he could check, too. One of the last of the big body checkers."

There was always speculation in the Toronto media about Stanley's age. Would the year just ended be his last? What had made him last so long in a bruising game? Conditioning, tactics, good northern Ontario bloodlines and Imlach's patronage were all advanced as theories.

Writer Margaret Scott thought she had the answer. "Allan Stanley spends the hockey season living by a strict code of self-discipline," she ventured in October 1963. "Like bull fighters, he has his lightest intake of food on the day he performs." Imagining Stanley as a bullfighter was like projecting Eddie Shack as a psychoanalyst.

Stanley's value to the Maple Leafs in the next decade lay in his ability to subordinate himself to Imlach's alchemy, an element in the chemical reaction that propelled the Leafs to the top in short order after nearly a decade in the wilderness.

As a veteran, he also helped teach the younger defensemen the art of playing defense. "I fell in love with Allan from the first day I met him," remembers Bobby Baun, with a smile. "As a guru, as a person who would help you . . . He really taught me you didn't have to run around all over the place to make things happen. I was certainly a better skater than he was—so were Horton and Brewer—but he used his head in playing. I think that's the reason he excelled and stayed so long."

After a short time as partner to Baun, Stanley was paired with Tim Horton, the nearsighted bundle of muscle and determination who had been with the Leafs since 1954. They perfected the art of playing defense between themselves.

"I haven't had a coach, I dare say, that taught us anything," Stanley states. "We worked it out. I was an upfront guy. I stayed on the blueline no matter who the hell came down the ice ... make them go the long way around me or else shake loose the puck. Tim picked up the garbage if I could get a hold of somebody."

The tall, lanky Stanley and the perfectly sculpted Horton were a Mutt and Jeff team who revelled in their comic roles as well as their status as the NHL's best defense pair on the NHL's best team.

"One time I asked Tim, 'Everybody likes to receive a pass at a certain time. When do you like to receive it?'

"He looked at me and said, 'Sam ... I'm going to put my stick down like this. And if you don't hit it with the puck, I'm never going to see it with these eyes.'" In fact, Horton's eyesight was so poor he saw only shadows as he skated beside Stanley all those years.

Off the ice, they were an inseparable team as well. The tales of Horton's escapades with Stanley in tow are legend among the players of the time. When they were in Toronto, the pair would usually gather up many of their teammates after practice and head for George's Spaghetti House on Dundas Street at Sherbourne.

"They were very close," recalls Lori Horton. "You'd never know what time they'd be home, because they were always at George's. They would sit there for lunch, and sometimes they'd come home at two in the morning, sometimes they'd be home for dinner. This was a daily thing. They'd come home in time to go on the road together. It was not very nice for the wives, but for the hockey team it was almost ideal."

On the road, Stanley played Horton's sidekick in the many pranks that Horton instigated. Sometimes, as Carl Brewer remembers, it meant initiating a rookie to major-league life.

"When we were in Montreal, we'd end up at the Venus de Milo Room on St. Catherine Street all the time," recalls Brewer. "This one day, Noel Price decided he was going to drink with Tim and Al, the big boys. They'd already had quite a few when I left to see a movie. I came back from the movie, and they were still there, sipping. Noel was looking a little grey.

"So I went off to another movie. I came back from that one, and Tim and Al were still sipping, but Noel was bleary-eyed. We had to carry Price back to the hotel, and he couldn't practise the next day. But when we left, Tim and Al were still sipping, no worse for wear."

For some reason, Horton couldn't get to sleep at night on the road without a visit to the rooms of Dick Duff or Dave Keon. The visit consisted of Horton—inspired by a few beers at dinner—flipping the bed and personal property of a Leafs player into the air, and perhaps a little head massage for good luck. The only recourse the victims had was to lock their door and barricade the doorway.

Locked doorways were a red flag waved at Horton, however, and thus the annual ritual of training camp in Peterborough became Horton lowering his shoulder and going through the locked door to surprise his victims. "Then Tim and Allan Stanley, his frequent partner in crime, attempted to prop the door up for a few hours until the carpenter arrived next morning," remembers Billy Harris.

Sometimes, Horton and Stanley enlisted others in their mischief. "The defense corps was pretty close," says Stanley. "All the defensemen went, and we used to get Keon ... he used to come with us. We'd say, 'You're a defensive forward, you can come.' We had blowouts, but really, we used common sense when we did it. The odd person maybe abused it."

Stanley's job was to make sure Horton, the star of the defense, didn't abuse it. "Allan always had that calming effect," remembers Baun. "Timmy would be getting all hyper, too much beer. You've heard those stories of him being Superman breaking doors down. Allan was the one who calmed him down. He was the only one who could cool him out."

"I'd tell him, 'Moderation, Tim, moderation,'" says Stanley, with a hint of sadness in his voice. "And he'd say, 'Yeah, you're right. Have your two-four and go home.'"

On several occasions, that meant cooling Horton down in a police station or with hotel security. Whatever he did, however he did it, Stanley helped preserve his partner long enough for Horton to play into his forties. And Stanley, too, was still playing hockey at the age of forty-three when he was finally separated from Horton, going to the Philadelphia Flyers in 1968.

Stanley knew from more than just the aches and pains that it was time to go. "I saw big changes, attitudes in players. After coming from Toronto with all the discipline—where you went downtown with a tie and a blazer—it seemed to be completely different. The players did what they wanted."

Stanley periodically left the Flyers in that final year as he negotiated the purchase of the Beehive Lodge in Bobcaygeon, preparing for his career after hockey. When the Flyers were eliminated in four straight by Scotty Bowman and St. Louis that year, the end had come.

"He was Silent Sam," remembers Brewer. "He enjoyed a quiet beer, a very significant part of those teams. To tell you the truth, I was surprised later when he put his name on the lawsuit. There didn't appear to be anything in his personality to predict it."

Except that Allan Stanley was first and foremost a team man—a trait he'd prove again when retired players chose sides to fight the NHL in the pension battle.

7

TIM

When Tim Horton was starting up the chain of donut stores that bear his name across Canada, he enjoyed getting his hands dirty, pitching in with the building and outfitting of the stores. On one such occasion, Horton—who had the granite physique of a stone mason—was laboring in a trench, digging out foundations for a new store.

As he strained to shovel out the dirt, a group of young schoolchildren happened by with their teacher. One eager pupil looked down in the trench to see the famous Horton features looking back through a film of mud and dirt.

"Look, miss, it's Tim Horton," he piped up. "Tim Horton, the famous hockey player, is shovelling in that ditch."

"And let that be a lesson to you, class," replied the teacher, "of what happens when you don't stay in school and get your education."

Ron Joyce, Horton's partner in the donut business, tells that story to illustrate the legend of Myles Gilbert "Tim" Horton. Marked for success throughout his hockey career, Horton's life was then extinguished just as it was about to blossom once again. The marquee player in the Maple Leafs' defense quartet, he is as integral to any story of the pension fight as the men who put their names to the suit.

Horton was born at the northern outpost of the Ontario Northern Railroad in Cochrane, Ontario, in 1930. Cochrane is linked with the world by Highway 11, which cuts a jagged path through the middle of Ontario's rugged mining country. A sizeable chunk of Maple Leaf talent was born or grew up in that land of rock and scrub within a hundred-mile radius of Highway 11. Allan Stanley, who was to be Horton's defense partner for eleven seasons with the Maple Leafs, and Frank Mahovlich, the most talented scorer on the Leafs, were born sixty miles south on Highway 655 in Timmins. Dick Duff, who played with Horton and Stanley on two Stanley Cup winners, was brought up nearby in Kirkland Lake. Eddie "The Entertainer" Shack, the colorful and often comic sparkplug on the Leafs, was a product of Sudbury. And George Armstrong, later the Leafs' captain, was reared in Falconbridge, just outside of Sudbury.

Horton's father, Aaron Oakley Horton, worked for the CNR. The railways took the ore and minerals mined from the Cambrian Shield and carried them to Sault Ste. Marie, where they were made into steel and shipped all over the world. In the same way, hockey players were extracted like the ore and sent to the hockey markets down south.

When Tim was fifteen, Oak Horton moved his wife and two boys—Horton's brother, Jerry, was a highly rated prospect in the Boston system, who remained in northern Ontario to play senior hockey—from Cochrane to Sudbury. Horton had reached his adult size of 5 foot 11 by the time he was eleven, and the youngster with the impressive physique was soon a star defenseman for the Sudbury Wolves. He was a fine skater, but most of all he had a booming shot from the point.

His size and talent naturally brought him to the attention of the Leafs' scouting department. Through the efforts of Bob Wilson, a bird-dog scout in North Bay, the young Horton (who'd never been out of the North) was signed by Toronto to its protected list. As an out-of-town prospect, he needed a place to live while in Toronto, so he was enrolled at St. Michael's College at the busy corner of Bathurst Street and St. Clair Avenue. Though St. Mike's is a Catholic school, Horton, a Protestant, was nonetheless admitted into residence, proving that a good hockey player is worth more than a good convert in hockey-crazy Canada.

The improved competition in the Toronto junior leagues accelerated Horton's development, and in 1949 he turned pro with the Leafs' farm team in the American Hockey League, the Pittsburgh Hornets. By all accounts, Horton was a painfully shy character off the ice (his years of door-smashing lay ahead of him), but he attracted attention from the fans at old Duquesne Gardens, the home of the Hornets.

He also caught the eye of a figure skater who was trying out for the Ice Capades at the Gardens as well. Nineteen-year-old Dolores "Lori" Michalek, who had left high school to try out for the travelling ice show, was introduced to Horton by his friend, Adolph Donadeo, as they stood alongside the ice.

"He was standing there watching the game," remembers Lori Michalek Horton, the daughter of a Pittsburgh housepainter. "Adolph said, 'You know Tim Horton,' and introduced us. Tim took me home that night, and that was it. I gave up my career."

After spending the summer apart (Horton in North Bay, Lori in Pittsburgh), the couple began courting while Horton started his pro career with the Hornets. After two seasons in Pittsburgh, Horton and Michalek set a date for their wedding. Unfortunately, it conflicted with a playoff game between Pittsburgh and the Providence Reds. Another date was chosen, but it too conflicted with a potential Calder Cup playoff date. Horton finally took matters into his own hands, leading the Hornets to the Cup with a goal three days before his wedding day, making any further postponements academic.

In that fall of 1952, he received the long-awaited call-up from the parent Maple Leafs. (Conn Smythe labelled him "the best defense prospect in Canada.") At about the same moment, the Maple Leafs had begun their descent into frustration and futility. His rink-length dashes with the puck and his heavy shot off the point soon won Horton steady work on the Leafs' blueline. As a further good omen, he was given the Number 7 sweater previously worn by Hall of Famer Max Bentley.

In spite of Horton being recognized as an NHL second team All-Star in 1953-54, the first few years of his career in a Leafs uniform were uncertain ones for him, remembers his wife. "There were stories going through the papers about how Tim hadn't reached his potential," she recalls. "He just never felt he'd made it. Every year, he'd worry about being cut and sent to the American Hockey League. When he finally got a one-way contract, that was unreal ... he was actually going to stay in Toronto."

Horton's relief was short-lived, however. Just as he began to establish himself on the Toronto defense, he suffered an injury that seriously jeopardized his career. In a game at Maple Leaf Gardens against New York in March 1955, Horton was carrying the puck up the ice. Awaiting him was the rock-solid figure of Bill Gadsby, the Rangers defenseman who looked like Jack Palance before Jack Palance ever did.

The two men collided with a sickening thud. Horton spun away from the check but his right skate blade got caught in the ice, fracturing the tibia just above the ankle. As he pitched forward on the broken leg, his head bounced off Gadsby's shoulder, fracturing his jaw.

"You could hear his leg crack all over the Gardens," Lori Horton recalled years later. "But two men behind me yelled, 'Get up and skate, you phony!' ... I went into shock. I would have sat in the Gardens all night if an usher hadn't led me away."

The break was so severe and so close to the ankle that there was some question if Horton would ever skate again, let alone play. But he steadfastly refused to give up and set to work rehabilitating the leg. Bob Baun, still a junior with the Marlies, had come to know Horton while the two worked at Smythe Sand and Gravel, and he helped Horton in his recovery.

"I was his chaser," says Baun with a smile. "He could hardly walk at the time, so I'd walk around the track with him at the Central YMCA, play a little basketball, and we'd swim for hours at the pool together."

Horton did play a few more seasons after his recovery—twenty more NHL seasons, in fact. And he dispelled the notion of his being injury-prone, playing 486 consecutive games during one stretch for Toronto (still a Leafs record). "He seemed indestructible," recalls Allan Stanley. "He had that sense about him."

But it wasn't until 1958, the year Imlach arrived, that Horton truly felt comfortable with the Leafs. "Tim never knew where he was going with Bill Reay," says Lori Horton. "One time, he had the Asian flu that left him with a high temperature, very weak. But he was still expected to show up for the game. And he had to go down there and play hockey. He darn near died.

"After all that, they benched him for the next two weeks. He just never knew where he stood, and this was important for Tim, to feel secure."

Adding to the insecurity under Reay was the threat of being traded. On one occasion, Horton was told that he was going to be traded to the Canadiens and to go home and wait by the phone. Horton sat all day, waiting for the call that would uproot his young family and move him to Montreal. The call never came, and Horton never asked what had happened.

In 1957, Hap Day, the Leafs' GM, went so far as to call Horton "expendable" and seek Smythe's blessing on a deal. "I would like permission to try and make a deal for either or both of [Jimmy] Thompson and Horton," he wrote. Smythe traded his captain, Thompson, and Horton survived in Toronto.

The arrival of Imlach marked the revival of Tim Horton. "Punch Imlach is the best thing to have happened to Tim Horton, in a hockey sense, since Tim made the second NHL All-Star team in 1953-54," wrote *The Toronto Star*'s Red Burnett in 1958. "Right now he looks like the Horton of old, the dashing defender who lifted fans out of their seats with his length-of-the-ice rushes and solid blocking."

But even Imlach had his doubts about his strapping defenseman at first. Horton heard his name mentioned in trade talks during Punch's rookie year as coach. "Punch Imlach, the hard-cookie assistant manager, says he'll trade any defenseman except Carl Brewer for some scoring strength," wrote Scott Young in *The Globe and Mail*. "One of the deals rumoured has been with New York. In the past, they have expressed warm interest in Tim Horton, a colourful and muscular rusher of a kind well-liked in good old N.Y."

Fans of the Maple Leafs were always thankful that Imlach came to his senses before dealing his "colourful and muscular rusher." Imlach himself recanted any notions of moving Horton during the next fifteen years. Not only did he coach Horton for eleven more seasons with the Maple Leafs, but he recruited a forty-three-year-old Horton to steady the defense with his new team, the Buffalo Sabres, in 1973. Like any successful, long-running act, Horton and Imlach were inextricably linked in the public consciousness.

"George preaches a strange gospel," Horton told reporters once. "But it seems to work."

Perhaps it worked because the near-sighted Horton was unable to see or hear that gospel at times. Horton "never said much," recalled Punch. "Or listened much, for that matter. He's a stubborn so-and-so ... he's going to play it the way he wants to play it. Period. There is not much you can do about it."

And Imlach was unlikely to get through to Horton with any chalkboard talks either, remembers Bobby Baun. "He was blind as a bat; how he never got hurt I'll never know."

Imlach instead let the fortuitous pairing of the single-minded Horton with Allan Stanley work its unique magic. That piece of non-coaching may have been the best strategy of his years in Toronto. When Stanley joined the team in 1958, he and Horton were soon paired up, on and off the ice. While he never knew how to handle other players on the Leafs, Imlach knew enough not to meddle with his top defense combination.

"We liked hockey talk," says Stanley, who is now retired from the lodge he and his wife ran for almost twenty years. "We were always trying to be a better defense pair."

They were the touchstones for the Maple Leafs of that era, the two constants on defense, even after Brewer quit and Baun was banished to the bench. Their willing acceptance of the status quo under Imlach gave Imlach the necessary foothold in the dressing room, the bulwark against a revolt when other players were critical or upset with Imlach.

Although not driven to perfection like Bert Olmstead, Horton earned his teammates' respect in other ways. "Tim always had time for people, he was always organizing something," remembers Brewer. "One year at training camp in Peterborough, he had an old '51 Buick convertible. One night, he took a bunch of us, we all snuck home to Toronto from camp. On the way back, the roof blew off the convertible. The last forty-five minutes we almost froze. Of course, Tim drove fast and that didn't help either."

Horton's biggest claims to fame were his scoring (prolific by the modest standards for defensemen of the day), and his strength on the ice. "There is a particular sort of spine-chilling feeling reserved only for the spines of goaltenders and defensemen," gushed a 1964 magazine article. "It hits whenever the puck squirts out to Tim Horton on the blue line, and he winds up for a slap shot. Horton's terrorizing shot has been estimated to boom towards the net at a speed of around 100 miles an hour."

In the days before Bobby Orr, defensemen had only two rules. First, stay back in your own end of the rink. Second, when in doubt, consult rule number one. Yet Horton scored 126 goals in his career, 11 of them in the playoffs. And, until Orr redefined defensive play in hockey, he held the NHL record for points by a defenseman in the playoffs with 16 in the 1961-62 playoffs (still a Toronto record).

"Horton's puck-carrying ability, plus a booming slap shot, always have made him an important part of the Leafs attack," said a 1962 *Hockey News* feature. "These skills have made him a prime favourite with Toronto fans. He is one of the best rushing defensemen in hockey, and his slap shot is one of the hardest there is."

As Horton's skating began to slow, he changed his focus to a more defensive style that finally earned him recognition on the All-Star teams again. (He was named first- or second-team All-Star five times between 1963 and 1968.) His prodigious strength crumpled forwards along the boards and moved even the biggest men from in front of the net.

One has only to see a picture of Horton in the dressing room from that period to see where the strength came from: he had a defined physique that body-builders train years for. Bobby Baun remembers that Horton was nicknamed "Clark Kent," for his awesome strength and his Coke-bottle glasses.

"He was so equipped, his strength was just awesome. Nobody, not even Gordie, was as strong as Tim. If the Dubin Inquiry into the use of steroids had begun in 1960," Billy Harris later remarked, "Horton would have been asked to testify. Tim had a very muscular body and a reputation of being perhaps the strongest hockey player of his day."

"He did wrist-curls with 150-pound weights, as if they were powder puffs," marvelled Paul Henderson, who played with Horton for two years in Toronto.

"Actually, he didn't do weight work until later on in his life," recalls Lori Horton. "I bought him barbells for Christmas one year. He was already in his thirties. He did them daily after that, but he was naturally built that way. He didn't have to work at it."

Gordie Howe of Detroit was widely recognized as the game's top player, in no small part because of his strength and his mean streak (he once shattered the nose of 200-pound Lou Fontinato with a single punch). But Imlach insisted Horton was the strongest, toughest player in the NHL.

"You can't call him a really tough player, because he's not mean the way Howe is," explained Imlach. "Tim has to be riled up. But when he is, he's the best. I've seen enough movies of him in action to know."

Unlike the tempestuous Brewer, who was always stirring up trouble on the ice, Horton was slow to get angry or fight in games. When a player finally coerced him into a fight, Horton usually eschewed punches and applied a killer bear hug, squeezing his victim like a tube of toothpaste. A Horton embrace could crack ribs and leave opponents gasping for breath days later.

"I tried Horton once," said Derek Sanderson of Boston, "and he just put the bear hug on me. Never again."

One famous instance of the Horton temper boiling over came in 1961, and it forever endeared him to Imlach. Fontinato (who is a constant in this sort of story from the '60s) had jumped Bert Olmstead and was applying a liberal five-finger editorial to Olmstead's head. Despite the fact that Olmstead and Horton had themselves fought each other at one time, Horton leapt off the Leafs' bench to protect his teammate. It touched off a wild brawl as Horton pummelled Fontinato and any other Rangers foolhardy enough to get close. "One of the liveliest brawls seen at the Gardens in recent years," Jim Proudfoot of *The Star* clucked approvingly.

"That was the kind of support I like to see for anybody on one of my teams who gets in trouble," said Imlach, defining the Smythe doctrine. "It isn't a personal thing at all in hockey. When Horton fought Olmstead, he was helping out one of his teammates then, too."

Horton's high spirits were more often in evidence off the ice in his Leafs days. "He was unassuming, a nice, level-headed, intelligent guy," says Stanley. "Until he had a few extra beer and then went 'Hee-hee-hee' in that voice of his ..."

As part of the juvenile, often cruel behavior that is second nature to sports teams, Horton liked to terrorize his smaller teammates Dave Keon and Dick Duff (whom Horton called "the Singer Midgets"). Hotel rooms across North America with loose door frames, wobbly beds and uneven floors bear witness to Horton's idea of good fun.

"When Tim came to your door, you answered it," recalled former teammate Paul Henderson. "When you heard Tim giggling outside your door, you yelled out, 'Wait a minute, I'll be right there.' Tim would pick up half the cost of a new door, but you had to pay for the rest. That's why Tim got prompt attention."

Occasionally, the police took a dim view of the hijinks. In Quebec City in 1963, Horton and Bob Pulford were returning to their hotel along with team physiotherapist Karl Elieff after postgame libations when, in the words of Billy Harris, they "decided to have a contest to see who could kick over the most garbage cans along Grande Allée."

The considerable din naturally attracted the Quebec police. The trio was arrested and taken to the local police station. The incarcerated Horton had only one option: phone Imlach, who had coached in Quebec and still knew some influential people in the city.

An annoyed Imlach toyed with the idea of letting Horton and friends stew in the cells for the night, but typically he realized that he could turn the situation to his own advantage down the road. Confident that Horton would now owe him a marker, Punch finally came down and bailed him out. If Horton was chastened by the episode, it didn't show, however. He capped the night back at the Chateau Frontenac by breaking down the solid-oak door of Dave Keon's room and ransacking the place.

Horton and Pulford were later found guilty of disturbing the peace and fined fifty dollars each or *ten* years in jail. While he thought something might have been lost in the translation, Horton paid the fifty dollars.

One problem Tim couldn't take care of was the appearance of stories about the incident in the Toronto papers Lori Horton read. "It was in the paper the next morning, so it was hard to miss," she says today with a rueful smile. "He was a character. But there was a point where he let his hair down and had a good time. I'm not sure I liked that part of it."

Mostly, the press was kind to Horton, ignoring his predilection for disturbing the peace. "The years have been kind to him physically," gushed one article. "His hair has the same hue, his face is unlined and his skating has the same old zip ... his appearance has changed little since his rookie year, though there is one significant difference: he keeps getting better and better."

Listening to Lori Horton today, one gets a portrait of the other side of Tim Horton and the Leafs during that period, the wives who struggled to keep their families together while their husbands indulged in sports and superannuated hijinks. While she recalls the time as "golden" and Tim's teammates as "family," she acknowledges that daily life was a grind. Horton's eldest daughter, Jerilynn, was four days old before Tim saw her; in all, he was away for the birth of two of his four daughters. And Horton was away from home for the first five Christmases of his eldest daughter's life.

One New Year's Eve, Lori Horton decided to surprise her husband by joining him in Detroit, where the Leafs were planning to spend the night after playing the Red Wings. "At midnight, New Year's Eve, I was driving home to Toronto alone by car while Tim was heading back with the team by train. The coach had decided not to stay over in Detroit."

The coach, of course, was Punch Imlach, and no one battled him harder than Lori Horton. "Wives were better tolerated in other cities than in Toronto," she says. "Punch always said that the perfect hockey team would be made up of bachelors. He had no regard for the wives at all. He was inconsiderate. Once, he decided to take them to Peterborough after a playoff game, but he never bothered to tell anyone until after the game. We're going to Peterborough, that's it, no planning ...

"I used to write him nasty letters all the time. Tim never knew until he was traded to New York in 1970. They gave him a pile of letters this thick," she says, holding her thumb and forefinger six inches apart. "They were all letters from me to Punch Imlach. We both wanted Tim, but at least I was willing to share."

The press at the time skirted such issues. Stories dwelt on the Hortons as the "model family"—bruising Tim with his wife ("a dainty, feminine type," according to one report of the day) and four daughters, all of whom did modelling at the time. They had designed their own home, and Tim was on his way to a business career after hockey.

A cover story in *The Toronto Star Weekly* in February 1964 showed an attractive Lori Horton going through the range of emotions at her lucky number 7 seat in the blues at Maple Leaf Gardens. "Vivacious" and "attractive" are the words used to describe her in the article, but if you read the quotes carefully, you can sense Lori Horton's true feelings.

"After ten years of being a hockey wife," Lori told writer Sylvia Fraser in 1964, "I know better than to let anything get in the way of hockey. Nothing except illness comes ahead of hockey. That's our bread and butter and we know it."

There was also a dark, troubled side to the "perfect" marriage. The same year *The Star Weekly* article appeared, Horton's wife suffered severe whiplash in a car accident. The painkillers prescribed for the injury soon became an addiction for Lori Horton. For twenty-five years, she drifted in and out of a drug- and alcohol-related nightmare.

Horton and the children had to rescue her from overdoses and binges. She consumed painkillers and anti-depressants like candy, and she spent a small fortune feeding her habit. At one time, she would make the round trip to New York in one day simply to pick up pills at clinics there.

By the time of Horton's death in 1974, their marriage had been on the verge of breaking up several times over her problems with drugs and his drinking escapades. Tim's death that year pushed Lori

Horton over the edge of an emotional precipice. Only in the last few years has she managed to clean up her life and piece together a role for herself.

The Hortons' marital problems seemed controllable back in the 1960s. They both understood that hockey would end someday, and Tim spent much of his later career with the Maple Leafs auditioning for a second career. "It was part of his personality," recalls Lori Horton. "He always had a business, it was always on his mind. A real entrepreneur ... the guy was always looking for something."

A brief stint selling advertising for car dealers at *The Toronto Star* led him to his first business venture—a Studebaker dealership on Yonge Street in Willowdale called Tim Horton Motors. "The new '62 Lark is ... as stingy on gas as Johnny Bower is on goals ... yet the Lark moves like Dick Duff and Billy Harris—fast, sure," boasted the ads.

"In the early '60s, Tim always had these old junkers," recalls Baun. "He'd have an old Buick convertible or an old Chev, and he'd always be pawning them off on the rookies coming into training camp."

The car dealership lasted two years before his business partner grew tired of operating solo during the hockey season. By then, Horton was already sizing up the next opportunity: fast-food outlets.

"When Horton goes on road trips, he spends his free time sampling fare at drive-ins, comparing food and looking for ideas," reported a magazine article in 1963.

"He'd always ask me to go to look at some place, a fast-food place, a McDonalds," says Allan Stanley. "He'd go in there and ask some questions, see how they operated."

At some point, most of Horton's teammates joined him on his scouting expeditions to restaurants, where he'd scratch out rough blueprints on napkins and coasters. After seeing the hamburger joint owned by former teammate Gord Hannigan in Red Deer, Alberta, Horton decided to get into the hamburger business.

He bought a chain of three drive-ins, named them Tim Horton's Hamburgers and decorated them with hockey paraphernalia and a life-size image of himself in uniform on the signs. He received the typical support from the press. "Horton attended to his new hamburger businesses," gushed the Maple Leafs' program of October 1963, "which have suddenly caught fire (financially, that is)."

"Monday, he never practised," recalls Allan Stanley. "He told Punch that Mondays he was off because he had things to do for the business. At the same time, he told his partners that hockey comes first."

It was a formula for business disaster. All the goodwill in the hockey world couldn't save him from the vicissitudes of business once again. Despite the early enthusiasm of his partners, Horton soon found himself in financial trouble because he could not contribute enough of his time to the business. Not even the famous Horton name could rescue his chain of hamburger restaurants from bankruptcy.

Yet there was a small glimmer of hope left from the episode. Horton had a partner in one of the stores named Jim Charade, a man who'd had some limited success in the donut business years before in Montreal. Using Charade's recipes and Horton's name, they decided in 1965 to take a stab at the donut business.

Donuts might well have been another casualty, too, had it not been for a squarely built former Hamilton policeman named Ron Joyce. He had tried to buy a couple of Dairy Queen outlets in the city but was rebuffed. So in February 1965, Joyce settled for the first Tim Horton Donuts franchises that opened in Hamilton. From that modest beginning, Joyce became a dynamo who built a multi-million-dollar chain with six-hundred stores and counting. But you can still sense his trepidation as he recalls the company's modest beginnings. "Tim didn't know anything about the donut business; neither did I," he says from his office in the modern headquarters of Tim Donut Ltd. (the corporate name for the chain) in Oakville, Ontario. "Neither did Jim Charade. There were a ton of problems at first. Eventually, Tim bought Jim's shares, and in 1967, the year they won their final Cup, I became his partner."

Joyce found a way to make a business partnership with Horton work where others had failed. He was the high-voltage worker bee, Horton the laid-back king bee. They shared a fondness for hunting and fishing and having a cold beer when the day was done. And they were both competitive.

None of which guaranteed smooth sailing, of course. After being absent from the business for most of one hockey season, Horton took it upon himself to order the equipment for a new store in Stoney Creek, Ontario. He misread the plans, however, and ordered all the fixtures backward. When the error was discovered, the franchisees hit the roof. An enraged Joyce called Horton to complain, spewing rage at every turn.

"The way I see it, Ron, I can do one of two things," said a deadpan Horton. "I can drive to the Skyway Bridge in Hamilton and jump off. Or I can order new equipment. What do you want me to do?" Horton's insouciance cooled the crisis, and the equipment was eventually ordered, this time the right way around.

Through the determination and luck of the partners, Tim Horton Donuts survived one emergency after another. Part of Horton's responsibility was to find capital for the company, but in the early stages, money was hard to come by. During a chance conversation with Harold Ballard on a train trip to Montreal with the Maple Leafs, Horton bemoaned the high interest rates he was faced with in dealing with the banks.

Ballard responded, "Go down to my bank in Toronto and tell them you want $50,000 from my account."

"I don't know what collateral I could offer, Harold," said Horton.

"You don't need any collateral with me. Your word is your bond," said Ballard. The loan helped the fledgling operation to survive.

The 1966-67 season was the toughest in years for Horton—the demands the game was making on his new business and on his personal life were beginning to tell. The team had suffered through a ten-game losing streak, Imlach was sick and it looked as if he had come to the end of the line. For the first time Horton seriously considered retirement.

But to everyone's surprise, the Leafs won the Stanley Cup that year, an accomplishment engineered by Imlach and his ageing veterans. Thirty-seven-year-old Horton was suddenly rejuvenated by the win and decided to go back for a seventeenth NHL season. Unfortunately, the euphoria of the previous spring was quickly shattered for Horton and the Leafs. The 1967-68 season was a disaster.

After winning the Stanley Cup, the Maple Leafs failed even to make the playoffs the next year. Horton himself was named a first-team All-Star, but there was little solace in the award. It was clearly the end of the team that had ruled the '60s, with veterans like Baun, Mahovlich, Pulford, Sawchuk and Stanley, Horton's partner, all gone by the end of the year.

Having lost top young prospects like Garry Unger, Arnie Brown, Peter Stemkowski, Jim Pappin and Gerry Cheevers from their system, the Maple Leafs had few replacements available for their long-time stalwarts. Expansion teams were coming into Maple

Leaf Gardens and winning in a building where the home team had dominated for years.

Despite his loyalty to Imlach, Horton decided he would return to play only if his salary was increased dramatically. When Imlach balked at paying him $45,000 a year, Horton stayed away from training camp in Peterborough.

"It wasn't the money, really," says Allan Stanley. "It's the principle of the thing. You try like a son of a gun to get what you think you're worth, and they're telling you you're a lousy hockey player. Then, as soon as you sign the contract, you're expected to forget it and go out and do all these wonderful things for the team. Tim wanted to prove a point."

Instead, he decided he would build a new donut store. Newspapermen would trundle down to the construction site to find out when Horton would give in and report. But Horton held firm. "One day I was making donuts," says Joyce, "and he took these terrible ones, just scrap donuts, placed them in a box and gift-wrapped them. Then he sent the box to Punch in Peterborough with a note that said, 'With donuts like these, who needs hockey. Love Tim.'"

After missing much of training camp, Horton finally agreed to a three-year deal worth $42,000 a year and reported to the club. The 1968-69 season was another fine one for Horton. He made the first All-Star team for the third time in his career. The team, however, had another turbulent year on and off the ice. There was constant speculation from the press (and Stafford Smythe) about Imlach's future with the team, and traded players like Mahovlich and Unger were having great years in Detroit.

The Leafs barely squeezed into the playoffs, thanks to a late surge and the collapse of their competition. In the playoffs, though, the team was destroyed by Bobby Orr and the powerful young Boston Bruins. In the wake of the final game, Smythe fired Imlach as coach and general manager. For the thirty-nine-year-old Horton, Imlach's firing seemed like a natural segue into his life after hockey.

"If this team doesn't want George, I guess it doesn't want me," Horton told the press when he heard of the firing.

"Imagine a first-team All-Star today deciding to retire, because his coach had been fired," wrote an admiring Imlach in 1982. "I never ran into any."

But Horton's retirement was motivated as much by personal reasons as by blind loyalty to Imlach. Lori Horton was hoping that getting her husband away from hockey would stabilize their home lives. "His home life was very turbulent," says Baun. "Tim used to call her Rose when things were good, and when they were bad he used to call her Rose but without very much affection. It was a very interesting relationship but very turbulent. I gather when he left Toronto it got worse."

And Ron Joyce was needing Horton at the office as the business grew. "He had a lot more pressures on him by then," says Baun. "He started to drink more at that time ... I heard that through training camp from 1968 on. The whole crew was starting to drink more. They had so many changes when Frank [Mahovlich] and Pully [Pulford] left. I heard they were starting fires in their rooms and drinking all night long."

"He was a really, really nice guy when I met him," admits Lori Horton. "I liked him a lot better at the beginning."

As the summer of 1969 dragged on, the hue and cry over another Horton retirement haunted a Maple Leafs organization struggling to ensure continuity for their young players. But Horton was steadfast, even after hearing he'd been named to the All-Star team.

"It's a nice way to end my NHL career," he told *The Globe and Mail.* "I was serious when I first said I was retiring. I'm just too busy with my donut business."

When he encountered Harold Ballard on a Toronto street that summer, Horton issued a facetious challenge, saying that he'd play again if they doubled his $42,000 salary. To the shock of Horton and nearly everyone else, the team agreed to do so, even though his contract still had a year remaining. (For public consumption, the Leafs cloaked the salary increase in the cryptic clause "special considerations.")

Horton still held out as long as he could to avoid going to training camp. ("Tim always said he'd play for free," says Lori Horton. "They had to pay him for training camp and to practise.") But finally he relented, becoming the highest-paid player in team history. Tim Horton was back for an eighteenth season with the Maple Leafs, noting, "I only stayed in shape enough to run faster than my wife."

Not that his return did anything to improve the Maple Leafs. Despite his steadying influence, the club's young defense floundered, and it was evident that forty-year-old defensemen were not part of the program to turn things around.

"It has become obvious that the Leafs are going to finish last," wrote Jim Proudfoot in *The Toronto Star.* "For that reason, the

Toronto club has been attempting to deal for some young skaters (they received future considerations in the deal). Horton went on the block, inasmuch as the $85,000 gamble hadn't worked."

On their way to a sixth-place finish out of the playoffs, Toronto dealt Horton and his salary to the New York Rangers, who were gearing up to challenge Boston for the Stanley Cup. Horton had the right to cancel the trade, but approved the move.

King Clancy wept when told of the deal by Jim Gregory (Imlach's successor as general manager) and Toronto fans mourned, but Horton seemed rejuvenated by the trade to the Rangers. "To tell you the truth, I had begun to think in terms of another season or two," he told *The Star*. "It's always subject to my business around Ontario, of course, and that's getting big. But I can't deny the hockey involvement helps."

Horton played almost four more full seasons in the NHL after his trade from the Maple Leafs, holding out each year to give his business more attention and to avoid training camp. In his fourth and final year, however, Tim Horton was stopped by a force more powerful than Bill Gadsby or bankruptcy, in a highway accident near St. Catharines.

8

BOOMER

If they'd all been negotiators like Bobby "Boomer" Baun, the pension lawsuit against the NHL would never have been necessary. Baun was renowned for two formidable skills in his NHL career: his ability to crunch forwards like Dixie cups with a bodycheck and his ability to coax impressive salaries from NHL general managers in lean times.

Perhaps the greatest bargaining session of Baun's illustrious haggling career occurred in a hotel parking lot in Oakland, California, one pleasant October afternoon in 1967. While his wife Sally and his five children sat in a taxi with its engine running, Baun went toe-to-toe over his contract with his former Maple Leafs teammate Bert Olmstead, now the general manager of the expansion Oakland Seals. Olmstead was as tough and unforgiving as the Saskatchewan prairie he'd been raised on.

Olmstead had drafted Baun from the Maple Leafs in the expansion draft of 1967, and the hero of four Stanley Cup triumphs was to be the anchor of the Seals' defense. Baun, who relished the move to the coast as a way to escape the purgatory of Punch Imlach, had already purchased a home in the Oakland hills and had moved his family to the West Coast with him.

There was just one small problem. Baun had agreed to succeed his old teammate Bob Pulford as the president of the new National Hockey League Players' Association. Old comrade-in-arms or not, no Oakland Seal was going to be leading a players' union while Bert Olmstead was the manager of the team.

But Baun had his own ideas on the subject of the NHL Players' Association. He was adamant that he would serve his fellow players as their president. Olmstead retaliated by refusing to sign Baun's contract, fining Baun $1,000 a day until he resigned. Thus it came to pass that Baun was without a contract and $13,000 in debt on opening day of the 1967-68 NHL season.

Olmstead forgot that while the tenacious Baun knew all the tricks on the ice, he had a few more up his sleeve when it came to negotiating contracts. So, with the debut of the Seals just hours away, the star defenseman—who'd been a key selling point for the team—was waving seven airline tickets to Toronto under Olmstead's nose. Unless he got the contract he wanted, he was hitting the Nimitz Freeway to the Oakland Airport and heading home to Toronto with his family.

Olmstead wouldn't budge. An exasperated Baun finally climbed into the airport cab.

"Where do you think you're going?" barked Olmstead.

"Home to Toronto," replied Baun.

"You can't do that," said Olmstead as the cab started to pull away.

"I have no contract and I'm $13,000 in the hole because of fines," shouted Baun as the cab picked up speed in the parking lot of the Nimitz Freeway Hotel.

In the cab's taillights, Olmstead saw nights of opposing forwards dancing through the Seals' goal crease, bullies from the opposition taking liberties in his end, double figures on the scoreboard ...

"Here, sign the goddamn thing," he pleaded.

"What about the $13,000 fine?" teased Baun.

"Forget the $13,000," said Olmstead. "You win. Sign the contract."

Bob Baun was more than a canny negotiator. He was also the NHL's Renaissance man—and the least likely Renaissance man you could ever hope to meet. Even today, he has the earnest look of the village smithy, with his forearms like great hawsers and battered nose splayed across his face. You'd cast Baun as one of the luckless Okies in a Steinbeck novel, not the man who first plumbed the mysteries of the NHL Pension Society, not the man who started a retired players' alumni association with his own guts and money, not the man who has a collection of priceless art and wines.

But Bob Baun likes to surprise people. Surprise is the salesman's greatest technique, and "Boomer," the man who reinvents himself every decade, is a great salesman.

"On the ice, he was a bull in a china shop," says his former partner Carl Brewer. "Off the ice, he tried to make out like a connoisseur of all the good things in life. He carries it off rather well, I think."

"In the old days with the Marlboros, you had to wear a shirt and tie every Sunday to the game," remembers broadcaster Harry Neale, his teammate in Junior A. "Baun was always spiffy. I had one jacket for the whole season; he had one for every Sunday. He even taught me how to tie a tie. Bob Baun was a big-leaguer before he made it to the big leagues."

If his demeanor was unlike that of any other hockey player, the origins of Baun's career in hockey were grassroots Canadiana.

Born just outside of Saskatoon on September 9, 1936, Baun moved with his family to the east end of Toronto in 1940, just as the relentless suburban sprawl began transforming the very British town of Toronto into a far-flung city. Many families arrived in Toronto hungry for a better life for their kids in the green, pleasant neighborhoods of suburbia.

Ken Dryden, who grew up in the west end a few years after Baun, expressed that sense of "manifest suburban destiny" in Toronto, observing how "first-generation postwar parents moved from cities to suburbs to build a clean, healthy, church-going, family-oriented, college-educated world for their children. We felt immensely privileged growing up when we did, where we did. We felt that in the 1950s, in ... a middle-class suburb, when being middle-class and suburban was considered a virtue, there was no better place to be."

And while it was hardly their expressed goal, families like the Bauns and later the Drydens fuelled an explosion of hockey talent from the city and its new suburbs, which had always been considered by Conn Smythe as an unlikely place to build the right mettle in a hockey player.

Bobby was the eldest of three children in the family of Ted Baun, the only son in the comfortable middle-class family. His hockey schooling began on the outdoor rinks not far from where he lives today. His first team was Birchmount Baptist in the Scarborough church leagues, under the eye of George Kitchen, who was later an executive with the Canadian Amateur Hockey Association.

Baun was short for his age—the man who flattened NHL stars for two decades weighed just 109 pounds when he entered high school. But he was an eager competitor. "Lorne Wideman was a semi-pro baseball player and the principal of our public school," remembers Baun. "He would hit us flies at recess. For a nickel, a dime, a quarter ... I was very competitive, I would always be there for the money. Used to drive him crazy. Even though I was young and small, I'd dodge in front of the big kids to catch the ball. I was very aggressive."

It wasn't long before Baun the little buzz saw was competing with older hockey players at the old Scarborough Arena Gardens, the outdoor rink where he played. With his neighborhood friends like John Cochrane and Don James—whom he still sees—he began to establish a name for himself in sports in Scarborough.

By fifteen, Baun had filled out to a robust 160 pounds, and he was rising through the ranks playing in the Toronto Hockey League. He was also gaining experience in a Saturday industrial league at the Arena Gardens. "It was up to twenty years old ... a renegade league. We used to pack the arena every Saturday night."

One of Baun's high school friends who played with him in the Saturday night industrial league was a pretty fair athlete in his own right. Mike Nykoluk, later the coach of the Maple Leafs, was two years older than Bobby when they met at Scarborough Collegiate. They played football together (Mike's brother Danny later played for the Toronto Argonauts of the CFL) as well as hockey and baseball.

Mike was a good enough hockey player to be scouted by the Toronto Marlboros. The Marlies wanted Nykoluk to try out with their Junior B club, the Weston Dukes, who played their games miles away on the western side of Toronto. Nykoluk liked the opportunity but hated the idea of those long, cold drives across Toronto to play hockey. He came up with a brainstorm.

"I won't go to training camp unless I can bring my friend Bobby Baun," Nykoluk told the Marlies. Wanting Nykoluk and figuring they could accommodate his pal somewhere in their vast system, the Marlies said, "Sure, bring your friend along."

Nykoluk made the Weston Dukes, but Weston wanted Baun to get a little more experience. They arranged for him to play with the Dukes' farm team, the Toronto Marlboros minor midget club. "At that time, we had Bob Nevin, Bob Pulford, Billy Kennedy, Harry Neale on the team," says Baun. "We were the finest minor midget team in the country. Fourteen fellows from that club turned pro."

But Baun barely had time to work up a sweat in minor midget. "When I was playing minor midget hockey," recalls Harry Neale, "we always had guys coming out to practise. This one Thursday, this guy who weighed about 190 pounds—as square as can be—came out to practise with us. It was Bobby Baun from Scarborough. The next night, I went to the Weston Junior B game, and Bobby Baun was playing there, the same guy who'd been at our practice. I thought, 'That's strange, he wasn't that good ...'

"Then I go to the Marlboros Junior A game on Sunday, and Baun's playing there! In three days, he blew by the midget team, the Junior B team right up to the Marlies. It took me two years to catch up to him."

"A couple of their defensemen were hurt," explains Baun today. "So Reg Hamilton, the Marlies' coach, said, 'Let's see what you can do.' I never went back to Junior B."

By season's end, Baun was playing in the OHA (Ontario Hockey Association) final against the powerful Barrie Flyers team that featured future NHL stars Doug Mohns, Leo Labine, Don McKenney, Réal Chevrefils and Jerry Toppazzini. Not that the Marlies were short of talent themselves: Billy Harris, Al McNeil, Gary Aldcorn and Bob Pulford were in the lineup along with Baun and Nykoluk that first year. Barrie won the final against the Marlies and went on to win the Memorial Cup in 1954, but it was the last setback the Marlies would suffer for two years.

"It was just a fun time all our junior career because we were winning all the time," recalls Baun. "Stafford [Smythe] and Harold [Ballard] would have a trip to Quebec every year. We'd stay at the Chateau Frontenac. It was one big party. We'd go there with a twenty-five-game winning streak and leave with a fifteen-game losing streak. But Harold and Stafford were just two of the boys at that time in junior. They were real characters, the original Mutt and Jeff team."

Baun and his sidekick, Al McNeil, were team leaders and practical jokers. One of their favorite stunts came during team meals at the old St. Charles Restaurant on Yonge Street. While the players had a pregame steak before boarding a bus to the game, their rotund coach, Turk Broda, would tuck into Chinese food. Invariably, McNeil would summon Broda to the phone before he could eat any of his dinner: "It's Staff on the phone, Turk. He needs to speak to you right away."

The dutiful Broda would trundle off to answer the bogus phone call; Baun and McNeil would then dispose of Broda's meal. The coach returned to his empty plate, and while the team howled, Broda could only contemplate a long bus ride on an empty stomach—which in Broda's case was a considerable chasm. What made it so funny to the players was how often it worked.

In 1955, the Marlboros, under Broda, clinched the OHA title against the St. Catharines Tee-Pees before 12,545 fans at Maple Leaf Gardens; next they polished off the Quebec Frontenacs in five games for the eastern championship.

They then travelled out west by train to play the Regina Pats, the western champs. There is a wonderful photograph taken at Union Station in Toronto as the team of anxious teenagers embarked on their journey. A young, crew-cut Bobby Baun leaps out of the picture, giving a rousing war whoop in the back row, looking manic in his best travelling clothes. In the front row of the photo sits the management team of Harold Ballard and Stafford Smythe. They look as ready for mischief as Baun does.

The Pats won the first game of the Memorial Cup series in Regina, but Toronto then stormed back to win four straight for their first Memorial Cup since 1929. Billy Harris remembers that an extremely nervous Stafford Smythe left the Regina Exhibition Stadium for the hotel during the fifth game with the Marlies trailing the Pats by two goals.

"Stafford decided to go to bed, but he couldn't sleep," recalled Harris. "So he dressed, then walked back just in time to join the celebration." The Marlies had scored three in overtime to win the Cup.

The next year, the Marlies played in the Memorial Cup final back east. Harry Neale was new to the team that year, and he says Baun left nothing to chance in the effort to repeat as champs. "He believed in witchcraft or the occult," says Neale, "so we had to go get our tea leaves read. The girl who did the reading told us that we were going to win it all. For me, I wasn't so sure; we had some tough teams to beat. But Baun, well, that was it, he was convinced." The tea leaves—and Baun—were right; the Marlies won their second straight Memorial Cup.

By the time the Marlies took the Cup that year, Baun had filled out to a solid 182 pounds. He was also becoming intimate with the hockey scene at Maple Leaf Gardens. When he wasn't playing for the Marlies, he was working at Smythe Sand and Gravel or shovelling snow in front of the Smythe home.

"I came up to the Marlies in Baun's last year," says Brewer. "He was a well-known player, teamed with Al McNeil. I got to know him a little bit. He drove a Cadillac even then." Baun—who has never lacked for earning power or cars in his life—had saved enough of his money to buy a Cadillac in junior. One fine day when Conn Smythe had left the sandpit early, Baun decided to wash his Caddy in the garage recently vacated by Mr. Smythe.

"I thought he had left for the day. The next thing I knew, the automatic zapper sounds and up goes the door. There's Mr. Smythe trying to get in. He was just storming."

Later that day, Baun was summoned to Smythe's office, presumably to get the sack for insubordination. But after some blustering, Smythe got to the point.

"Whose car is that?"

"It's mine, sir," replied Baun.

"How did you get that?"

"I paid my own money, sir," said Baun.

"Well ... don't let me catch you in the garage again," harrumphed an obviously impressed Smythe.

"That year at the Memorial Cup dinner, he tells the story," Baun says with a laugh. "'You talk about young guys not making money in hockey,' says Mr. Smythe, 'well, I've got a young fellow here on this team driving a Cadillac, and I couldn't get in my own garage because of it.'"

After the 1956 Memorial Cup, Baun was summoned to the Maple Leafs' training camp to begin his pro career. It was perhaps the best and worst time to be a rookie with the Leafs. The team was in total disarray at the management level. Conn Smythe was eliminating his long-time friend and ally Hap Day from the picture so he could hand over the running of the team to his son Stafford. Coaches and managers arrived and departed with amazing speed. In Baun's first three years, he had four general managers—Day, Howie Meeker, King Clancy and Punch Imlach—and four coaches—Clancy, Meeker, Billy Reay and Imlach. The team reflected the changes, finishing fifth and then last in the two years before Imlach arrived.

As well, Baun and the young Leafs saw how Smythe tore into the infant NHL Players' Association in 1957-58. If he could trade the team captain and the top scorer, what would he do to a young defenseman? "It was my second year. There was a whole group of us there the same age. Six of us were twenty or twenty-one years old," says Baun. "Conn had all the young guys led down the garden path. We didn't know our backside from page nine."

But it was also a great time to be young and a Leaf, because there were opportunities for jobs throughout the team. When he assumed

Day's old post as manager of the team, Stafford Smythe decided to cast his lot with the junior players he'd managed and developed for the Leafs. Youth would be served at Maple Leaf Gardens under Smythe and the new "Silver Seven" management team of Ballard, John Bassett and four other businessmen who'd bought controlling interest of the team from Conn Smythe. Scott Young puckishly described the collection of party boys and industrialists who had just inherited the mantle of the Canadian institution as a "seven-man political, military and economic junta ..."

Looking back, it seems as though Baun was a fixture on the Toronto defense from his first day at the Gardens. But he remembers it differently. After his impressive rookie year, his confidence suddenly deserted him.

"I had a bad training camp my second year, the year I got married. They sent me down to Rochester to play for old Bucko McDonald. We went on tour against the Montreal Canadiens, and Bucko wouldn't let me off the ice. I'd play forty-five minutes a game against the Stanley Cup champions for five nights running. By the time that was over, I'd got my confidence and there was no looking back."

In fact, Baun was soon rated as one of the hardest hitters in hockey, and there can be little doubt of his unique contribution to the success of the Toronto defense.

"Bobby had that low center of gravity," recalls Eddie Litzenberger, who played with and against Baun. "He would just get underneath you. He really hit hard. He and Leo Boivin in Boston were the hardest hitters."

"Boomer, he always took the man," marvels Stanley. "If you couldn't get out of the way, man, you got him. Bang."

Gordie Howe still says the hardest he was ever hit in a hockey game was in Baun's first year. He caught Howe right in the middle of the shot. "I made it to the bench, but I didn't know if it was our bench or theirs," Howe told Harry Neale years later when Neale coached him in the WHA. "I wasn't just going to lie there on the ice no matter what."

Howe—who had a legendary memory for pain inflicted on him—waited a while for his revenge. In fact, it took him ten full years. Baun was by then playing in Oakland, and he tried to hit Howe in the middle of a shot again. This time, Howe left his stick up in the air, virtually impaling Baun in the throat. As the stricken defenseman lay on the ice, struggling for breath, Howe skated over to him. "Now we're fucking even," he casually informed Baun.

Baun's steadiness and physical presence proved the necessary counterpoint to Carl Brewer's mercurial, enigmatic temperament when the two were teamed up as a defense pair by Punch Imlach early in 1958. "Boomer and I played together for seven years, did a lot of things together," says Brewer. "I hate to describe him as a defensive defenseman, because he did it all with a lot of skill ... if people knew how hard he worked at his game, the angles ... he was an artist out there."

Baun's willingness to play with pain was what made him a legend in the 1960s—the Maple Leaf with the Purple Heart. And his rugged, take-the-body style exacted a steep price. Baun's greatest moments are often colored blood-red with pain, and it was a serious neck injury that finally forced him to retire on his second tour of duty with the Leafs in 1972. Baun now laughingly admits that when he quit, he had cosmetic surgery to repair the scars left by his seventeen-year career. Only his battered nose remains as it was in that period, like a gallant duelling scar.

Stories of Baun's heroism abound, although not all reached the newspapers (and thus legendary status). A typical episode of his true grit occurred in a Chicago hotel in the early 1960s. Baun had been casually eating his dinner in his hotel room bed when he was victimized by a nocturnal visit from Tim Horton and Allan Stanley. Pillows, sheets and cutlery were sent flying. Unfortunately, the horseplay left Baun with a deep gash on his left foot as a souvenir.

The players involved—worried that Punch Imlach would find out and fine them—hushed up the incident, and Baun had his foot clandestinely stitched up by a sympathetic doctor. He then gamely travelled home to Toronto on the plane, biting back the pain the whole way, but showing no outward signs of the injury.

The gash, however, was at just the point on his foot where Baun laced up his skates. Billy Harris remembers what Baun endured. "I sat beside Bob in the dressing room, and for two weeks after practices he would quietly slip into the washroom where he would wash the blood that continued to seep from the cut ... I could feel that pain, and it wasn't my foot. Bob never missed a shift or practice."

Sally Baun was also left in awe of her husband's pain threshold. When Baun scored the famous game-winning goal against Detroit on his broken leg in the finals of 1964, she got to see the part of the story the public was never shown. The goal, she explains, "was on Thursday. On Friday, he was in agony—a complete invalid—and on Saturday he could barely get out of the house."

Baun played that night in Toronto as the Leafs won their third straight Stanley Cup. "Some players probably wouldn't have done it," Sally Baun explained at the time. "I don't know whether Bob was heroic or just plain stubborn. I think that those who do such things just can't help themselves. They are built up to such a high pitch."

On another occasion, Sally Baun was in hospital after delivering the couple's third child. She had listened to the Leafs' Sunday night game from New York the night before. The next morning she turned on the radio to hear the announcer say that Bob Baun was having emergency surgery and might be dying. Even for the normally sanguine Sally Baun, this was too much. Mrs. Baun went into shock.

Ironically, Baun was a few floors away at the same hospital when his wife heard the news of his imminent demise on the radio. His wounds had been cared for and he was out of danger even as she contemplated a lengthy widowhood with three kids. The couple was reunited shortly thereafter and allowed to recuperate together. "We used to wheel around the corridors together," she sighed.

These days, Baun himself is loath to discuss his blood-and-guts reputation. He will only allow that "it was the respect I had for those people I played with at the time" that kept him plugging away. As well, he was close to many people in management at the time, men like Don Giffin, the man who later bankrolled Harold Ballard's rise to ownership of Maple Leaf Gardens, and Toronto lawyer Jim Blaney of Blaney, Pasternak, Smela and Watson.

Baun was a charter member of the Blue and White Investment group started by Blaney and his young colleague Alan Eagleson. It was in Blaney's office that Baun's interest turned to the business world and the prospect of starting a players' association that would last.

"We used to have twice-weekly meetings at Blaney's office," explains Baun. "The old Marlboro group, we used to meet there. Jim hardly ever went home for dinner, so we'd be shooting the breeze about business and other things almost every night of the week ... that developed into the talk about the players' association."

Blaney was ultra-conservative, not a union man, yet even he knew that the autocratic labor scene in the NHL had to change if the sport was to prosper. Still, he was reluctant to take the initiative in starting another players' association. On the other hand, Eagleson, whom many of the hockey players like Baun and Bob Pulford had known for years, seemed a natural. Eagleson had ingratiated himself with the players by helping them get off speeding tickets and parking tickets in court. With his rollicking, brazen style and his sharp tongue, he seemed perfectly suited to harness the fractious players.

Eagleson was also to possess the trump card of Bobby Orr, the teenaged phenomenon he'd signed as a client in 1966. Through Orr, Eagleson would controll the game's number-one attraction and—in hockey's tribal climate—wield ultimate power in the world of power politics. "There were BIG egos," remembers Baun. "They all wanted to be boss cows ... Boom Boom Geoffrion, Dickie Moore ... there had to be a catalyst like Eagleson who could smack them down with his mouth. Then they'd all be quiet and listen."

While Eagleson's autobiography, *Power Play*, states that a chance meeting with the Boston Bruins in a Montreal hotel room in 1967 started the NHL Players' Association, in truth it was those meetings with the Leafs' young firebrands like Baun, Brewer and Pulford at Blaney, Pasternak in Toronto that really launched Eagleson's career in hockey.

"Once Al got control and left Jim [Blaney]'s influence, some of the wrong things happened," says Baun. "Al had no one to control him. The players certainly weren't going to control him. I was only there for a short time as president. Al didn't want me there any longer. I thought the players should have been controlling him, not him controlling the players."

While the Players' Association he fostered didn't work out as planned, Baun's other interests flourished. Through Blaney and his other business contacts, Baun also came to meet the movers and shakers of Toronto business as the city began to take off in the 1960s. "It was an interesting time to meet the Eatons (who owned part of the Leafs) and learn about the family background. And the Bassetts ... you know, a lot of people really think Toronto is a big city. But the Establishment is not very big."

Baun used his contacts to establish himself in business. He operated a contracting company called Baun & Cawker Construction that specialized in additions, alterations, kitchens and all repairs. "An Outstanding Performance Guarantees Customer Satisfaction—says

Bob Baun, star defenseman now in his eighth season with the Leafs," proclaimed the advertisements for Baun & Cawker.

Like a lot of Leafs, Baun was also playing the penny-stock market. He says that it nearly cost the team its Stanley Cup in 1964. "That was the year Texas Gulf and Sulphur had that big strike up in Timmins. We were involved in penny stock at the time. Everybody had a phone on their backsides and one in each ear. We didn't care about the playoffs, we were making $5,000 or $6,000 a week.

"Most of us had $25,000 or $30,000 in our pocket at that time. So we weren't concentrating too much ... we almost lost that year because of that damn stock."

Baun later parlayed his business experience in a big way in the insurance business, making—and losing—a small fortune before settling down to run franchises of Tim Horton Donuts. With his wide-ranging business and cultural interests, Baun became the eclectic hockey player, the dilettante defenseman who collected art and fine wine, dabbled in the stock market and generally pursued all that was good in life.

Most of all, he enjoyed the reaction his wide-ranging interests evoked in people. "A lot of people want to put you in a square," he says. "I don't think you can put people in squares. I remember when I did some cooking on TV—jeepers—I did a lobster soufflé on TV. They couldn't believe I attempted to do a lobster soufflé on TV." But Baun had taken Cordon Bleu cooking courses in France. And, despite not having drunk wine until he was twenty-five or twenty-six, he stocked his cellar with Chateau Latour and Lafite and Mouton Rothschild from the great 1961 vintage. Brewer now jokes that he regrets not starting to drink wine himself until after he'd parted company with Baun and his considerable cellar. As Brewer says, Baun didn't spend money, he burned it.

Baun's other teammates were similarly taken with the refined tastes of their teammate. "Allan Stanley had a great influence on me on the ice," says Baun. "But I influenced him, too. When I'd go out dining with him, whatever I'd order, he'd say, 'Me too, I'll have the same.'

"Here I was, ten years his junior, but he'd always listen to everything I had to say about business or arty things—the finer points of life. He used to say, 'I don't know where you came from ...' But he'd always call me up and say, 'What do you think about this, Bob?' It was interesting."

Everyone found Baun simply the most different hockey player they'd ever met. He collected Eskimo and wood carvings from Quebec, a lot of paintings and prints by Andrew Wyeth, and he listened to progressive music.

"The Bob Bauns have a large collection of records," reported Margaret Scott in the Maple Leafs' program of January 1964. "Bob has a definite preference for progressive jazz, two of his favorites being Al Hirt and Dave Brubeck ... when it comes to vocalists, Bob's ears are attuned to Sarah Vaughan and Ella Fitzgerald."

As Harry Neale had observed, Baun was also very conscious of his clothing. Eagleson remembers the impression Baun made at NHLPA meetings. "At most meetings, everybody would be in a T-shirt except me. I'd be wearing a jacket and tie. But Boomer ... like as not would come in evening dress."

Baun was eccentric, and in some ways he needed to be. Despite his undisputed value to the Leafs, he was the only member of the defense quartet not to be named to the All-Star team or to win a major award. He was not a scorer, either, or a charismatic figure on the ice. That was for Brewer and Mahovlich and others. Baun's job was to do the dirty work in the corners and flatten the forwards who ventured too close to Bower in the Leafs' net. "He hit a lot, he was rough," recalls Brewer. "But he did things with a lot of skill. We had a lot of mutual respect on the ice."

While his public profile was modest, Baun's place within the team community was unchallenged: he was the man to see at contract time. His exploits in negotiating with Imlach became well known, and he began to share his bargaining tips with his teammates. Because he could not use gaudy scoring statistics to make his case with Punch, Baun worked out his own series of statistics on his play that reflected his value to the team. He used this data in dealing with Imlach, and when it failed to make the case, he was not afraid to hold out, either.

In fact, Imlach partially blames Baun's holdout in training camp of 1965 for causing Brewer to quit the Leafs. Baun was fighting Imlach for a better contract that fall while a troubled Brewer was with the team in Peterborough for training camp. When Brewer became embroiled in an argument with Johnny Bower between periods of an exhibition game in Peterborough, Baun wasn't around to help settle his friend and partner's jangled nerves. Imlach confronted Brewer in the dressing room, telling him if he wasn't ready to protect Bower in net, then he should take off his uniform. Brewer did just that, walking away from the team for good.

Baun returned to the Leafs, however, and continued to counsel younger players on how to deal effectively with Imlach's negotiating tactics. One night in 1966, Imlach was walking down the hall of the Empress Hotel—the club's training camp headquarters in Peterborough—when he encountered a knot of young players lined up outside Baun's door.

"What the fuck are you assholes doing out here?" demanded the solicitous Imlach.

"We're waiting to speak to Mr. Baun about our contracts," stammered one of the younger players.

Imlach then did a fair imitation of the explosion at Krakatoa, dispersing young hockey players with a lava-like stream of vituperation. The idea of Baun, his loyal soldier, plotting behind his back to pry more money from the coffers of Maple Leaf Gardens...!

"That was the beginning of the end for me," admits Baun.

By 1967, Imlach had Baun riding the bench regularly; he used Larry Hillman and Marcel Pronovost in his place on defense. For a competitor like Baun—the man who'd scored a game-winning goal for Imlach on a broken leg—this was impossible to accept.

The tension between Baun and Imlach reached a climax during the playoffs that spring. Baun was rarely seeing any ice time, and had remained after practice at the team's hideaway in Peterborough, doing stops and starts to stay in shape. Imlach ordered him off the ice for a team meeting. "We're not going to wait around for you," added Imlach.

"Punch was with the reporters, being smartass like Punch could. I skated over to the boards in front of the reporters and said, 'Fuck off, I'm getting ready in case you might need me. You may want me to look like an asshole, but I'm just going to make sure that I don't.' He just stormed away."

Needless to say, Baun's ice time didn't increase after the blowup in Peterborough. When the Leafs won the Cup, Baun's response was to skip the parade and reception at Toronto's City Hall, a move that obviously stung Imlach. "I know his pride was hurt, because he'd spent most of the playoffs on the bench," Imlach wrote later. "He'd been with me long enough to know there was nothing personal in that. He said he didn't show up because he hadn't done much towards winning the Cup. But he showed up to collect his playoff money, all right. I thought him staying away took a little of the lustre away from the guys who did win it."

If Imlach had had any doubts before, Baun's no-show convinced him to leave Baun available for the expansion draft. Instead of giving Baun a spot on the roster, he protected Larry Hillman and Marcel Pronovost. Baun had the last laugh—he managed to play five more years in the NHL for Oakland and Detroit, while Hillman and Pronovost were gone from the Leafs within a year.

Being dropped from an expansion team was an ignominious end to the Toronto career of a player who perhaps best personified the workmanlike Leafs of that era. But it was by no means the end of Bob Baun's contributions to the NHL.

"I march to a different tune than most of those guys from that time," he remarks, "because I'm inquisitive as hell."

9

CARL

During the Stanley Cup finals of 1959, a select group of NHL stars huddled together in the stands, observing in minute detail the activities of twenty-one-year-old Carl Brewer on the ice surface below. Brewer had come upon the NHL in 1958 as suddenly as a summer storm. He lit up the sky with dazzling bolts of energy and thundered menacingly everywhere he skated, leaving fallen limbs and hockey sticks behind him.

Now this skating storm cloud was being charted by his peers: goalie Gump Worsley of the Rangers, center Jean Béliveau of Montreal and Gordie Howe, the *sine qua non* on right wing for the Red Wings. For most of the practice, they observed in silence as Brewer tore up and down the ice, dealing out passes and punishment with equal alacrity. As the practice came to a close, the rotund Worsley turned to journalist Scott Young and muttered, "You know, I think Brewer is just zany enough to be real good."

Howe and Béliveau, who—like Worsley—intrinsically understood what makes greatness in a hockey player, could only agree. Something about Brewer impressed and unnerved even the game's dominant players.

If you measure the impact of a man in the NHL by the length of his service or the number of records he established, then Carl Brewer's greatness went largely unrealized. "He probably wasn't recognized to be as good as he was," says Harry Neale, Brewer's teammate in junior hockey. "He was an All-Star every year ... if he wanted to be." The problem was Brewer didn't always know what he wanted to be.

A three-time All-Star, he left the NHL at his physical and creative peak in 1965. He could skate like few defenseman before Bobby Orr, controlling the pace of a game or upsetting it with a flash of ferocity. And yet he couldn't master the passions that gave him his muse. "I took hockey seriously," he says today. "Perhaps too seriously."

Brewer skated on a razor's edge that few of his teammates or rivals could understand or appreciate. Only his defense partner, Bobby Baun, matched the quixotic Brewer's curiosity and intellect; but where Baun was burnished and made whole by his pursuits outside hockey, Brewer was buffeted and bruised by the same process. He stood defiantly outside the old boys' club that dispensed hockey's jobs and perks, a man who would not be controlled.

Ironically, it was his status as an outsider that enabled Brewer to convert Baun's work on hockey players' pensions into a legal challenge. A man closer to the power structure might have considered the risks differently—toes stepped on, jobs lost, friendships ruptured. After years of life beyond hockey's pale, Brewer was ideally positioned to challenge the system.

Brewer is not one to let his psychological make-up be probed too deeply, but it can be said that this unconventional man started from very conventional roots in Toronto's Riverdale neighborhood. Born October 16, 1938, and brought up in the working-class streets around Pape and Gerrard that had spawned Punch Imlach and Billy Harris, Brewer was the middle son in a family of three boys and a girl. Though small, he had the strong, sloping shoulders of a good athlete. Friends remember that while his older brother Frank was perhaps a better athlete, Carl was a dedicated worker who would shoot the puck alone against the boards even after the ice had melted in the spring.

His mother was of Irish-Catholic descent, while his father, Carl Senior, was Protestant. Under the dictates of the Church of Rome, the Brewers were brought up as Catholics, but they went to the Protestant schools. "When we were going for our catechism studies after school, the Catholic kids wouldn't believe that we were Catholic, too. They wanted to fight us," Brewer says with a sly grin. "The Brewers didn't lose too many fights."

Brewer was also a naturally bright student. "He was a serious student, in the brainy class," remembers Toronto school principal Ernie Priest, who grew up with Brewer in the east-end Withrow Park neighborhood. "He took Latin, he took Greek, he was with all the brains at Riverdale Collegiate, which had a good academic reputation then. He was looking for an 80 in subjects while the rest of us would take a 50 if there was one that wasn't being used."

Carl Brewer, Sr., and his twin brother, Willie (nicknamed "Wee"), were considered fine all-around athletes in the 1930s, playing soccer, hockey and baseball in the parks around Toronto's east end. Brewer's favorite story from that time recalls when his uncle was hurt in a soccer match. His father, who was not playing in the game, dashed into the dressing room to find his brother had been knocked *hors de combat*.

"My dad had a mustache," says Brewer. "He shaved it off right there, put on my uncle's uniform and went out and played the rest of the game. No one noticed the difference."

Carl inherited more than his athletic ability from his father. "Carl was like his dad, I've heard," says Baun. "He worried too much about himself. If only he'd had Gordie Howe's focus ..."

Sports were as natural as breathing to the Brewers and the young men they went to school with or played against in the church leagues and the Toronto Hockey League. Like his father, young Carl was small and fast as a youngster, making him a fine offensive player in hockey and a quarterback in football at Riverdale. He also played a lot of soccer, a training device later used to great effect by Anatoli Tarasov and the Soviets. "At that time, say 1946 to 1950, all the kids were immigrants around us," he says. "The kids from Lithuania and Latvia and Ukraine played soccer every day, so I played soccer every day and became proficient at it."

He was also a fine second-base prospect in baseball. "He was a fabulous player, a great second baseman because he was so smart," says Ernie Priest. "He could hit, had a fine glove, he could steal a base, even come in and pitch. He could've been a professional, he had that savvy."

"I tried out for the Cleveland Indians when I was seventeen," Brewer says. "They wanted to sign me, but I told them I wanted to play hockey instead."

Everyone wanted to play hockey in Toronto during the halcyon days of Conn Smythe's Maple Leafs in the late '40s and early '50s. Brewer's neighborhood spawned several pro hockey stars in those years, while at least another half-dozen others were considered good enough to have played pro had they pursued a hockey career.

Brewer, who was an accomplished skater and player, soon caught the eye of Cliff Cooper, his coach in pee wee hockey and an operative in the Maple Leafs' local farm system. He began climbing the ladder of the Toronto Marlboro system, from bantam to midget and then to junior.

Because of his smaller stature and the glut of fine young defensemen like Bobby Baun, Al McNeil, Ron Casey and Harry Neale in the Marlies system, the Marlies tried to put him on the wing when he came to the Junior A level. "Carl Brewer played for the Marlboros when we won our second straight Memorial Cup," remembers Neale. "He couldn't make the defense so he played left wing and really helped us."

In spite of the success of the team, Brewer didn't appreciate being moved up to forward. "I was obviously the best defenseman in midget, because I played the whole game," he says matter-of-factly. "But all the other defenseman were bigger and got called up first. So I was overlooked. I remember that." He was also one of the youngest players on those teams, something that would remain a problem for him when he was called up to the Maple Leafs.

During his years with the Marlies, Brewer's sense of self-worth grew in tandem with his skill. Along with Baun, his future defense partner, he was a member of the powerful Marlboro teams of Turk Broda and Stafford Smythe that won the Memorial Cup twice in the mid-'50s. Under Smythe, Brewer and the Marlies developed the winner's sense of invincibility that would carry over when they hit the NHL.

Brewer also developed his unique showmanship. In one game at Maple Leaf Gardens, Brewer was assessed a delayed penalty, but it took a while for the Marlboros to touch the puck and end the play. In the meantime, Brewer had slipped off the ice and crouched low behind the bench. "The referee came over to the bench and says, 'Number 2 ... penalty!'" recalls Harry Neale. "But there's no Brewer. Turk Broda says, 'Number 2? We didn't dress Number 2 today' ... Meanwhile, the guys on the bench are howling with laughter.

"After fifteen seconds, the referee threatens us with two penalties if Broda doesn't produce Brewer. So Carl finally comes out from behind the bench and skates to the penalty box. But he skates like he's got a rope pulling him into the box ... he was crazy in his own right."

Brewer also honed his sharp tongue in Junior A as well. In one game, the Marlboros were reduced to three defenseman: Brewer, Neale and Casey. "We can't take any penalties, especially no misconducts,"

Neale warned Brewer. "Carl was always yapping, and sure enough he gets a misconduct. Casey and me had to play ten straight minutes. Just before the end of the penalty, I skated over to the penalty box and said, 'Don't worry about the other team when you get back out there, worry about me and Casey, *we're* going to kill you.'"

Stafford Smythe was of the same generation as many of the players he developed in the Marlboros' system. And unlike his father, Conn, he was liked by most of the young men who played for him. "I liked Stafford, he was a friend of mine," says Brewer. "He lacked some personal graces perhaps, but he was a players' guy."

By 1958, the big club decided to take a first-hand look at Brewer during training camp. While others had their doubts, Brewer realized that he belonged from the first day he skated with the big club. His impressive performance convinced the management of the last-place Leafs that Brewer was a player they could build on immediately.

Punch Imlach, newly installed as the gatekeeper of Conn Smythe's fortune, routinely offered Brewer the standard pittance for a nineteen-year-old rookie: a $1,600 bonus and "peanuts" for a salary. Brewer balked. "I knew that two guys I'd played with in junior, Wally Boyer and Bobby Newman, had gotten $5,000 bonuses from Hap Day, and they hadn't made the team. So I wouldn't sign the contract, I held out."

The contract wrangle was an ordeal for the stubborn young Brewer. "You're a kid, you're scared to death, how do you tell the Toronto Maple Leafs to go to hell?" says Brewer. "Because all they knew was how to intimidate the shit out of kids. Your dad is intimidated by the scene as well. He makes just enough money to keep the family, he's thinking, 'Take the money, take the money.' Just to be a Leaf ..."

Punch Imlach figured that, like all cocksure rookies, Brewer would soften up eventually with a little friendly persuasion. He had Brewer travel with the team to play a five-game trial (the maximum number of games a junior could play before the NHL club was obliged to sign him). Still Brewer wouldn't sign. "He thought I'd capitulate on the train to Detroit. I didn't. In fact, I thought more of quitting than ever."

Brewer's first contract squabble (though not his last by any means) finally ended when Imlach offered a two-year contract for $16,500 and a $4,000 bonus. But while the Leafs had their man under contract, they were soon to discover that Carl Brewer was never under their control.

Brewer made an instant impact in his rookie season with the Maple Leafs. "Being still a junior in his first year with us, he had a lot to learn," Imlach remembered later. "He developed very quickly. He was a pretty good hockey player by the end of the season. He did a remarkable job for a first-year man."

Newspaper reports applauded his "hell-for-leather form that has made him one of the finest young defensemen to come into the league in years."

"Carl could move the puck," says his defense partner, Bobby Baun. "He was a wonderful skater, good hockey brain. There wasn't anything he couldn't do. If he'd wanted to fight, he'd have been as good a fighter as anyone, because his reflexes were so good. And he was strong, too."

Brewer also developed a reputation as an *agent provocateur*, racking up 125 minutes in penalties his first season and 150 the second, a figure that led the League. Much of that time came via misconducts when Brewer's dialogues with referees landed him in the penalty box. By his third year, he was being variously described as "the target for most of the NHL's most notorious hatchet men," and "the NHL's badman—a strange achievement for the well-mannered young man he is off the ice."

Pictures of the time often show Brewer with his glove in an opponent's face or his stick probing their digestive tract. He was described as the "Leafs' bad man" by Peter Gzowski, who was a horrified witness to Brewer's handiwork on Stan Mikita of Chicago in 1964. "He rammed the business end of his hockey stick into Mikita's stomach. It was as vicious a spearing as I had ever seen. Mikita ... clutched his stomach and fell as if axed."

"I don't feel I did anything underhanded," Brewer explains today, his face impassive, his voice soft and measured. "There were only a couple of times in my recollection when I speared somebody. It was just tough, aggressive, hard hitting."

Brewer sowed fear and loathing in opponents via a repertoire of irritations that Scott Young soon dubbed "Brewerisms—that massive collection of unnerving gambits by which this young man has persuaded his National Hockey League adversaries to never drowse while in his vicinity." On one occasion, Brewer disarmed Jim Morrison of the Rangers using the "More-In-Sorrow-Than-In-Anger ploy." After Morrison had skewered Brewer with his stick, Brewer skated over to him and "leaned his chest on Morrison's shoulder, and spoke earnestly. Brewer kept his stick on the ice and did not look warlike at all.... This peaceful scene was broken up when Lou Fontinato reached around and placed one large and sweaty glove over Brewer's mouth. Then there was a bit of shoving."

Brewer gave Young an explanation in the Leafs dressing room. "I just went to him and said, 'What did you spear me for, Jimmy? I expect spearing from some of the more ruffianly players on your team, but not from you. You're not the spearing KIND of player, Jim. Whatever got in you to spear me?'... I told him if he kept on spearing me, I would have to take some retaliatory measures, much as that would go against the grain with me."

Young observed: "And he [Brewer] shook his head ... more in sorrow than in anger—although undoubtedly realizing that here was another fine Brewerism, the fatherly lecture, a needle as effective in its way as a spear."

Indeed, it was Brewer's refreshing wit, plus his inspired play alongside Baun, that caught the attention of hockey people. After one of his many misconducts for verbally abusing referee Eddie Powers, Brewer was asked what he had said to provoke the ten-minute penalty. "You might say I made a few deleted remarks," Brewer told reporters, using the word "deleted" to save editors the effort of cleansing his comment for the next day's papers. And when he visited Europe, he sent back postcards written in German. "He has a fair knowledge of the language," said an approving George Gross in *The Toronto Telegram*. "I wouldn't put it past him to use it in one of his arguments with referee Frank Udvari next season."

Whatever his tactics, Brewer was soon recognized as one of the League's top players on its best defense corps. By 1961-62, he was an All-Star, the first of four nominations he received in his career (once as a first-team player). "...Carl Brewer, who may be the fastest defenceman and who is almost as good at his specialties of shoulder fakes, lob shots and holding sweaters as [Allan] Stanley is," was how Gzowski described him, his pacifist nature notwithstanding.

Eddie Litzenberger became an expert on just how fast Brewer could skate after he joined the Leafs in 1961. Punch Imlach always paired Litzenberger—who depended on skill, not speed—with Brewer in tandem skating drills. "I hate Carl Brewer," laughs Litzenberger today. "One of Punch's drills was to skate as fast as we could in pairs. Now, the two fastest skaters in the NHL those days were Don McKenney in Boston and Carl in Toronto. Guess who got Brewer? I spent the better part of three years looking at his backside."

At the tender hockey age of twenty-three, with a Stanley Cup and an All-Star award, Brewer had reached the summit of the hockey world. It was a world that soon proved too limited for Brewer. Even as a young man back in Riverdale, Brewer had had a serious streak that was atypical of jocks. "We'd sit in the park, fourteen, fifteen years old, and he thought about the big questions of life," recalls Priest. "World issues, life after death, religion ... he was very intense."

Contributing to Brewer's intensity was his Catholic faith. In fact, the two passions were irrevocably intertwined throughout most of his career. "Right up until the time I was married in 1962, I was considering leaving hockey and becoming a priest," says Brewer. "Up until the end of my second year, I was considering it. It was part of my life. And there was a precedent for it in Toronto. Les Costello had done it a few years before."

For now, the transition to the NHL was easier for Brewer on the ice than off. "It was an older team—Horton, Bower, Stanley, Olmstead— and I was just a kid. Being Catholic, being devout, I showed deference for my elders. I was too intimidated to invite myself to lunch with them. Seniority on the team got you a lower berth on the train. When I finished seven years later, I was still riding in an upper berth."

"The defense corps was pretty close; they went everywhere together," says Allan Stanley. "Except Carl, he didn't really hang with any group. He was the odd guy out, not like the rest of us."

One reason Brewer wasn't like many of his older teammates was that he didn't drink. "I never touched a drop of alcohol until I had been in the NHL for years," he says. "I didn't drink, so what was I going to do? Sit there and watch them be silly all afternoon? You can't talk to a drunk. Of course, I made up for that drinking later on."

Not that his teammates didn't try to tempt Brewer, of course. "I'll never forget the first time Carl had a beer," Baun says with a chuckle. "It was a little bar called the Pentagon on 42nd Street in New York, just around the corner from the Commodore Hotel. Allan Stanley said to Carl, 'You won't last ten years in the NHL unless you have a beer.'

"Well, Carl was almost done by this time in his career, he was a psycho ... Carl looked at him, picked up the beer, and Al didn't even see it go down. It was gone like that, and then Carl was out the door."

Brewer's teammates seem to have been divided on their troubled teammate. Some wanted Brewer to bear down and stop upsetting the team with his holdouts and feuds with Imlach. Many others sympathized with his problems. They all agreed that his enormous talent was being dissipated by his conflicts with the Maple Leafs' coach, and that he was a tough man to get to know.

Brewer bridles at the idea that he was a loner in his career: "I considered myself as good a team player as there ever was." For once, Imlach agreed with Brewer. "He was a team guy," Imlach recalled. "He and Bobby Baun stuck close together, with a lot of loyalty between them, and then the two of them had a lot of loyalty to the team."

All the same, the inquiring mind of Carl Brewer led him away from the narrow regimens of hockey. He was heading towards marriage. (His father-in-law, Harold Rea, later chaired the Task Force on Canadian Sport in 1968.) He wanted to get a university education. He wanted to teach. He wanted to come to grips with his faith. But fate stepped in and pushed Brewer's life in another direction.

Carl's father, upon whom he had relied for guidance, died in 1961. There was suddenly a void in the life of the twenty-three-year-old, with his mother and younger brother to look out for. Alan Eagleson, the peripatetic Toronto lawyer who later achieved fame—and Brewer's censure—for his duties with the NHL Players' Association, filled that void.

Eagleson had met Brewer through Bob Pulford, the Maple Leafs' young center and Eagleson's boyhood friend. Brewer and Eagleson were both restless spirits, both products of Toronto's lower middle class and both prideful to a fault. They hit it off. Eagleson made Brewer a member of the Blue and White Investment Group that included Maple Leafs players like Pulford and Baun and local businessmen like Herb Kearney of Hearn Pontiac and George Graham of Ostranders Jewellers.

It was the prototype for how Eagleson would marry business and sports for the next quarter-century. The businessmen got access to their sports heroes, while the players received endorsement opportunities away from the prying fingers of Punch Imlach. "Like Carl, this watch is built to take it," purred an Ostranders ad from 1963 featuring Brewer.

For his part, Brewer let Eagleson handle his legal work and try to negotiate a new contract with Punch Imlach for him. (Imlach's comment to Brewer before snubbing Eagleson: "Can he skate? Can he play hockey? Then I don't want to talk to him.") This bond with Brewer gave Eagleson credibility with other hockey players—especially Bobby Orr—and a toehold in the business of representing those players, a business he was soon to dominate. He made Brewer and his wife the godparents of his daughter Jill.*

What Brewer got besides money from Eagleson is a little less clear. Whatever it was, Imlach believed the result was counterproductive for Brewer. "He's very nervous and tension gets to him easily," Imlach said after being fired from Toronto. "He's a guy who could be told that I'm taking advantage of him, and he isn't getting enough money ... he can be led, and I think he got the wrong guy for him. He needed somebody who, instead of aggravating his problem, would cool his problem down. But this guy Eagleson aggravated the problems all the time, made them bigger."

Imlach was right; Brewer was high-strung, often lost hair during a season and suffered from skin rashes. He especially hated flying. But having recognized the need to soothe his temperamental young defenseman, Imlach failed to take his own advice. The antagonistic coach and his sensitive player were soon on a collision course over matters large and small.

By the time the Leafs had won their first of three straight Cups in 1962, nearly everything Punch did got under Brewer's already inflamed skin. "The day we won that first Cup was a significant day for me," remembers Brewer. "Duffy [Dick Duff] and Ronnie Stewart and I were singing. And Imlach came into the dressing room in Chicago and said, 'All right, for fuck's sake ... get ready and get the fuck on the plane and get home.'

"Why did I have to get on the plane? The season was over ... If I'd known better, I'd have stayed in Chicago for three days and gotten pissed. Instead, I just got on the plane ..."

Then, in the final game of the 1963 Stanley Cup finals, Brewer fractured his left arm while trying to check André Pronovost of Detroit. He gritted his teeth in pain long enough to see the Leafs clinch the Cup before going to have his broken arm set. But his relationship with Imlach stayed fractured. "After I broke my arm in '63, I was

---

* By 1982, the two men were so estranged that Eagleson dumped Brewer as godfather to his daughter.

treated like dirt by Imlach," he says. "I was ignored, looked down upon as if I was an ant on the floor. So I held out at training camp."

Brewer wasn't expected to play until December, but Imlach wanted him under his thumb in camp. Brewer, whose broken arm had required bone grafts, dodged coming to Peterborough until the last minute. When he got there, he let fly with news that he was quitting hockey to finish his degree at the University of Toronto. The papers had a field day with the story. Imlach had a splitting headache.

Having amused himself long enough at Imlach's expense, Brewer finally signed a new deal, telling George Gross of *The Toronto Telegram*, "My ultimate goal is still to become a teacher, but it will take longer than if I could study full time." (Gross's summation: "Brewer IS a tough man.")

Even the condition of his laundry annoyed Brewer at times. While holding out in 1961, he enrolled at McMaster and played football. "At McMaster football training camp, you practised three times a day and got clean underwear each time," he recalls. "At Leafs training camp—the NHL, the pros—you got the same wet underwear in the afternoon that you wore in the morning. It was hard to figure out."

Brewer was not alone in loathing Punch. Frank Mahovlich suffered from Imlach's caustic style until Imlach traded him to Detroit and Montreal, where he thrived. Dick Duff and Bob Nevin, two players who'd grown up in the farm system with many of the Leafs, were shipped off to New York for Andy Bathgate, leaving many to say they had been sacrificed to Imlach's hunches and his unbridled ego. Bathgate, in his turn, blasted Imlach when he left the Leafs. "There's a limit to an athlete's endurance," he told reporters in 1965. "Imlach pushed a few of the players past that limit mentally and physically." Several others were chafing under his unbending regime.

By 1965, Brewer was burned out. The reasons were many and varied and not all involved Imlach. Brewer was deathly afraid of flying, for instance, and he was coming to the realization that the often brutal and lonely world of pro hockey, with its insecurities and drinking, wasn't the ideal training ground for a compassionate, understanding human being to practise his faith.

His partner, Bobby Baun, observed Brewer first-hand. "I know he blamed Punch for things, but Carl just worried too much about himself, and it was a shame. It was his heart and his head that finally killed him. He didn't understand the name of the game. If you want to be a tough guy, then you pay the price to be one."

Allan Stanley was aware of problems, too. "Carl is a sensitive guy. He didn't know whether he wanted to play or go to school or whether he wanted to do anything. I guess he couldn't take what Punch gave out."

Even Imlach—who acknowledged Brewer as a great defenseman—had had an inkling of what was to come. "I was told one time by a doctor on our hockey club, 'Someday he's going to quit on you. Mark my words, he's just going to walk out.' Well, he had him pegged."

The showdown occurred in training camp in October 1965. The Leafs' run of Stanley Cups had ended the season before, with the club ingloriously knocked out in the semifinals by Montreal. After wrestling all summer with the decision of whether to return to the Leafs, Brewer had reluctantly appeared in Peterborough. He was moody and confused, and with his defense partner, Baun, holding out, he was disoriented on the ice. One moment he told teammates that he was quitting, the next that he thought he'd work things out. He was unmotivated and looking for a challenge. Things finally came to a head after the first period of an exhibition game in Peterborough.

Imlach's pre-game speech to the players dwelt on loyalty to the team, a thinly disguised jab at Baun and the other players holding out for better contracts. When the game finally started, Brewer says he "was in a fog. The first period was just a disaster." He had coughed up the puck several times, and goalie Johnny Bower was facing an awful barrage as a result.

In the dressing room, Bower confronted Brewer. They had a heated argument. ("I don't blame him, he was right," admits Brewer today.) Imlach then blistered the team. "If any of you don't want to play, stay in the room," he shouted with a few other words thrown in for emphasis. When the Leafs returned to the ice for the second period, Carl Brewer was getting into civilian clothes, his career as a Leaf over until 1979.

It might have been just another holdout on Brewer's already lengthy record of run-ins, until Imlach and the hockey establishment gave Brewer the challenge he was looking for. "I probably stuck with the retirement because Imlach said I'd be back ... Stafford Smythe said he'll be back in a couple of weeks ... Ballard said he'll be back before Christmas ... Clarence Campbell says no one quits the NHL. I guess I liked making those guys look bad."

Brewer had no immediate plans. He was a second-team All-Star from the previous season, turning his back on a $20,000-plus salary. CBC TV showed some interest in turning him into a sportscaster. He had not completed his degree and the school term at the University of Toronto had already started. The waiting game began.

Brewer sat on the sidelines as the Leafs struggled in the 1965-66 season, finishing fourth and then bowing out in six games to Montreal in the semifinals, their second straight year of frustration in the playoffs. Perhaps if he could escape the Leafs, thought Brewer, he might start somewhere else afresh. But that would be impossible under the NHL's restrictive "reserve clause" that bound a player to the team that owned his last contract. A move to another NHL team was impossible without the consent of Imlach and the Leafs.

Wherever he went in Toronto that winter, Brewer was constantly badgered to return to help the languishing Leafs. Finally, he met with Imlach in the summer of 1966 to discuss terms for a possible comeback. Any sentimental return to the fold was extinguished soon after Brewer left Imlach's office.

"I turn on the radio and there's Joe Morgan [sportscaster on CKEY] giving the blow-by-blow of my interview with Imlach," he says in his hushed monotone. "Figures, everything like that. Imlach saying Brewer is too greedy, he's asking too much. This was all supposed to be confidential, and they have it on a sportscast the minute I leave Imlach's office."

Instead of rejoining the Leafs for the 1966-67 season, the twenty-seven-year-old Brewer finished off his Bachelor of Arts degree at the University of Toronto, and—along with Eagleson—began plotting to regain his amateur status once again. He wanted to play for the Canadian national team under Father David Bauer, who'd made his mark coaching at St. Mike's and was now leading a gallant but futile challenge to the Soviets using a team of amateur volunteers. Bauer emphasized an innovative system that stressed defense and sophisticated passing—a style that wouldn't come to the NHL for fifteen seasons.

"I wanted to study under him for a year," Brewer says. "I was intrigued by that. I wanted to play with the national team, but I also wanted him to help me save my faith. I was still struggling at that time. I was disappointed with the result, but I'm sure my personality had something to do with it. I was scary to a lot of people, I can acknowledge that now."

After a lengthy battle and threats of legal action against the NHL and its president, Clarence Campbell, Brewer was given his amateur status again to play for Canada in 1967, although his playing rights in the NHL were retained by the Maple Leafs.

Young fans who see today's Canadian teams regularly win the Canada Cup and the world junior title might not understand the longing in this country for hockey revenge that Father Bauer's teams expressed in the '60s. Most often those teams were outmanned, and when they weren't, they were often given the short end of the hockey stick by international referees and bureaucrats. It was a practice that ended only when Alan Eagleson coerced, co-opted and cursed those same referees and officials into submission in the 1970s.

Brewer saw the chicanery first-hand. "We were a good team; everyone said we should've won the world championship. But the Russians beat us on two lame goals. They called back two of our goals in the game, and the Russians tied for first with the Czechs. It would have been nice to have won to vindicate Father Bauer's system. Outside of Eddie Shore, he was the best hockey brain ever produced in North America."

Canada failed to win the world title that year (no Canadian team has won the world championship since 1961), but Brewer was stimulated by his taste of international hockey and Father Bauer's system. "It was so advanced over anything I'd ever seen in the NHL. The drills, the push of the puck, the defensive game, systems for moving the puck ... that really was an exciting experience for me."

The next year, 1968, was an Olympic year, and while the International Ice Hockey Federation had allowed a former pro like Brewer to play, the International Olympic Committee, under the crusty Avery Brundage, would not. Besides, his relationship with Father Bauer hadn't worked out as planned: "I wasn't the right kind of personality for him."

With his NHL rights still being held by the Maple Leafs, going back for the 1967-68 season was out of the question. So Brewer took a $35,000 offer to become player/coach of Muskegon in the International Hockey League, bringing along his younger brother Jack for good measure. "We had a very successful team, *incredibly* well coached," Brewer says with a grin when recalling his year in Muskegon.

While he continued his exile in the bushes of the IHL, Brewer was still a valuable commodity in the NHL. Towards the end of that 1967-68 season, Imlach—desperate to spark the Leafs and save his job—made one of the biggest trades in NHL history. The Leafs received Norm Ullman, Paul Henderson and Floyd Smith from Detroit for Frank Mahovlich, Garry Unger, Peter Stemkowski and the rights to Carl Brewer. ("*I've* never been traded," he says, "the *rights* to Carl Brewer have.")

But instead of heading straight to the open arms of the Red Wings, Brewer again took the road less travelled. He moved his wife and sons to Helsinki, Finland, for a year, to coach and to scratch his itch to see the world. "It was a fabulous experience. I became a hero in Finland, because the team was so successful." The unconditional approval and the absence of Imlach had begun the healing process for Brewer.

His friends on the Red Wings hadn't forgotten him, either, or what he could do to spark their sagging playoff hopes. Mahovlich, Baun (who'd been traded from Oakland) and Sid Abel, the Detroit GM, urged him to join the Red Wings when the Finnish league ended in February 1969.

At the urging of Baun, Brewer went to Detroit when he returned from Europe. He had decided not to play for the Red Wings that spring, but he also knew if he didn't sign a Detroit contract soon, his rights would revert to the Maple Leafs.

"I went to a party. Bruce Norris, Sid Abel and John Ziegler [then Detroit's team lawyer] were there. Bruce was pissed out of his mind. I knew they'd give me anything. Ziegler gave me a blank contract to sign, said I had to sign by midnight or my rights would go back to Toronto."

Brewer signed the blank contract, then negotiated the details later. They provide an eye-opening portrait of how the NHL worked in the era before salary disclosure. Brewer, who hadn't played an NHL game in two years but had leverage, received a $92,000 base salary plus bonuses up to $130,000. As well, the Red Wings guaranteed to make up the years Brewer had missed on his NHL pension when he left the Leafs. Bob Baun, his old partner, was making $67,000. Gordie Howe, who'd carried the club and the NHL for two decades, made just $45,000.

And so the prodigal son returned to the NHL with the Red Wings in the fall of 1969. Brewer proved he hadn't lost a thing during his layoff from the NHL. He and Baun patched up a porous defense, spearheading the Red Wings to the third-greatest point total in the team's sixty-seven-year history. He was named to the League's second All-Star team and returned in triumph to Maple Leaf Gardens, where the Leafs missed the playoffs.

"It was a great year. I enjoyed watching Gordie, Frank and Alex Delvecchio play together on one line ... they were beautiful to watch."

Just when it looked as if Brewer had found happiness in Detroit, however, complications intervened. Part of his contract called for his brother Jack to play in the Red Wings system. But Jim Bishop, the new general manager of Detroit, failed to honor part of Jack Brewer's contract. So for $500 and principle, Carl Brewer traded in his sweater once again ... to sell Koho hockey sticks, which were making inroads into the Canadian-dominated market.

When the call to arms came again in the 1970-71 season, it was from his former Red Wings teammate Garry Unger, who had been traded to St. Louis. The Blues wanted him to finish the season and play next year with them. "I could have had a five-year contract from them, all guaranteed, but I said to Sid Salomon, the Blues' owner, 'I don't seem to be able to stick around places too long, I don't want to tie you up.'"

Instead, Brewer signed only a two-year contract, something he now regrets. "What a jerk, principled to a fault," he says now. "Hiding behind your merits, what a jerk." Brewer finished the year with the Blues, but halfway through 1971-72, he suffered a knee injury. It was—except for a spin with the Toronto Toros in the World Hockey Association and a very brief stop with the Maple Leafs in 1979—the end of Brewer's playing career.

Perhaps the greatest testament to Brewer's extraordinary skills is that so many teams were willing to give him a chance despite his reputation as a maverick, as a man who would not budge an inch on principle. Look over the lists of the greats in the NHL. Only Carl Brewer carried that kind of reputation and made it work. In the NHL's labor climate, that was a triumph unsurpassed until Eric Lindros came along.

10

HOGTOWN
HEROES

April 25, 1962, was an unusually warm spring day in Toronto, with temperatures soaring into the high seventies. *The Toronto Star* headline that day announced, "U.S. Fires First A-Test Shot Over Pacific." Italian police were investigating a report that Elizabeth Taylor had taken an overdose of sleeping pills after a fight with Richard Burton. The wife of Peterborough police chief W. J. Shrubb told the Royal Commission on Crime how gambler Vincent Feeley had left forty dollars on a table for her after the two had been drinking at local hotel. And "Mr. Bimbo" won the fifth race at Aqueduct, paying $15.30, $6.20 and $4.50.

But the only news of any consequence in the city on the north shore of Lake Ontario was The Parade. Almost one hundred thousand Torontonians had jammed the streets of Hogtown to celebrate the first Stanley Cup for their beloved Maple Leafs in eleven years. The ticker tape was knee-deep on some parts of Bay Street, in the heart of Toronto's stuffy, pinstriped banking center, while the hockey fever gripping the staid, old Toronto avenues forced nearby law courts to adjourn when magistrates were drowned out by the celebration.

"Even the Queen never got a crowd like this," marvelled Metro Toronto Chairman William R. Allen.

Fans had begun lining up as early as 9:00 a.m. for the noontime parade, and unprepared Toronto police suddenly faced crowds thirty deep by the time the Leafs made their way up Bay Street in their open limousines. Workers on their lunch breaks and kids skipping school shouted "Go Leafs Go" till their throats were raw, and many of the Maple Leafs were forced to abandon their limousines and complete the trip to the Cenotaph in front of City Hall on foot.

En route, the players' watches, handkerchiefs, ties and some pockets and lapels were ripped off them by souvenir hunters. When Eddie Shack finally made it past his adoring fans to the podium, a brave teenager leaned over and shouted into the public-address system, "I've touched him! I've touched him!" The crowd went wild with delight.

Still clad in his Leafs jersey, twenty-four-year-old Carl Brewer rode through the streets of his home town in awe of the crowd and afraid someone might steal the big roll of cash in his pocket that he'd just withdrawn for a trip to Florida. "The parade was incredible," he remembered thirty years later, the memory of the pressing crowd and the warm spring day as fresh for him as yesterday. "Here we are going in this parade and wondering if anyone is going to show up. That was very ... How many guys win a Stanley Cup ... how many?" His voice trails off, words fail him.

"A Myth Is Buried By 100,000 People," wrote *The Telegram*'s Hal Walker. "Good old Toronto the Good, cold and unemotional. Still wearing hoop skirts. Staid and trademarked with a legend which says you can shoot a cannon up Yonge Street on Sunday morning and you won't harm a soul.

"Hogtown's real warm heart came out in the real warm sun yesterday afternoon in the most glittering spontaneity of affection ever lavished on any individuals, including royalty.... Try and tell the Leafs that Toronto people are cold and unemotional."

Cold and unemotional Toronto people were not, but Toronto's burghers kept a check on their emotions and generosity—true to the frugal Scottish roots of the city. Every player on the Toronto's first Stanley Cup winner in eleven years received a simple pair of cufflinks as a token of the city's gratitude when they signed the guest book in City Hall. The watches and jewellery snatched by the crowd were never replaced. None of the Leafs—flush with $4,250 in playoff bonus money—stopped to complain, however.

Just three days earlier, Punch Imlach's team had defeated Bobby Hull and the Chicago Black Hawks (the defending Stanley Cup champions) in six games, expunging more than a decade of frustration for Torontonians. It had been the first Cup for the Leafs since Bill Barilko's fateful shot sent him winging his way to immortality in 1951.

Many had begun to think he'd taken the Leafs' chances of ever winning again with him on his star-crossed flight.

Such was the delirium that enveloped the grey old city by the lake those last days of April 1967 that only 3,500 fans turned out to see Sweet Daddy Siki and Bull Dog Brower retain their tag-team title at Maple Leaf Gardens, while movie cinemas reported half-empty auditoriums the night of the final game. Even the ladies of the night apparently gave up and went home to watch the Leafs.

And the triumph reached across the province. In Kirkland Lake, news of native son Dick Duff's winning goal was credited with keeping up the spirits of miner Russell Baskin, who lay trapped under tons of rocks at the Macassa gold mine. Baskin, who knew Duff, asked for the score of the game when rescuers finally pulled him out fifty-eight hours after the cave-in.

For the record, the Maple Leafs had beaten Chicago 2-1 on goals by Duff and Bob Nevin, all the while dodging a hail of eggs, rubber balls, hats, paper planes and red ink tossed by the 16,666 announced patrons of Chicago Stadium. (The Chicago fire inspector inexplicably always stopped counting at that point, missing the many thousands in standing room.)

For a jittery Stafford Smythe, the Stanley Cup final was no easier on his stomach than the Memorial Cup finals had been years earlier in Regina. He spent much of the evening of Game Six in the men's toilet in Chicago Stadium, listening to the muffled roars of the crowd and the churning of his nervous stomach. The newly named president of Maple Leaf Gardens finally emerged ashen-faced but elated at game's end to proclaim, "You see what happens when they give me absolute authority?"

At the other end of the spectrum that night was Bill Stanley, the fire chief of Timmins, Ontario, and parenthetically the father of Allan Stanley. When the final whistle sounded, Stanley Senior vaulted the boards along with the players and skittered out to center ice to pose with his thirty-seven-year-old son next to the Cup his brother had won forty-seven years before with the Vancouver Millionaires. "It was a long wait but worthwhile after all," grinned Allan, who had played fourteen years in the NHL before reaching the prize. His father nodded in obvious agreement.

It had been a victory for the character of the team as much as for its talent. Bob Pulford had scored three goals in the fifth game with the Black Hawks despite having torn ligaments in his shoulder. The shoulder was frozen before every game of the finals to allow him to play. Trainer Bobby Haggert then helped him into his street clothes in the dressing room beneath ancient Chicago Stadium while his teammates celebrated.

Forward Ron Stewart needed novocaine to deaden the pain of the ribs he'd cracked in a car accident, while goalie Johnny Bower was knocked out of the series with Chicago when he tore groin muscles stretching for a Bobby Hull blast in Game Four. Bert Olmstead's shoulder was separated. Every member of the team nursed some small injury as he surged decisively to the Cup on the home ice of the Black Hawks.

None of this was lost on the hockey fans of Toronto, of course. Their gratitude was heartfelt, overwhelming and permanent.

The first taste of what the Stanley Cup win meant to their home town came just five hours after the team received the Cup from Clarence Campbell at center ice in Chicago. Over two thousand fans "shouting, cheering and behaving in a most un-Toronto way" welcomed the team at 3:30 a.m. as they deplaned at Toronto's Malton Airport. "Certainly the crowd lacked the normal phlegmatic approach usually associated with Toronto crowds," intoned *The Telegram* in its night edition.

George Armstrong fulfilled a promise he'd made before the playoffs, awarding the puck Dick Duff used to score the game-winning goal to "Dodo" Imlach, Punch's wife, while Imlach himself waded into the sea of fans clutching the Cup to his chest. It took more than an hour for the last of the Leafs to leave Malton as fans hoisted them on their shoulders and escorted them to their parked cars.

For players like Baun, Pulford, Brewer, Harris, Mahovlich, Nevin and Duff, who had emerged from the Leafs' farm system and developed under Imlach, the win in Chicago marked the climax of their demanding, difficult ascent to stardom. For the imported players like Red Kelly, Eddie Litzenberger and Bert Olmstead, who had won the Cup elsewhere, it was a confirmation of their status as money players. And for Punch Imlach, the first Stanley Cup win in the hostile din of Chicago Stadium announced his elevation to the status of hockey savant, a label he would embellish and cultivate until he was fired seven years later by Stafford Smythe (whose stomach never got upset when he fired a hockey coach).

Certainly, Imlach's arrival in 1958 had heralded the change in Toronto's hockey fortunes.

As he carried the Stanley Cup into Toronto for the eighth time in Maple Leaf history that April morning in 1962, Punch Imlach was universally being acknowledged as the man who'd made the difference. Imlach was, according to one account, "the closest thing the NHL had to a tribal strong man. With Punch, the team was everything, individual glitter a weakness, a flaw in the system."

"He'll go to any length to achieve his goal in hockey life," wrote Jim Vipond of *The Globe and Mail*. "The players treat him as if he was their crazy uncle," observed a bemused Scott Young. Others, including Imlach himself, compared him to Vince Lombardi, the coaching legend of the Green Bay Packers. Billy Harris disagrees with the Lombardi comparison. "What Punch didn't realize, or forgot after 1963, was that there was another dimension involved in coaching," Harris contends. "Vince Lombardi was a master at not only challenging the team, but the individual as well."

How much responsibility Imlach can claim for the turnaround has, of course, become the subject of heated revisionist thinking. "In my opinion, I think we would have won more without Imlach," contends Carl Brewer. "The Leafs should have won six Cups in the '60s," harrumphed Conn Smythe.

However you look at it, Imlach's triumph in Toronto was certainly no overnight success story. After guiding the Maple Leafs from oblivion to the 1959 finals in his first year as coach, Imlach began a streak characterized by equal measures of good management and good luck. Even his most virulent critics grudgingly give him credit for his work leading up to the first Stanley Cup in 1962. Yet it still took five long seasons to make it to the top.

He made the most of the bountiful raw materials handed to him by the Leafs' farm system. He masterminded a series of terrific trades that netted him key players like Kelly, Shack, Olmstead and Larry Regan for virtually nothing. And he resuscitated Stanley and Bower, whom many in the NHL had given up for dead. Until 1962, Imlach seemingly never made a poor personnel decision.

After their stunning trip to the finals in 1959, where "Rocket" Richard and the Montreal Canadiens' dynasty beat the Cinderella Maple Leafs in five games, Imlach kept retooling his club. In February 1960, Toronto added the great Red Kelly from Detroit for a modest price: reserve defenseman Marc Réaume. Then, in a typical Imlach hunch, Kelly was switched from defense—where he'd been an eight-time All-Star—to center, where he shone for another seven and a half seasons.

Back in his home town, where he'd played for St. Mike's, Kelly responded to Imlach's coaching. His leadership and stability helped Toronto to its first winning record in six years. Kelly often neutralized the big centers on the opposing teams and played his new position as if he'd been doing it for years—although he needed the occasional snooze between periods in the trainer's room to recharge his batteries.

With Kelly on board and the young players blossoming, the Leafs once more made it to the finals in the spring of 1960, and once more they had their doors blown off, this time in four straight by the mighty Canadiens. The Habs outscored the Leafs 15-5, winning their fifth consecutive Stanley Cup, a record that has never been surpassed.

Losing to the Habs was no disgrace for the Leafs, but Imlach fine-tuned his team once more in the fall of 1960, introducing a fearless five-foot-nine, 165-pound center from Rouyn, Quebec, via St. Mike's, who could score, skate forever and play both ends of the rink like a veteran. Dave Keon scored twenty goals that season and won the Calder Trophy as the top rookie of 1960-61.

Along with ex-Marlie Bob Nevin (who was finally getting a full-time spot next to Kelly and Mahovlich), Keon helped the Leafs battle Montreal the entire season for first place. It was a regular season of team and personal accomplishments. The most dramatic element of that tumultuous year was the pursuit of "Rocket" Richard's record of fifty goals in a season by Frank Mahovlich—a mark that had stood since 1944. Mahovlich had thirty-eight goals in thirty-five games and seemed a cinch to shatter Richard's mark, but he faltered late in the season, winding up with forty-eight goals. Bernie Geoffrion, meanwhile, put on an incredible surge, scoring eighteen goals in his last thirteen games to tie Richard's record.

Mahovlich's late slump mirrored that of the Leafs in general, who suffered a rash of injuries to Keon, Stewart and Bower and slipped back to second place. No matter, concluded the scribes, they'd be better in the 1961 playoffs. If any team was going to prevent Montreal from making it six straight, it would be up-and-coming Toronto.

But it was Chicago that succeeded Montreal as Stanley Cup champs, not the Leafs. An overconfident Toronto was upset by

Gordie Howe and the fourth-place Detroit Red Wings in the semifinals. For the first time in three seasons, since Imlach took over the team, the shocked Leafs were on the sidelines for a final series.

The setback was probably the inevitable reversal of fortune the Maple Leafs needed before they could win it all the next year. It focused the players even more on winning, and it seemed to give credence to the need for Imlach's strict training regimen. Most of all, however, it prolonged the suffering of the loyal fans at Maple Leaf Gardens, who hadn't seen a Stanley Cup in a decade.

In the fall of 1961, Imlach added a few more spare parts to the team that had failed the spring before. Larry Hillman, Al Arbour, Eddie Litzenberger, Don Simmons and the bull-rushing Eddie Shack were brought in to keep the veterans on their toes and to fill in when injuries cropped up.

The most significant roster change occurred in the executive suite, however, as Conn Smythe sold his controlling interest in Maple Leaf Gardens to the unholy trinity of his son Stafford, Harold Ballard and John Bassett, the publisher of *The Toronto Telegram* and owner of CFTO TV. He retained the post as chairman of the board of Maple Leaf Gardens while Stafford became the president.

"My wife thoroughly approved of the deal," said the Major. He then added, "Stafford has had his hair brushed two times in a row, and that's something that never happened before he became president of Maple Leaf Gardens." No wonder the forty-year-old Stafford still suffered from an inferiority complex!

"We always thought Stafford's problem was trying to emulate his father," says Litzenberger. "That was pretty tough to do. As a result, Staff got an air about him, a bit of strain."

The Montreal Canadiens were still the dominant team during the regular season in 1961-62, finishing first for the sixth time in seven years, thirteen points up on Toronto. But the playoffs were another matter for Montreal once more in 1962, and the defending Stanley Cup champs from Chicago used their physical style of play to eliminate the smaller, artful Habs in the semifinals for a second straight season.

The Leafs, meanwhile, had their own troubles in their semifinal, this time with Gump Worsley and the unlikely New York Rangers, who were very infrequent playoff visitors in those days. The Leafs breezed past the Rangers in the first two games of the series at

Maple Leaf Gardens, but then New York, under playing coach Doug Harvey, swept a pair at Madison Square Garden.

The sweep came despite the efforts of Lori Horton, who had ventured to New York for the games. She sat in lucky seat number 7—to match her husband Tim's sweater number—but could barely hear herself think. "I've never heard such a thunderous rumble," she reported after returning from New York. "I don't know how they kept it up for six periods. The noise was terrific."

In Game Five back at Maple Leaf Gardens, Worsley was astounding, stopping fifty-six shots to keep the game tied through regulation. The rotund Worsley made save after save on the perplexed Leaf shooters to send the game to overtime. But Red Kelly finally tucked a rebound under the Rangers goalie to put New York away for the night. Worsley later confessed that Kelly's goal was the darkest moment of his hockey career until then—a frightening thought considering the brutal clubs Worsley played for in the 1950s.

There was still considerable tension in Toronto as Game Six approached. "Mrs. Les Nevin, mother of Leaf winger Bob Nevin, admitted going to bed on three successive hockey nights and nursing splitting headaches brought on by tension and agitation when her favorite squad met the New Yorkers," newspaper reports said.

Mrs. Al Arbour, "a pretty girl with short dark hair, compelling dark eyes and pearly teeth," apparently suffered the torments of the damned when her husband coughed up the winning goal in Game Four. "I know Al has sufficient inner strength to overcome a personal reverse," she grimly informed writer Margaret Scott.

Leafs fans needn't have worried. With the HMCS York Navy Band (under the direction of Lieutenant Robert Plunkett) supplying the tunes, Toronto dispatched the Rangers 7-1 before an enthusiastic throng of 14,000 at the Gardens. (The game was moved to Toronto because the circus was occupying Madison Square Garden.) Now only Chicago stood between Punch Imlach and his coveted Stanley Cup.

The matchup of Chicago and Toronto in the 1962 finals was the first playoff series between the teams in twenty-four years, but the previous series had been memorable. In 1938, the Hawks had rescued goalie Alfie Moore from a nearby tavern to replace the injured Mike Karakas. While Chicago coach Bill Stewart and Conn Smythe tossed punches at each other under the stands, Moore knocked Toronto cold, setting the Black Hawks on the way to the Stanley Cup.

Rudy Pilous's 1962 Black Hawks were the defending champions as they headed to Toronto for the first two games of the finals. Through the vagaries of free trade NHL-style, Eddie Litzenberger—the Chicago captain in 1961—was now a Maple Leaf, but the Hawks were still well-armed. With stars like Bobby Hull, Stan Mikita, Kenny Wharram, Murray Balfour, Pierre Pilote, "Moose" Vasko and the redoubtable Glenn Hall in goal, Chicago was a potent foe.

With the pugnacious Reggie Fleming aboard as well, the Hawks were also an intimidating team, especially in front of their rabid fans at the Chicago Stadium. But with Bert Olmstead around, the Leafs weren't likely to back up to the Hawks' tough guys. And with Imlach isolating his team in a hotel away from the fun and temptations of the big city, the Leafs were guaranteed to be ornery.

Besides, the omens looked good for the superstitious Imlach, whose team had the extra home game by virtue of finishing second. The Leafs were undefeated on home ice in the 1962 playoffs, and Chicago had won just once in two years in Toronto. The Hawks didn't improve on that mark in the 1962 final. Toronto easily won the first two games at Maple Leaf Gardens. Then the clubs headed west to that boiling cauldron of fan craziness called the Chicago Stadium.

Hockey in Chicago had almost died of neglect in the long period of ineptitude experienced by the Hawks between 1942-43 and 1958-59, when Conn Smythe dumped his surplus or troublesome players on Jim Norris's club. In those seventeen seasons, Chicago made the playoffs just three times, and fan support nearly evaporated.

But there were at least twenty thousand maniacs in the building April 15, 1962, and with Al Melgard booming away on his enormous pipe organ, they sent down such a wall of noise that most of the Leafs could barely hear themselves breathe. The effect was paralyzing on a visiting team. The fans "raise such an incredible rumpus that visiting players get the distinct impression they are unloved," noted Rex McLeod in *The Globe and Mail*. "Complications from this realization, of course, hinder their play."

Complications ensued for the Leafs in Chicago. They were beaten twice by the Black Hawks to tie up the series. "I wish we had that kind of crowd behind us in Toronto," said a miserable Imlach. "They're worth two goals to a team." Even then, Toronto fans were notoriously hard to excite.

Perhaps worse than the loss of the games to Imlach was the loss of Bower. Extending to make a save on Bobby Hull, he had severely pulled a hamstring, leaving the goaltending chores to lefthander Don Simmons. The Chicago crowd jeered Bower as he limped off for the rest of the series.

It looked as if Chicago was going to use the Bower injury as a springboard, because back in Toronto, the Hawks took a 3-2 lead in the second period of Game Five. Then All-Star defenseman Pierre Pilote broke in alone on Simmons. For the pessimistic Toronto fans, falling behind by two at home like this would confirm their worst fears. The Leafs were never going to win another Stanley Cup.

But Simmons made a big save, and the revitalized Maple Leafs seized the momentum. They came back in swarms at the Hawks net to crush Chicago 8-4. The Leafs now had two games to finish off a tired Chicago team and win the Cup. But as Imlach reminded his club, the last game is the toughest to win.

As the teams met at center ice for Game Six, Ron Stewart—the pride of Calgary, Alberta—looked across at the great Bobby Hull, a fifty-goal scorer from the regular season and the man he'd been assigned to shadow the entire playoffs. Stewart, a notoriously unserious character, grinned. "Don't tell me Pilous intends to have you shadow me again, Bobby," he whispered. Stewart's confidence mirrored that of his team.

Game Six was a classic. Toronto outshot Chicago 27-12 through the first two periods, but Glenn Hall was unbeatable in goal. The game remained scoreless after two periods. In their dressing room, the tired Black Hawks felt they'd taken the Leafs' best shot and now the breaks would go their way.

In the Maple Leafs dressing room, Billy Harris's mind was turning over as well. "What does a hockey player think about during the intermission when he realizes that within twenty minutes he might be a Stanley Cup champion? After two periods of hockey at the Chicago Stadium, a player thinks of one thing. Do I have the energy to climb the thirteen steps up to ice level?"

The two exhausted squads battled evenly until 8:58 of the third period when Dick Duff coughed up the puck to Murray Balfour of Chicago in his own end. Balfour's pass to Hull resulted in the eighth goal of the playoffs for "the Golden Jet." Chicago had its break, its change of fortune. More importantly, it had a 1-0 lead. The stadium erupted, and for twenty minutes, fans bombarded the ice with eggs, hats, programs, peanuts and missiles of every description.

The crowd's attempt at intimidation had just the opposite effect on Toronto, however. The sagging Leafs made use of the delay to regain their poise and their breath while the crew at the stadium tried to clear the ice surface of debris. Sure enough, Bob Nevin tied the score just ninety-five seconds after play finally resumed. Four minutes after that, Duff atoned for his mistake on the Chicago goal, scoring the winner from Armstrong and Horton, who set a record for playoff assists with thirteen in twelve games.

It now fell to Baun, Brewer, Horton and Stanley to protect the lead. While the gallery gods of Chicago screamed for the equalizer, the defense corps and Don Simmons in net held the fort for the final six minutes, and Toronto had its first Stanley Cup in eleven seasons.

As the Leafs poured over the boards to congratulate each other, they had done more than become a winning hockey team. They had transcended the steamy ice of noisy old Chicago Stadium. Their triumph that spring was carried coast to coast on CBC TV, just as the subsequent Cups of the '60s would be. For a generation of Canadians old enough to stay up for the end of the hockey game but young enough not to understand the Cuban Missile Crisis, the Toronto Maple Leafs were the apotheosis of TV's growing power and importance in Canada.

As the Leafs matured, their success was magnified by a medium also just maturing in Canada. And they would, in turn, magnify the medium of TV itself, as their triumphs became triumphs of TV's ability to reach this country.

Author Dan Diamond revealed how effortlessly "Hockey Night in Canada" had married itself to the spectacle when he recalled a boyhood chat he'd had with Foster Hewitt, the legendary voice of the program. "What was significant was ... that I, a young hockey fanatic, considered Foster Hewitt, not Frank Mahovlich or Tim Horton, no, that I considered a middle-aged broadcaster ... my foremost link with NHL hockey. Millions of others felt exactly the same way."

Tom Woycik is now a training consultant in Toronto, but he remembers the ritual of Saturday nights, a ritual repeated endlessly by families across the land. "We'd have our bath and put on our pyjamas. They always picked up the game at the end of the first period and we'd try to guess the score of the game when it came on at 8:30.

There was this great tension waiting to hear the score. 'Welcome hockey fans, the score here at Maple Leaf Gardens is the Toronto Maple Leafs 3, the New York Rangers ...'"

Through the power of this new, unlimited eye, and Hewitt's voice, the Leafs were soon the sporting equivalent of comedians Wayne and Shuster—a symbol of vitality and change for Toronto and English Canada. As important to the legend of the 1960s Leafs was their timing. For the Baby Boom generation that came of age in that decade, the last years of the "Original Six" would be a touchstone, and the Leafs, as the best team for much of that decade, would be the marker. It would be another year before this heralded generation discovered the Beatles, five years until Trudeaumania, Woodstock and the counterculture of Yorkville, and ten years before Canada finally got the chance to play and beat the Soviets. The Leafs were there, first, on the medium that mattered.

The players had no idea at the time, of course, that they were anything more than a very good team in a hockey-mad city. Allan Stanley can only remember the added lights and the heat they generated when arenas became TV studios.

Carl Brewer says he was "totally unaware" that he'd become a national TV star as well as a hockey player. "I was aware that the Maple Leafs were legendary, and for me, from the east end of Toronto, I was privileged to be there. But I had no sense of being a TV star."

The players were relentlessly marketed, pushing everything from cars ("Bob Pulford takes delivery of his new Pontiac Parisienne Convertible") to peanut butter ("Look under the lid for free hockey cards") to razor blades ("This one blade shaved all these Maple Leaf hockey players"). Even their wives became celebrities. "If the Stanley Cup could be won by a beauty contest, the Toronto club would probably have a lifetime lease on the silverware," gushed a 1963 magazine piece. "Leafian wives wear chic clothes, the latest hairdos and look like a bevy of Hollywood starlets when they have a pre-game pow-wow...."

But to millions of kids who were soon growing their hair long, protesting in the streets or practising transcendental meditation, the heroes of Saturday night were bona fide TV stars. Their pictures went up on walls, their skating styles were endlessly imitated and their battles were made holy in schoolyards from coast to coast.

By this time, Toronto was no longer the sleepy British village of Conn Smythe's youth. It was a multicultural stew with a half-million

Italians, and large numbers of Greeks, Portuguese, Ukrainian and Caribbean citizens now looking to the Leafs as a symbol of belonging in their new land.

Lawyer Walter Stasyshyn recalls the importance of the Maple Leafs to the new Ukrainian immigrants in Toronto. "They gave us a place to belong," he says. "You had a guy like Mahovlich, an ethnic guy; to us that was something to embrace. He was a hero. He represented people who were not accepted by Canadian society as anything but working class. He was a Slavic personality.

"We didn't have the money to socialize then so we'd listen to games ... Saturday night became a social focal point of the whole week. Life centered around Saturday night to an amazing extent, not just here in Toronto, but across the country."

For a city that needed reinforcement to withstand the comparisons to cosmopolitan Montreal with its Expo 67 and sense of *joie de vivre*, Toronto clung to the success of the Maple Leafs like a drowning man to flotsam and jetsam. And when Dick Duff sent the Black Hawks to defeat in the unremitting din of Chicago Stadium, it marked the beginning of an era of success and influence that would see the Leafs become the team of the decade and Toronto the largest, most influential city in the country.

11

FAREWELL TO ALL THAT

On the night the Toronto Maple Leafs won the Stanley Cup in April 1962, a lone figure sat quietly in one corner of the dressing room in Chicago Stadium, oblivious to the singing and hollering of his teammates. Bert Olmstead was thirty-six years old, bone-weary and staring at a life without hockey. He had just won his fifth—and final—Stanley Cup, one of only three Maple Leafs who'd won the Cup before. His aching shoulder, which had kept him out of much of the final series, throbbed painfully as he dragged on his cigarette.

The exhausted Olmstead embodied the effort the Maple Leafs had expended in the previous four years to reach this triumphant apogee. From the moment of his arrival in 1958 from Montreal, where he'd been a key ingredient on the great teams of "Rocket" Richard and Doug Harvey, the Saskatchewan farmer had bullied and strong-armed his Toronto teammates into the kind of team that wins titles, not headlines.

He was old-school hockey down to his long underwear. A man who made his living battling in the danger spots, the corners, he gave up his body to feed the big scorers in front of the net. His style had been described as a "human eggbeater" and "a perfectionist." And no opponent left a confrontation with Olmstead unscathed.

"No hockey player ever demanded more of himself than Bert Olmstead," recalls Billy Harris. "And he demanded almost as much from his teammates."

"Bert was such a ball-burner, he put that team on the map because he was such a head-knocker," remembers Bobby Baun. "He'd say,

'Smoke Punch—get him out of here—I'll show these guys how to play the game.' His retention of the game was incredible."

Not everyone saw Olmstead in quite as flattering a light. "They were all scared of him," recalls Carl Brewer. "Everyone thought he was a god, and I thought he was just a very average hockey player. He hated my guts, and I hated his. If Olmstead had been Santa Claus, there would be no fucking Christmas."

Scared of him they may have been, but for a young team looking to become a great team, having an uncompromising presence like Olmstead around was as critical off the ice as on. And his experience manifested itself in subtle ways.

The night before the sixth and deciding game, for instance, Olmstead had led a group of players out for a beer at the Morrison Hotel in Chicago. After a round, a number of the Leafs got up to return to the hotel. "Sit down," barked Olmstead. "Let's have one more—we'll sleep better." They did, and the next night the Toronto Maple Leafs christened a new era in hockey. But Olmstead's reward for his leadership and inspiration was a pink slip.

Olmstead retired to his farm in southern Saskatchewan when Punch Imlach unceremoniously cut him loose following the '62 Cup triumph. He tried his hand at coaching and managing hockey teams, but he couldn't abide players who didn't burn with the intensity he'd possessed during his fourteen-year Hall of Fame NHL career. He could not find a way to fill the gnawing chasm left by retirement. And the team experienced a similar loss.

Without Olmstead, for the next six seasons the Maple Leafs slowly, inexorably, drifted into mediocrity. The Leafs tried without success to find a player who commanded the kind of respect and fear that Olmstead had in the dressing room. Dave Keon, Frank Mahovlich and Tim Horton were the team's top players, but none was a forbidding figure in the mould of Olmstead. Other veterans were either too busy with their off-ice activities to come to the fore or simply not talented enough to command respect. And with Imlach's considerable ego, it was unlikely he'd allow any challenge to his authority to take hold of the club.

As Imlach and the Leafs' front office lost touch with the team in the next few years, the absence of a "gamer" like Olmstead within the club to agitate and demand performance from his teammates would force the Maple Leafs into dramatic trades (such as the Andy

Bathgate deal in 1964) and demotions (Eddie Shack, Jim Pappin and others wore out a groove between Toronto and the Rochester farm club) to shake up their talented team.

These moves in turn served to alienate the core of the club. Players saw their friends and comrades humiliated or discarded. The young generation of promising players, like Mike Walton, Jim Dorey and Brian Conacher, arrived in a divided, politically charged atmosphere of fear and loathing that culminated in Imlach's firing in 1969. No Leafs prospect fulfilled his promise during that period ... at least, not with Toronto.

The process of drift started innocently enough in the fall of 1962. Many players felt that winning a Stanley Cup and all those sold-out houses during the playoffs at the Gardens would result in substantial salary increases. After all, hadn't the Maple Leafs been sold to the "Silver Seven" for the staggering sum of $4.5 million the year before? With the Eatons and Bassetts now involved in ownership, there must be more money than ever in the till. But the players were bitterly disappointed to find Imlach as recalcitrant as ever in negotiations when training camp rolled around in Peterborough. Not only was he keeping the padlock on the Maple Leafs' vault, he was armed with a barrage of statistics with which to denigrate any vigorous negotiators.

Then, at a cocktail party on October 4, 1962, at the Royal York Hotel in Toronto, Chicago owner Jim Norris made his million-dollar offer for Frank Mahovlich, an offer accepted by Harold Ballard. Conn Smythe nearly had a coronary when he heard the news the next day. Owners and general managers around the NHL were similarly stunned. They could see the price of players skyrocketing should this deal go through. And if the enormous sale price wasn't bad enough, the public disclosure of the figure was a disaster. Players would be lining up for new contracts ten minutes after Mahovlich pulled on a Chicago sweater.

Writers and broadcasters were also shocked, but predictably dwelt on the emotional aspects of the sale, not its financial implications. The value of hockey talent subordinated itself to the value of forty-eight-point type in headlines. "How Could Toronto Even Think of Trading Its Brightest Star?" was a common theme. "Could Mahovlich and Bobby Hull Co-Exist On the Same Team?" mused others. Scott Young proclaimed the whole deal a publicity stunt and was eventually fired from his job on "Hockey Night in Canada" as a result.

Some players, however, saw the deal in dollars and cents, *their* dollars and cents. A top NHL star like Mahovlich on the open market was worth a million dollars, but he was being paid about one-twentieth that amount. Players who'd swallowed their pride and signed for less when Imlach claimed that the Leafs were on the way to the poorhouse, now had a sobering reminder of just how profitable NHL franchises like Toronto or Chicago were; and how much they could pay players if they wanted to; and that the sportsmen who ran the NHL didn't always tell the truth if it wasn't in their interests. (In 1960, for example, Maple Leaf Gardens paid out $176,539 in dividends; within seven years that figure rose to over $2.29 million.)

Stafford Smythe was told in no uncertain terms by his father to get out of the Mahovlich deal, and while it took a few days to extricate themselves from Ballard's handshake commitment, the Maple Leafs managed to hang on to "the Big M," who had scored eighty-one goals in the previous two seasons.

The near-selling of Mahovlich was a sensational but typical example of the discrepancy between a player's real value and what he was paid in this period. Punch himself gave a textbook example of how hockey's grey market operated in *Hockey Is A Battle*.

In 1967, Imlach traded with Boston GM Milt Schmidt, sending Eddie Shack to the Bruins for cash and Murray Oliver. Shack, naturally, was interested in finding out how much cash had changed hands. John Anderson, Imlach's assistant, told Shack that Boston had paid about $30,000. The real figure, wrote Imlach, was $100,000 in *U.S. funds*, which was highway robbery for Toronto.

"If Shack had known he'd been sold for $100,000 in U.S. funds, plus Murray Oliver, he would have been down to see Milt Schmidt with a lawyer, demanding $50,000 a year," Imlach snickered. "I couldn't do that to Uncle Miltie after what I'd already done."

"I don't remember feeling poor until 1967, when we were traded to Boston," remembers Shack's wife, Norma. "That's when we woke up. Anytime you were traded, it was a guaranteed good raise, because the new team obviously wanted you. We saw then how much money there was to be made."

The Toronto players were not the only ones who noticed, either. The seeds of the Players' Association, still five years in the future, were germinated by the "Mahovlich For A Million" episode and fed on countless other humiliations. Gordie Howe remembers being thrown out of the Olympia in Detroit for asking for $500 more when his wife was expecting their first child. And the solemn promise that he'd always be the top-paid player in Detroit was a bond that he later discovered from Bobby Baun was simply a cruel exploitation of the game's greatest player and ambassador.

Lacking a firebrand to stand up to the owners, the players buried their frustrations in a multitude of minor challenges to the authority of the six NHL clubs.

"No unity is what it was," says Lori Horton. "A real lack of unity. They just didn't have the nerve to stand up. The poor guys who did, like Jimmy Thompson, were traded away."

To the outsider, the Maple Leafs seemed as determined and focused as ever in 1962-63. They rallied from being nine points down to Chicago to capture first place—the only Toronto team between 1948 and the present to finish first in the regular season. Then they took just ten games to crush Montreal and Detroit for the first Stanley Cup won on Maple Leaf Gardens ice since 1951. Dave Keon led the way with seven goals and five assists in the playoffs.

Once more, the fans of Toronto took to the streets in the victory parade. "City Salutes the Conquering Leafs," roared the headlines in *The Toronto Star*, "40,000 Jam Bay Street Eight Deep." A jubilant Eddie Litzenberger—who had just won his third consecutive Cup—joked to reporters, "You can say I'm getting tired of meeting all these mayors."

There was still a fierce pride in how they worked together as a team, in a job well done, remembers Brewer. "We were fortunate to play on a team that had great defensive forwards ... Pulford, Keon, Armstrong ... you were never alone; they played the whole ice. If you couldn't do the job defensively, you weren't considered part of the team."

And the camaraderie was as strong as ever. Once, George Armstrong accidentally put the puck past Johnny Bower in his own net. The team was sitting in the dressing room afterward, contemplating the dire consequences from Imlach, when Armstrong looked over at Bower. "I don't know what all those guys are talking about," said a poker-faced Armstrong. "You aren't so tough to score on. I wish I played against you all the time." Everyone broke up laughing.

But to the trained eye, the Maple Leafs that Imlach had built and nurtured since 1958 were rapidly becoming ungovernable. Outside interests were diverting the players' attention. Red Kelly, for instance, was commuting between Toronto and Ottawa, where he was now a Liberal member of Parliament. (He won the election in 1963 over a Progressive Conservative by the name of Alan Eagleson.)

Horton was getting deeper into his restaurant business, while Brewer, Pulford and Harris were pursuing their university educations. Baun and Duff, among others, were becoming involved in investments and the stock market.

"Almost every Leaf has a second (and sometimes third and fourth) business," marvelled *Maclean's* magazine beneath a picture showing the entire team standing next to the boards at Maple Leaf Gardens in their civilian attire. "Each of them earns no less than fifteen thousand a year, some of them as much as thirty thousand dollars."

Many of the Leafs were also getting married and starting families. And all the players were drinking deeply of the draft that comes from being world champions in a city that adores them. "It was awesome to see the people," Allan Stanley remembers of the parades that became an annual staple of Toronto life. "We didn't think they'd show up like that. It was a great, great feeling to be in the parades."

Underpinning everything in this era, however, was the growing desire of NHL players—advertised by their owners as the greatest in the world—to unite as a group. The times, as Bob Dylan noted, were a-changing—even in the NHL. However, the maturity and self-assurance born of winning the Cup only brought the Toronto players face-to-face with Imlach. For Punch, it was still his way or the highway.

The long practices, the abrasive behavior, the superstitious hunches that Imlach believed had made the Maple Leafs champions now began to grate on many of the younger members of the team who felt they had earned the right to manage themselves. Even Olmstead, the consummate pro, had complained of the workload before Imlach sent him packing. If a new day was dawning, Imlach was still firmly in the dark.

While he rarely blamed a player in the press, behind the dressing-room doors Punch would still assail the players' ears with language "chosen almost equally from the Bible and a novel called *Lady Chatterley's Lover*," according to Scott Young. Imlach's harangues dwelt on the team approach. "I always tried to deal with the team as a team, rather than a group of individuals," he wrote. "There are exceptions, but they have to be big ones to cut any ice with me."

Imlach claimed he rarely singled out players publicly for blame, but when he did criticize someone for a bad play or wandering attention, he soothed their feelings with some patented Imlachian philosophy: "If I swear at you, if I call you a stupid son-of-a-bitch sometime, take it as a term of endearment. That's the way it's meant to be taken." When the bitching about commitment and dedication got too much, Imlach only had to point to the chairman of the board, Conn Smythe, who, as a forty-three-year-old family man, had dropped his comfortable life and business in Toronto to serve King and Country overseas in World War II.

Perhaps no Leaf was more sensitive or suffered the boos more often than Frank Mahovlich, the talented left-winger who became the prime target of Toronto hecklers when his enormous talent didn't always square up with his production. But he endured the ordeal alone.

"Imlach never spoke to Frank Mahovlich or me for most of the season," said Andy Bathgate upon departing the Leafs in 1965. "And when he did it was to criticize. Frank usually got the worst. We are athletes, not machines, and Frank is the type that needs some encouragement, a pat on the shoulder every so often."

While the rest of the club was composed of overachievers—men like Johnny Bower, who confounded age and limited ability—Mahovlich was gifted with the rare combination of skill and size. At six-foot-two and well over 200 pounds, he had a scorer's touch in a big man's body—the prototype for a great player. He was looked upon as Toronto's answer to Bobby Hull or Gordie Howe. King Clancy dubbed him "the Big M" for Moses, the man to lead the Leafs to the Promised Land. But Mahovlich kept getting snagged in the bulrushes.

After flirting with "Rocket" Richard's sacred fifty-goal record in 1960-61, he was never forgiven for coming up short again. "Life was never the same after that," he admitted. "They expected too much of me." Despite leading the team in scoring almost every year, Mahovlich was the only Leaf of that era to be consistently booed at the Gardens.

"If the crowd booed a guy, he was doing something wrong," commented Imlach in a poorly disguised stab at Mahovlich. "So because he's a sensitive guy, should I go in and tell him a bloody lie, that the crowd didn't know what it was all about ... that he's the greatest thing on skates, and stuff like that?"

A man of sensibilities and pride, Mahovlich bridled under the profane Imlach and his punishing training regimen. Having come from a warm, supportive family background, Frank seemed lost in the glacial atmosphere fostered by Smythe and then Imlach. It grew worse upon the retirement of Olmstead, who had taken Mahovlich under his wing.

One of Mahovlich's particular torments occurred when the team lost. "We'd catch a plane back to Toronto on Monday morning, and then he would take us directly from the airport to the rink for a practice," Mahovlich explained. "Why didn't he just have us practise on the ice right after the game?

"Our teams in Toronto, we struggled to get through the season. I think the reason was that Punch kind of drove us into the ground. He whipped us too much. [Scotty] Bowman had the ability where he could get his team to a peak and keep it there. Punch couldn't do that. He couldn't keep his team at a nice pitch. It was always up and down and struggle, struggle, struggle. Seems to me those Canadiens teams in the '50s didn't have to go through that, or Bowman's teams in later years."

Mahovlich's production steadily declined under Imlach after the record-setting campaign of 1960-61, and the already shy left-winger began to withdraw totally into himself. Then, on November 12, 1964, after being booed by Toronto fans even though he'd been chosen the second star of the game the night before, Mahovlich disappeared from the Leafs. The public was given a series of excuses for his absence, but Mahovlich was in fact under a doctor's care for "deep depression and tension."

After two weeks of rest, Mahovlich returned for the rest of the 1964-65 season, without divulging the real reason for his layoff. He finally told a Toronto reporter a year later what had happened, and that his tension with Imlach was at the root of the problem. "My doctor told me to pull an imaginary curtain around myself whenever Punch was around," he explained.

The curtain didn't protect him for long, because in November 1967, Mahovlich walked off a train bound for Detroit and checked himself into hospital, once more for deep depression and tension. After rest and therapy, Mahovlich returned once again to the Leafs to complete the season, but his Toronto days were effectively over. He was finally traded to Detroit in a blockbuster deal the next spring.

Free of Imlach and the Toronto pressure-cooker, "the Big M" experienced a rebirth in his career that saw him set personal scoring records in Detroit and win the Stanley Cup twice more with the Montreal Canadiens.

Carl Brewer, Johnny Bower, Eddie Shack and Mike Walton all had well-publicized run-ins with Imlach. It was a pattern that repeated itself in the late 1970s, when Imlach—brought home as general manager for a curtain call by Harold Ballard—feuded with most of the team.

Brewer feels Imlach's high-pressure tactics were not needed once the Leafs of that era hit their stride. "The team was good, solid, dedicated to the purpose of winning," he says today. "They had some fun, but they were dedicated to winning. Turk Broda [the Marlboros coach] or Sid Abel [the Detroit coach and GM] would have been a better coach. More of a relaxed atmosphere with the idea of treating people like human beings."

The Red Wings under Abel in the '60s were less talented than Toronto but spent the day of playoff games at the racetrack or playing tourist. The Leafs, meanwhile, were skating and practising, often as early as 9:30 a.m. after a night game. Several of the Red Wings players seemed genuinely concerned that the older players on the Leafs would completely break down before the playoffs finished.

"That Imlach must be nuts," said Bill Gadsby. "The business of working out every day, it's killing them."

In 1964, a well-rested Detroit team almost upset the heavily favored Leafs, with many giving Abel credit for his handling of the Red Wings. "Sometimes, we hoped that we'd lose to Detroit," says Brewer. "We wanted to play our best, of course, but we thought by losing, Imlach's methods would be disproved. Unfortunately, our talent was too much for them. Imlach still took the credit."

Brewer bolted the Maple Leafs in the fall of 1965. Andy Bathgate, the playoff hero of 1964, had departed that same summer. Bathgate cited several teammates, including Mahovlich, Peter Stemkowski and Ron Ellis, as victims of battle fatigue. "There's a limit to an athlete's endurance. Imlach pushed a few of the players past that limit both physically and mentally." To which Imlach replied: "There is no limit to what you can do."

Whether the Leafs of that era won in spite of or because of Imlach will never be known, of course. What is certain is that his methodology created a resentment that accelerated the collapse of the Leafs. "A lot of them worked for him, but they didn't like what he was doing," says Allan Stanley.

Imlach wanted control over every aspect of the player's career, too. He created a system whereby *he* divided up all the endorsement money coming to the Leafs players from certain accounts controlled by the Gardens. And players were stopped from endorsements deemed improper by Imlach and Smythe. To say nothing of dress codes, beard bans, mustache maxims and curfews.

The dissonance generated by Imlach's daily attempts to assert control over his players helped eliminate any realistic chances the Leafs had of winning a fourth or fifth Stanley Cup in 1965 or 1966. The distractions of the Mahovlich illness and Brewer's defection further eroded the focus of the team.

Another disruption of the Leafs "dynasty" was a result of Imlach's decision to trade away the team's future for short-term success in the present.

"Any possibility of the Leafs establishing a dynasty vanished on Saturday, February 22, 1964," wrote Billy Harris. "Bob Nevin and Dick Duff were found guilty without a trial. When team production falls below what is expected, perhaps the coach is responsible, but to prevent that theory from catching hold, Imlach traded Duff and Nevin to the New York Rangers."

After the veteran Bathgate helped the Leafs to the 1964 Stanley Cup, Imlach began importing ancient players en masse. Dickie Moore, Terry Sawchuk, Pierre Pilote and Marcel Pronovost added to his already-greying roster. Some of these players contributed to the "surprise" Stanley Cup of 1967, but their ice time—combined with that of Stanley and Bower and Armstrong—denied an opportunity to develop the next generation of stars who might have helped the Leafs win titles in the '70s. Players such as goalie Gerry Cheevers, defensemen Arnie Brown, Rick Seiling and Pat Stapleton, forwards Jim Pappin, Peter Stemkowski, Garry Unger, Wayne Carleton along with Nevin and Duff—all very productive NHL players in the 1970s— were discarded by Imlach in favor of older players.

And none of the younger players Imlach did retain proved to be the next Keon, the next Horton. Kent Douglas and Brit Selby both won Calder Trophies as top rookie, but neither blossomed into a star. Both were gone before the end of the decade. The same thing happened with "can't-miss prospects" such as Mike Walton, Brian Conacher and Gerry Meehan. Of the prospects, only Ron Ellis stayed with the Leafs to become a solid, if unexceptional, pro.

By the playoffs of 1967, the Leafs seemed a spent force. They had been supplanted by Montreal as the dynasty of the 1960s, losing ignominiously in the playoffs two years in a row. The 1966-67 season had been as turbulent as any season in living memory for observers of the Leafs.

Mahovlich had been disabled once more by depression and exhaustion. The team suffered through a ten-game winless streak that culminated with Imlach himself being hospitalized for exhaustion. King Clancy then revived the team, leading them to a ten-game unbeaten streak during Punch's absence, but upon his return, the Leafs limped into the playoffs in third place.

The Leafs were colder than mackerel, said the pundits. They didn't stand a chance against the mighty Habs or the first-place Black Hawks, who had set an NHL scoring record that season in finishing first by a colossal seventeen points. They were too old and too worn out. It would be over in a few days.

Then a funny thing happened to Toronto's old nags on their way to the glue factory. Veteran goalies Johnny Bower and Terry Sawchuk discovered a secret elixir that allowed them to relive their past glories one last time. The venerable tandem proceeded to stone the mighty Black Hawks of Bobby Hull, Stan Mikita and the young Phil Esposito—a team that had scored sixty more goals than Toronto during the regular season. In one game, Sawchuk turned aside forty-nine shots in just two periods. The Black Hawks seemed stupefied by the brick wall in the Toronto net. They collapsed, stunned by Toronto's two great goalies. The rest of the Leafs took heart from Bower and Sawchuk, pulling together to dispatch the baffled Black Hawks in just six games.

Montreal was next, and Imlach, now restored to full health and confidence, tempted the fates by labelling Montreal's young goalie Rogatien Vachon a "Junior B" goalie. Had Montreal been some upstart club prone to losing its nerve, Imlach's barbs might have been expected. But this was a team led by the incomparable Jean Béliveau and Henri Richard, winners of fourteen Stanley Cups between them. It had a defense corps anchored by Jacques Laperrière and J. C. Tremblay. And it had the inscrutable Toe Blake behind the bench. That seemed more than enough to compensate for Vachon's inexperience.

If they needed more incentive, the Habs were hoping for a third straight Cup to cap the Expo 67 celebrations in Montreal. Imlach's bravado and the Canadiens' clear advantage in talent once again appeared to have doomed the Leafs.

But no one told Bower, or especially Sawchuk. The two men burnished their Hall of Fame credentials in the final series. Bower shut out the Habs in Game Two and was largely responsible for the Leafs being ahead 2-1 in games midway through the series. Then he pulled a hamstring muscle in warm-ups before Game Four. He was through for the playoffs.

The Leafs' luck appeared to have finally run out. Montreal—smelling blood—pumped six goals behind Sawchuk in Game Four to tie the series at two games apiece. A rout seemed inevitable as the teams headed back to the Forum in Montreal. But Sawchuk miraculously rebounded in the next two games. Suddenly, he was the game's best goalie once more, the man who'd led Detroit to three Stanley Cups in the 1950s.

He allowed the confident Canadiens just one goal in the two remaining games, while the Leafs veterans victimized Vachon at the other end for seven goals. As if to reward the loyalty of his Old Guard, the players who'd stuck with him when no one, including his boss Stafford Smythe, wanted them any longer, Imlach hand-picked the players to hold Montreal off the scoresheet in the final fifty seconds of Game Six. Kelly, Armstrong, Horton and Stanley joined Pulford for the final faceoff. They scored to clinch a 3-1 win and the Leafs' eleventh Stanley Cup.

The Leafs were the unlikely winners of the final Stanley Cup before expansion. The two goalies plus the loyal veterans corps had put Imlach on top of the hockey world one last time. "They had the champagne on ice," Eddie Shack says with a cackle. "I said to Henri Richard, 'Hey Henri, we sure stuck that one in your crease, eh?'"

Even in triumph, however, the 1967 Stanley Cup champions were a museum piece. The length of the playoffs would be extended the next season, and a veteran team like the Leafs would not be able to sustain an edge for the four or five draining weeks it would now take to win a Cup. Within a year, only Horton would be left of the great defense corps, while Bower, Keon and Pulford were the sole reminders of the team that won the first Cup in 1962.

By the end of the 1967-68 season, more than the playoffs had changed. Expansion had altered the face of the sport for fans. The NHL of the "Original Six," with its time-honored rivalries, was dead. To win the Stanley Cup that season, Montreal faced the fledgling St. Louis Blues in the finals, not the Leafs or the Black Hawks or the

Bruins. It was over in four brief, forgettable games on the steamy ice of Montreal and St. Louis.

However much the face of the game had changed for fans, behind the scenes the business of hockey remained immutable in the hands of its power brokers. "Hockey is a playpen," says Bob Baun. "The playpen was established when the Norrises and the Wirtzes kept the League going. They thought their legacy would last forever." They were almost right; the stranglehold of the "Original Six" owners wasn't broken till Bill Wirtz stepped down as chairman of the NHL board of governors in 1992, twenty-five years later.

Imlach tried to remain a constant as well, fighting battles on every side against beards, beads and player agents. He was doing the owners' bidding, unaware that Smythe and Ballard would pull the rug out from under him when he could no longer drag a Stanley Cup out of his disgruntled troops.

"The turning point came in my last season," remembers Allan Stanley. "We came back off the road at Christmastime, and he called a practice. I've never seen a team so upset.

"There was one player sitting to my right, quiet and everything. He hears Punch's voice at the door coming in, and he stood up. Everyone was watching him, he was absolutely white. And he grabbed Punch, he was going to kill him. Red Burnett of *The Star* had to pull him away. He had kids at home; these are family people.

"If there was any one incident that made people quit on him, I think that was it. And a number of them did quit on him; they wouldn't work for him any more. It was obvious."

The Maple Leafs crashed from being champions to being out of the playoffs in that one tumultuous year. The signs of player antipathy to Imlach were rampant. Jim Pappin went home rather than accept demotion to Rochester. Frank Mahovlich was traded. And twice, Leafs players were mugged on the ice by opponents while their teammates stood to the side watching—a cardinal sin in Punch's philosophy. In one incident in Boston, seemingly half the Bruins' team took a turn pummelling Brian Conacher while he lay on the ice. "I should have seen it, I should have known right then," Imlach later remarked. Conacher, meanwhile, was never the same as a player after the incident.

The next season was only marginally better. Operating under an ultimatum from Smythe to get out of coaching and concentrate on the general manager's job, Imlach cobbled together a fourth-place finish from a team led by Keon, Ellis and Norm Ullman. The makeshift defense corps was Horton with Mike Pelyk, Jim Dorey and Pierre Pilote. Bruce Gamble was now the workhorse in goal with Bower finally showing his considerable age.

The year was filled with disputes over Mike Walton (the talented but high-strung center who had married into the Smythe family) and Alan Eagleson, the head of the new Players' Association. The team made the playoffs with a late surge, and hope for a reprise of the 1967 miracle began to circulate.

The playoffs, however, sealed Imlach's fate. His borrowed-and-blue team met the Boston Bruins, led by Bobby Orr. This time there was no Sawchuk or Bower to save the day. The Bruins used the Maple Leafs as target practice, scoring seventeen goals in the first two games of the series. Toronto was easily eliminated in four, vanquished by the NHL's next great team.

There was a case to be made for superior force overcoming the Leafs, some argument that the young players in the system would improve the club in the next season. But the relationship between Imlach and Stafford Smythe was poisoned, and it was Smythe, not Imlach, who owned the team. So, in a small room under the Gardens, Smythe demanded Imlach's head on a platter just moments after the final bell in Game Four at the Gardens.

After four Stanley Cups, eleven seasons and countless controversies, George Imlach was replaced by Johnny McLellan as coach and by Jim Gregory as general manager. While Punch would return to the Stanley Cup finals again with the Buffalo Sabres, the Maple Leafs have yet to make a final series in twenty-six years.

Whatever problems Imlach had created for the Leafs by the spring of 1969, it is the Toronto ownership, not Imlach, that bears most of the blame for that quarter-century of futility. In the beginning, the Leafs ownership group that succeeded Conn Smythe was seen as a happy-go-lucky band of hockey fans travelling on a busman's holiday with their celebrated team. Parties and fun were the order of the day.

"I got a long-distance call at midnight from the other committee members," John Bassett wrote Conn Smythe in December 1957. "The other committee members were in great form after the magnificent weekend."

But as time passed, the management group grew rowdier and less inhibited. And with time, Stafford Smythe came to believe that he could run his team better than Imlach was running it.

In fact, the increasing distraction provided by the management of the team had undermined the hockey atmosphere in Toronto for years before Imlach's firing. Stafford Smythe was openly critical of his coach/GM during that time, demanding he give up his coaching job. In response, Imlach adopted his live-for-today philosophy to avoid giving Smythe a reason to fire him.

And the increasing value of the Gardens pushed profits ahead of the hockey program. Fuelled by Harold Ballard's promotion efforts, Maple Leaf Gardens had become a money machine. In 1961, shares were valued at $26.50, but four years later, they were worth $114.75 before being split five for one. Easy money created predictable results.

Players like Bob Baun watched as Stafford Smythe and Ballard used profits from the Gardens to do major construction on their cottages, while player salaries remained depressed. "I was in the construction business so I had a good idea where the money was going," Baun says today. "I made it my business to know what was happening. Stafford and Harold were selling tickets on the side and putting the money in their pockets. They were doing things at home and charging it to the public corporation. That's how it travelled down the line so Punch wouldn't get more money to sign players."

Imlach retaliated against Smythe by buying the Rochester farm team and funnelling fringe players to the Americans. "Then him and his buddy Joe Crozier ended up selling the team to Vancouver when it came into the NHL," says Baun. "That's where they made the big sting as far as money goes [$2,820,000, according to Imlach]. That irked Stafford. But he couldn't say anything, because *he* knew that *Punch* knew what Stafford was doing with the books ... it was a merry-go-round.

"I knew what Punch was doing, and that's one of the reasons I was left unprotected in the 1967 expansion draft."

Others, like Allan Stanley, tried to ignore the front-office politicking. "We knew everything that was going on," he says, "but my attitude was 'Who the hell cares? It has nothing to do with me.' I was here to play hockey."

Smythe, incidentally, got revenge on Imlach. In 1967, Smythe led the move to deny an expansion franchise to Vancouver when it appeared that a group including Imlach and Foster Hewitt was best positioned to win the franchise. Then in 1969, when Vancouver finally won an NHL team, Smythe made certain that Medicor, a group from Minneapolis with no hockey background, received the franchise. Imlach and his partners were again shut out.

The good times for Smythe and Ballard in the Gardens front office came to a crashing halt in 1968, when the RCMP raided the Gardens and seized company documents. They also raided the homes of Ballard and Smythe. A shareholders' report soon revealed that $212,800 had been spent on improving the two men's homes. Later it was revealed that they had created a phony bank account to siphon money from the Marlies as well.

The skimming had not been especially clever. The phony bank account was in the name of "S[tafford]. H[arold]. Marlie" while invoices for sprinkler heads were billed as interior repair work done at the Gardens. Finally, an invoice for construction materials destined for the Gardens had a map drawn on the back to show the driver where to deliver his load. The map led to Ballard's cottage.

In June 1969, John Bassett convened a meeting of the directors of Maple Leaf Gardens to have the two men removed from the board. Bassett himself cast the deciding vote against the pair. But purging the two men was merely a symbolic stance unless they were stripped of their ownership as well. While Bassett managed to get Ballard and Smythe off the board, he couldn't obtain their controlling interest in Maple Leaf Gardens.

A fight for control of the Gardens began, a fight that wasn't resolved until businessman Donald Giffin arranged to have Ballard and Smythe buy out Bassett and the other partners in 1971. After a bitter takeover fight, Bassett recognized the inevitable and gave up his dream of control of Maple Leaf Gardens, turning his attention instead to the Toronto Argonauts of the Canadian Football League.

Smythe and Ballard had little time to celebrate their good fortune, however, before the RCMP announced the charges against the pair for defrauding the Gardens of approximately $475,000. Stafford Smythe, who finally had risen to the rank and prestige held by his father, immediately launched into his defense of the charges, all the while vowing the authorities would never put a Smythe in jail. He also began to drink heavily.

By late summer of 1971, Smythe had developed severe stomach

problems. He entered hospital for surgery for a bleeding ulcer and had much of his stomach removed. Complications arose after surgery. As he lay dying, he told his father, "See, Dad, I told you they wouldn't put me in prison." On October 13, 1971, Smythe died in Toronto's Wellesley Hospital.

Filled with a father's grief, Conn Smythe could still not help but wonder whether Stafford had not willed himself to die to avoid the pain and humiliation he was undergoing.

With Stafford Smythe dead, Harold Ballard was left to face the RCMP charges alone in 1972. Ballard was convicted of forty-seven of the forty-nine charges and sent to prison for three years for his part in the deals. (He served eighteen months of his sentence, joking about the country-club atmosphere he enjoyed at the prison.)

Ballard ended up with a much bigger prize, however. Once again, Don Giffin came to Ballard's aid. By agreement, Ballard had first option on Smythe's stock, but he didn't have enough cash to complete the sale. Giffin helped supply the money, enabling Ballard to buy out the remaining stock owned by the Smythe family. As executor of Smythe's estate, Ballard then simply sold the shares to himself. When he emerged from Millhaven Prison in 1972, Ballard was master of Maple Leaf Gardens, and hockey in Toronto was entering the Dark Ages.

Conn Smythe later noted with some irony that while his son Stafford had died rather than face humiliation, Ballard had rolled with the punches in the criminal investigation and had survived and prospered as the boss of the Gardens for twenty years afterward. Which man had taken the proper route? wondered old man Smythe, who probably already knew the answer to his question.

12

THE LONG
GOODBYE

As Stafford Smythe lay dying in Toronto's Wellesley Hospital in October 1971, his life's work was rapidly coming undone. The RCMP investigation and charges of fraud were soiling the reputation of one of Toronto's proudest families. The Maple Leafs, which had been in the Smythe family for almost forty-five years, were about to become the possession of his partner and friend, Harold Ballard. The Players' Association, which his father had fought so hard to abolish, was now firmly in place (although it would soon become a house union under Alan Eagleson). And the men of his great Maple Leafs teams from the 1960s were being cast to the four winds. Frank Mahovlich, his enigmatic star, was finally enjoying life, winning Stanley Cups with the Montreal Canadiens. Bob Pulford was in a Los Angeles Kings' uniform, Eddie Shack toiled for former teammate Red Kelly (now the coach in Pittsburgh), Bob Nevin had just finished six years as the captain of the Rangers, Dick Duff was in Buffalo with Punch Imlach, while Ron Stewart played in Vancouver.

George Armstrong, Johnny Bower, Kent Douglas, Don Simmons and Eddie Litzenberger had joined Bert Olmstead in retirement, while only Dave Keon would remain as the final Maple Leaf from the glory days, until he jumped to the Minnesota Fighting Saints of the WHA in 1974. The four men who had stood so firm on the blueline in the glory years were similarly dispersed. Carl Brewer and Allan Stanley were about to be joined by Bob Baun in retirement. Tim Horton had lasted the longest of the quartet with the Leafs—until March

1970—when he was finally sent to the New York Rangers for future considerations.

The Rangers experiment had begun well enough for Horton. The fickle Rangers fans greeted Horton warmly ("I remember how they booed Allan Stanley out of Madison Square Garden," Lori Horton told the New York press), but despite the presence of excellent players like Brad Park, Rod Gilbert, Jean Ratelle, Vic Hadfield and goalie Eddie Giacomin, the Rangers couldn't parlay Horton's experience into the Stanley Cup the Manhattan fans had coveted for thirty years. So after just one year, the Rangers and Horton came to a mutual parting of the ways after the 1971 playoffs.

"There wasn't any closeness with the Rangers team as there was in Toronto," says Lori Horton. "Of course, he'd played in Toronto for years. But he never felt the closeness."

As the summer of 1971 came to a close, it looked as if the illustrious career of Tim Horton was coming to a close as well. He was forty-one years old, a cinch for the Hall of Fame, with nothing left to prove. Horton still had the itch to play, but no one in the NHL seemed willing to scratch that itch.

Privately, Ron Joyce was relieved that he'd finally have his partner around full-time to help him build the donut business. "He was always there to talk to, but he wasn't there to do the day-to-day during the season," recalls Joyce. "I used to have to fly to New York to talk business with him."

Lori Horton, as well, hoped that her growing family would have their father back on a full-time basis. It might also revive their troubled marriage. But even as Lori nursed such ideas, Horton's old teammate Red Kelly—now the coach and general manager of the Penguins—was working on a brainstorm in her home town of Pittsburgh. Looking for ideas to resurrect his blundering hockey team, Kelly hit upon the idea that Horton might be just what his underachievers needed to escape sixth place and return to the playoffs.

Horton liked the challenge when Kelly approached him. Reluctantly, Ron Joyce supported his partner. "Red Kelly wanted Tim on the team," says Joyce. "I remember we all went down for the signing of the contract ... our lawyer, Tim, Lori, we chartered an aircraft from Buttonville and flew down for the signing of the contract."

Going back to Pittsburgh, the town where she and Tim had met twenty years earlier, somewhat soothed Lori's trepidation about her husband's return to the NHL. "It was my home town, so I thought it would be a breeze," she says. "But it wasn't as successful as we hoped it would be."

For the first time in almost fifteen years, Horton missed most of a season due to injuries. "It was not one of his great years," remembers Joyce. "He suffered a couple of injuries—one to a tendon in his knee, another to his collarbone. At the end of that year, he truly was willing to pack in hockey."

The Penguins made the playoffs without Horton that season, and so, feeling extraneous, he told Kelly that he was retiring. Once more, the people surrounding him quietly hoped that this truly was the end of his hockey days. Horton would now give his full energies to the business he'd created for his post-hockey career. But once more a Maple Leafs' connection intervened. Punch Imlach, who had risen like the phoenix to create a strong young team in Buffalo with the Sabres, had designs on Horton if he was leaving Pittsburgh. "I was going to draft the best young defensemen available, and they would need an anchor," Imlach wrote years later. That anchor was Tim Horton, who would stabilize rookies like Jim Schoenfeld and Larry Carriere while they learned the ropes in the NHL.

Horton was tempted. While it meant another year away from the business, the $100,000 he brought in on his contract would help with some of the financial shortfall in the donut business. And he could still hear Punch's siren song. Money, he said, "wasn't the only thing. George was very persuasive."

Allan Stanley also believed that after years of having terms dictated to him, Horton very much liked the idea of a player controlling negotiations. "I asked him after I retired, 'How is it now, the attitude?' And he said, 'Remember when you used to walk out of camp when you were only $200 apart? Just $200 apart and you'd leave camp?' Tim wanted to retire the last two or three years, but Punch wouldn't let him. He kept stuffing his pockets full of money."

Horton signed for his twenty-third NHL campaign and reported to training camp, arriving early and amazing even Imlach with his desire. Imlach's hunch about Horton's beneficial influence paid off for the Sabres, who'd only entered the NHL in 1970. Powered by the "French Connection line" of Rick Martin, René Robert and Gilbert Perreault, the team finished fifth overall in the NHL standings that season. At one point, the dashing young Sabres went unbeaten in twenty-one straight games at the club's ancient home rink, the Auditorium.

In the playoffs, the Sabres pushed Montreal to six games before losing to the eventual Stanley Cup winners. But the season had been a smashing success for a team just three years old. Horton was voted the team's MVP by his teammates. "Tim was the principal factor in giving us the mix we needed," remembered Imlach. "Horton had done a tremendous job in helping those kids."

"Jim Schoenfeld worshipped the guy," says Joyce of the Sabres defenseman who was just two years old when Horton made his first All-Star team. "He became Jim's mentor. He taught him all the moves. Tim was not as fast as he once was, but you had a tough time getting through him on defense."

Once more, Horton had hit the perfect note on which to retire. While Imlach announced that he wanted him to return to Buffalo, Horton gave every appearance of quitting for good that summer of 1973. Sabres training camp opened in September, and despite repeated appeals from Imlach, Horton wouldn't budge.

Three days before the end of camp, Imlach issued an ultimatum: if Tim Horton didn't show up that day, Punch would assume he was going to retire to his donut business. Horton never showed up.

Of course, he couldn't resist for very much longer. Having antagonized his old boss enough, he phoned Imlach the following day. His demands for another year, relayed to an amazed Punch, included a $150,000 salary and a new Ford Pantera sportscar. A sportscar fan, Horton wanted a sleek $17,000 package of speed and handling to clinch the deal. Imlach gulped, but said yes. Tim Horton would attempt one more season at the age of forty-four.

"I was disappointed when he returned to Buffalo, because we were really starting to make the business work," says Joyce, who was running the company single-handed much of the time.

"I was really hoping he'd retire that season," says Lori Horton. "But for some reason it was the car that really convinced him to go back. By this time, he could afford the car himself. But it wouldn't give him the pleasure of having Punch Imlach buy the car for him."

Imlach knew that Horton liked to drive fast. Always superstitious, Punch later claimed to have had a sinking feeling about "one of those hopped-up sports jobs that went like a bat out of hell." In fact, Tim had received a speeding ticket on the way to St. Catharines the day he negotiated the contract. But his need for Horton on the team outweighed his anxieties, and so he went along with the deal.

Imlach got a first-hand idea soon after of how fast the Pantera could move. "One night, he just about scared me to death on a ride out to the airport," confessed Imlach, who did not scare easily.

"Tim loved to go fast," says Joyce. "I think it's part of being an athlete. A lot of them drive fast. Certainly, I had a few occasions when I would just as soon not have been in the car with him driving."

The 1973-74 season was not the cakewalk everyone in Buffalo had been hoping for. Gilbert Perreault missed twenty-three games with a broken ankle, and his linemates slumped without his deft playmaking. The team that had seemed on the verge of greatness the previous spring, now struggled to make the playoffs.

In January, there was personal tragedy to go along with the hockey problems when Tim's father, Oak Horton, died.

Then, on February 18, with the team just returned from a long road trip, Horton's jaw was broken by a shot during practice. Despite the swelling and the intense pain, he was determined to play two days later in Toronto against the Maple Leafs, who were battling Buffalo for the final playoff spot. After all, Maple Leaf Gardens was still a special place for Tim, and it was a chance to beat Dave Keon and his old team. His daughters would be in the crowd, and so would Ron Joyce and a group of businessmen he'd be meeting after the game. Former teammates like Bob Baun would be in the stands, while his old defense partner Allan Stanley would tune in via television from his home in Bobcaygeon. Horton's wife and mother—who had just returned from a vacation in Florida after Oak Horton's death—would watch on TV from their Toronto home.

So, despite the numbing pain, Horton made the trip with the team. The Toronto team doctors examined his jaw before the game but refused to freeze it. Instead, they gave him painkillers. Horton played the first two periods, but by the third period, the pain had become too much even for him. He sat out the final twenty minutes, but still a favorite son around the Gardens, he was chosen one of the three stars in the game. Afterward, he told Imlach's wife "Dodo" that whenever someone hit him, it felt like a shot going through the top of his head.

After the game, he spent time talking with Baun, Keon and the Imlachs. He told them he had to get back to Buffalo to have the jaw examined the next day by the Sabres' team doctors. He begged off the business meeting Joyce had set up at George's Spaghetti House and drove the Pantera back to the Oakville head office of Tim Horton Donuts.

That's where Joyce found him a couple of hours later. "I'll never forget it," he remembers. "He had his topcoat on and a big ice pack wrapped around his head. He looked so funny—I broke up. But his jaw was out like this—and he was in a lot of pain."

Horton was in too much pain to sleep, so the two friends and partners sat in their office, chatting about business and having a few quiet drinks. Horton phoned his wife. Joyce, who had to be in Sarnia by 8:00 the next morning, finally convinced Horton at 4:00 a.m. to come to his home for some sleep. Horton agreed, and said he'd come along after he locked up the office.

Joyce set out for home in his Lincoln Continental. Soon he saw Horton in his rear-view mirror, speeding up the QEW Highway towards St. Catharines and Niagara Falls. "He had to be going as fast as the car would go. He went by me at a terrific rate of speed. I thought, 'That's the last I'll see of him tonight.' I didn't know it was the last I'd ever see him."

"I don't know what kind of painkillers they gave him," says Lori Horton. "He sat up all night and talked and had a few drinks, which is a tough combination."

Accounts differ about what happened when Horton reached the Lake Street exit near St. Catharines. Police say that he must have dozed off slightly, causing the wheels of the Pantera to stray off the road. When Horton tried to regain control of the car at its high rate of speed, the Pantera flipped over, rolled across the median and ended up on the northbound lanes of the highway.

Lori Horton says this theory doesn't explain the skid marks some people reported seeing on the road. "He'd just come through a series of curves, so he couldn't have been asleep. It was the straightaway where he lost control. The police never released the reports to me. I really don't know exactly what happened."

What everyone agrees on is that Horton wasn't wearing his seatbelt and was thrown from the car as it rolled. The Pantera then rolled over him, breaking his neck. He died almost instantly. It was 4:30 a.m.

Police at the scene found the name of Joe Crozier, the Sabres' coach, on the body. Along with a Sabres official, Crozier was called in to identify Horton's body at the St. Catharines morgue. They then had a Buffalo executive phone Imlach at his Toronto home, where he'd spent the night. Imlach, in turn, phoned Ron Joyce.

Despite being awakened from a deep sleep, Joyce vividly recalls the conversation.

"Punch said, 'Ron, I want you to call Lori and the girls. Tim has been in an accident.'

"I said, 'God, how bad is it?'

"He's dead."

Joyce gathered himself and headed to the Horton home in North Toronto. By the time he arrived, "Dodo" Imlach had phoned to break the news to Lori, the girls and Tim's mother and brother, who were both staying at the house. "The news was on the air," Lori recalls. "And the phones just started ringing ..."

In Bobcaygeon, Allan Stanley was roused from bed by a call from a friend in Boston. "He phoned and asked if I'd heard about Tim. I said, sure, I'd seen him play on TV the night before. Then he said, 'Tim was killed.' I said, 'What do you mean he was killed? I saw him play on the TV last night!'"

Carl Brewer was a member of the Toronto Toros of the WHA at the time. He heard the sad news on the radio. "I was numb," he says. "I mean, Tim was Tim ... he always had time for people. It was very emotional. The end of our innocence, I guess."

As the news spread through the hockey community that morning, the tributes poured in. The men who knew him best had their own private thoughts. Punch Imlach went to see the crushed Pantera in a St. Catharines garage. "I stood there remembering the very first time I saw Tim in a game, how strong he was, and thought that he could never be hurt," Imlach recalled in *Heaven and Hell In the NHL*.

Billy Harris recalled seeing the Buffalo-Toronto game the night before and missing Horton in the third period. "He was conspicuous by his absence," noted Harris of his old teammate. "Tim played for the Rangers, Penguins and Sabres, but will always be remembered as Number 7 of the Toronto Maple Leafs."

"No finer person, teammate or hockey player ever lived," said George Armstrong, who played with Horton for twenty-two seasons, longer than anyone else.

The members of those Maple Leafs teams rallied to Lori Horton's side. "Right after Tim's death, Allan Stanley, Eddie Shack, Bobby

Baun ... those guys were there," she says. "Eddie was always there. And Boomer, of course."

The night of the day he died, the Sabres had a scheduled game. They wore black armbands and they were clearly distracted, earning only a 4-4 tie with a late comeback. Two days later, Horton was buried in Toronto with Stanley, Baun, Duff, Armstrong, Keon and Harris as pallbearers. Not surprisingly, the rest of the Sabres' season was a writeoff, and they missed the playoffs.

Added to the rough times with drugs and alcohol she had been through in her marriage to Tim, Lori Horton now had the impossible task of coping with his death. She tried to involve herself in the business with Ron Joyce, but by mutual consent they agreed it was unworkable. Her addiction to alcohol and drugs grew worse. She was taking twelve to twenty amphetamines a day and drinking as well.

She finally sold her interest in Tim Horton Donuts to Joyce, but even that ended badly. Lori sued Joyce in 1992 over the sale, claiming she was taken advantage of while in a vulnerable personal state. She also sued her former lawyer, Jim Blaney, the same Jim Blaney who'd counselled Baun and Brewer and others in his law office nearly fifteen years before.

Joyce insisted that she had received a fair market price from an independent appraiser. In early 1993, a judge agreed with Joyce, noting that 1984—the year Lori Horton finally decided her finances had been mismanaged—was also the year she'd spent the last of her settlement money from the company.

"I worry about Tim's family, because I know what has happened to Lori," says Baun, who is also close friends with Joyce. "It's not a pretty picture what she has gone through. She went through all the money that she had. Everything. But she's a lot better now than she was."

Tim Horton Donuts has become a resounding success story. From thirty-nine stores in 1974 when Horton died, the firm now boasts over six hundred outlets. Joyce says he hopes to have one thousand stores and a billion dollars in sales by 1995. They run a series of summer camps for underprivileged kids under the Tim Horton Foundation. The company also was successful enough to bankroll the failed bid by Hamilton for an NHL expansion franchise in 1991. ("We didn't know till we got to the meetings in Florida that we didn't have a hope in hell," he adds.)

"Tim Horton back in hockey, sure, it's a significant part of our heritage," says Joyce, but he also notes that "a lot of our customers now don't even know who Tim Horton was. He's been dead eighteen years. I'm not a strong believer that the name Tim Horton sells donuts any more. It's more the philosophy of the chain."

When Carl Brewer attended Horton's funeral, he was a thirty-four-year-old member of the Toronto Toros of the WHA, a band of players almost as quixotic as Brewer himself. With players like Gilles "The Cat" Gratton and Wayne "Swoop" Carleton, the Toros had many kindred spirits.

Since his triumphant return to the NHL with Detroit in 1968-69 when he was voted to the All-Star team, Brewer had bounced along the fringes of the hockey world, signing on as a hired gun here and there to whichever team could pay him and put up with his independent nature. As often as not, his stay with a team was brief and ended with Brewer thumbing his nose at authority on his way out of town.

By the time he left the Toros in the mid-1970s, Brewer had come a long way from the quiet, intense, nineteen-year-old rookie who didn't drink anything stronger than a milkshake. "When he came back from Europe," marvelled Baun, "as part of the deal with Detroit, he had to have a bottle of whiskey, fly first class ... Jesus, he was something." In truth, drinking helped Brewer unwind after games and put up with the flying he so hated. Often, he started in the dressing room after a game to calm his nerves before a flight. He used to tell teammates, "I don't know whether I drink to fly or fly to drink."

Brewer had one constant obsession in those restless years: the elimination of hockey's reserve clause, the device that bound a player for life to the team that held his rights. His years under Imlach had taught him the importance—to say nothing of the power and financial benefit—of controlling his own destiny.

In 1967, Brewer had tried to sign as a free agent with the Oakland Seals after having missed the previous two NHL seasons. Officially, the NHL considered Brewer to be on the Maple Leafs' retired list and still Toronto property. Having been out of the NHL for two years, however, Brewer felt he was free to sign a five-year, $250,000 contract with the Seals.

"I didn't really want to play hockey again," he explains today. "And I certainly didn't want to have to fly again, particularly from fucking Oakland. But I was willing to do it if they signed me as a free agent and challenged the NHL's whole reserve system."

The Seals, desperate for talent, seemed keen on the idea. But NHL president Clarence Campbell quickly educated the new Oakland owners about the realities of life in the League. After this fatherly chat, they decided not to test the reserve clause, and the Seals gave up the plan to sign Brewer. And so he went to play for the Canadian national team under Father David Bauer with stints in Muskegon, Finland, Detroit and St. Louis, and the Toros to follow.

There finally seemed to be some light at the end of the tunnel for Brewer when the U.S. Department of Justice's Anti-Trust Division began to investigate the NHL in the early '70s. In response, the League unilaterally amended its rules to allow players to change teams, then imposed such onerous compensation upon the teams who signed free-agent players that virtually no one moved. Players were also still tied to the last NHL club they played for.

Particularly galling for Brewer, the NHL Players' Association, led by his former friend and mentor Alan Eagleson, had agreed to the punitive compensation scheme in collective bargaining.

And so Brewer was forced to exploit the few grey areas available to hockey players saddled with the reserve clause in those days. He had also begun dabbling in business—importing Koho hockey sticks into Canada from Finland and investing in real estate. He did well enough that he has never had to hold a steady job since. Brewer's real wealth was—and remains—a closely guarded secret. From outward appearances, teammates and enemies could never be certain if Brewer was a millionaire or a pauper—which is exactly how Brewer likes it, of course.

Brewer combined his various businesses with old-timers' hockey in the years after leaving the Toros, keeping himself in shape for a final shot at the NHL—a shot even he probably expected would never come. But fate and Carl Brewer are inseparable companions, and late in 1979, Punch Imlach—once again Toronto's general manager and once again desperate for talented defensemen—granted Brewer a trial with the club he'd walked away from fourteen years earlier. It was a move that stunned both the team and the hockey fans of Toronto. But Imlach rationalized the unholy alliance with his old adversary, saying, "We were so thin in reserves that anybody who could help, even *might* help, should be welcome."

While his prospective teammates and the media howled at the idea of a forty-one-year-old "has-been" cluttering up the Leafs' defense corps, Brewer auditioned for two weeks with Moncton of the American Hockey League. He was rusty, but he flashed enough of the old skills to justify bringing him up to Toronto. Imlach awarded him a prorated $125,000 contact. Even parsimonious Punch admitted that the salary was "a ridiculous one, but one I'd based rather senti- mentally on our old Stanley Cups."

Whether it was Brewer's presence in the lineup or not, the Leafs marked the return of the bald prodigal son by losing in convincing fashion 8-2 to Washington at the Gardens in his first game. Brewer was the only Leafs defenseman not on the ice for any Capitals goals that night. None of which endeared him to Darryl Sittler or the new generation of Leafs. Dave Hutchison, the man he'd replaced in the lineup, spent his practice time taking runs at Brewer. Börje Salming, the Leafs best defenseman, refused to pass Brewer the puck. "I couldn't believe this could happen on a hockey team," he says. "It's kind of funny when you think about it. If I was coaching a team, no player on my team would get away with that shit."

"It was such chicken stuff it was unbelievable," said Imlach, who offered this assessment of what Tim Horton would have done had Dave Hutchison taken a run at him: "Hutchison never would have lived to tell the tale."

Ironically, the players considered Brewer a spy for Imlach in the dressing room. "If they had any intelligence at all—which obviously they didn't—they would have appreciated that Carl Brewer is no one's pipeline," he says. "There was only one guy I wanted to get along with: Tiger Williams. The first game I played, Tiger told me, 'Carl, some of the guys don't want you around. Don't worry, I'm with you all the way.'"

It was an impossible situation, of course. Floyd Smith, the Leafs' coach, tried to placate his troubled dressing room by rarely playing Brewer, but nothing worked in the poisoned atmosphere. When the nightmarish season ended, Brewer told reporters that nothing on earth could make him come back for another year. The final chapter of his playing career had ended with a whimper, not a bang. There would be no Hall of Fame induction to look forward to, no big press conference where the Leafs honor their retiring star.

But Brewer returned to the Leafs on another matter in 1982, claiming he was owed $8,287.32 for the two weeks he'd spent in Moncton. "Imlach shook my hand on a deal," he says. "Now, it was kind of greedy to look a gift horse in the mouth—I'd played about three minutes and got paid $85,000—but I didn't care. Mainly I wanted to get Imlach into court, because on the stand he'd have to tell the truth."

By this time, Imlach had suffered a serious heart attack and was being eased out as general manager of the Leafs by Harold Ballard. But he took up the Brewer challenge. "Brewer didn't have five cents coming to him," Imlach insisted. "He had come to me and said he'd play for nothing if I'd just let him end his career as a Maple Leaf."

Once more, the two men squared off, this time in front of Justice Keith Gibson. And once more, Imlach trumped his former player. "Punch was brilliant on the stand, he really was," Brewer says with a laugh today. "He controlled the whole situation—swearing, it was incredible. The judge was in awe. You have to give him credit. He was marvellous. So I lost the suit."

"Once Judge Gibson reminded me that I was in a court of law, not a dressing room," crowed Imlach afterwards. "This was because I said a few things like 'hell', 'bloody' and 'bugger-all'. But he was very fair."

Brewer didn't dwell too long on his loss. During the trial he and his companion Sue Foster (Brewer and his wife separated in the early 1980s) had noticed that, according to the option clause in his contract, he had remained under contract to the Leafs after his playing career ended. So he sued the Maple Leafs for the years of salary and benefits he felt he was entitled to for that period. At the end of a protracted legal wrangle that lasted until 1986, Brewer won approximately $45,000, enough to cover his legal costs. "I had a lot of fun doing it," he says. "Proved to be in their hair, so to speak."

The suit inadvertently launched Brewer into his next crusade. "I think probably the reason I took on the whole pension thing was because I was denied my rights to the pension. When the lawsuit finished, I tried to apply for further pension benefits and was denied them. I was under contract, but they said I hadn't played any games to qualify for the pension. It would have been so simple for Eagleson to get me those two years of pension, and all this shit wouldn't be here today." Eagleson probably thought Brewer would go away after a few months. He was wrong.

Challenged by Eagleson in 1986 the way he'd been challenged by the Leafs in 1965, Brewer set his formidable sights on Eagleson and the NHL Pension Society. He had his next project, one that would consume his life for the next seven years.

Where Carl Brewer tried to keep the NHL's feet to the fire after his retirement, Allan Stanley had steered clear of the past. He'd been gone from the NHL for five seasons by the time he served as Tim Horton's pallbearer in 1974, retired longer than any member of the defense corps. His final year in Philadelphia, 1969, had convinced him that the end of his playing days had finally come.

"It was a different year. After Toronto with all the discipline, it seemed to be completely different ... the players did what they wanted. We didn't have a good year; St. Louis blew us out in the play-offs in four straight. I just said, 'I've got to think of something else. This can't go on forever.'"

Stanley began negotiating to buy the Beehive Lodge in Bobcay-geon, a summer resort on Pigeon Lake in the Muskoka cottage country of eastern Ontario. With the Flyers' consent, Stanley flew north four times during the 1968-69 season to complete the negotiations for the sale. "Sometimes, the club would fly home from L.A. and I'd fly up here—take four different flights. But I only missed one practice."

In the summer of 1969, the forty-three-year-old Stanley finally called it quits after twenty-one years in the NHL and purchased the lodge. When he and his wife, Barbara, took over running the Beehive Lodge, Stanley had done nothing but play hockey all winter and golf all summer for most of his adult life. He was mindful of that old expression that says there are two things every man thinks he can do better than anyone else: build a fire and run a hotel.

Stanley and his wife suddenly found themselves running not only a hotel but a dining room, a resort, a coffee shop, a golf course, a rink and a hockey school—all at the same time. When buses to and from the rink got too expensive to rent, Stanley bought one. The hours, he recalls, were endless.

"I opened the golf course at 7:00 a.m. We had eight hours of ice time at the rink, and I took half of that for hockey school. At 4:00 p.m., I'd go to the dining room and set up the bar. I was the bartender.

You wouldn't get home till 1:00 or 2:00 in the morning. The only time I came home was to sleep."

After six years of working eighteen-hour days from April till October, Stanley conceded that the workload was too great, and he and his wife closed the dining room until they could find a manager to take it over. Someone was finally found to manage the dining room and some of the other duties, and Stanley began to relax a bit—half a dozen years after starting his "retirement."

He accepted a brief opportunity to return to the NHL as an assistant coach with the Buffalo Sabres at the conclusion of the 1976-77 season. The Sabres had reached the Stanley Cup finals two years earlier, but Punch Imlach thought they were losing their desire. Stanley was called in by his old boss to help embattled coach Floyd Smith light a fire under the team as it headed into the playoffs. But Stanley found modern players too pampered.

"There are too many players here who think work, body contact, and aggressive play are dirty words," he wrote to Imlach at the conclusion of the season. "The players seem very complacent and talk tired all the time. Not from overwork, it would seem to me. To acquire a couple of hard-nosed hockey players who think it's worth fighting for would make our big guns better hockey players."

Suitably disillusioned with modern hockey, Stanley returned to Bobcaygeon, obtained his real estate licence and began developing a subdivision near his home. "That relieved a lot of the pressure," he says. "It gave me time to think of something else."

That something else proved to be an alumni association for retired NHL players. While the NHL Players' Association under Alan Eagleson was now firmly ensconced, the NHLPA neither represented nor served the retired players who had once been its members. "I represent the current players, that's my responsibility, not the retired players," Eagleson told CBC TV in September 1991.

Retired players—in particular those who'd been instrumental in starting the NHLPA—were searching for a body to represent their unique needs and give voice to their concerns as pensioners and former athletes. Several initiatives trying to fill that gap started about this time. The garrulous former Bruins and Rangers star Phil Esposito—who'd been the president of the NHLPA— attempted to form a foundation to assist needy retired players.

At first, there was considerable support for the concept. Esposito claims his foundation helped find jobs for eighty former players and got medical care for others. And it helped to coordinate alumni groups in various NHL cities. But it soon ran into problems. Foremost among the stumbling blocks was financing. Esposito approached NHL president John Ziegler for help, but Ziegler explained that the League was already helping players through its own Crisis Fund. It was the first Esposito had ever heard of such a fund in his twenty-five years in the NHL.

Despite the large number of retired players, there was no permanent financial base on which to build the foundation Esposito envisioned. "We all tried to tell Phil that the Rockefellers may be able to support a foundation, but we can't possibly make enough money the way we retired players are to support a foundation," says Baun.

Egos also came into play, just as they had when the players competed against one another on the ice. "Phil had all his entourage, all we got was lip service," says Stanley. "Look, I'm against building a foundation under anybody's name. I'll build a foundation for the NHL alumni, under the name of all the players, not one name. Not Gordie Howe, not Phil Esposito, not 'Rocket' Richard. I don't think that's what it's all about."

Esposito's foundation had competition from another ex-player, competition that had its genesis when Allan Stanley phoned his old teammate Bob Baun. "I said, 'I'd like to have lunch with you one day. I have something to discuss with you. We need an alumni.'"

Like the other Leafs, Baun had been shaken by Horton's death. But he'd had his own troubles since retiring. He had gone to Oakland in the expansion draft, then to Detroit, and finished up his career with Toronto in 1972. The Maple Leafs had been bounced in the first round of the playoffs the year before. Desperate for a veteran to shore up their young defense corps, the Leafs had summoned him for one last hurrah. But Baun would play only a part of the season before a serious neck injury forced his retirement.

Baun accepted the end of his career with equanimity. Except for a stint coaching the Toronto Toros in 1975, he left hockey behind. When he could no longer play the game, he left it for his cattle farm in Pickering, Ontario. He built his home by himself on the property. "My father came in and looked at the place I'd built," says Baun, "and he said, 'I don't know where you came from sometimes ...' He was amazed."

On the farm outside Toronto, with his wife Sally and three boys, he lived the life of a gentleman farmer, developing his herd of prize cattle, collecting wine and art, enjoying the good life, just as he'd done when he played.

Then, just after Horton's death, the federal government began expropriating property for the proposed international airport in Pickering. Real estate values collapsed, and Baun was soon wiped out. (The airport was never built.) The cattle, the farm and much of the art and wine were liquidated by the banks. As he passed his forty-second birthday, Baun was broke.

If he was adept at spending money on the finer things, Baun was also born with the gift of making money. A friend in the construction business who'd heard of Baun's problems invited him to sign autographs at one of his building sites. After three weeks, he approached the builder, offering to sell some of the houses.

"So he gave me twenty houses at the end of the subdivision, ones he wanted to get rid of. I sold eighty houses in six months and made $150,000. That got me back on my feet again."

From developing real estate, Baun moved into selling medical insurance. Jim Blaney, his friend and lawyer, introduced Baun to Mark McKee, who had been a pal of Howard Hughes back in the 1940s. Despite the wide disparity in their ages, Baun and McKee hit it off, and Baun began to handle the cancer-insurance policies McKee was attempting to bring into Canada.

For five years, Baun was a super salesman, selling cancer insurance from coast to coast. Baun would go into an area, enlist door-to-door salespeople, teach them the sales pitch and then send them into the field. He collected a percentage of their sales. The money was good and the lifestyle even better for Baun. When his bid to buy out the Canadian company failed, he signed a lucrative deal with a major brokerage house that would pay him $250,000 a year to sign up new customers. He also got into the donut business on the side, purchasing a Tim Horton franchise for his wife in Pickering, just alongside Highway 401.

"It was an exciting five years for me. I really enjoyed the insurance business," he says today, standing in his Tim Horton store. "I was always used to the high lifestyle. But in order to make the money I needed, the donut business wasn't conducive."

Financial setbacks nearly wiped out Baun once more, however, and it was the donut business he eventually fell back on. "I had to go back to square one," he explains.

During this period of boom and then bust, Baun was also taking business courses at the Wharton School of Business and the Harvard Business School. "All these guys had their MBAs. I was a grade ten dropout," he says with a laugh. "At the start, I'd be in the bottom of the class. At the end, I'd be in the top five. These guys could have all the letters they want, but if you worked harder than them, you could bring yourself up to them very quickly."

Through the courses he took, Baun met a number of financial movers and shakers. And by picking the brains of those around him, he learned a good deal about pensions. Like Stanley, he began to recognize the need for an association to represent retired players and to protect the value of their pensions. So, in 1979, he started up the NHL Alumni Association.

"The person who should have started it was Al Eagleson. It was a natural transition from active players to alumni. Sooner or later, we were all going to be alumni. I could never understand why he didn't start it ... other than, if he started an alumni association, there would be some strong people like Red Kelly or Ted Lindsay or myself who would put controls on him. He didn't want any part of that."

So while he tried to balance the demands of his business interests, Baun took on the job of wrestling the many strong personalities in the hockey world into a cohesive unit. "Hockey players are notorious for saying yes, yes, yes ... It was very difficult for them to stick together, mostly because they had their egos in the way."

When Baun met his old teammate Allan Stanley for lunch, they discussed the dream of uniting retired players in an organization that would promote their interests and provide a touchstone in their lives. So many hockey players had crashed financially and personally when they left the game; there had to be someone, something there to help them.

All Baun and Stanley needed was an issue to unify the players, one common thread that would cut through the animosities of the past. The NHL pension plan, the pot of gold they all thought they'd earned back in the '50s and '60s, seemed to be the universal that cropped up whenever the players got together.

As the two men finished lunch, they realized they had found the key to uniting hockey players. The door it opened was at the NHL Pension Society in Montreal.

13

"A GREAT BOON TO THE PLAYERS OF THE LEAGUE"

Allan Stanley's home sits atop a gentle hill in Bobcaygeon, Ontario. As he looks out his window, he can survey the Beehive Lodge and the pleasure boats as they navigate Pigeon Lake. "I always said, if I took all the worst days of my hockey career and put them together, they couldn't touch the frustrations of my first two years in business." A man accustomed to the cloistered life of an athlete— practice at 11:00, games at 8:00, someone else to sweat the details— Stanley had encountered a foe stronger than Gordie Howe, faster than Bobby Hull and more persistent than Henri Richard upon leaving the game in 1969.

"It is like living through an Arctic summer for the first time," Ken Dryden wrote of the athlete's life. "Arriving in May or June, and feeling the wonderful, endless sunlight, knowing but forgetting, that sometime it will end. Then one day in July, long after it began to happen ... you feel the sun slowly hemorrhaging away. And unable to stop it, suddenly you know what's ahead."

Like most athletes, Stanley had found himself largely unprepared for the working world, a world where middle-aged hockey players with creaking knees and little education were twenty years behind their age group on the corporate ladder—at the bottom, not the top, of the socio-economic heap.

While Stanley—and most of his peers—would never give back a day spent on the playing fields, they all acknowledge that there were few worldly goods they could take with them into the next life as private citizens. Those few contacts Stanley had managed to carry with him into civilian life could never compensate for the years he had spent pursuing glory instead of a trade or the toll that pursuit had taken on his body.

For all the heartaches of his first years in business, Stanley had in fact been lucky to survive the transition. Around him, many contemporaries had fallen by the wayside. Camille "The Eel" Henry, the slick playmaking star of the New York Rangers in the 1950s and '60s, battled arthritis while working as a school janitor in New York. Réal Chevrefils, a promising forward with Boston in Stanley's day, had drunk himself to death. Bill Speer, who played alongside Bobby Orr on the Bruins' Stanley Cup winners of 1970, had crashed through the ice on a skidoo in an alcohol- and drug-induced haze not far from Stanley's house in Bobcaygeon.

Some of this was the inevitable churn of life, of course. As they say in sports, "The sun can't shine on the same dog's ass every day." And some was the product of leaving the arena of sports—with its euphoric highs and its catastrophic lows—for a world of more modest inclines and descents.

But hockey players experienced a cruel deception that athletes in other sports had not encountered. Told for years by Clarence Campbell, the owners and even their own union leader that they would come into the best pension plan in sports when they retired, they instead had received payouts at subsistence levels and lower. The financial cushion they had dreamed of was just a bag of straw on a cold cement floor.

"Clarence Campbell would take up one day each year telling us how we had the greatest pension plan in sports," remembers Frank Mahovlich. "Then when I retired, I saw the baseball players driving Cadillacs while we drove Fords."

Worse, the players didn't have the slightest idea what had gone wrong with their pension. They had paid out as much as 20 to 25 percent of their after-tax income in some years, that they knew. And interest rates were soaring into double digits in the 1980s as the stars of the 1950s and '60s began collecting their pensions. The only conclusion was that they had trusted, and that trust had been misplaced. Now Stanley and Bob Baun tried to put the pieces together for their entire generation of players.

They at least had a jumping-off point. By 1981, Baun had gained access to various pension authorities in North America through his studies at business school and his contacts in the financial world. He was picking the brains of people such as Jim O'Donnell from Mackenzie Financial, Robert Munro at William Mercer Inc., and Lorraine Mahoney from Allan Smart Services in Toronto—all experts in the pension field. It was only natural that his curiosity about the subject would lead him towards his own NHL pension.

"He was in the insurance business at the time," remembers Allan Stanley. "He was exposed to presidents of companies and people in the pension business. Bobby was a pretty charming guy, and he had people looking into his pension for no money. I don't believe it cost him any money."

"I knew there was something wrong, because I'd been saying there was something wrong since Clarence Campbell," says Baun. "I used to be one of those guys putting his hand up all the time to ask questions."

Those players who'd witnessed the crushing of the Players' Association in 1957 had long harbored suspicions about how the NHL had handled their pensions over the years. To the largely unsophisticated players, the plan always seemed shrouded in secrecy and baffling legalese. What little they knew came from dressing-room chats with Clarence Campbell or the odd details their player representatives on the board gleaned at meetings.

Doug Harvey, at the time the top defenseman in the NHL, was one of the more vigilant and persistent questioners about the NHL pension plan in its early days. "What the fellows are interested in," he asked the 1957 meeting of the NHL Pension Society, "is if they went into a pension scheme on their own at twenty-two and paid $900 a year until thirty-two ... is it true—as they come to me and say—their payments would be better?"

Harvey was chastised by Frank Selke, his general manager with the Montreal Canadiens: "How can an intelligent man say that if he put money into some other investment he would have the same return in twenty years?... Where can you get the services of men like these directors and Mr. Campbell for nothing?" So much for impartial expert advice.

Ted Lindsay, as always, was more abrupt. "Players want to know what they are going to get each month, and we would like to see that in black and white," he told the same meeting in 1957. "We are not lawyers, but hockey players, and it is a little bit above their heads."

"Oh, hell, I listened to Clarence Campbell come by training camps every year," says Stanley. "He expounded on what a great plan this is, how generous the owners are ... very seldom did anybody ask a question. I remember Gus Mortson asked a question once, got one of those traditional answers. You know, mind your own business, or don't be stupid. And he said, 'Mr. Campbell, you never made a decision in favor of a player in your whole darn career.' That's the only question I ever heard in twenty-one years."

So when Baun and Stanley went searching for issues to attract players to their new alumni association, the pension plan was at the top of their list. Baun and Stanley had contributed between $900 and $1,500 a year into the plan (as much as 15 percent of their after-tax income some years). Yet Baun was entitled to only $7,622 a year after seventeen years in the NHL, while Stanley was eligible for $12,000 after twenty-one seasons.

Others had similar complaints. "Any conversation that we had, any meeting that was attended, the major theme was to do something about the pension," says Stanley. So Baun enlisted his circle of business associates to help him research and analyze the pension plan run by the NHL Pension Society.

What they discovered shocked them. While interest rates in the early 1980s were often as high as 20 percent, the players' pensions were still being calculated assuming the old rates of 3 and 4 percent return from the 1950s. According to Lorraine Mahoney, "If I had walked across the street with the death benefit reserve from 1982 [the pooled investment fund out of which the players' pensions are paid], Bob Baun's pension would immediately have gone up five times ... not double, not 50 percent, but 500 percent."

Under the NHL's guidance, the value of the pension plan in the early 1980s had plummeted against the cost of living, while inflation had gouged massive holes in what should have been a considerable investment. "I have to tell you that the NHL plan was the bottom of the barrel in terms of inactivity and non-action on behalf of the players," says Mahoney, who has underwritten group-annuity contracts such as the one used by the Pension Society as far back as the 1960s.

"The NHL should have been negotiating with Manufacturers Life to increase pensions—not only those for the current players—but also those already in payment. I think that over the years the assumption was 'It's not broken, don't fix it.' But in fact it was broken quite badly. When you analyze what those death benefits would have provided [compared to what the players got], it was a joke."

While some former players expressed disbelief that the NHL could have let such a thing happen, anyone familiar with the League's attempts to intimidate its players and assure the docility of its work force should not have been surprised.

The NHL Pension Society was in fact a rear-guard action launched by the League in 1947 to head off an independent players' pension fund proposed by Detroit insurance executive C. Jean Caspar. Caspar seemed a natural person to organize the project after his previous insurance work with the players.

"We had an insurance policy [through Caspar] that paid us if we got hurt, if we got cuts," remembers Leo Reise, who played for Chicago, Detroit and New York in his career. "We got five dollars a stitch and all this sort of stuff, and after a while he developed the idea that the pension program would be good for us."

Support was quick in coming for Caspar's idea, and the Detroit club actually donated some of the seed money to get it started. But when Caspar proposed the pension plan to the NHL, owners like Conn Smythe weren't quite as accommodating. After an independent pension plan, they reasoned, could a union be far off? And then collective action? Such left-leaning ideas were anathema to the capitalist captains of the NHL, particularly at the onset of the Cold War.

Newly installed NHL president Clarence Campbell was dispatched by his masters to start another pension plan, this one tightly controlled by the owners. Despite his high-brow, Oxfordian trappings, Campbell was extremely conversant with hockey players and their vulnerability. An accomplished amateur player, he'd been an NHL referee prior to World War II, where he'd served as a war-crimes prosecutor. He cut an impressive figure in his tailored business suits, could spew legalese with the best of them, and had little compunction about using a heavy hand to please the owners—such as when he suspended Boston's Don Gallinger for life from the NHL in 1948 for gambling. Needless to say, Campbell was never asked, nor did he offer, to discipline any wayward owners (such as the embezzling

Ballard and Smythe) during his thirty-year tenure as the "head" of the NHL.

Eddie Litzenberger remembers a meeting with Campbell in 1961 when he was holding out for a better contract with Detroit. Campbell had been brought in by the Red Wings to soften up Litzenberger in negotiations. "He told me how lucky I was that God blessed me with talent, how lucky I was to be in the NHL," Litzenberger says with a chuckle. "I looked at him in his blue suit, his green socks, his red tie with the hanky out to here ... and I said, 'Mr. Campbell, one of us is wasting our time.' And I left."

There was just one problem with Campbell, a problem that would become manifest with the pension plan: he was a lawyer, a man of ideas, not a businessman. This made him perfect for the owners, who *were* businessmen and didn't want Campbell interfering with their money decisions. By the same token, this lack of business savvy made him unsuitable—by both inclination and training—for running the pension fund

Not that Campbell or the owners were deterred by this flaw, of course, as they forged ahead with their plans. Despite considerable misgivings from some corners, the players—with no single voice to unite them—were eventually "won over" to Campbell's version of the pension plan. "They had a bit of a selling job to sell it to the players," remembered J. D. Ford, the Pension Society's first auditor.

"Actually, the NHL instituted the plan pretty much on their own," testified Leo Reise. "It wasn't a case of negotiating between players and management ... It developed with the NHL taking the idea that Caspar had, saying they wanted to develop a pension, and that is the way it worked out. There wasn't a negotiation between people."

The brand-new NHL Pension Society was constituted in 1947 with Campbell, Conn Smythe of Toronto and John Reed Kilpatrick of New York as the original "members" of the enterprise. The affairs of the Society were to be administered by a board of five directors, two of whom were to be participants in the plan (i.e., active or retired players). Syl Apps of the Maple Leafs became the first vice president from the players' side.

On May 12, 1948, the letters patent of the Society were issued. "Philanthropic, charitable, provident and benevolent" were the words they used to describe the aims of the Pension Society. The letters patent also specified that "the business of said Corporation shall be carried on without the purpose of gain for its members and that any profits or other accretions to the corporation shall be used to promote its objects."

Those objects, it stated, were "to provide for the payments of pensions and/or annuities to players, coaches, trainers, and referees employed by the National Hockey League or any of its member clubs." The business of the Society was then described in a series of by-laws and regulations.

Effusive praise for the plan came in a letter to all NHL players co-signed by Campbell and Syl Apps in March 1949. The plan, it stated, "will be a great boon to the players of the League for years to come. It will likewise serve to increase the attractiveness of our game as a career and enhance its prestige with the ever-increasing numbers of players and fans throughout the world."

Contrary to Leo Reise's assertion that the plan had been unilaterally imposed, however, the letter from Campbell and Apps contended that, in the two years since Caspar had presented his ideas, "many conferences and meetings have been held and much study and negotiating has been necessary to bring the plan into being.

"It is the confident opinion of the Officers and Directors of the Society that the Plan is so calculated and designed to provide for the participants the maximum possible benefits and protection from the resources available," the letter closed.

One attractive selling point of the plan in the early days was that players could start drawing their pensions as early as age forty-five. While taking their money at forty-five dramatically reduced the value of the pensions, it did provide a small transitional income for players between their retirement from hockey and the time when they could collect Canada Pension or Old Age Security.

In truth, this early access to their pensions was one of the few perks players had won when the League appropriated Jean Caspar's idea. Otherwise, the owners were in complete control.

For one thing, while players contributed the bulk of the money, the NHL decided where and how to invest it (Campbell had the deciding vote on the board of directors). There was no independent trustee to guard the players' interests, just NHL executives like Campbell and John Reed Kilpatrick, president of the New York Rangers. Inexperienced in pension matters, these men opted for extreme fiscal prudence and complete control by the League.

Secondly, the players were forbidden to hold the NHL liable if anything went wrong with the pension plan. The NHL, meanwhile, was protected by its contract with Manufacturers Life from any losses or shortfalls in the plan. In short, the players took the risk that the plan would survive and flourish, not the owners. The owners' reluctance to share in the losses of the plan would prove an important point in court when they sought to partake of the profits years later.

Finally, until 1967, there was no established bargaining agent for the players in their dealings with the owners, just a loose collection of athletes who had been taught to loathe each other on and off the ice.* "We were taught to hate each other, and we did a great job of it," remarks Gordie Howe.

The formula seemed simple enough at the time. Under the regulations, the ninety or so players who played a full NHL season would contribute $900 a year, and the NHL Pension Society would guarantee them a benefit of $90 per year of service for life at age forty-five. So if you played ten years in the NHL, you'd be eligible to receive $900 a year at age forty-five.

To help support the plan, the individual NHL clubs also promised that two-thirds of the revenues from the annual All-Star Game and twenty-five cents from every playoff ticket sold would be directed to the pension plan—although this formula was not incorporated in the regulations of the Society. The NHL's contributions to the plan averaged $61,000 per year until 1957, when the League began matching players' contributions.

The monies were to be held by the Pension Society until players qualified for the plan—a procedure known in insurance language as "vesting." The money was then invested in individual annuities with the Canadian Department of Labour Annuities Branch. Many of the early investments made by the Pension Society were in CNR bonds, bearing about 2.57 percent interest—a very cautious rate of return. The directors of that time "were afraid of getting black eyes, so they played it pretty safe," recalls J. D. Ford.

In 1952, the Society entered into a group-annuity contract with Manufacturers Life known as Group Annuity Contract No. GA550.

---

* Active players received representation under the NHL Players' Association in 1967, but retired players still have no agent or representative on the board of the Society.

This group annuity would allow the NHL to purchase pensions on a multiple rather than single basis. There were two important benefits to the NHL from the group annuity, both of which produced surplus monies in the pension plan: "premium discount" credits—or reductions in the rate the Society was charged for the purchase of annuities; and "experience rate" credits—interest and capital gains generated by the principal funds contributed to the plan.

Surpluses could develop in other ways as well. Any players not meeting the plan's vesting requirements of five (later three) years had their contributions returned with interest, but the NHL's contributions on their behalf remained in the plan. This type of surplus was used by the League to reduce its future obligations to the plan.

According to Leo Reise, the players believed as far back as 1947 that all surpluses in the plan were to go to them. Reise, an accounting student at the time, had discussed surpluses with Clarence Campbell when the Pension Society was being organized. Today, Reise says the players wanted surpluses used as soon as they appeared to enhance their pensions. The NHL president, however, wanted the surplus money to build up a contingency fund for a rainy day.

"He came up with another program that he [had] to build a society," remembered Reise. "I said ... there shouldn't be anything left over for anything else. It should all go to the players."

But Campbell won out, and in the first ten years of the plan, surpluses were transferred to a contingency fund until $65,000 had been set aside. As well, a past-service fund was established to pay for benefits earned by active players who'd accumulated service before the plan's inception.

While the plan was far from perfect, most players decided it was better than anything they'd had before and went along with the Society. Players suspicious of the NHL's motives were directed by Campbell to the undertakings in Regulation 32 of the plan.

"Change or modification in the Plan shall not in itself have the effect of diverting from any Participant any benefits arising from contributions previously made by such Participant or from any contributions made by the League, Member Clubs or Society for the benefit of such participant.

"All monies," it concluded "will be held by the Society for the benefit of the participant exclusively under the Regulations of the Plan."

It was the understanding at that time of J. D. Ford, too, that no monies would ever revert to the owners. "Not at that time. Certainly not," he testified.

Clarence Campbell proved a vigilant watchdog for the NHL owners and a resented figurehead to the players. In the early years of the plan, Campbell's conservative zeal in tying up surpluses in reserve funds and low-bearing investments left even some owners shaking their heads. With his underworld connections and boxing interests, Chicago owner Jim Norris was used to playing for higher stakes; to him the fund was moving at a pedestrian pace.

"I would almost feel like taking a little bit of a gamble and buy other bonds and get a better yield," he told the 1950 meeting of the Society. "I know that may be considered a little risky, but I do it, and I think we should turn it over in our minds."

When Campbell admitted, "We have taken a very conservative view," Norris replied tersely, "Very conservative." But Campbell—advised by his self-described "mouthpiece," J. D. Ford—continued to play it safe so the NHL wouldn't be confronted with a deficit in the future. "We were pretty new in the game at the time, and none of the owners wanted to get saddled into vesting these monies," says Ford.

While Norris was allowed to voice opinions, Campbell grew very testy whenever his running of the Society was challenged by players such as Harvey and Lindsay. When Harvey, the Canadiens' eleven-time All-Star defenseman, attempted to contrast the Pension Society's efforts with other plans, Campbell petulantly remarked, "You say that you have some plan which you would like to submit—if you do, I would put it in the hands of some competent person to examine it. Everyone will be glad to know whether the plan can go on doing a job for another ten years—if it cannot, we are just wasting our effort."

Once again, Chicago's Jim Norris seemed at odds with Campbell on an issue. "I would think it might be worth analyzing to see if they come up with a better plan. My experience is that this is terrific ... I would like to know myself. It is very good." Despite Norris's enthusiasm, few comparative studies of other plans were ever undertaken.

When Lindsay, the Detroit captain, asked, "Do you think we run our pension plan as well as a big company [does]?" Campbell defended his performance on the grounds of thrift. "I do not say we can do it better, but we do it for free, and that is one thing they cannot do," he replied.

"There [have] been thousands of dollars devoted to this Society without charge," echoed John Bain, the Toronto accountant who advised the Society. "I don't know of anyone who has had any remuneration, including myself."

Of course, the reason Campbell and other officers and advisers took no remuneration from the Pension Society was that they were already being compensated by the NHL for their other duties, a point the players failed to realize or make note of. With remuneration from the League, their loyalties lay with the NHL, not the Pension Society.*

Little wonder that Montreal's general manager, Frank Selke, purred, "I had faith in these fellows to do the job."

But with the players' contributions alone worth approximately $90,000 by 1957 ($684,000 in 1992 dollars), not even the plodding Campbell could prevent a sizeable surplus from accumulating in the fund. By 1954, the size of the surplus was such that the annual meeting of the Society drafted a special by-law "Re. Disposition Of Potential Surplus." It began: "Whereas by the Regulations of the Society all monies paid into the Society must be used for the benefit of the participants and cannot be refunded...." The by-law then went on to state that an accounting should be done of the surplus as of October 1, 1957, and it should then be distributed on an equitable basis to all the participants in the first ten years of the plan.

Those present at that 1954 meeting appear to have been concerned that any such surpluses in the future be distributed to players in the same fashion. Characteristically, they were worried about greedy players, not owners, later seizing benefits already earned by players in the plan. General John Reed Kilpatrick, who represented the New York Rangers, summed up their concerns: "Someone might say, '$65,000 going back to the first fellows?—let us accumulate it and increase the current benefits so that we don't provide any surplus ...' That is very far-fetched, but it is possible."

---

* When American lawyer Marcus Grayck, who drafted legal opinions on the plan for the NHL, was asked in court in 1991 if he had ever been to a meeting of the NHL Pension Society, he said no, but he had been to a meeting of the NHL Board of Governors. "I was presented this watch by the NHL upon my retirement at a meeting of the Board of Governors," said Grayck. "It reads on the reverse side..."

"You don't have to read it," replied the players' lawyer, Mark Zigler.

Kilpatrick went on, "I don't think we ought to set it up in such a way that we are afraid they will be crooks ten years from now—that is going a little far—but if we go over the policy and the principle and say: 'This is the way we have taken this action, because we contemplate that the policy of the Society will be along the same honest distribution lines that we have shown today.' I may be a little overcautious, but I would like to see that."

Kilpatrick would never know how prescient he'd been, even though he was fingering the wrong culprits. The directors drafted a resolution supporting the by-law and declaring that "no action should be taken hereafter in defeasance of it." Thus, in 1957, a net dividend of $310,243 in surplus monies was distributed to the players, representing $315 per player per year of service.

That same year, the NHL also agreed to match the players' $900 annual contribution to the plan, while guaranteed benefits went from $90 to $180 per player per year of service.

While it had disposed of this first surplus efficiently enough, the question of who legally owned the surpluses still dogged the Society. Thus, legal opinions were sought on the matter, and in the Annual Report of 1958, the minutes make reference to an opinion having been secured by the board of directors. "The opinion received was that this surplus belonged to all the 'Participants' and that the money could only be disbursed to provide additional pension benefits for the 'Participants' on an equitable basis." (No record of this opinion could be found in 1991.)

An independent insurance company hired to do a review of the plan after its first ten years of operation came up with a similar opinion. "After vesting, no circumstances or contingency can deprive the Participants or his dependents of the value of the League's contributions on his behalf," found Sun Life officials.

And it appeared that the Society agreed. In 1962, an accumulated surplus of $257,879 (or $560 per player per year of service) was once more equally divided among those who had contributed between 1957 and 1962. The same occurred again in 1967, when a dividend of $857.93 per player per year of service was declared for the years 1962-66. And in 1968, a further $591.73 per player per year of service was distributed. (This amount would typically deliver another $50 per month in real pension benefits upon retirement.) What players made in these modest gains, they saw taken away later.

In 1964, player contributions went up as well to $1,500 annually (the NHL matched the amount for its contribution) while the guaranteed benefit increased to $300 per player per year of service.

When the NHL finally got around to adding six new American teams in the 1967 expansion, the Pension Society realized that U.S. tax laws obliged it to establish the plan formally as a "foreign situs trust" to qualify for tax deductions under American jurisdiction. In 1966, lawyer Marcus Grayck of the Chicago office of Baker and McKenzie was instructed by J. D. Ford to draft a suitable trust agreement. He did so, under the proviso that the new National Hockey League Club Pension Plan and Trust contain virtually the same regulations and administration as before.

"There was no intention to change the funding of benefits, surpluses or anything at that time," said Ford. "His agreement was supposed to bring it on all fours."

As of 1967, the scheme was to guarantee a pension benefit of $300 a year at age forty-five for each season played. As well, the Society formalized the arrangement for distributing all surpluses to the players, mandating that it be done at five-year intervals.

And the new plan strengthened the language that protected the players' unique interest in the plan's funds. Article 4, for instance, said amendments to allow the clubs or the NHL to use the funds or assets of the plan were forbidden. As well, "... no funds contributed or assets of the Club Pension Plan shall ever revert to or be used or enjoyed by the League or Member Clubs until after the satisfaction of all liabilities ..." Exactly what those liabilities were, of course, would become a bone of contention when the players finally had their day in court.

The NHL expansion in 1967 also marked the end of a remarkable thirty years during which the NHL had shrunk from a ten-team to a six-team league (three of them owned by the Norris family), while the number of games ballooned from 240 to 420 a season. Neatly, the owners had consolidated their power and maximized their profitability in that period. The "Original Six" teams were not unlike autonomous city states. Not all observers at the time thought the compact, incestuous formula worked to the benefit of the sport.

"Professional ice hockey's survival under the policies of greedy promoters who care little about the players and even less about the fans demonstrates the great paradox that even when this splendid and exciting game is awfully bad, it's still pretty good," Dan Parker wrote in *Sports Illustrated* in October 1957.

Ten years after Parker's scathing indictment of the NHL, the desire to find new markets and increased TV profits finally convinced the six established clubs to open the door and shed a little light on a game—and a business—closeted for too long. The six new clubs brought in under expansion meant new jobs for over 120 players, effectively doubling the number of players eligible for the pension plan overnight. The desire to expand also motivated the NHL finally to recognize Alan Eagleson's NHL Players' Association, "so long as it [continued] to represent over two-thirds of active players" in the NHL. (This recognition, however, was not done under any applicable labor legislation of the time, and to this day, the NHLPA is simply an organization voluntarily registered with Labour Canada. Most of its collective-bargaining agreements with the NHL have ignored key requirements of modern labor legislation.)

While it was a new day for hockey, the NHL governors had no intention of changing their business practises just because Alan Eagleson had popped into the scene. On pain of death, there would be no power-sharing between Jim Norris or Conn Smythe and the NHLPA. After all, an effective players' union—such as the one being organized by former United Steelworkers executive Marvin Miller in major-league baseball—could prove to be a major-league irritation to the paternal manner in which they'd run their business for fifty years. Having an aggressive players' association privy to the NHL Pension Society's innermost workings also might give them a window into the League's windfall profits from expansion and TV deals. If players knew how much the NHL was making, salary and other demands might shoot through the ceiling. Or the NHL might find itself charged with unfair labor practises or bargaining in bad faith, as if it were a steel company or a railroad, not a benevolent collection of sportsmen.

So it became incumbent on the owners, now fleshed out to twelve, to recognize the NHLPA but keep its prying eyes away from the business workings of the League. One simple move would go a long way to accomplishing this: the elimination of players from the board of directors of the Society, which controlled the administration and supervision of the plan.

Then the owners would have just one man to deal with: Alan Eagleson.

14

THE EAGLE'S NEST

"Al was proof to me that if you have the nerve to pull things off, there is not much you can't pull off," remarked his friend and former law partner Bob Watson.

In the years between his emergence as a savvy lawyer in the 1960s and his legal problems with the FBI in 1992, there didn't seem to be a deal or contract that Alan Eagleson couldn't pull off. Audacious to the point of foolhardiness, Eagleson developed a reputation as the slickest deal-maker in Canada. A lawyer, former member of the Ontario Legislature, former president of the Ontario Progressive Conservative Party, player agent to hundreds of NHL and other sports stars, self-made millionaire and hockey promoter, Eagleson was the man who marketed Bobby Orr and created the Canada Cup hockey tournament. Perhaps his greatest achievement of all was the creation of the legend of "The Eagle."

He was, without question, the best-connected man in Canada; his list of clients and friends ranged from former prime minister Brian Mulroney to Supreme Court justices to business executives to sports heroes. As well, he proved to be a most elusive target to his enemies, who for twenty-five years tried to curtail or stop his activities.

For a quarter-century, Eagleson performed maneuvers worthy of a contortionist, placing himself simultaneously on two, often three and sometimes four sides of the same deal. In his capacity as an agent, he concurrently represented players and management in the same negotiation. As international negotiator for Hockey Canada, he was promoter, talent-supplier and advertising executive all at once. As head of the NHLPA, he represented all the players, some of the players and none of the players, depending on the exigencies of the situation. His nerve in attempting these feats of sophistry and paralogism was surpassed only by his ability to convince so many that the result was in their own best interests.

"He was a bully, and he was profane, and he was ignorant," remembers Derek Holmes, who managed Team Canada in the 1970s. "Then, he'd be totally charming—he was a chameleon in that sense."

Eagleson did it all—or as much as he could—on a handshake basis, counting on loyalty and friendships to clinch the deals. It gave him the freedom to operate on the fly, an ability to improvise. "My agreement with Eagleson was based on a handshake," recalls former client Glen Sharpley, who played for Minnesota and Chicago in the 1970s before an eye injury forced him to retire. "There was nothing in writing; that's the way he always operated."

"It was all done on a handshake," remembers a business client. "He said that if I didn't do it that way there was no deal."

Eagleson's greatest accomplishment was to control the fractious NHL players when no one else had been able to do so. Through Brewer and the Maple Leafs he represented, he knew the innermost fears of the men who played the game. He could swear faster, talk louder and generally intimidate the stars of the NHL better than any goon who played the game.

"He was smart; he always had one big star on every team," says Norma Shack. "In Boston, it was Espo [Phil Esposito]. He won Espo over, and Espo would stand up at a meeting and say, 'He's a good guy, he's good for us,' and everyone would say fine. That happened in every dressing room."

It didn't hurt that Eagleson also had at least a half-dozen personal clients in each dressing room to spread the good word about his services. By using Orr, he convinced scores of NHLers that he was the man to get them top dollar in their contract talks with management (though he often did little or no negotiating for his journeymen clients). Later, by convincing the acquiescent Wayne Gretzky into multiple Canada Cups, he could convince other players to play for peanuts in the name of patriotism. Eagleson became the man who could get a journeyman client included on Team Canada or help a borderline candidate into the Hockey Hall of Fame through his contacts.

plan than was needed to guarantee the annual $300 benefit per player. While Eagleson was later to claim that the pension plan required $3,000 annually to maintain each player's benefits, the NHL knew the contribution needed was in fact closer to $1,800. The extra sums being contributed were creating large surpluses, surpluses that Manulife was reluctant to part with.

Manulife's contribution schedule had convinced the NHL that it could assume the players' contribution obligation itself and still save hundreds of dollars on its contributions each year. The NHL would tell the players the plan was fully funded as before, even though about $1,200 a year less was actually being contributed. Eagleson's strategy in the Owner/Player Council played right into NHL hands and cost the players millions of dollars.

When he sat down in 1969 to negotiate the terms under which the NHL assumed complete financing of the Pension Society, Eagleson was already on friendly terms with Charley Mulcahy, the secretary of the Boston Bruins* and the point man for the League in the negotiations. The proof of the League's conviction that it could do business with the bespectacled Torontonian was soon borne out in the results of those talks.

Eagleson entered the Owner/Player Council meetings apparently hoping to get the owners to invest more of the pension plan's assets in equities, which would bear higher returns. Ever-cautious, J. D. Ford advised the League that equities were too risky an investment for pensions. Eagleson countered by saying that if the League wouldn't invest their money as the players wished, then perhaps the NHL should simply make the players' contributions itself.

If the players weren't going to contribute any more, Ford and the NHL gladly replied, then maybe they shouldn't be on the board of directors telling the owners how to invest *their* money. This didn't sit too well with Eagleson, who contended that the players still wanted some say in how surpluses in the plan would be invested in the future.

No problem, replied the NHL. After we take over the players' annual contributions, there won't be any more surpluses. ("I would have to be blind to think there couldn't be," Ford admitted afterward.) At this point in the negotiating, Eagleson appears to have

---

* Mulcahy was later a director of Bobby Orr Enterprises, the company Eagleson set up to handle Orr's investments.

folded his hand, accepted the deal and decided to start up a separate, NHLPA-run investment fund that would use the annual $1,500 contributions the players had just saved.

Perhaps Eagleson truly believed that the owners' assumption of the players' financial contributions to the plan was a bargaining achievement. To the players he represented, most of whom didn't know a pension plan from a plough horse, having their annual $1,500 payment apparently assumed by the owners (as well as increases made to their insurance coverage) might well have appeared a coup for their new president.

But anyone with even a passing acquaintance with pension plans would have red-flagged the price he had paid. In exchange for the owners taking over the players' contributions and guaranteeing a $300 benefit per player per year of service, the NHLPA would be barred from making any additional requests with regard to benefits and television revenue for three years. *And* the players agreed to cease their representation on the board of directors of the Society. In short, they would trust the NHL to administer their plan fairly.

At least one of the NHL owners at that time understood what getting the players off the board meant. "It was a godsend for the owners," says Bill Putnam, a former owner of the Atlanta Flames and Philadelphia Flyers. "We had about two hours of meetings over three days ... I doubt the players really knew what happened. It was a charade, really ... disgraceful."

Later, John Ziegler, the president of the NHL from 1977 to 1992, would claim the decision to remove players from the board was initiated by the players. "The players asked not to participate," he said in a 1991 interview. "We didn't ask them. This was the Players' Association request." (Ziegler was not present at those 1969 meetings, however.)

Norm Ullman, one of the players involved in the negotiations at the time, remembers it differently. "It was the owners' idea to put us out of the Pension Society," he told *The Lawrence* (Massachusetts) *Eagle-Tribune* in 1991. "It was just done. I don't think the players had any notification of changes."

Lou Angotti was another of the players present during the negotiations. "I don't recall the players ever giving Al [Eagleson] the mandate to let players be taken off the pension board," he recalls today. "The thing that disturbs me, knowing what we know now, is that we trusted Al. Anything he said was gospel."

No one else could remember Eagleson having the right to negotiate *retired* players off the board, either, since he was not recognized in any official or unofficial way as their bargaining agent. But he did so, and the NHL accepted his actions.

Ford remembered how much the players trusted Eagleson at meetings of the Owner/Player Council. "There was [sic] quite a few of them at the table, but he was the one doing all the talking, as was always the case ... even when they were at the meetings they never said boo. They were just lumps in their chairs."

The players' removal from the board became crucial, because although it called itself a "pension society," the NHL plan bore little resemblance to typical Canadian pension societies. Pension societies are generally extremely democratic organizations. At Canada Steamship Lines, for instance, each plan participant is a member with a vote at annual meetings, of which the trustees are obligated to notify them. Changes in regulations and by-laws are reported to every member, as are the purchasing and selling of the securities in the plan.

Until 1969, NHL players at least had annual meetings they could attend, although little of any substance was offered. After 1969, players received no notice of annual meetings, nor did they have any rights at such a meeting. It was the very essence of an undemocratic institution. Investment decisions and amendments to the pension plan went unreported, and requests for such information by players were refused. Had they received such information, for instance, players might have seen that almost $1,200 a year less was being contributed to each player's pension.

In having the players withdraw from the administration of the Pension Society, Eagleson had simply given away one of the most powerful weapons the players had in collective bargaining. Without the players' presence on the board, the owners were now free to use surplus funds to take "contribution holidays" (let the surplus funds cover their annual obligation to the pension plan) and to carry on unencumbered by the annoying questions they had had to field through the 1950s and 1960s. And since pension improvements were about all players received from collective bargaining in the next twenty years, the mistake was magnified.

When pressed by critics of his achievements in collective bargaining, Eagleson has always claimed that it's unfair to judge events in the past by today's standards. "There's no sense second guessing ...

we did what was right at the time, and that's the best you can offer."
Yet comparisons made to events transpiring at the same time in baseball do not suggest Eagleson was doing what "was right at the time."
Marvin Miller had taken over the Major League Baseball Players'
Association in 1967, the same year Eagleson created the NHLPA. In a
similar labor climate—and with owners who enjoyed an antitrust
exemption from the U.S. Congress—Miller had made baseball players into the best-paid athletes in team sports.

At Miller's insistence, baseball players had remained on the board
of directors of their pension fund. When a dispute erupted in 1972
between the players and owners over a surplus that had accumulated in their pension plan, the players went on strike and won the
right to keep all the surplus in the settlement. According to Miller,
the MLB Players' Association's chief counsel until 1983, this was only
made possible because players had access to financial records
through their participation on the Pension Board, a right hockey
players had given away.

With dissent exiled from the Pension Society, all hockey owners
had to do was meet the minimum contributions calculated by Manulife and smile benignly—which was easy to do considering that
Eagleson's negotiating coup of having the NHL assume the players'
pension payments cost the League millions of dollars less than what
Eagleson was telling NHLPA members.

While many attribute dark motives to Eagleson's behavior in these
1969 negotiations, his failure to see the big picture is consistent with
future collective bargaining he did for the NHLPA. The results of
many of those negotiations suggest that Eagleson was out of his
depth when it came to pension, insurance and economic issues. In
part, this was due to the overwhelming claims made on his time by
his many other business and political concerns. No mortal could sustain Eagleson's pace and keep everything in order. The NHL players
consistently suffered the consequences of his fall-back-and-bluster
style at the bargaining table.

As well, Eagleson operated the NHLPA for most of twenty years
with just a skeleton staff; research and preparation were almost
unheard of in advance of collective bargaining. Eagleson bragged to
the NHLPA player representatives that this thrift saved millions, but
it never made up for what was lost in the way of salaries and benefits. Hockey players fell farther and farther behind their compatriots

in other sports as a result. But it was not until they had retired and started to collect their pensions that they realized the magnitude of those losses.

The bargaining process between the NHL and the NHLPA usually consisted of a series of disjointed policy quotes and veiled threats to journalists from Eagleson in the months leading up to the meetings, most of which were quickly swept away by an avalanche of propaganda from the NHL (which did believe in preparing for bargaining). A few crumbs of insurance or pension improvements were then loudly hailed as a breakthrough, and Eagleson went back to his myriad other concerns.

In truth, Eagleson, the legendary deal-maker, never seemed to thrive in the adversarial atmosphere of labor law, where you choose up sides for life. It somehow cramped his style not to have a vested interest on both sides of the deal. As well, he had more in common with the business people he saw across the table than the young hockey players he was paid handsomely to represent. It did not take long for his allegiances to soften in such an atmosphere.

Whether they fully understood the implications of what they'd given up in the 1969 pension negotiations or not, there was no objection from the NHLPA membership to any of the terms Eagleson had negotiated. He triumphantly reported to them in a letter on December 15, 1969, urging his members to invest the $1,500 they had saved in the Sportsmen's Mutual Fund he had just created as a registered retirement savings plan vehicle. (The Sportsmen's Fund, much to Eagleson's chagrin, did not attract much of the money the players saved and did not become a significant asset to the NHL Players' Association.)

NHL president Clarence Campbell also wrote the players to report on the same negotiations. Campbell's letter contained one additional point not mentioned in Eagleson's letter. According to the NHL president, "There will be no more *surplus funds* available to provide dividends in the form of additional pension benefits."

Campbell conveniently forgot to say in his letter *which* of the different types of surpluses in the pension plan the players would not be receiving again. The difference was crucial: while surpluses from excess contributions ("premium discounts") would no longer arise with the NHL taking over full funding of the plan, even the League's auditor admitted that the NHL knew there would still be surpluses generated by dividends on the plan's earnings ("experience rate" credits).

Campbell's letter is the only reference from that period to players forgoing any surpluses. The minutes of the 1969 meetings of the Owner/Player Council contained no mention of players agreeing to give them up. And when the Pension Society's board of directors met in 1970 for the final time with player representation, there was likewise no mention of the players renouncing future claims to surplus funds.

On the contrary, the business of the meeting contained two very specific motions by Norm Ullman dealing with the disposition of surpluses to players in the future. Ullman moved that the approximately $370,000 in surpluses arising from premium discounts on the purchase costs of annuity contracts in 1968 and 1969 be distributed equally among the players in the form of additional pension benefits. "And further, that any additional surpluses which may develop hereafter from these contracts shall be distributed on the basis of the same formula." The motion was unanimously accepted by the board of the Pension Society.

As well, it was reported that Manulife was releasing $412,793 (CDN) and $224,343 (US) from its reserves due to relaxation of government restrictions and improvement of the projected earnings. Once more, Ullman moved that this surplus be distributed equally among the eligible players' pensions, and that "any future distribution of dividends as a result of releases against players' contracts by Manufacturers Life Insurance Company be distributed on the same basis." Once more, the motion was unanimously accepted and the distributions were made to the players' pensions.

Clearly, the players thought they were staking out a proprietary interest in future surpluses from both premium discounts and experience-rate credits—with the owners' blessing. There is an obvious discrepancy between these actions taken at this meeting and Campbell's assertion that the players weren't entitled to any future surpluses, a claim the NHL later would use to justify reserving almost $20 million in surpluses to itself.

While the players felt protected as a result of the 1970 meetings, NHL owners had a separate agenda. They began making plans to grab experience-rate credits (the dividends produced by the plan's investments) for themselves. Unbeknownst to the players, in 1971 they began tracking the credits earned since the NHL took over complete funding of the plan in 1969 to produce experience credits available to the *owners* as reduction in premium.

In the twenty-four years since the negotiations, little has been done to clear up what transpired at the 1969 Owner/Player meetings over the pension plan. There was no formal, written agreement in which the players agreed not to claim any more surpluses. Campbell is dead, and Eagleson never expanded upon what he wrote to the players in December 1969 when he wrote his autobiography, *Power Play*.* And players were never asked to vote on the changes.

J. D. Ford claimed that—Campbell's letter notwithstanding—the NHL never questioned the players' entitlement to any surpluses that accrued based on their own contributions before 1969. And it did not dispute the players' ownership of at least a portion of the surplus when it divvied up the huge surpluses of the 1980s. According to Ford, Campbell simply believed such surpluses would be largely dispensed with when the owners took over full funding of the plan: "The purpose of this stuff is to set it up so that we could try to eliminate surpluses as much as possible."

The owners—under new NHL president John Ziegler— would later interpret the evidence of this period differently when first Bobby Baun and later Carl Brewer attempted to find out what happened. NHL lawyers would challenge the retired players by saying they had made a bad deal in 1969 and now—like spoilsports—wished to reinterpret the agreement.

The one aspect that all agree on now is that players lost the ability to monitor the Pension Society's activities first-hand as a result of Alan Eagleson's first big showdown with the NHL. The NHL would do nothing to inform or consult them for twenty years as they rewrote the agreement.

---

* Eagleson did praise Campbell's "early and unflagging" efforts on the pension, however, saying the NHL president "knew how essential it was."

15

DARK
AGES

For Bob Baun, the man who'd helped put Alan Eagleson in power, the decade that followed Eagleson's coronation constituted the Dark Ages of hockey. Retired from the game and ignored by its power structure, the former president of the NHL Players' Association could see that something had gone drastically wrong within the sport to which he'd given his heart and soul, and within the NHLPA, the democratic "voice of the players" he'd helped establish in 1967. He had only to look at his pension to see evidence that something was amiss.

"I knew we were only getting about 3.5 percent on our money," Baun says. "It was all my money in there, and that was wrong. If it had been their money, I would have said maybe you've got some control over it, but it was all my money. I was watching the interest rates go up. I said [my pension] was wrong for the amount I was getting back."

An exasperated Baun brought his questions about the NHL Pension Plan to investment expert Lorraine Mahoney in 1981. The only clues about the NHL Club Pension Plan and Trust—investments and its *modus operandi*—consisted of the bits and pieces of correspondence from the NHL and the certificates issued to the players. Even to an experienced businesswoman like Mahoney, there was little to shed light on how the plan had been handled. But she found enough to warrant more study.

"One of the things they hadn't caught in the certificates was a thing called a death-benefit reserve," recalls Mahoney. "To me, it represented the underlying value of the pension plan. Whatever is there by way of reserve provides the pension. Looking at the reserve versus what they were paying him just didn't make any sense. The reserve that was there at the time was capable of generating a much larger benefit than they were paying him." In fact, Mahoney estimated that there was more than $40 million in the fund at the time.

By the time Mahoney uncovered these shocking discrepancies for Baun in the early 1980s, much had changed in the hockey world Baun once knew. Old faces were gone, new teams had emerged and a competing league had surfaced, however briefly. In fact, only the ways of doing business with players remained the same.

John Ziegler, the former club lawyer for the Detroit Red Wings, had succeeded Clarence Campbell as president of the NHL. (Campbell died in 1980.) Bill Wirtz of the Chicago Black Hawks and Ed Snider of the Philadelphia Flyers had become the two most influential owners in the League. Kenneth Sawyer (who would later become NHL vice president of finance) had replaced J. D. Ford as the secretary-treasurer of the Pension Society.

European players were making inroads on the rosters of NHL clubs, forever altering the style of play and the Canadian hegemony when it came to talent. The Cleveland Barons (formerly Oakland Seals/California Golden Seals) had folded, but the addition of four other teams from the World Hockey Association meant there were now twenty-one teams in the NHL, with over four hundred players on their rosters. And Eagleson had graduated from being the Rexdale real-estate lawyer to being the self-styled "hockey czar," controlling not only the NHL Players' Association but international hockey events like the Canada Cup as well.

As Baun knew from his own turbulent experience in business, the world beyond hockey was changing as well. In contrast to the favorable conditions of the late 1970s, the economy of North America in the early '80s suddenly experienced a debilitating recession coupled with crippling interest rates that surpassed 20 percent in 1981, the highest rates of the century. The consumer price index went up twenty-three points in 1980-81, seriously eroding the value of investments and fixed incomes. All over North America, pension managers were looking for ways to protect the value of their assets from the threat of inflation.

At the NHL Pension Society, however, life went on as usual. There was nothing done to protect the buying power of Bob Baun's pension, or Allan Stanley's pension, or Carl Brewer's pension.

Increases in pensions were still being calculated at interest rates needed to guarantee the puny benefits promised in the 1950s and 1960s. Pensions were never boosted by surpluses in the plan that arose from the skyrocketing double-digit rates enjoyed by other investments in the late 1970s and early 1980s. Instead of safeguarding the buying power of the players' money in their care, the NHL was taking "contribution holidays" and preparing to withdraw almost half a million dollars from the fund. (This in spite of the many earlier undertakings to players in the letters patent, by-laws and trust agreements that no assets would ever revert to the member clubs.) Credits produced by the retired players' investments also funded the vesting of hundreds of new players into the plan. (The fifteen new clubs added since 1967 produced a 350 percent expansion of the participants.)

As Lorraine Mahoney points out, "When credits started to emerge from the plan, they should have started to do cost-of-living upgrades, transition-and-bridge benefits, widows' benefits, all sorts of things." The NHL Pension Society had gone from being "a boon to all present and future hockey players" to an "enormous cash cow for the NHL," in the words of Mahoney.

The NHL's laissez-faire attitude towards the retired players' pensions had completely compromised the value of those pensions. The personal contributions of players in the original plan had been devastated by the rampaging inflation of the 1970s and 1980s. According to the 1988 Ontario Task Force on Inflation Protection for Pension Plans, a $1,000 pension in 1965 would have seen its real value decline to $261 in 1985, and a $1,000 benefit in 1980 was worth just $634 by 1985.

The effect on money from the early days of the plan, when Baun and Brewer and Stanley began contributing, was even more stark. The $90 benefit promised in 1947 was worth just $11.84 in 1992 dollars, while the $180 benefit level of 1957 was worth only $38.55 in 1992. Conversely, retired players earning that $90-a-year benefit in 1992 would have needed $684 of today's dollars to purchase the same goods. The $300 benefit, which began in 1964, would need to be $1,229.16 to keep up with inflation.

While fully indexed pension plans are rare outside of governments, many private plans administered in Canada have a policy of voluntarily increasing pensions by 50 percent of the value of inflation. Players' unions in other sports had made upgrading retired players' pensions a key part of collective bargaining. Yet the NHL Club Pension Plan and Trust, which Clarence Campbell had repeatedly labelled "the best in all of sport," never lifted a finger to protect the pensions of retired hockey stars against inflation in the '70s and '80s. Nor did Alan Eagleson make retired players' pensions an issue for the NHLPA in his twenty-five-year term as its executive director.

The NHL also ignored provisions in its contracts with Manulife that might have upgraded those pensions. According to the policy, Manulife was obliged to purchase the normal annuity stipulated in the collective-bargaining agreements, or "... if greater, the amount of the annuity that the member's Basic Contribution will purchase ..." In other words, Manulife was obliged to provide players with the full value of the monies contributed on their behalf by the NHL or themselves, even if it exceeded the basic "defined benefit" of $90 or $180, or whatever was the standard at the time.

In practice, the only improvements made were at the owners' whim, and by 1981, nothing in the way of a surplus distribution had occurred in a decade to bolster the pensions of the participants in the NHL pension plan. J. D. Ford, the auditor for the Society, recognized this problem, but when asked in 1992 if the NHL had done anything to protect the value of retired players' pensions, he replied, "No, nothing was done."

"And nothing was contemplated?" he was asked.

"Not that I am aware of."

Inflation of the participant base was another concern. Even the Pension Society acknowledged that the wholesale influx of new participants was hurting the value of their predecessors' pensions. "As you pointed out yourself," Yvon Chamberland, actuary for the Society, wrote J. D. Ford in 1976, "older participants are paying for the newer ones through forfeited dividends."

"It just wasn't right that these people weren't getting it [the benefit of the credits]," acknowledged Ford in 1992.

The overriding theme of the NHL Dark Ages for Bob Baun was the complete disregard for the participants in the plan. Major changes were incorporated without a word to those most affected, and no input was sought from outside the narrow corridors of the Pension Society. Baun later discovered, for instance, that when the NHL finally got around to incorporating the changes brought about by its 1969 "deal" with Alan Eagleson, it had had to do a major restructuring of the pension plan. The guaranteed annual benefit of $300 a year promised by the NHL to the players upon retirement exceeded the maximum amount allowed by law in Canada.

To honor its 1969 "deal" with the neophyte NHL Players' Association, the Pension Society was obliged to register the plan with Revenue Canada, the Pension Commission of Ontario and the applicable authorities in the United States as a "defined contribution" scheme rather than a "defined benefit" scheme.*

While to the layman such terms seem comparable, in legal terms the difference was significant. Calling the NHL pension plan a "defined contribution" scheme put the member clubs' ownership of any surplus in question. In the "defined contribution" scheme, players were entitled upon retirement to whatever pension benefit could be obtained from the proceeds of the contribution made years earlier—just as the Manulife contract had promised. The owners would get nothing.

While the plan was officially registered as a "defined contribution" scheme, the NHL continued to run it as a "defined benefit" plan and successfully stonewalled the players. Twenty years later, in a 1991 interview, John Ziegler was still carrying on the charade, insisting that the surplus in the pension plan arose when the NHL had been "overcharged" while purchasing defined benefits for retired players.

"It's like you go buy a set of [four] tires and you pay $100 apiece," offered Ziegler. "And then there was a sale on, and they forgot to tell you that ...You go back and you say, 'Gee, I hear you have a sale on and you charged me $100 [instead of $75].' And they said, 'You're right ... here's $100.'"

The NHL's brief prepared in 1992 in response to the retired players' lawsuit echoed Ziegler's whitewash without the whitewalls. It insisted that the change to "defined contributions" in 1972 had simply been a bookkeeping procedure, and the pension plan had remained a "defined

---

* The vast majority of privately funded pension plans in Canada have been "defined benefit" schemes. The "defined benefit" scheme favored the NHL clubs; once they had produced the promised benefit to a player of $300 a year, they could claim any excess money over and above that figure. Thus, it was in the NHL's interest to continue portraying the plan as a "defined benefit" scheme. With that much money on the line, no Revenue Canada regulations were going to stop the NHL and the Pension Society from publicly describing it as a "defined benefit" plan.

benefit" scheme. But because neither Bob Baun nor any of the other participants had been informed about the changes, let alone about their implications, no one could call Ziegler and the Pension Society to account for this unilateral change in the rules.

While it had plenty of time to alter the pension-plan regulations behind the players' backs and redirect money for the NHL owners' uses, the Pension Society had little enthusiasm for its duties as trustee for the players' interests. For example, it continued using the Manulife group-annuity contract started in 1952 to fund the plan well into the 1980s, even though such vehicles had been considered as "dead as the dodo" by pension and investment experts since the 1960s.

The group-annuity contract was inflexible, unresponsive to changes in the marketplace and a money-loser for players. Money purchase plans, group RRSPs and deferred profit-sharing schemes had long since become the vehicles of choice for pension purposes. "The group annuity was the most arcane way of doing things by the 1980s," observes Mahoney.

The NHL's group annuity remained, in spite of advice from its own advisers who said that Manulife "was surprisingly amenable to changes and have indicated that they would be prepared to transfer the value of the group-annuity policies to a pooled fund policy without any significant change."

"I surmise that nothing was happening because the NHL did not understand how pension plans work," observes Mahoney. "I couldn't discover in any of my dealings [with the NHL] the involvement of a professional, anyone in the whole relationship who had a knowledge of pensions on the NHL side."

A likely explanation for the Pension Society sticking with the group annuity was that it guaranteed the owners would never be asked to make up deficits in the plan in poor investment years. In the late 1970s and early '80s, for instance, returns on investment in most major Canadian pension plans were negative, and so the sponsors of those plans were forced to contribute additional money to guarantee them. The NHL, with its group annuity scheme, was not forced to make up shortfalls.*

---

* The blame for the low level of pensions doesn't rest with Manulife's investment department. Figures from the 1970s show Manulife had one of the best investment track records in Canada.

"It was a case of let sleeping dogs lie," Mahoney contends. "No one was complaining or rocking the boat from the NHL." As well, under an RRSP scheme, the League would lose control of the money in the plan. "It would permit the player to surrender the plan and take his money out even if he is still an active player," the NHL was told in a 1972 memo from actuaries looking into plan changes.

With the pension plan causing them few restless nights, the NHL executives who doubled on the board of directors of the Pension Society had time for other matters. They spent most of their time and energies in the '70s fighting the twin plagues of competition from the upstart World Hockey Association and investigations from the U.S. Justice Department's Anti-Trust Division.

The WHA (which had begun operations in 1972) was the only positive labor development to emerge for hockey players in their fifty years of dealing with the NHL. For the first time, there was a free market in hockey talent, as the rival league signed stars like Bobby Hull, Gerry Cheevers, Derek Sanderson, Bernie Parent and dozens more. Especially galling to owners like Harold Ballard in Toronto were the raises of 300, 500, even 1,000 percent offered to their players by WHA clubs.

This seller's market sent a shiver of dread into unreconstructed monopolists like Ballard and Bill Wirtz of Chicago, who tried to play hardball with the players in negotiations. Ballard lost a half-dozen players to the WHA as a reward for his intransigence, while Bobby Hull reluctantly left Chicago when Wirtz balked at matching the million-dollar offer for the greatest Black Hawk of all time. Hull could only shake his head to see Chicago reject the same million-dollar price tag it had placed on Frank Mahovlich ten years earlier.

The talent raids by the WHA catapulted hockey players to the top average salary in North American team sports by 1977. Increases to benefits and salaries—which had failed to arrive with the inception of Alan Eagleson's NHLPA—were instead created by a rival league. Despite teams folding or being transferred during the seven-year war between the NHL and the WHA, it remained a lucrative time to be a hockey player.

"It was hard to believe there was money to be made in hockey," marvels Jim Dorey, who jumped from Toronto to New England of the WHA. "You didn't need a summer job all of a sudden; you could work and concentrate on your hockey career like athletes do today, which made for a better presentation for fans."

That honeymoon ended in 1979 when four of the WHA's remaining six teams (Winnipeg, Quebec, New England and Edmonton) agreed to join the NHL. The NHL called it an "expansion" but in reality it was a merger of the two leagues—a merger facilitated by the ubiquitous Alan Eagleson, the man representing the only group who stood to lose from the loss of the WHA: the players.

Eagleson had already assisted NHL owners during the war with the WHA. In 1977, NHL clubs claimed financial ruin and asked Eagleson to help them institute a buy-out provision, where owners could dump players at one-third the balance of their contracts. Instead of leaping to the defense of his members, reminding the public that even the last man on an NHL roster represents the top 2 or 3 percent of all the employees in a very lucrative business, Eagleson actively participated in purging what he called "fringe players," men who were not so fringe that they couldn't pay his NHLPA salary.

"Owners never balk at paying a great hockey player what he's worth," Eagleson argued. "What really upsets them is paying an average player an inflated salary. The players who are out of work are players who in some cases should never have been employed." Eagleson's sympathies in this matter were clear and at loggerheads with the members' best interests.

With absolutely no concession to the NHLPA, Eagleson allowed the NHL to reopen the 1975 collective-bargaining agreement so that the buy-out clause could be put into effect. Owners were thus allowed to escape their legally binding contracts with players they only recently had been so desperate to acquire. It was "something the NHLPA can be proud of, done strictly in the interests of the game," Eagleson crowed. What the union leader was doing helping owners put his members out of work became a moot point in the flurry of self-congratulation.

Eagleson's conflicting interests were never more clearly illustrated than in the NHL-WHA merger of 1979. As part of its collective-bargaining agreement with the NHL, the Players' Association could reopen negotiations in the event of a merger between the WHA and the NHL. It was a golden opportunity for the players to obtain the same concessions on free agency, arbitration procedures and benefits that the National Basketball Association players had won when the NBA merged with the American Basketball Association in 1976. Eagleson had said as much at various times, promising that he would invoke anti-trust law if the players didn't get what they wanted in any merger.

Predictably, the NHL owners cried poor in 1979—just as the NBA leaders had done in 1976—saying a third, maybe half the League, would fold if liberalized player movement was allowed under a revised CBA. Chronically inept franchises like Pittsburgh and Detroit were on life-supports. Hockey in Canada might be jeopardized.

"Unless we can maintain some form of equalization for free agents and keep collective bargaining intact," John Ziegler proclaimed as he circled the NHL wagons, "several owners will be forced into a position of re-examination, deciding whether it's worth their while to continue."

There was rhetoric in the owners' camp about toughing it out if the players said no. But everyone within the NHL knew differently. They needed the players on board to avoid anti-trust scrutiny.

While a U.S. Senate subcommittee had examined the financial picture of basketball before the NBA-ABA merger—and found the NBA's claims of poverty to be largely rhetoric—no substantive documentation was ever presented to back the claims of hockey's owners. Nor was any rationale ever advanced for why incompetent businessmen should be propped up or their franchises not moved to markets that might support hockey better.

In its pre-merger propaganda, the NHL trumpeted box-office figures and its modest TV revenues as the whole truth and nothing but—all the while ignoring the fact that most teams received revenue from owning their own buildings, concessions or parking, along with other lucrative revenue sources. Nor did owners discuss with players the multitude of tax breaks they received that allowed them to depreciate player contracts, the purchase price of their franchises or their contributions to the pension plan.

When the owners failed to remember these perks, Eagleson did nothing to jog their memories. "Either he knew and did nothing about it, or he didn't know and is a fool," says Brewer. "And I haven't heard anyone describe Alan Eagleson as stupid."

Eagleson had begun negotiations on the WHA merger talking tough, saying the players wanted more freedom of movement and $12 million of the expansion fees; later he said the NHLPA wouldn't settle for less than $9 million. By the time of the meetings in Nassau, however, he was downgrading those estimates, saying a package of $7.5 million in benefits—with no freer movement for free agents—would do the trick. (NHLPA documents later revealed that the benefits cost the League nowhere near $7.5 million. In fact, the cost was as little as $200,000 a year.)

Eagleson convinced the voluble NHLPA president, Phil Esposito— who has never been confused with a labor-relations specialist—that approving the benefits package and eliminating the WHA as painlessly as possible for the NHL was in the "best interests of hockey." Of course, Eagleson had no research to prove such a claim as he begged Esposito to "search your soul" for the answer; still, Esposito swallowed Eagleson's entreaty hook, line and sinker.

Having been advised by their executive director that hockey Armageddon awaited the players if they drove too hard a bargain, the players meekly acquiesced to the cash-strapped owners' demand for a merger. Phil Esposito's brother Tony, the Chicago goalie and a future NHLPA president, acknowledged the owners' triumph but saw it as necessary in the circumstances. "But I'm worried about the game, with so many owners losing so much money. When we agreed to the new deal, we gave the owners a chance to get things straightened out a little," he intoned.

Five years after the deal was done, Edmonton's general manager, Glen Sather, told *Sports Illustrated* "... that whatever the players wanted, they could have gotten. They would have gotten some concessions [if they had held out for them]."

A subdued Phil Esposito confessed, "I was like his [Eagleson's] puppet. I admit that."

If the NHL was hurting for money before the merger, it wasn't hurting for long after it. The League received a whopping $24-million transfusion from the four WHA clubs joining the fold; it dumped extraneous player contracts onto the new teams; and it regained its monopoly position with the players. Had it been in Eagleson's power, he'd have given the League a major TV deal in the United States as well. The WHA merger positioned the NHL perfectly for the 1980s, a decade of unparalleled growth and prosperity for the owners.

NHL players, meanwhile, soon fell from first to fourth in terms of salaries and benefits among the North American team sports. Instead of free agency, impartial arbitration and revenue sharing, the NHL players had won a small increase in the annual pension benefit (the extra $250 per year in pension benefits cost the NHL a one-time payment of approximately $2,900 for a twenty-five-year-old player in

1979) and a few fringe items as a result of the merger. The changes were so slight that the League merely extended the current collective-bargaining agreement from 1980 to 1982. It would take ten years—and the elimination of Eagleson from the bargaining process—before NHL players would start to recoup the losses to their income and freedom of movement suffered under the Eagleson-orchestrated merger.

Eagleson had talked tough with the owners before the negotiations, but when it came time to deliver on the WHA merger, this man of action was inexplicably rendered mute. "I wanted to find out what the players thought," he said afterward. "I studiously sat back and avoided [taking part in] any discussion."

Had he taken a proactive part in the discussion, Eagleson might have jeopardized his business relationship with the owners; he needed their cooperation and sufferance in his other interests, including international hockey. In the end, it appeared that he had sacrificed the players' causes, not for the best interests of hockey, but for his own best interests.

The NHL players did better by the merger than the WHA players, however. The WHA players never voted on whether to accept the merger, and many lost their WHA pensions. The NHL, on the other hand, paid the WHA Players' Association director Ron Roberts (a former college aquaintance of John Ziegler's) $250,000 to "wind up the business of the WHAPA."

While their so-called union leader waxed and waned on their behalf, players received help from outside the hockey fraternity in ending the restrictive "reserve clause" that Carl Brewer disputed. The U.S. Justice Department became interested in the NHL and its monopolistic practises in the late 1960s when rejected bidders for expansion teams turned to Washington for help. In particular, the Justice Department was concerned with the terms of the reserve clause.

By 1971, it had launched a full-scale investigation. Agents of the U.S. government seized documents from the NHL head offices in New York and Montreal in 1972. Interest on Capitol Hill in Washington coincided with WHA lawsuits that claimed the NHL was in violation of the Sherman Anti-Trust Act, using monopolistic tactics to prevent players from switching to the rival league.

Faced with a congressional investigation of the NHL, or even an FBI probe, in 1974 Clarence Campbell unilaterally announced a new compensation scheme for players who had played out their option and wished to sign with a new club. The compensation to the team signing a player was so punitive, however, that under its guidelines only a handful of players considered trying to move, while even fewer went through with the futile exercise. But it convinced the Justice Department to discontinue its investigation.

The NHL Players' Association's acceptance of the sham free agency followed the next year when it concluded its first collective-bargaining agreement with the NHL in 1975. If the terms of the agreement were questionable, then its legality was even more in doubt. The agreement, and subsequent collective-bargaining agreements until 1992, neither conform nor purport to conform to any of the labor codes in any of the jurisdictions where the NHL carries on business. No secret ballots were held, printed copies of the agreement were often unavailable at the time of acceptance, election of the officers of the NHLPA was never ratified by the full membership—the list would make John L. Lewis spin in his grave.

"I don't recall ever hearing about a vote," says Bobby Hull. "The only vote I ever heard about was on a raise to Eagleson. There was nothing positive for the players."

16

FOREIGN AFFAIRS

The inaugural collective-bargaining agreement negotiated between the NHL and the NHLPA in 1975 was remarkable for more than its historic significance. Typically, the agreement co-signed by Alan Eagleson and Clarence Campbell did not contain any ground-breaking advances won by the players: there was no movement away from the dreaded reserve clause, nor any breakthrough on power-sharing with the owners. The 1975 agreement did, however, introduce the idea of funding increases to the NHL pension plan using profits from international hockey ventures sanctioned by the NHL and NHLPA—the first agreement of its kind in pro sports.

While Alan Eagleson showed little inclination to immerse himself in pension law, he knew the law of the financial jungle like no man alive. When unlikely hero (and Eagleson client) Paul Henderson scored the winning goal in Game Eight of the 1972 Canada-USSR showdown series—a goal that propelled Canada into ecstasy—Eagleson appears to have been the first to recognize that international hockey could become a financial wellspring for himself, his clients and the NHL itself.

Fans tired of the plodding dump-and-chase style of game employed in North America had seen the future of hockey in the Soviets' swift, creative offense, and Eagleson realized that they would pay premium prices to see Kharlamov, Yakushev and Tretiak against the NHL's best. Advertisers, in turn, would fall all over themselves to be associated with any event that had the national impact the 1972 series demonstrated.

The gross revenues for the 1972 series from TV and radio broadcast rights—which Eagleson had purchased through an unholy consortium of Bobby Orr and Harold Ballard—were $2.19 million, and the series showed a book profit of $800,000. Half of this reportedly went to the NHL Pension Society, enabling owners to increase the annual pension benefit from $300 to $500 per player per year of service. A golden egg like this was simply too good for the NHLPA's executive director to resist.

So, in just three years, agent and union leader Alan Eagleson transformed himself into the ringmaster of a hockey and commercial circus that pitted hockey nations—instead of NHL clubs—against each other as the top attraction in the sport. After years of frustration, Eagleson and his hand-picked team of players, coaches, officials and lackeys showed Canadians what it took to win consistently at the world level; whether Canadians wanted to keep paying that price became less and less certain.

As with most of Eagleson's coups, international hockey was a single-minded display of opportunism, effort and bare-knuckled aggression. When Henderson leapt into the arms of Phil Esposito and Yvan Cournoyer at the Luzhniki Ice Palace in Moscow that September evening in 1972, he had reversed a long, painful journey through the national psyche, and halted a public flogging administered to the pride and prejudices of the country. Hockey was, is and always will be "our" game to Canadians, yet for an interminable period Canadian teams had been beaten, robbed, cheated and otherwise humiliated by the Soviets and their cronies in the International Ice Hockey Federation (IIHF). As Carl Brewer learned when he joined Father David Bauer's team in 1967, the cards were hopelessly stacked against Canadians.

The thirst for revenge, and for regaining Canada's rightful place atop the hockey world was so profound that Pierre Trudeau made overhauling the hockey establishment a plank in his political platform in the election of 1968. The goal was to organize, promote and maintain a hockey program of the calibre that would supply a steady stream of players to wreak havoc on the invidious Soviets and Czechs and Swedes. It was one of those rare political promises destined to be kept. And it served to allow the Tory fox—Alan Eagleson—into the Liberal Party's henhouse.

Upon taking office, Trudeau directed John Munro, then federal minister for sport and fitness, to create an advisory committee that would chart Canada's future hockey direction. The committee—headed by Carl Brewer's father-in-law, Harold Rea, a Toronto businessman—proposed a body that would include all of the traditional elements of the hockey establishment in Canada, or "snowbankers" as Clarence Campbell referred to them. The NHL, the Canadian Amateur Hockey Association, the corporate sector, the three levels of government—all were to have a part in the newly founded "Hockey Canada," but none was supposed to dominate. However, with Alan Eagleson aboard as the NHLPA representative, the chances of that balance of power remaining intact were slim.

In its early days, Hockey Canada seemed a godsend. It soon obtained the rights to host the 1970 world championships in Winnipeg and received agreement to allow a limited number of professionals to compete for Canada. But the best intentions soon foundered on familiar shoals. The new hockey board was jolted when the IIHF—run by Bunny Ahearne from that hockey hotbed of London, England—and the International Olympic Committee—run by crusty patrician Avery Brundage—reneged on the promise to let pros play. In frustration and anger, Hockey Canada pulled Canadian teams out of international play and gave up the world championships in Winnipeg.

This impasse was just the opportunity Eagleson needed to impose himself on the situation. While other earnest Hockey Canada types used established political channels to negotiate Canada's return to the international arena, Eagleson worked the back rooms and corridors of the Soviet bloc on his own, using his personal brand of negotiations. Eagleson understood that cold, hard cash was the way to oil the machinery run by the Soviet hockey commissars. Make them plenty of western currency, he reasoned, and they will come around to Canada's point of view.

Eagleson's method successfully circumvented Ahearne and froze the old schemer out of the hockey equation. While the diplomats tippy-toed, Eagleson strong-armed the meeting of "our best" versus "their best." But not everyone was left in awe.

"The relationship between us and Al was one of antagonism, constant antagonism," lamented Hockey Canada board member Lou Lefaive, who'd been left in Eagleson's dust. "Anybody who suggested that there was something wrong was immediately labelled as being a Communist."

Eagleson employed the same tactic with the NHL. Using the NHLPA and his own personal clients as a lever, Eagleson persuaded Clarence Campbell and the NHL to allow players under contract to

League clubs to battle against the Soviets. He softened the blow by permitting the exclusion of NHL defectors like Bobby Hull, J. C. Tremblay and Gerry Cheevers from the team. ("As an old hockey man, I am proud that there are no contract breakers representing our country," intoned the patriotic Conn Smythe.) He appeared to have won a total victory from a group of businessmen not given to philanthropy.

Eagleson's blunt, no-holds-barred approach—coupled with the requisite "oil" in the right gears of the Soviet system—eventually produced the long-awaited agreement for the 1972 series. The turbulent eight games in which Canada lost, then won, then lost, then won the series by the slimmest of margins made many reputations and careers, but none more so than Eagleson's. From his inescapable presence behind the scenes to his wrestling with the KGB in front of an international TV audience, his was the single enduring personality that shaped the most memorable event in Canadian sports.

"He is what Canada is," proclaimed fellow Hockey Canada board member Chris Lang. "Trudeau isn't, Eagleson is!"

Unfortunately for Eagleson—whose dishevelled shirt-tails and raised finger led one writer to call him "a walking diplomatic disaster"—his efforts weren't seen in quite so flattering a light back home. While Henderson and the other players received the credit for the win, he was vilified by many of his countrymen who found his brawling, profane image offensive and embarrassing.

Stung by what he perceived as the ingratitude of Canadians, Eagleson pulled back from international hockey. Having strong-armed Team Canada to an artistic and financial success in 1972, he needed to consolidate his power as the international hockey impresario so that he might never be second-guessed again. Inadvertently, it was something Eagleson *didn't* do that helped him achieve that goal. Once again, Hockey Canada's shortcomings offered him a chance at total power.

Starving for cash and struggling with its mandate to upgrade the level of hockey in the country, Hockey Canada decided to mount another Canada-USSR series in 1974. But Eagleson objected to the timing; for a litany of reasons real and imagined, he was going to sit this one out. Without the executive director of the NHLPA, there would be no NHL players. Undaunted, Hockey Canada moved ahead, using an all-star team assembled from the World Hockey Association.

Without Eagleson to "convince" the Soviets and to assemble the corporate support, the series foundered. The Soviets won the series handily, and there was no financial windfall for Hockey Canada. (Gross revenues from TV were only $190,000.) It wasn't helped by the concurrent announcement from Marc Lalonde, the new federal minister of sport, that the government was handing over the responsibility for organizing a World Cup of hockey in 1976 to none other than Alan Eagleson, the reluctant cold warrior.

At the last moment, Eagleson came on board to keep the 1974 series from degenerating into a complete financial disaster, but his belated cameo appearance only made his absence from the planning process more pronounced. By simply withholding his services, Eagleson had superseded the Ottawa bureaucrats and the well-meaning leaders of Canadian amateur hockey as the most powerful figure in the sport. With the political backing of the federal government—a Liberal government at that—Hockey Canada was now almost totally dependent on him to actualize dreams of having ex-pros help develop Canadian minor hockey skills programs.

"Once he liked an idea, he would begin to run with it," wrote Douglas Fisher, the putative chairman of Hockey Canada at the time. "But if he didn't push for it ... it never happened."

Eagleson didn't push for using former pros to teach kids, but he did use his position to exert complete control over the board of Hockey Canada. "He gave people the impression—rightly or wrongly—that he could bring the players to the table," remembers Derek Holmes. "Up until that time, no one could." In practice if not in theory, he dictated Canada's hockey policy on training camps to trading cards from 1975 onward, and woe unto those who tried to challenge that authority for the next seventeen years.

But Hockey Canada was just one of Eagleson's many hats. By 1975, he was pursuing his own agenda on other fronts as well: he was fund-raising for the first Progressive Conservative leadership bid by a Quebec corporate lawyer named Brian Mulroney; starting his own private law practice after departing Blaney, Pasternak; running a sports agency consisting of hundreds of clients; and taking on the Canada Cup responsibilities. There was simply no time in this busy schedule for drawn-out research and negotiations with the NHL on the first collective-bargaining agreement in 1975, and no inclination to engage in any long-term planning. What Eagleson needed for the 1975 agreement had to be simple, quick, and look like a triumph for both sides.

Eagleson's proclivity for short-term gain at the expense of long-term pain was both his greatest strength in times of crisis and his greatest weakness in times of stability. In a 1979 letter, Douglas Fisher summed up that duality: "An aspect of Alan I found astounding, and I still wonder at, is his inability to do any synoptic thinking or planning ahead. Despite his quicksilver, he's not reflective about the long-range future."

Thus, the idea of increasing NHL pension benefits through the profits from international hockey (as had happened in the 1972 series) was heaven-sent for Eagleson. It was simple, it was quick, and Eagleson would look like a hero to everyone. The players thought he'd won an important concession from the NHL by getting a share of international money, an accomplishment he would cite to justify continuing his other conflicting jobs outside the NHLPA. Meanwhile, the League—which was already enjoying benefits thanks to Eagleson's 1969 "deal" with the players—would get some fresh money from international hockey with which to further reduce its pension obligations.

The first tour by Soviet club teams—Red Army and Wings of the Soviet—dovetailed neatly with the first NHL-NHLPA collective-bargaining agreement in 1975. As a trade-off for allowing star NHL players to participate in the tours—and more importantly in the first Canada Cup the next year—owners received an infusion of cash from the international hockey venture to offset soaring salaries and dwindling attendance.

The formula worked out in the 1975 agreement called for international hockey profits in any year to be divided according to a prescribed formula among Hockey Canada, the NHL and the NHLPA. A 1988 NHLPA memo to players from Eagleson promised that players would be the sole beneficiaries of the NHL and NHLPA's portion of those profits. "The National Hockey League and the National Hockey League Players' Association shares will be directed towards pension contributions," wrote Alan Eagleson.

Calling NHL players "joint venturers in international hockey," John Ziegler echoed the sharing theme. "All of the profits [of international hockey] go into the players' pensions," he told the Empire Club of Toronto on April 6, 1989. "Not only regular pension but also supplemental pension." This lofty promise was never set in writing by the NHL, however.

Any of the NHLPA's profits from international hockey that were not applied directly to the NHL pension plan were to be gathered in the NHLPA's "Bonus Pension Pool" for investment and later distribution to players who had been active in the League in those years. (Sometime in the middle 1980s, the name of the "Bonus Pension Pool" was changed without explanation to the "Employee Benefit Plan.")

For 1975, the NHL owners agreed to use these monies to increase the pension benefit from $500 to $750 per player per year of service. Players' contributions from their international hockey profits provided half the added amount. In effect, the NHLPA underwrote $125, or one-sixth of the annual benefit, through its own participation in these games.

With the WHA merger in 1979, the owners upped the annual benefit to $1,000 per player per year of service; once again, the NHLPA contributed half of the increase from its share of international hockey. Now, the NHLPA contribution provided $250 (or one-quarter of the annual benefit) from its portion of international hockey profits.

There were several wrinkles to this deal, of course. One concerns how much must be invested today to guarantee a payoff upon retirement. While these pension increases seem impressive on the surface to the layman, they are less generous in reality. For instance, to guarantee a player the promised $1,000 a year for life at age forty-five, the NHL had to set aside a one-time payment of $2,498.22 at 8 percent interest when that player reached twenty-five.

Another wrinkle was that players were now coerced into playing for next to nothing in the international games by the NHL and Eagleson under the guise of enhancing their pensions. "The thing that all the players have to remember," Team Canada coach Mike Keenan (then an Eagleson client) told *The Toronto Star* in 1991, "is all these monies are for the pension plan." That message apparently sank in with Eagleson's membership. "We end up with more money in the pension because of the international games we play," Cam Neely of Boston declared before playing a team from the Soviet Union in December 1990.

Yet, no matter how much was grossed by players in international hockey in any year, it didn't increase their NHL pensions by one cent. The profits from Canada Cups and Soviet tours simply helped to pay the NHLPA's obligations as already promised in the collective-bargaining agreement. The hard-won patriotic efforts by Wayne Gretzky and others simply defrayed the owners' obligations of maintaining the $1,000-a-year benefit.

As well, players didn't have to play a single international game to guarantee the increases collectively bargained with the League. When the NHLPA issued a flyer entitled "The NHLPA Bonus Pension History" in 1983, it neglected to mention that the NHL was liable for the full amount of the increase if international hockey did not produce a profit. So if there had been no revenue from a Soviet tour or Canada Cup in some year, the owners were still obliged to pay the full benefit.

Finally, despite rhetoric to the contrary from Eagleson and Ziegler, the NHL was never obliged in writing to contribute its share of international hockey money to the NHL pension plan. Pension Society director Ken Sawyer—who was an NHL vice president at the same time—testified in 1992 that the NHL had always reserved the right to do what it pleased with that money, and had used its share from the profits of international hockey for other purposes when it saw fit. In 1993, new NHL commissioner Gary Bettman wrote to Carl Brewer, saying that the NHL's share went to NHL clubs for "general purpose use." The "joint partnership" of the NHL and the NHLPA was really a hollow promise.

The 1975 collective-bargaining agreement marked the final participation in the Pension Society by seventy-year-old Clarence Campbell, who by this point was coming to the end of his thirty-one years as NHL president. As Campbell's health deteriorated and the NHL board of governors became wracked by factional fighting over his successor, the administration of the Pension Society was allowed to drift. Despite the significant changes brought on by the inclusion of international hockey money in the plan in 1975, there was no meeting of the board of directors in 1976. After the retirement of Campbell in 1977, the board failed to meet again for four full years, until 1981.

Not that representation in the 1980s produced greater vigilance on the part of the trustees. In fact, the management of the Pension Society displayed an absurd streak worthy of Monty Python. While a member of the Hartford Whalers' administration, Gordie Howe was elected as an associate member of the Pension Society from 1982-86. Howe was subsequently elected to the board of directors of the Society from 1984-86. Yet, Howe never attended a meeting in that time. The former star was never asked by anyone if he wished to serve, nor was he ever notified of his election. When he finally was apprised of the honor bestowed on him, Howe phoned the Pension Society to say he was unqualified for the position and would not accept the draft of the NHL to serve. Undaunted, the Society continued to list him as a director, though he never once attended a meeting of the august organization. Howe's name continued to be listed as a member of the Society's board until 1986. (In cross-examination, Ken Sawyer could only point to one meeting where Howe's name appeared. It was the meeting that had nominated Howe to the Board.)

Or consider the letter to Ken Sawyer of the Society from Arthur Gans, a lawyer representing the Maple Leafs, in 1986: "I suspect I was more confused at the conclusion of Thursday's meeting in respect of the pension-fund issue than I was at the commencement of same. I see, however, that I am a member of the Pension Society and I believe I have an affirmative obligation to insure that I not only understand the issue at hand, but receive and review all relevant documentation..."

If the experience of Gans and Howe is typical, it appears that the Pension Society was also a *secret* society to a number of its members, so secret they didn't know they belonged. The confusion at the board level mirrored the confusion at the participant level, and little seems to have been accomplished in the seven years bridging Campbell and Ziegler.

In fact, the only real activity in the Pension Society in the second half of the 1970s and early 1980s consisted of the Society's actuary Yvon Chamberland trying to extract better experience-rate credits—the dividends on investments in the plan—from Manulife, a process that was like pulling teeth.

Chamberland knew that Manulife had built up a large reserve since its last release in 1971, but the insurance company was slow to release the funds. As long as Manulife held so much of its money, the Pension Society would never be able to move to another insurance company. Chamberland urged Ford to "get tougher" with Manulife about releasing the reserves it held.

After years of work, the dogged Chamberland finally met with success in freeing up some reserves. Manulife informed the Pension Society it was releasing $2,993,262 in experience-rate credits calculated as of June 30, 1982.

While the NHL confidently asserted its rightful claim to part of this surplus distribution in court ten years later, the League appeared less certain in 1981. In January, the Pension Society once again sought the advice of American lawyer Marcus Grayck on ownership of these latest surplus funds—the first to emerge since 1971.

Grayck, who'd had a major hand in drawing up many of the previous trust documents, advised the Pension Society that the players should be entitled to any credits earned on their own contributions before 1969. On all contributions made by the NHL clubs, Grayck concluded, the NHL had "carte blanche."*

However, when Grayck drew up his opinions on surpluses in 1971 and again in 1981, the NHL failed to supply him with the crucial minutes of the 1970 Pension Society meeting at which Norm Ullman's motions dealing with the future dispositions of surplus were made. Nor did he know that two subsequent distributions of experience-rate credits in 1971 and 1972 had gone exclusively to players' pensions.

The instructions from Ken Sawyer, the new vice president of the Society, to Grayck neatly skirted these precedents and asked him to assert once again that players had no rights to any surpluses that accrued after they stopped funding the plan themselves in 1969. Based on the available information, Grayck concurred.

Fortified by this opinion, Sawyer ordered Yvon Chamberland in July 1982 to seek permission from the Pension Commission of Ontario to allocate the surplus from the experience-rate credits that would allow for an absolute withdrawal of money from the plan by member clubs. In seeking this permission—without notice to the plan's participants—the Society said that "at least $1 million" would be allocated to the players' pensions.

In fact, only $915,398 was allocated to the players when the Pension Commission of Ontario approved the move. Of the remaining amount, $469,841 was refunded directly to the "Original Six" NHL clubs based on the earnings on their contributions to the plan before 1969; the rest was allocated within the plan to all the NHL clubs to pay for their 1981 and 1982 contributions.

There was no consideration given in this process to the players or the NHLPA, whose participation in international hockey had been the source of much money used to fund the plan improvements since 1975. There is also no evidence that the Pension Commission had any

---

* At one point in Grayck's cross-examination by Mark Zigler, counsel for the retired players in their lawsuit, he took offense to a remark Zigler made about U.S. law. "I resent any insult you make to my nation in your recent and just made remark," protested Grayck. "I will not tolerate you despoiling my flag. Please do not do that again."

serious misgivings about the request for withdrawing money completely from the plan, despite the many undertakings and precedents in the regulations, by-laws and restated agreements that all monies would stay in the plan.

Just in case someone should ask, however, the Pension Society's board of directors passed a resolution on December 9, 1982, stating that, in future, all surpluses would be distributed along these same lines, with players getting only the portion relating to the years when they contributed directly to the plan.

Bob Baun and Lorraine Mahoney were certainly unaware of this raid on the pension fund when they met in her Toronto offices for the first time in 1981. "He said, 'I can't understand why I am getting this pension,'" Mahoney says. "It didn't seem right to him. His pals were in a similar situation. Guys like Dave Keon."

Baun and Mahoney requested disclosure from the Pension Society to uncover the value of the NHL Pension Fund and its investments. What they received were the annual two-page information returns from the Society—"a joke" according to Mahoney—and claims that a pension plan underwritten by group-annuity contracts precludes any valuation of the plan. Disclosure that might reveal the true value of the plan—which now must be revealed by law—was never provided. "The documents should have been voluminous," says Mahoney.

Visits to the Pension Commission of Ontario revealed little more about the financial underpinnings of the Society. It was only Baun and Mahoney's knowledge that the pensions were being funded by a group annuity contract that offered any insights. Baun used his contacts in the insurance industry to obtain the information about the group annuity Manulife had been using to fund his pension since he started in the NHL in 1957.

"When I saw the contracts, I understood what the problem was," Baun says. "The contracts were just forward-averaging the annuities they'd bought with surplus, and that's all they were doing ... taking our surplus and buying current pension plans for all the players as they came through. They [the NHL] weren't using their money at all ..."

Through his newly formed Professional Hockey Alumni (PHA), Baun began to look for ways to reform or restructure the pension plan's funding. His meetings and correspondence with John Ziegler and the NHLPA resulted in well-meaning nods in the direction of the retired players but little action. Everyone agreed the plan's funding was outdated, but there seemed no outward sign from the NHL or Manulife that they planned to make it more competitive.

In an attempt to break the logjam, Baun had Mahoney write to the Pension Society on June 3, 1983, requesting that the portion of the reserve held in his name be transferred into a Registered Retirement Savings Plan.

In his reply to Mahoney on July 15, Ken Sawyer—who was the NHL's vice president of finance in addition to his duties with the Pension Society—upbraided Mahoney, saying she misunderstood the way the plan operated in asking for a transfer of Baun's reserve. (According to many players, the "you don't understand" response was standard from Sawyer and his staff to other participants through the years.)

Mahoney fired back on July 20, 1983, that she had reviewed the information supplied to Baun "in lieu of the disclosure requirements which are now law in the Province of Ontario," and that she was "under no misunderstanding whatsoever concerning the operation of the plan.

"In actual fact, I am well aware of the tremendous shortfalls of this particular pension plan. Indeed, the uncompetitive plan provisions and the woeful level of accrued pensions are precisely the reasons that Mr. Baun wishes to transfer his present accrued reverse away from Manufacturers Life Plan."

Sawyer replied that the death benefit on Baun's Certificate of Entitlement did not represent the market value of his pension, and that the $7,612.28 annual pension he'd accumulated reflected the low yields on the long-term investments made on his behalf in the '50s and '60s.

Sawyer didn't explain the discrepancy between how well the investments were doing as represented by the death benefit and how poorly they were performing in the pensions he and his staff were entrusted to protect and defend. Further, Sawyer explained that nowhere in the plan were lump-sum withdrawals permitted, because the thinking behind the plan was to provide a "retirement income" to players, not sums of cash.

In short, Sawyer's letter reveals a petty bourgeois possessive streak about the plan married to a 1950s sophistication about pensions that typified the attitude of the trustees who managed it. "There seems to be an attitude from Mr. Sawyer that this is his fund, not ours," Carl Brewer observed in a 1990 letter to John Ziegler.

Typical of this "ours, not theirs" attitude at the NHL Pension Society was a phone call made by former NHL player Jim Harrison in 1992 to the Society's Montreal headquarters. When Harrison asked the status of the lawsuit filed by the retired players, the woman at the Society's office snorted, "It's ridiculous, the players don't have a chance."

Baun's request in 1983 that the value of the fund be evaluated and his share of the pension money transferred to an RRSP is now permissible by law—and usually encouraged by pension advisers. "What Sawyer was saying to me in 1983," says Mahoney, "is that 'I am not willing to have the plan amended.' In actual fact, they could have caused the plan to be amended to give portability provisions to the players."

Baun, meanwhile, soldiered on, spending considerable sums of his own money to pursue pension reform for the players through his Professional Hockey Alumni. In a June 18, 1984 letter to Alan Eagleson, Baun outlined the Professional Hockey Alumni's detailed plans for restructuring the NHL pension plan, including: changing the investment vehicle after a comprehensive study of alternative methods of funding; re-examining the appropriateness of age forty-five as a commencement age for receiving pensions; offering players a choice of equity funds, bond funds, mortgage funds, etc., as a vehicle for funding their pensions; and establishing a pension committee to meet periodically with the fund's investment manager.

Despite requests to modernize the plan, the directors of the Pension Society resisted any significant restructuring until 1986, when the clubs finally acknowledged the defined-contribution nature of the plan and abandoned the group-annuity contract as the funding vehicle for the pensions.

"Baun did the right thing ... he did remarkable work," says Carl Brewer. "He was in the insurance business at the time; he had a real understanding of it. But he did what every other hockey player had done for the forty years previously ... the Glen Harmons, the Bob Goldhams ... the guys who were interested in the pensions, interested in the benefits of the guys. They all did the same thing. They wrote the nice letters and got obfuscations in return."

Perhaps Baun might have succeeded where others hadn't. But before the Professional Hockey Alumni met with success, Baun suffered another financial setback. His job with a brokerage firm disappeared. "I ran out of money," he says. "I had put $125,000 in the PHA, and I was $100,000 short. I will never see that money. I had to absorb it. I couldn't put in any more money."

"We ran out of money," echoes Stanley. "Couldn't even put a mailing out. That was it."

Baun's financial problems mirrored the problems he'd had trying to establish the PHA as the voice for retired players since 1979. Formative meetings in 1982-83 were lively but only modestly attended, and while the zeal was there, the wherewithal was not. "They wouldn't spend a nickel to see the Pope go down Yonge Street on a white horse," Baun said in 1990. "They wouldn't stick together when I started this Alumni Association. I was looking for support from within ourselves. We had some of the best pension people advising us, but the players said, 'What's in it for Baun?'"

While Baun's group tried to garner support for pension-plan reform and attempted to represent destitute players and their widows to the NHL, the Phil Esposito Foundation in the United States was attempting to assist and speak for players there, and Brewer was fighting his individual battles with the NHL over pension rights.

"We were all disjointed. It was like the old days when we tried to start the Players' Association," recalls Baun. "Egos came into play, and everybody wanted a say. We were all working against each other."

"I didn't get the opportunity to support Baun," says Brewer. "He had his own group of people he was working with. He was trying to bring a group of people together, but it didn't work out. Fiscal responsibility took over and it died out."

"The retired guys get different stories from everybody," says Stanley. "Nobody knows the real story. Communication is such an important thing if you want to get something done when you're spread coast to coast. You've got to have experience, you've got to have somebody who can put up with the workload, and you've got to have the money to do it." Unfortunately, having just two out of those three conditions meant the end for Baun's group.

A crestfallen Baun, bitter about the many former NHL stars who stood aside as he struggled to keep the PHA going, relinquished his dream of heading the association. Senator Keith Davey, who was on the board of directors for the PHA, suggested that perhaps Baun's former teammate Larry Regan might take over the running of the organization. At the time, Regan headed the federally funded Canadian Oldtimers Hockey Association (COHA), an amateur group in Ottawa.

"Senator Davey asked me if we'd take it over, because we had an organization going here in the COHA, a pipeline across the country already," says Regan. He has spent most of his energies since 1986 negotiating benefits from the NHL for down-and-out players and their widows. He insists that he did have meetings with the Ontario government about the pension, but that the minister involved, Peter Kormos, was demoted and nothing came of it.

"Larry is not a crusader," states Brewer. "He's always been management, so what role was he going to play? He's going to play the role of management."

"It was a matter of time till we got into [the pension suit]," says Regan in his defense. "It seems we always had someone on the line for approval of benefits from the NHL, and we didn't want to rock the boat too much."

For almost six years, Regan kept the NHA's boat steady, drifting through very calm seas, occasionally casting out a single line here and there. (The biggest change was in the organization's name from the Professional Hockey Alumni to the National Hockey Alumni.) When he did attempt to raise questions about the pension issue in 1989, John Ziegler came crashing down on him.

"Had you informed your group of the facts rather than your misinformed opinions, we wouldn't have the present situation where a number of your members are suspicious, ..." Ziegler chided Regan in July 1989. "Until you are willing to correct this situation, we have no choice but to regard your self and your organization with suspicion."

Stung by Ziegler's acid remarks, Regan sought to demonstrate his good faith for the NHL president, listing the newspapers he'd turned down for interviews over the pension issue. He vowed to step aside if he was becoming an issue. Regan eventually stayed on in the job but quietly dropped active interest in the pension as a subject for discussion with the National Hockey Alumni.

With Regan indecisive, it fell to others to try to revive Bob Baun's dream of justice and self-respect for retired players. It's a dream that, the pension suit notwithstanding, is largely unrealized. "I guess I'm still disappointed in ourselves that we can't stick together, can't pull it all together," laments Baun. "It means so much to the little guys, the ones who live in the little towns across the country, who can't play in the golf tournaments or old-timers' games."

While the rise and fall of Bob Baun's dream was being played out among the participants in the NHL pension plan, events were rapidly overtaking the Society that administered it. Having successfully seized or diverted almost $2 million of the surplus funds generated by experience-rate credits in 1982, the NHL clubs amended the trust documents in December 1983, spelling out the divvying up of future pension booty among the groups with a stake in the plan. They made it retroactive to January 1, 1982, so as to cover the surplus distribution that year.

This amendment legitimized the NHL's use of experience-rate credits that emerged since it took over funding of the plan in 1969 to "reduce Member Club contributions to the Club Pension Plan." The fact that the plan had been funded since 1975 by international hockey profits generated by the players apparently didn't concern the Pension Society.

This act of administrative sleight-of-hand was merely the warm-up, however, to an even bigger grab by the men charged with running a Society of "philanthropic, charitable, provident and benevolent character." It was to be a performance that would have made Conn Smythe grin from ear to ear.

17

ZIGGY
AND IGGY

As Alan Eagleson approached collective bargaining with the NHL in 1986, he was still juggling his conflicting interests with the skill of a circus acrobat. Friend and foe alike wondered whether there were enough hours in the day for him to serve so many causes. He seemed to be everywhere, with everyone, doing everything. The media—at least those not on the well-stocked Eagleson bandwagon—hinted at elaborate networks of influence and money, then gave up in sheer frustration. The players he represented just shook their heads sadly when questioned about Eagleson, as if asked to contemplate astrophysics.

"Years ago, I tried to figure it out, to get to the bottom of it," said Ken Dryden, as thoughtful and perceptive a man as ever strapped on hockey equipment. "But what I found was a web of political, hockey and business connections, spreading out in all directions. It was too convoluted, too complex ... and so I just gave up. I couldn't do it alone."

The "secret" to his success was rather simple: seize the moment and let the future take care of itself. While his long-term vision might have been suspect, no one could play the short term better than the now fifty-two-year-old Alan Eagleson. He found the cracks and fissures in every opportunity and inserted himself into them. Soon, it was impossible to build without Eagleson as the mortar.

By 1986, as collective bargaining dawned, there was every reason for Eagleson to feel confident of continued success. For the NHLPA's executive director, the previous two years had been a very good indeed. The Canada Cup had returned in triumph to Canada from the Soviet Union, his Progressive Conservative Party had swept to a stunning majority in the House of Commons under Brian Mulroney, and his sports agency business had finally recovered from the defection of Bill Watters, his recruiter extraordinaire, and from an exposé by *Sports Illustrated*.*

The minor brush fires of discontent within the Players' Association following the WHA merger had been snuffed out, and the players' pension plan—which Eagleson so proudly plumped as his major bargaining plum—continued to receive largesse from Eagleson's many international hockey involvements both at home and abroad—although how much, no one knew. While some retired players weren't too keen on the pensions they were receiving, there certainly didn't seem any reason to start banging on the ornate desk of NHL president John Ziegler in New York, demanding pension reform in the NHL.

Eagleson's co-stewardship of pro hockey in North America with Ziegler was at its zenith, a marriage of power and influence recognized throughout the hockey world. Together, the two men had been able to extend the 1975 collective-bargaining agreement through the WHA merger and the recession of the early 1980s with few significant changes—no small feat considering the revolutionary changes occurring in other sports. Ziegler referred to the NHLPA's executive director as "my friend Alan Eagleson" and bragged about their joint trusteeship of pro hockey.

"They [the NHLPA] had to make some sacrifices in the beginning for us to be even able to put a business plan into effect, and they did that," Ziegler said in a 1989 speech to Toronto's Empire Club. "One of the things I'm proud of—and I know Al Eagleson is too—is that we have taken the owner-player relationship and used it as the means to solve problems. We do not go out to confront or compete."

Ziegler went on to favorably compare hockey's huggy-kissy labor relationship to those of other sports. "They've not solved it; they've tried to solve it by confrontation. Just look at Mr. Garvey with his football association when he was leading them to two strikes; it cost those players more than $100 million in salaries they will never get back. That's what confrontation does at the bargaining table." (Not coincidentally, as

---

* While *Sports Illustrated*'s "The Man Who Ruled Hockey" had scored some solid hits on Eagleson's integrity, it had failed to land a knockout blow against his power—reason enough for Eagleson to say that "*Sports Illustrated* spent $750,000 to try to nail me. They weren't successful."

Ziegler condemned Garvey, the former NFL Players' Association boss was trying to unseat "my friend Alan Eagleson" as head of the NHL Players' Association.)

"Ziegler and Eagleson were like this," says Bob Baun, intertwining his index and middle fingers. "You'll never see it again in any other sport. It was difficult to know how the relationship worked, but everyone knew that it did."

On the surface, John Ziegler and Alan Eagleson did seem an unlikely pairing. Where Eagleson was loud, profane, dynamic and direct, Ziegler was urbane, deliberate, cranky, a consensus-seeker who, at times, seemed a little prissy in the jocular hockey world. "He didn't like getting too close to a lot of sweaty hockey players," observes a high-ranking hockey official. "He always seemed offended by a bunch of guys with no teeth and scars on their faces."

The tanned American lawyer—with his rheumy, darting glance and corporate style—would seem to have personified all Eagleson thought was wrong with hockey. But what the two men shared had little to do with hockey and everything to do with the exercise of power. While Ziegler let Al have his international hockey money-makers, Eagleson allowed John to be the unopposed arbiter in all contractual disputes between players and management. Hockey was secondary to political stickhandling, which was just as well for Ziegler, who by the end of his tenure as NHL president visited hockey rinks only under duress or as part of his latest image makeover.

John Augustus Ziegler, Jr., was born in Grosse Pointe, Michigan, on February 9, 1934, and was a "hockey nut" growing up. While he played football and baseball as well as hockey at Lakeshore High School in the tony Detroit suburb of St. Clair Shores, the five-foot, eight-inch Ziegler continued playing hockey well into his thirties. "I wasn't that good in hockey, although I love the game," he remarked upon taking over the NHL presidency in 1977.

Ziegler graduated from the University of Michigan Law School in 1957 and went to work as a litigation specialist at the law firm of Dykehouse and Wise. At first, he was assigned to the drudging work of law, but he soon sniffed out the real action for a young lawyer in Detroit. Dykehouse and Wise handled accounts of the Norris family, and Ziegler the hockey fan set his cap to get himself in the door at the vast Norrin Corporation, particularly with the Norris family's prized sports possession, the Red Wings.

At the time, Norrin and the Red Wings were guided by the unsteady hand of Bruce Norris, whose father, James Senior, had established the multinational corporation with holdings in grains, shipping, liquor importing and cattle breeding. Bruce's older half-brother, Jim Junior, owned the Black Hawks and ran the boxing empire his father had established. His sister, Marguerite, had been forced aside in the family business when Bruce took over.

Tall and handsome, the athletically built Bruce Norris was also a party boy of the first order when he first set his bloodshot eyes on little John Ziegler in 1959; he was prone to consuming great quantities of booze and entertaining untold legions of women. (He was married four times.) He was also squandering much of the family fortune on poor deals and worthless investments. And his King Midas in reverse was working on the Red Wings as well, turning the team that had won seven straight NHL titles in the 1950s into a pathetic shell.

Ziegler decided that to get next to Bruce Norris and to win his business and his trust, he had to out-party the competition. So Ziegler became Norris's top corporate caddy, holding his coat until the wee small hours of the morning. He went so far as to move in next door to Norris's home in North Miami, Florida.

The strategy worked, and Ziegler, with his Kennedy-esque bangs and Gucci shoes, was soon Norris's top legal counsel and a senior partner in his law firm. Better yet for Ziegler, he was rising as rapidly in the Red Wings pecking order as the team was descending to the bottom of the standings. By 1976, Ziegler was the chairman of the board and the Red Wings' representative on the NHL Board of Governors. With his smooth, unhurried style, he was soon a rising star within the League.

As Clarence Campbell's health deteriorated in 1976-77, Ziegler cemented his credentials to succeed him by working with Eagleson to keep the financially destitute Cleveland Barons afloat. With the NHL unable or unwilling to advance any more money to Cleveland, Ziegler convinced Eagleson as the executive director of the NHLPA to advance enough money to the Barons to complete the season.*

---

* Not that the NHL held a grudge against Barons' owner Gordon Gund, of course. He and his brother were later permitted to buy the Minnesota North Stars; when they had run that franchise into the ground, the Gunds were next handed the plum expansion franchise in San Jose, California. Despite early enthusiasm, the Sharks seemed headed for the same fate as the Barons and North Stars.

Without approval from the NHLPA membership, Eagleson scrabbled together $600,000 from the NHLPA and his individual clients and lent it to the NHL. The bail-out allowed the Barons to finish the season before expiring for good, and the $600,000 was returned, minus a finder's fee for the lawyer who'd put the deal together for the individual clients. That lawyer was, of course, also the executive director of the NHLPA, Alan Eagleson.

After a drawn-out nomination process, Ziegler was hired to a four-year term as NHL president on June 22, 1977, at $225,000 a year. With its established factions and bitter in-fighting, the NHL wasn't willing to give Ziegler the type of wide-ranging powers enjoyed by NFL Commissioner Pete Rozelle. It simply needed someone to patch up the feuds, deal with the WHA once and for all and not get in the way of the real powers in the League.

The comments at the time were positive: "Ziegler is a diplomat, but very firm," said Washington's Governor Peter O'Malley. "A good man for the job."

"He'll be great, G-R-E-A-T in capital letters," said Harold Ballard, who would almost immediately rescind the endorsement. "Maybe he's not tough enough right now, but he'll get hard, believe me."

Ironically, no one seemed to connect Ziegler to the fact that the team he'd helped run for eighteen years, the Red Wings, were a complete financial mess with half-empty stands and a $2-million loss the season before. Fifteen years later, his connection to the NHL's woeful financial picture in 1992 *would* be made, however, and it would cost Ziegler his job.

In his early days as NHL president, Ziegler accomplished the tasks he'd been hired for. With Eagleson's help, he successfully sued for peace with the WHA, got the Board of Governors to stop their bickering and kept the politicians in Washington and Ottawa away from the League's anti-trust status. When the 1980s boomed, however, and a vision of marketing and global expansion was needed to take Wayne Gretzky worldwide, Ziegler would prove less satisfactory in the job, and the NHL would suffer as a result.

He became more and more detached as the decade wore on, and his public image was nearly obliterated when he was AWOL for several League emergencies. Most famous among these no-shows was the strike by referees during the 1988 playoffs, sparked by New Jersey coach Jim Schoenfeld's verbal assault on referee Don Koharski.

This assault culminated with Schoenfeld urging the well-upholstered Koharski to "Go have another donut, you fat pig!" While the referees were walking out in New Jersey, Ziegler was nowhere to be found for almost two days; he was variously reported to be in Hawaii, England and the Rocky Mountains. When he did return, he snarled that his whereabouts were none of the media's business.

At that point, the close alliance he'd formed with the accommodating head of the Players' Association helped protect him from his detractors within the NHL. (The media's howls of outrage never had any impact on NHL owners.) The two holidayed together in Florida, the Caribbean and in Europe. They were found golfing together or yachting together with Bill Wirtz, or in London on business at the same time. While the players could only assume that this proximity was part of a union chief doing business, the League's owners laughed all the way to the bank every time they witnessed the alliance of Ziegler and Eagleson, or "Ziggy and Iggy" as they were dubbed.

Ziegler, of course, played up the benefits of that cozy relationship to the players. "We have, again, the only case in professional sports, a partnership," Ziegler said. "Our players are entrepreneurs. They are, for example, joint venturers in international hockey." Joint-venture partners who were not allowed to see the books.

That partnership was still potent during the 1986 collective-bargaining agreement negotiations. Eagleson had always talked tough until he got to the bargaining table, when the players were delivered up for the slaughter. While Ziegler kept a consensus among the owners, Eagleson "studiously sat back" and left the players to decide for themselves. It was a simple but devastating formula for controlling labor in the NHL.

However, Ziegler had a wrinkle for his yachting buddy Al Eagleson in the course of negotiating a new agreement in 1986. Ziegler and his NHL bosses fully intended to use their favorite party trick, the players' pension plan, to dupe the gullible players one more time. Once more, they would use a surplus accumulated in the pension plan to buy players away from the kind of free agency that was creating millionaire athletes in other sports. The surplus this time, though, would reach a staggering $28 million by the time it was distributed in 1988. That enormous sum would be hard to keep under wraps.

The NHL had its legal opinions on the ownership of the money from lawyer Marcus Grayck in Chicago. And the current players represented by the NHLPA ... well, they had never been a problem in the past with Alan in control. But Ziegler and the NHL would need Eagleson more than ever to help with their plans to keep most of the surplus for themselves. It was a gambit that threatened to stretch the Ziegler-Eagleson axis to the breaking point.

The only wild cards in this equation were the retired players. But without a unified leadership, they would not present much of a challenge—even if they found out about the money, which was unlikely. It was all enough to give a hockey owner an overpowering sense of well-being.

This time, however, when the NHL went hunting for honey at the bargaining table, it stirred up a hornet's nest that neither the League nor Eagleson could manage. The private strategies became public, and the outrage generated by the owners' appropriation of most of the $28 million from the NHL Players Pension Plan and Trust overwhelmed the carefully constructed scenarios of the NHL within five years. Eventually, that outrage spelled the end of the Ziegler-Eagleson axis.

It started off simply enough, as most disasters do. After the frustrating six-year negotiations with Manulife that produced the 1982 surplus distribution, the NHL and Manulife wanted a simpler formula for dealing with experience-rate surpluses that emerged from the investments in the players' pension fund. Under Canadian law, the NHL's tax benefits for pension contributions could be denied if too large a surplus remained in the plan for too lengthy a period.

And so Manulife and Pension Society actuary Yvon Chamberland had settled on the idea of a "one-shot" experience-rate credit in 1985 to end the administrative nightmare. This one-time payment would be a calculation of all the present and future experience-rate credits that arose from the inception of the group-annuity contract from 1952 until June 30, 1982. When the payment was complete, there would be no more surpluses paid out by Manulife from the group annuity, no more messy negotiations and no question of the players getting any part of those earnings. The NHL would start a new plan for everyone not getting a pension already, one that produced no surpluses.

This "one-shot" payment was calculated by Manulife at $22,364,000 on January 1, 1985.* Six weeks later, having once more received a positive legal opinion on its ownership of the surplus

---

* When it was finally allocated on June 30, 1987, this figure had grown to $28,550,000.

from Marcus Grayck, Ken Sawyer accepted the offer from Manulife on behalf of the NHL Pension Society.

The NHL owners then used the same allocation formula they'd employed in 1983 to distribute the surplus: namely, players got experience-rate credits proportionate to the monies they'd contributed before 1969, while the owners would get to use the rest of the surplus as they saw fit.* The former plan—which contained the money of those players already drawing their pensions—was capped, and the old group annuity was finally led out of the barn to be mercifully disposed of. All other pensions were switched to a non-participating group contract, which offered no experience-rate credits.

To complete the paperwork, the NHL Club Pension Plan and Trust was restated for a third time, incorporating this owner-favorable distribution formula in the amendments and repealing any previous regulations, by-laws or amendments that allocated surpluses to participants only. Once again, this was done without notice to any of the participants in the plan.

Under this formula, the NHL was obligated to distribute only $3.8 million (CDN) and $584,562 (US) of the $22,364,000 from Manulife to the retired players in the form of pension benefits. The rest remained at the disposal of the Society's board of directors for "future obligations."

One can only imagine the glee with which John Ziegler greeted the news of a $16-million windfall in the plan. Since taking over from Clarence Campbell as NHL president in 1977, he had made available almost $20 million from the pension plan to his employers to lower their contributions and obligations. It was a considerable feather in his cap as he tried to maintain power within the factional owners' group.

He had also overseen the reinterpretation of surplus ownership within the plan. A confident Ziegler even went so far as to dispute the existence of a surplus in the pension plan. "This so-called surplus is a refund," the NHL president said in a 1992 interview. "We were overcharged for buying the annuities."

While Ziegler's options for use of the surplus were limitless, it was decided that the NHL clubs should once again keep the money

---

* The NHL miscalculated the players' percentage of contributions to the plan from 1947-69 and had to admit in court that it had shortchanged the players as a result in both 1982 and 1985.

within the plan, taking "contribution holidays" and funding future projects. These projects took the form of the "NHL-NHLPA Estate Security Plan," which would provide an estimated $250,000 at age fifty-five to a player who had played more than four hundred NHL games. It would be the League's trump card in the next round of collective bargaining with the NHLPA in the summer of 1986.

In preparation for those talks, Eagleson had been making his usual noises in the media prior to bargaining, warning anyone who'd listen or thrust a microphone his way that free agency would be his number-one issue. "If you don't indicate that you are going to be responsible and take a reasonable course of action," he warned the owners darkly, "we will likely be on strike during the training camp in 1986."

Had he not made much the same noises in 1975, '79 and '81, of course, the sabre-rattling might have actually scared the owners. But they knew by this time that Eagleson's negotiating bark was worse than his bite—even if the NHLPA membership had yet to figure it out. (In 1986, there would not be a single NHLPA player rep remaining from the group that negotiated the first collective-bargaining agreement in 1975, making Eagleson the only figure with ten or more years experience on the NHLPA side. The NHL, however, had a dozen owners who dated back to 1975.) The owners knew that when Ziegler trotted out his heralded "Estate Security Plan," the opposition would crumble.

This fund, which Eagleson knew about in detail as early as the summer of 1985, was estimated by the League to cost $9.4 million and would be funded out of the recently obtained surplus in the pension. For the record, Eagleson says he "generally learned" of the surplus discussions with Manulife around 1984-85, "but was not told any details." The first written record of Eagleson being told of the surplus came in a letter from John Ziegler on July 22, 1985. "As you know, there has been negotiated with Manulife what we consider a return of overcharging for pension payments," Ziegler wrote.

By September 13 of that year, Eagleson was acknowledging the presence of a "multi-million dollar surplus" in a letter to Ziegler. His tone became distinctly bullish, as it usually did until he got to the negotiating table. "As 25% owners in any such surpluses earned since the commencement of the 1975/76 season, it is the NHLPA's position that we have a right to at least 25% of any such surpluses," he wrote. "It is also our position that the past and present players have a moral right to all of the surpluses ...

"From everyone's point of view this surplus is a windfall. I submit to you and every member of the Board of Governors that such a windfall should be used to improve the lot of past and present NHL players at the pension level."

He remained adversarial in a second letter dated the same day to Ziegler, complaining about the League's refusal to disclose information. "The League takes the position that information concerning annual premiums paid by the member clubs and experience ratings are 'confidential.' Since the NHLPA pays a portion of those premiums, the information must be made available to the Association."

Had the surplus been of the size of the 1982 distribution— approximately $3 million—then perhaps the fight might have remained on this level of rhetoric, with Eagleson waxing indignant in word but indifferent in deed. But as the surplus grew to almost $25 million by the end of 1985, it became too conspicuous. Stories of enormous piles of cash spread on the wind like wildfire.

"I phoned Eagleson's office," recalls Allan Stanley. "Of course, he was always out. But I talked to Sam Simpson [the NHLPA Director of Operations]. I told him I'd heard there was $44 million in surplus. He said actually it was $25 million, and Alan was negotiating with the Ontario government as to what they can do with it now. What else could I say then? I certainly didn't know Eagleson was trying to make a deal with the NHL to fund the current players' pensions."

Depending on whom you question, the players representing their clubs on the NHLPA side at the 1986 talks may or may not have known that the funding for John Ziegler's "Estate Security Plan" was coming from the surplus. But one thing was for certain: by the time Alan Eagleson sat down in Toronto to discuss the use of the pension "windfall" for the so-called Security Plan, his claims of a "moral right" to anything had melted like ice chips on a hot stove.

Hours before negotiations on the 1986 collective-bargaining agreement were to commence, the dedicated executive director of the NHLPA decided to renegotiate his own contract with the players. Via NHL counsel Larry Latto, he informed the astounded player reps that he was going to resign unless he received a new contract immediately. The young and inexperienced reps had heard Eagleson's recent musings in the press about becoming NHL president—musings he neither denied nor attempted to clarify. They were perplexed and poleaxed. Their mentor and advocate might be staring *across* the table at them from the NHL side that afternoon if they didn't accede to his demand for a whopping new six-year contract. "He deserted us," said Pat Verbeek, the New Jersey player rep.

So they did what any rookie does when pressured in his own zone: they coughed up the prize. Eagleson received a guaranteed six-year contract starting at $200,000 (US) a year and going up 10 percent each year of the contract, a guaranteed $50,000 (US) a year pension at age sixty-five, bonuses, office expenses, travel allowances ... and the right to conduct his other businesses. It made him one of the best-paid, if not *the* best-paid, union leader in North America. Adding to the blow, Canadian patriot Eagleson was drawing all his money in U.S. currency while working in Canada, yet pensions paid to Canadian-based retirees were paid in the lower Canadian dollar.

It was the sort of negotiating coup he'd never managed to pull off when faced with Ziegler and the NHL owners, but now he had scored it at the expense of his membership. Having played hardball with his clients in the backrooms, Eagleson then proceeded to play soft-toss with the owners at the bargaining table.

Instead of insisting on principle that "such a windfall should be used to improve the lot of past and present NHL players," the NHLPA meekly accepted a sliver of the surplus, and that for current players only. In front of the media, Eagleson briefly protested the NHL's actions—like plucky Belgium defying the Blitzkrieg—then waved the tanks in.

The NHL's right to divide the $25 million according to its 1982 formula—which gave the owners virtual *carte blanche* in rewarding themselves—would have to be decided by a judge, Eagleson told the media. According to its executive director, however, the NHLPA was not about to launch a lawsuit any time in the immediate future.

As a token of their gratitude, the owners acknowledged the new pension plan for active players as a "defined contribution" or money-purchase plan with annual contributions of $4,000 per player per year of service (which was raised to $5,000 by 1987). In addition, the owners "allowed" the players $1,372,000 from the surplus—money attributable to the proceeds from international hockey. According to the NHL, this amount and a further $10.8 million were used to fund the "NHL Estate Security Plan." (A remaining $8,271,000 was left in the fund to meet the NHL clubs' current obligations to the plan.)

Magically, there was no reference made to the deal consummated back in 1969—the one that owners said gave them the right to *all* future surpluses—when the League allowed the NHLPA to share in a portion of the 1985 distribution. And Alan Eagleson never brought the subject up, either.

As the owners expected, the "Estate Security Plan" swayed the players from their demands for free agency and impartial arbitration. The NHL's glittering prize looked too good to be true, and in fact it was just that. (See Appendix B.) Never mind that only 8 percent of all NHL players reach the four-hundred-game plateau annually, or that the League had to set aside just $3 million—not the advertised $10 million—to fund the benefit, or that the $250,000 figure assumed an average interest rate of 10 percent through the history of the fund. The fact that it had been funded by the labors of Gordie Howe and Bobby Orr and Jean Béliveau—men unrepresented in the negotiations—should have been enough for Eagleson to call for rejection of the package.

But amidst the orchestrated hoopla, few asked how the NHL and NHLPA could barter the retired players' pension rights when neither organization even *claimed* to represent them. After all, Eagleson had insisted "that's my job, not to look after the retired players, but players on the job now." Having rationalized his involvement, he traded away the rights of stars from the past like Bobby Hull for stars of the present, like Hull's son Brett.

Jim Fox, the player rep for Los Angeles, was one of the few who disliked the owners' unilateral decision on how the surplus was divided. "My beef is that the NHL Players' Association did not fight harder for the money," he said later. "I would like to think the executive director of the NHL Players' Association would say it's 100 percent players' money as opposed to 'I don't know' or 'There's a case pending.'"

Eagleson calmed any rough seas, saying that counsel in the United States and Canada had told the NHLPA that the League had a right to redistribute the money within the pension plan. "The NHLPA accepted this premise," Eagleson blandly recorded in a 1990 letter, "and sought to negotiate for as much of this money as possible to be used for the security package."

"From our perspective," he told reporters later, "we think we negotiated a good deal for the present players. It's now up to a court to decide." But Eagleson and the NHLPA would not be the ones to pursue in court the thorny issue of what happened to the pension money of the men who'd made hockey—and him—rich. That would have to wait five long years.

"There's no point looking at it from a backward point of view," he replied in 1991 when asked why the NHLPA wouldn't have challenged such a fundamental issue for present—and retired—hockey players. "I wouldn't say we've done badly as a result."

And neither had Eagleson himself done poorly as a result of the 1986 negotiations. Besides his new multi-million-dollar, six-year contract as executive director of the NHLPA, he had apparently reinforced the power of the Ziegler-Eagleson axis, earning more "credits" with NHL establishment figures like Wirtz and Ed Snider for easing them through another potential minefield at little or no cost. These were credits Eagleson would refund later when he came to stage his international hockey events.

He wasn't through with the pension plan just yet, however. Three years later, in 1989, Eagleson rendered the NHL another service. New pension legislation in Ontario in 1987 had mandated that in multi-employer pension plans such as the NHL Pension Plan, participants (the present and retired players) must make up at least half the representation on the board of directors. The NHL wanted an exemption from the rule.

Clearly, this was the opportunity for Eagleson—had he so desired—to wrest some real concessions for the players by restoring to them the crucial seats on the board of the Pension Society. This was the chance to ensure that the League couldn't again grab a surplus without the players' knowledge, a reward for ending no-trade contracts and enshrining buy-out clauses, player concessions made "for the good of the game" when the NHL was hurting.

The NHL was far from hurting in 1989. John Ziegler was trumpeting the NHL as a $350- to $450-million industry (depending on the audience), with new arenas being built or planned in half of its cities. He bragged about turning a $100-million accumulated loss in 1978 into a $60-million profit. "From a business standpoint, we are proud of that turnaround." Wayne Gretzky's move to Los Angeles had revived hockey in that important media center, but salaries had yet to start the climb that followed disclosure. Yet without consulting either the executive board or the player representatives of the NHLPA, Eagleson simply gave away the board seats for nothing. He wrote to the Ontario Pension Commission in 1989 to support the NHL's exemption from the new law.

"The National Hockey League Players' Association represents all players who participate in the NHL Club Pension Plan," he informed

Murray Elston, the Ontario minister responsible for pensions, on August 1, 1989. "This letter will confirm the NHLPA's support of the application to have the NHL Pension Society exempted by regulation from the plan and fund administrator provisions of the Pensions Benefits Act, 1987 ... we understand that an exemption will permit it to continue in its present capacity in respect of the Plan.

"In our view, this is in the best interests of our membership."

The letter was signed "R. Alan Eagleson, O.C., Q.C., Executive Director." A handwritten note was scrawled across the bottom of the letter: "Murray, personal regards, Alan."

While Eagleson's 1969 surrendering of the players' places on the board might be excused due to inexperience, it is inconceivable that an older, better-connected Eagleson did not comprehend the gravity of the move in 1989.

"This is Alan Eagleson we're talking about," observed a businessman who studied Eagleson's business dealings. "Alan Eagleson, Q.C., Queen's Counsel. We're not talking about Mary from Milwaukee."

When questioned in 1992 about the Elston letter, Eagleson stonewalled. "I don't recall and I don't want to discuss anything on that matter," he said at his NHLPA going-away party in January 1992.

Murray Elston remembers the issue being raised when the application was made in 1987, but recalls that he accepted the advice of the Pension Commission to allow the exemption. "The dispute is between the two parties," he says. "We can't, as a government, step in and do all the bargaining. That would be impossible."

Dallas goalie Andy Moog, who was a player rep for Boston at the time the letter was written, insists that players were never consulted. "There was a different idea on my part how the pension should be administered," he says today. Once again, the NHL had scored a victory over the NHLPA, with Eagleson's help.

Many people hearing about these events for the first time are shocked—not that Eagleson attempted such brazen moves, but that he was never called to account for them. If Eagleson acted with impunity, seemingly unassailable in his position atop the hockey heap, he was merely reflecting almost two decades where players and their supporters were too timid or too disorganized to bell the cat.

His paltry accomplishments at the bargaining table and his quasi-feudal style of managing the Players' Association *had* inspired some modest reform movements. The NHLPA's 1979 capitulation during the NHL-WHA merger had produced a campaign by Boston Bruins defenseman Mike Milbury to hire a full-time director and possibly unseat Eagleson. But that movement had run out of steam after six months. And some player agents in 1985 sought to break Eagleson's absolute hold on all the levers of power at the Players' Association, but that too expired.

As Eagleson frequently bragged, *Sports Illustrated* had also attempted—unsuccessfully—to bring him down in 1984 with an investigation of his conflicting loyalties, secret deals and manipulative tactics. And on eight separate occasions, Eagleson had announced he was either quitting, about to quit or seriously considering quitting the Players' Association when criticism became too harsh. These had all been devices to stifle dissent, as were the thinly veiled references to succeeding Clarence Campbell as NHL president.

It certainly appeared that only the Eagle could stop the Eagle. No one in the hockey power structure possessed the sheer energy, organization and bloodlust to topple a street-fighter like Eagleson on his own turf. Thus it happened that when all the logical contenders had fallen, some unranked fighters took up the challenge.

The 1986 collective-bargaining agreement and events afterward galvanized two player agents, lawyers Rich Winter of Edmonton and Ron Salcer of Los Angeles, into action. They were unlikely rebels and a more unlikely team. The twenty-eight-year-old Winter, whose clientele has included players such as Grant Fuhr, Esa Tikkanen and Ron Hextall, was fired by a youthful passion to win the same respect and rights enjoyed by athletes in the other team sports for his players. While a student in Los Angeles, he had heard his first horror stories about Eagleson's running of the NHLPA from players such as Ian Turnbull and David Forbes. "At some point, we decided we had to pursue these claims," recalls Winter, "because something appeared to be drastically wrong."

An inexperienced Winter locked horns with Eagleson several times with no success in the next few years. He developed a reputation as a lone wolf in the agent business, ready to go to court in an instant to help his clients and himself. Among team owners and general managers, Eagleson helped foster an image of Winter as a hot-head who was hard to deal with.

Salcer, who operates out of the non-hockey environment of southern California, had been in the agent game longer than Winter and knew the vagaries of dealing with Eagleson. More than Winter, Salcer understood just how powerful Eagleson was and how hard he'd fight to keep his power and rank in the hockey world if challenged. But Salcer had finally become fed up with an association that he thought was run for the executive director by the players rather than the other way around.

In 1988, the two men burst into action. They recruited Ed Garvey, the former head of the NFL Players' Association, to be their hired gun, and they used a caustic campaign of revelations about Eagleson's "imperial" directorship that would leave him poised for extinction by the summer of 1989. The three men had a simple formula to attack and unnerve Eagleson. They had over two hundred members of the NHLPA give them signed authority to investigate the union. To give the threat some muscle, those players each plunked down $100. It was a simple tactic, yet one that had not been used before to depose the self-styled "czar of hockey."

After conducting a tour of all the NHL clubs, Winter/Salcer/Garvey began to assemble information about the workings of the NHLPA—"your association," they reminded players—that had either been suppressed or distorted in the past.

The forty-four-page catalogue they prepared for the annual meeting of the NHLPA in West Palm Beach, Florida, in June 1989, was a stunning indictment of Eagleson's twenty-two-year reign. It sought to expose the full extent of Eagleson's personal contract, his lending of NHLPA money to friends and clients, his questionable expenses, his conflicts of interest in representing management and players, his concealed ownership of the building the NHLPA rented as its headquarters in Toronto, his failure to prepare adequately for collective bargaining, and the sorry state of NHL players versus their colleagues in other sports.

"Rumor, innuendo, half-truths and absolute untruths," spluttered Eagleson about the Winter/Garvey/Salcer offensive. "They suggested impropriety by Alan Eagleson ... and many more outrageous things."

Of interest to the retired players like Baun and Brewer and Stanley—whose groups had never been able to produce such research and documentation—were the revelations about the pension plan. In particular, many of the retired players learned for the first time of the $28-million surplus in their plan that had been almost completely appropriated by the NHL and NHLPA in the 1986 bargaining.

The retired players' lack of success in obtaining this sort of information on their own pension plan wasn't for want of trying, of course. Baun and Brewer point to thick correspondence files directed to and from the Pension Society on their behalf. A number of other former players, such as Glen Harmon, Bob Goldham and Leo Reise, were similarly frustrated by the League, the Society and Manulife in their attempts to obtain investment and regulatory information about the plan.

"The present pension fund is fully funded and is audited every year, which is the extent of the NHL's obligation," was the League's standard reply to inquiries, despite the fact that this refusal was in violation of disclosure laws about pension societies in Quebec and Ontario (where the headquarters and the plan respectively were domiciled) and in the United States.

Players were given access to information only in the Society's Montreal office, and then only on their own files. Former Maple Leaf Jim Dorey remembers a typical visit to the Pension Society headquarters: "They'd give you the indication you weren't expected, even though you'd served notice you were going to be there," says Dorey, who's now in the insurance business in Kingston, Ontario. "Then the handshake, the quick coffee, the no-answer, run-around routine. In most cases, you came in on the train and were booked back on a train, and they took advantage of that out-of-town situation. The answer was always, 'We'll get back to you.' If the information did come, it wasn't specific to what you asked. And if you brought a lawyer with you, they'd say, 'He's not a hockey player, he shouldn't be involved ... we can represent you better than someone off the street.'"

Winter, Salcer and Garvey met with the same bureaucratic brick wall that the players encountered at the Pension Society. They assigned Hamilton lawyer John Agro to seek out pension information in Montreal on behalf of the more than two hundred players who had anted up money to conduct the probe, but Agro was refused permission to examine the documents by the Society.

"We had to send a letter to Mr. Sawyer from Grant Fuhr (Winter's client), authorizing Mr. Agro to look at the documents," the 1989 Winter/Salcer/Garvey report to players stated. "Sawyer would *not* send the documents so Mr. Agro had to make an appointment to see Mr. Sawyer, *pay for a flight to Montreal* and, to add insult to injury, *pay $114 for copying the relevant documents*.... As a player, in order to determine what is in your pension plan, review the documents, obtain a description of the plan, *you must travel to Montreal for the privilege.*"

The report went on to say, "By law, pension plans must send a summary description of the plan to participants, active and retired. You have never received one. Mr. Sawyer promised that the 'summary description' would be available the week of May 22 [1989].... Then he followed it up with a letter saying that *it was too complicated to get finished within a week. They have had 21 years to figure out the plan but now it is too complicated to complete the report when promised!* Who is kidding whom?"

The same report decried how misinformation about the pension had been used to ratify the collective-bargaining agreement in 1986. (There had been no secret ballot by the NHLPA's general membership in 1986, and printed copies of the agreement were not made available to the members.)

"Several players said they were asked to vote on the new CBA [collective-bargaining agreement]. When they asked, 'What did we get?' the response was, 'We got $250,000 at age 55' ... what we discovered, after a very difficult time getting to documents in the control of Mr. Sawyer in Montreal, is that the $250,000 benefit *did not cost management one dime.*

"The money was reallocated within the pension plan ... one doubts that the players who were being asked to vote on an agreement that gave away their ability to become free agents or to challenge the system in court were aware of that."

The report went on to tell players that the cost of funding their spectacular $250,000 (CDN) "Estate Security Plan"—assuming a 10 percent return every year—was only around $17,000 in present money for the players who make the required four hundred games. And that money, lent in the form of mortgages to friends, clients and even Eagleson's law partner, had come from the "Bonus Pension Pool" accumulated by international hockey profits—money that was destined for their retirement benefits.

The detailed analysis of the pension—plus the other facets of Eagleson's duties—motivated the current players and a number of the retired players like Brewer, who had believed they might never understand the full extent of what had happened to them since their retirement. And so they watched with particular interest as Eagleson marshalled his loyal troops to withstand the attack in West Palm Beach.

In his autobiography, *Power Play*, Eagleson claims that he was bushwhacked in Florida. "The frustrating part was that not knowing what kind of ammunition they had, I'd had no time at all to prepare how to fight back." Yet he had already fired off a rebuttal in March 1989 to all NHLPA members over some of the complaints raised by Winter, Salcer and Garvey. And from the documents requested by the insurgents, he had a good idea on most others. Just in case, he persuaded loyal clients like Darryl Sittler, NHL executives like Ken Sawyer and his Toronto lawyer, Edgar Sexton, to bolster his retinue for the showdown.

Still, it was a stunning scene that June weekend at the famed Breakers Hotel in Palm Beach, Florida. Garvey systematically tore Eagleson apart in front of the men he'd so dominated for the past twenty-two years. Confronted by the pugnacious Garvey, who had run a sports union himself, Eagleson was finally forced to fight on a level playing field.

There were no callow hockey players, no nervous agents quaking at his feet, no media sycophants to save him. To a man who had always controlled hockey players like chattel, it was a rout.

"We learned so much from the confusion over the questions Ed Garvey began to pose," Winter remembers of the meeting. "We discovered from a quick review of the Players' Associations statements that it was an absolute mess.... You had Eagleson admitting the possibility of being involved in private mortgage loans and then backtracking ... you had [NHLPA president] Bryan Trottier admitting in front of everyone that he knew nothing of the loans and that Eagleson had no one's approval at the level of the NHLPA. That turned the meetings around."

When Garvey told the meeting that the NHL had funded its $250,000 "Estate Security Plan" out of surpluses in the plan, Garth Butcher of Vancouver leapt to his feet: "You mean to tell me the money contributed for Bobby Hull, Bobby Orr, Gordie Howe and those players is being used to pay current players' benefits? Well, that sucks!"

The discussions raged all weekend, and Eagleson seemed to wither beneath the onslaught of his accusers. When the issue of one of the mortgages funded by the NHLPA was raised, Eagleson looked blankly to his operations manager, Sam Simpson. "Is that one of mine?" he asked, before requesting time to refresh his memory.

Eagleson was finally faced with a number of humiliating conditions for hanging onto his job. The players wanted his income taxes inspected, but he later declined to supply them. A search committee was struck to select his successor (Detroit agent Bob Goodenow was chosen in 1990), a full audit of the NHLPA finances and an examination of the NHLPA's private mortgage investments were asked for, and a meeting later that summer to discuss reforms was demanded.

Even at that, Eagleson needed the help of his hand-picked executive board to win the vote on firing him 16-12. (Had it been one team/one vote, he'd have been defeated.)

It was a shocking comedown for the man who had bullied his way to an enormous new contract from the players in 1986. A compromised, acquiescent Eagleson left West Palm Beach to reload and rearm himself for the next fight. He had one small consolation: an audio-tape of the meetings made had mysteriously disappeared shortly after the meeting. At least he'd never have to listen to Garvey's cross-examination again.

Ever the street-fighter, Eagleson lived to fight another day, winning a second vote of confidence later in August 1989 at a carefully choreographed meeting in Toronto. The Price Waterhouse "audit" was a key to Winter/Salcer/Garvey's attack, yet William Dovey and his Price Waterhouse inspectors told players at the meeting that they had only performed a "limited financial review." Eagleson had already told the players that his income tax statements were none of their business.

There was no draft report made available for the membership to study at the August 1989 meeting, nor was a final report ever submitted. Dovey made a verbal submission to players after walking the NHLPA's four-man audit committee through his research the night before. Had the players had a chance to study the draft report in any detail, the vote of confidence might have turned out very differently. While the NHLPA's revenues from dues and licensing were often less than a $1 million a year, the report showed that the man who had said that he was "not a spendthrift" had bought gifts ranging from Wimbledon tennis tickets to Bohemian crystal, often for a variety of friends and business partners. (See Appendix D.) He had directed NHLPA contracts to his family and friends and had billed the NHLPA up to $500 a night for nights spent in his own homes in London and Florida doing business. All of this was done in violation of the NHLPA Constitution, without the NHLPA executive board's knowledge or approval.

The report also says that "accounting documentation was consistently missing to support expense claims by Mr. Eagleson. In most cases, a letter from Mr. Eagleson's law practice would detail the expenses but no supporting receipts of invoices would be provided." It went on to say that while examiners from Price Waterhouse "have been able to identify the nature of expenditures ... we are unable to determine how the NHLPA benefitted from them."

As well, the reporting of related-party transactions—the Players' Association's many business dealings with Eagleson's own companies and interests—did not meet the required reporting standards.

According to Pat Verbeek and other players, Dovey told the assembled players that there were only a few hundred dollars in unsubstantiated expenses claimed by Eagleson, even though NHLPA documents showed the executive director being reimbursed for tens of thousands of dollars of expenses without receipts. But with Dovey saying in the written report that the Players' Association statement "generally meets or exceeds required reporting standards," Eagleson was able to claim vindication on charges he misspent money from the NHLPA.

A report on the mortgage loans by Hamilton lawyer William Dermody was similarly curtailed in scope. Dermody did not receive all of the property documents and previous NHLPA mortgages that would have revealed Eagleson lending money from the NHLPA's Bonus Pension Pool to his friends and business partners. A series of earlier interest-only loans he had made from NHLPA escrow funds to his business partner, developer Norman Donaldson, was not disclosed—loans that ended up going power-of-sale or that took years to pay off.

By this time, Bryan Trottier's memory had cleared enough to back Eagleson's story on the placing of the mortgages in question. Trottier met with Eagleson and Goldblatt to review the transactions prior to the meeting. Based on the available information, Eagleson won a unanimous vote of confidence from the players in Toronto.

"Once I won that vote of 29-0 on August 29, 1989, I was free," crowed Eagleson. "My attitude was, 'Boys, you won't get the chance again.' And they never will."

Despite their lost opportunity, the present players were buoyed by their success in humbling Eagleson. Retired stars like Carl Brewer—who'd known him as the manic young Toronto lawyer eager to ingratiate himself with hockey players back in the 1960s—were heartened to see the underdog players win for a change. If it could happen to the present players, maybe it could happen to them, too, if they took on the Pension Society.

The retired players understood the inherent contradictions of power in the world of hockey. Just as there is a need for a dominant player on a team, there was a need for a dominant type to channel all the egos in a players' association.

"There had to be a catalyst like Eagleson who could smack 'em all down with his mouth," explains Bobby Baun. "Then they would be very quiet and listen. That's what Al did, and that's what it took to get the thing turned around and going."

They knew that the lack of a catalyst for retired players was hampering them in their pension battles. However, they also realized that this same personality type would eventually have to be checked, because the exercise of power and influence in a glamorous business like pro sports can be a drug. But with the window of opportunity opened by the Winter/Salcer/Garvey initiative, the revelations about their pension, they were going to have to choose up sides quickly behind a player—or group of players—or lose the chance forever.

The next challenge was to find that person who would finally translate anger into action, opportunity lost into opportunity regained. Who could battle through the legendary egos among the greatest stars of the past to create a group strong enough and resourceful enough to do any good? Who cared so little about membership in the close-knit hockey power structure that he or she might not be swayed by the siren song of a position somewhere as a scout or a coach?

As it turned out, the answer to these questions surprised even the man who met the job description. Carl Brewer had always considered himself a team player, but he had been prepared to fight on and off the ice. Soon, he would have the fight of a lifetime on his hands.

18

"MAKING YOUR CHRISTMAS EVEN MERRIER"

In November 1988, Carl Brewer was sorting through his morning mail when he discovered a brief notice from the NHL Pension Society. Brewer's eyes went immediately to the bottom of the page. The form letter had been co-signed by John Ziegler, the president of the NHL, and Alan Eagleson, the executive director of the NHL Players' Association. Brewer knew from bitter experience that any message from the taciturn NHL Pension Society, especially one sanctioned by NHL power brokers Eagleson and Ziegler, was a smokescreen for much bigger action. Seeing their names together on this cryptic message set Brewer's antennae jangling.

> As a result of the negotiations between NHLPA player representatives and NHL owners, we are pleased to be able to advise of an increase in your pension. Although the agreement was reached in August of 1986, it has only been in the last 90 days that the final approvals from all Government authorities (Canada, Ontario, U.S.A) have been obtained. We hope this helps in making your Christmas even merrier.
>
> Yours very truly,
>
> R. Alan Eagleson
> John A. Ziegler, Jr.

Any missive from Eagleson and Ziegler, especially one dealing with his pension, was unlikely to make Brewer's Christmas very merry. Since hearing the results of Bob Baun's research into the pension in the early 1980s, when the first hints of the Pension Society's incompetence and indifference had surfaced, Brewer and his companion Susan Foster had been seeking to expose the true state of hockey players' pensions. Their suspicions were later reinforced when the first reports from Winter, Salcer and Garvey emerged, pointing in the direction of Eagleson's mismanagement and exploitation of hockey players.

And now here was this note, increasing Brewer's laughable pension by a small amount,* with no accompanying explanation of where the money had come from, how much had been made available to the players and why it had taken more than two years to process. Brewer had been retired for almost a decade with no increase in his pension during that time; now, suddenly, there was money available to boost it? Was it related to the $250,000 "Estate Security Plan" offered to players in the 1986 collective-bargaining agreement? Was it international hockey money? The arrogance of it made Brewer's blood boil, and he set out to rid hockey of the man he'd helped introduce to the NHL.

"A lot of people knew that something was wrong, and a lot of people tried to do something about it," says Brewer. "But Eagleson was brilliant, and they left. I never left. I was the only constant."

Like a hunter stalking his prey, Brewer had plotted and schemed and waited patiently for his quarry. It had been a highly frustrating chase thus far, with Eagleson and his sidekick Ziegler seemingly invincible behind the high walls of influence and power they'd surrounded themselves with. But with this letter and the new research emerging from Winter, Salcer and Garvey, Brewer could see his target moving back into the cross-hairs once more.

Over the next six months, he learned that other retired players shared his misgivings about their treatment by the NHL and the NHLPA, the league they had put on the map. "If it hadn't been for the Howes, the Orrs, the Mikitas, these kids wouldn't have twenty-two

---

* Brewer was entitled to $8,600 at age forty-five but has yet to take his pension. As a result, the amount he receives later will be approximately $17,500.

teams in the NHL, they wouldn't be making the money they are," says Bobby Hull.

Yet it was always the same with retired players, it seemed. They were willing to carp at length about a problem, but when it came to addressing it ... a few might write letters or bend the ear of some NHL executive at a charity function, but for the most part they either lacked the willpower or the resources or the bloody-mindedness to take on a nasty fight with the NHL.

"It's the mentality," says Bob Baun. "They won't help themselves. They still want somebody to do it for them. And nobody will do it for you."

And hoping the present-day players might take on the plight of their predecessors was a faint hope at best while Alan Eagleson steered the NHLPA. Besides, the retired players had all been young once, too, and the last thing that had concerned them during their playing days was helping retirees. "They want to play hockey, bottom line. The expression 'We'll play for nothing' is true," says Dallas goalie Andy Moog.

"All we ever wanted to do was play," says Hull. "My first year in 1957, I made $6,000. Had Chicago known, I'd have played for nothing. That's the way we thought; we were making our boyhood dreams come true."

Carl Brewer's boyhood dreams had lost their lustre by the time of the "Merry Christmas" message. While he has many good friends from his hockey days, peers from the 1960s still give Brewer a wide berth as he moves among them, his beefy presence accented by the gleaming bald head with its scars from battles past. The warm smile he displays when discussing his son Michael's accomplishments with Team Canada can turn to a cold stare in moments if Eagleson's or Ziegler's name is brought up. He's a loyal friend but an implacable foe, not unlike Eagleson himself.

Sue Foster, who sees beyond Brewer's Teutonic fierceness and channels his energies, is the gatekeeper to Brewer and his alter-ego. Strangers and lazy journalists get weeded out by the ebullient, middle-aged Foster, whose common touch provides a stark contrast to the dramatic, sometimes daunting Brewer. With her friendly smile and solicitous manner, Foster might just be mistaken for the mother of some junior hockey prospect. Together, Brewer and Foster make an unusual pair of revolutionaries when they enter a room. But it would be wrong to mistake their commitment.

"Through my various machinations, she's been there to guide and help me," Brewer says of his friend. "She probably knows more about the NHL than the lawyers. And she's tough enough to take on Eagleson. I couldn't have done it without her."

It can fairly be said that when the battle to oust Eagleson in Florida fell short and the NHL players' pension case stretched into the 1990s, destiny sought out Brewer and Foster, rather than the other way around. Charming, respectable men like Baun and Bob Goldham had failed to get the NHL's attention through mediation and compromise, and the current players couldn't stomach the long fight to remove Eagleson. An aggressive, unapologetic legal challenge now seemed the only alternative left.

Cold-eyed pragmatism was Brewer's and Foster's long suit. By his own count, Brewer went through twenty-two lawyers before he found Allan Dick to fight his battles with the NHL in the middle 1980s. If a fight in court was what it took, Brewer and Foster were the ones best equipped to handle the nasty surprises of the legal process.

On his own, Brewer contacted Ed Garvey and Ron Salcer after their near-miss in purging the NHLPA leadership in June 1989. "When you're an outsider, you're out of it ... you're really out of it," says Brewer. "I didn't know what was going on until the Florida meeting was almost a *fait accompli*. I was hoping they wouldn't give up after the second meeting in Toronto. But Salcer and Garvey got out of it. So I began communicating with Rich Winter—whom I didn't really know at the time—and flew out to Edmonton to see him."

While it may pale next to Stalin meeting Churchill at Yalta, Rich Winter meeting Carl Brewer in Edmonton in July 1990 inaugurated one of pro hockey's most dynamic collaborations. Not that it seemed so at the time—for Winter, the troubled conscience of hockey, and Brewer, its 220-pound gadfly, the get-together in the wake of the missed opportunities of 1989's turbulent summer was low-key.

Alan Eagleson was back on top of the hockey world, telling one and all that he'd been absolved of the dastardly crimes he'd been accused of in Florida. "Anyone that's dealt with me knows I deal from the top of the deck," he told a CBC interviewer. "If you don't like it, that's showbiz. I play my cards face up to everyone." And the causes that Winter had fought so hard for in Florida—free agency, impartial arbitration, severance funds, pension reform—were rapidly being drowned out in the media by the annual cacophony of training-camp clichés. Thus, it may have been the worst of times to talk about resurrecting another challenge to the NHL or the NHLPA.

But Winter, Brewer and Foster are nothing if not dogged. Winter had decided that Eagleson must be purged from hockey from the first day he phoned the NHLPA, representing defenseman Dave Lewis in a dispute in 1985. Winter had been expecting to see the legendary man of hockey spring into action on his behalf, but a nonchalant brush-off was all the inexperienced Winter got to see. For the intense young Mormon lawyer who'd once interviewed Eagleson for a research paper in school, it marked the opening salvo in an undeclared war.

"Rich Winter is a complex, unique person," says Brewer. "His dedication to this cause has been monumental. Nothing would've happened without him. I don't think he'll get the recognition he deserves, but he should be in the Builders Section of the Hall of Fame."

In the intervening years, Winter deluged Eagleson and the NHLPA with complaints, suggestions and oblique challenges. In a memo to NHL players in December 1990, Eagleson backhandedly acknowledged Winter's prodigious work: "Since March 1989, Mr. Winter has sent more than 100 letters to the NHLPA ... and has made innumerable phone calls to NHLPA offices ... he has caused the NHLPA to incur extensive legal and accounting fees."

Once, Winter even stole a client, Philadelphia goalie Ron Hextall, away from Eagleson. Eagleson responded by supplying complaints about Winter from the NHLPA files to the Flyers; according to Winter, he did this in order to discredit the agent. Hextall subsequently left Winter.

In January 1990, after attempts to oust Eagleson from the NHLPA had failed, Winter launched an official complaint against Eagleson with the RCMP. The RCMP decided it was a matter for Metro Toronto Police. The RCMP officer who forwarded Winter's thick file to the Metro Toronto Fraud Squad on February 12, 1990, indicated that "my review of the material indicates two possible offence areas, namely breach of trust ... and secret commissions ..." Metro Toronto Police, however, gave primacy to the Law Society of Upper Canada—the professional body responsible for disciplining wayward lawyers in Ontario—in a complaint against a lawyer.

So the young Edmonton lawyer sent a sixty-page complaint to the Law Society, little knowing how well Eagleson was connected in the legal world in Ontario. The detailed complaint received a polite shuffling of feet from the Law Society, but little action. Three and a half years later, the Law Society had yet to complete its report, first promised in the summer of 1990.

For Winter, this journey into the heart of the Toronto power structure was instructive but frustrating.

By the time Brewer went to visit Winter, even the zealous young lawyer was beginning to think he had a hopeless case. Any more chasing windmills and his law practice might completely disappear. "I had pretty much decided to get out of it," Winter recalls. "I phoned my wife and told her that Carl Brewer had asked me to help the retired players. We both laughed and said, 'Sure ...'" Within weeks, however, he was committed again.

The sad-eyed Winter does not internalize much, and neither does Brewer, when the subject is Eagleson and the NHL. So their meeting in Edmonton was not unlike a revival meeting as the two men and Foster volleyed outrage and indignation back and forth like Boris Becker and Stefan Edberg smashing tennis balls at each other. The issues ranged from the closed shop that hockey had become under the present leadership of the NHL and NHLPA to the crooked agents who were ruining the game. Despite the recent setbacks, they agreed to press ahead with the pension issue.

Brewer was so encouraged by the meeting that he flew to Madison, Wisconsin, to enlist Ed Garvey's help, this time in aid of the retired players. He then returned to Toronto to find an expert in pension law who might take on the case.

In the summer of 1989, Brewer had been referred by a mutual friend to lawyer Mark Zigler of the Toronto firm Koskie and Minsky. "Our firm has made a commitment to representing employees," says Zigler. "You get a great sense of satisfaction doing that. We could probably make a lot more money representing management."

Zigler and his firm had handled the much-publicized Dominion Stores pension lawsuit, in which the owners of the Dominion grocery stores had appropriated a huge surplus that had accumulated in the employees' pension plan. Koskie and Minsky helped restore the money to the employees' Pension Fund and brought about a later settlement with Dominion.

Brewer and Foster had met Zigler that summer of 1989, but had not seen him since. "I really didn't know exactly what was wrong, so I didn't know what questions to ask," Brewer recalls of that first meeting.

"He had some documents and letters from the Pension Society. I told him that if he was interested he should come back with some specific things he wanted answered about the pension," says the bearded, deliberate Zigler, who was about to find himself immersed in a hockey fight even Conn Smythe might have relished.

Arriving home from their meetings with Winter and Garvey, Brewer and Foster decided the time had come to contact Mark Zigler once more. Koskie and Minsky's offices lie just north of the Provincial Courthouse on University Avenue in Toronto. When Brewer and Foster arrived there to meet Zigler for lunch, they were still novices in the pension business, armed only with Baun's material—now almost ten years old—and the fiery rhetoric of the Winter/Salcer/Garvey report.

Brewer and Foster have acquired an instinctive distrust of most lawyers, but they liked Zigler well enough to take the next step and consider the financial implications of what they were about to undertake. While they both had comfortable enough incomes, the cost of taking on a lawsuit of this nature was considerable for Brewer, who was going through a divorce, and Foster, who lives alone with her son and daughter. It would involve not only paying the legal bills but raising enough funds from the recalcitrant retirees to take on the wealthy NHL in a protracted battle.

While Brewer and Foster sought to frame the references for Zigler's inquiry, Brewer continued to stump for the cause at old-timers' get-togethers and alumni banquets. "He was wearing himself to the bone, trying to get the guys interested in what was happening to the pension fund," says Foster. "He was terribly frustrated at the problems of trying to get people involved."

"We tried networking," says Brewer. "Talking to various people in the hockey world and keeping the dialogue going."

One of the people Brewer called on was a former colleague on the Leafs' defense. "Carl Brewer called me up one day and said, 'Let's have a game of golf over at Beaverton,'" says Allan Stanley. "I met him, played eighteen holes of golf, had a nice steak.... He told me about what he was doing with the pension. I said, 'It's about time somebody did something. It's certainly needed.' And Brewer said even if he didn't get any one else interested, he was going to do [a lawsuit] himself."

Stanley, who is as conservative in life as he was on the blueline, committed himself to the cause that same day. "We wanted to be treated as intelligent people, even partners. Not the horse-and-sparrow stuff we've been living on," he says. "You know, the horse eats the oats the first time, and then the sparrow comes along to eat them a second time off the road."

As Brewer and Foster struggled to spread the word, it became clear that to get widespread financial support for a lawsuit, Mark Zigler should produce a preliminary report on the status of the NHL Pension Society and the pension plan. With some evidence, they might finally create the groundwork for a legal challenge to find out how much there was—and how much there should have been—in the plan. In August 1990, Brewer and Foster came up with $10,000 of their own money to commission the report.

While having a pension expert like Zigler working on the report might have helped in some areas, it certainly didn't impress Ken Sawyer and the NHL Pension Society, who once again parted with documents with the greatest reluctance. The haphazard reporting of meetings and the unorthodox funding structure of the Pension Society slowed the investigations, too.

Zigler presented his report to Brewer and Foster in September 1990. It was the first unobstructed look into the pension plan for the participants since the players had been tossed off the board of directors of the Society in 1969, and it contained enough shocking revelations not only to convince Brewer and Foster to start a lawsuit, but to convince a number of his former peers to get off their wallets, too.

Among the revelations in Zigler's five-page document:

1) The presence of the $25-million surplus in the fund—the same surplus that had funded the NHL's "Estate Security Plan" in the 1986 collective-bargaining agreement.
2) Plan documents and regulations going back to the 1950s had expressly reserved surpluses for the players, and players had been the only ones to receive surpluses until 1982. Yet the NHL had grabbed most of the $25 million surplus in 1986.
3) Profits from the All-Star Game (which players played in for free) had gone to administration of the pension plan, not to enhance pensions—as players had been led to believe.
4) There was no trace of the NHLPA having deposited a solitary dollar into the plan from international hockey, supposedly the cash cow of hockey finance. (This money was later revealed to have been deposited in the plan via the NHL clubs.)

The report was political dynamite for Brewer and Foster, the type of broadside they had been looking for for almost a quarter of a century—finally, tangible evidence that the NHL had not only neglected the players' pensions but seemed to be diverting money to itself. "I knew for certain there was going to be a lawsuit then," says Brewer, "but I just didn't know what form it would take."

Where other movements to reform the pension had foundered for lack of documentation and money, this time hockey's jungle telegraph began to beat as never before, fuelled by outrage over Zigler's findings. Brewer and Foster began spreading their findings with the alumni groups, and they convinced Ed Garvey to resume his activities, this time as counsel to the retired players. The money, too, began to flow, slowly at first, but then in greater amounts as players were solicited to join Brewer's group.

"Carl came over to the house," remembers Norma Shack. "He had Ed Garvey's newsletter and a letter from Mark Zigler. Mark was suggesting we get a group together and go from there." They kicked around possible names to join the lawsuit.

One of those names was Andy Bathgate, the former Hart Trophy winner in New York, who quickly realized that it was time to act. "It wasn't the first time we'd been asked to put money towards this kind of thing," he says. "But it was something that had been bothering me for a long time. I felt it was worth one last kick at the can. So I spoke to my wife and we committed right away. And I brought along some new people, like Keith McCreary."

The decision by the Bathgates convinced Eddie and Norma Shack to commit their names and money to any lawsuit. "I remember calling Andy in Whistler, British Columbia, to ask him if he'd commit himself," says Norma Shack. "He said, 'If you've got to make a commitment in life, you can't sit back.' So I said if Andy will commit, then we will, too. Ed said go for it."

"I said they won't talk to us, so let's sue the bastards," recalls Eddie Shack. "Norma read the stuff and said, 'Let's get involved. Carl said it'll cost each person in a lawsuit $5,000.' We said sure. After, I started to wonder what was I getting into it for? It's a lot of money ... then we worked out the golf tournaments, the trading-card deal, and it started to work out all right."

In turn, Norma Shack called the Howes and Bobby Hull. "They were in different parts of the globe," says Norma Shack. "They said they'd get involved if I thought it was important. I said, 'I think it's that important.'" Gordie and Colleen Howe and Bobby Hull were soon on board.

It was decided that a strategy session on the pension plan should be held for as many of the retired players as could be assembled in Toronto. Rich Winter would fly in from Edmonton, and Brewer would brief the assembled retirees on Mark Zigler's findings. So it was that the NHL pension plan lawsuit had its modest beginnings in the basement of Hector's Restaurant in midtown Toronto in October 1990.

Hector's is a chrome-and-neon joint on busy Eglinton Avenue that specializes in finger-food and draft beer for the lunchtime crowd. As historical spots go, it's a modest one. Winter and Brewer stoked the enthusiasm of the retired stars. A temporary steering committee was formed to exploit the enthusiasm of the group. "Carl hit the right nerve," says Stanley. "A couple of the wives were really hot about the pension. I think that really helped a lot, getting a couple of the wives saying we should do that."

"The first meeting in Toronto went over very well," says Brewer. "My idea had been the same as Baun's ... to bring hockey players together for social, fraternal and beneficial results. To network, help people, be brethren. There were about thirty guys who showed up. It's always the same guys ... just as it's always the same guys who don't show up, no matter how much you talk to them, no matter how much they bullshit about their unrest." Brewer would not—and will not—name names: "They know who they are."

The enthusiasm of the small group was such, however, that the steering committee decided to broaden the movement. "Three months later, we had our next meeting," recalls Brewer.

To call the session the retired players held in Toronto on December 11, 1990, a "meeting" is like describing the Stanley Cup as a silver bowl. Months of phoning and pleading and planning by Brewer, Foster and Norma Shack (who was assuming a major role in organizing the players) had produced the greatest synod of hockey stars ever. For one night, they brought together the generation that made "Hockey Night in Canada" the most successful long-running dramatic series on Canadian television. A fan of the NHL's "Original Six" who happened by the Ramada Hotel that winter night might have echoed Mark Zigler's sentiments. "I felt like I had died and gone to hockey heaven," he says with a laugh.

More than one hundred former NHL players, referees and their wives turned up that night at the Ramada, which sits at the juncture of the 400 and 401, two major highways in Toronto. There was a symbolism inherent in the crossroads motif, but hockey players living on modest fixed incomes tend to be more concrete in their thinking, and so it passed without comment.

There were the greats: Gordie Howe, Bobby Hull, Frank Mahovlich and even Bobby Orr, the "silent partner" who chooses his spots carefully and infrequently since his public and private split with Eagleson in 1980. There was the second rank of stars: Andy Bathgate, Bill Gadsby, Red Kelly. And one could assemble the heart of the 1960s Maple Leafs amidst the Ramada's "urban tedious" school of interior decorating: Johnny Bower, Carl Brewer, Allan Stanley, Frank Mahovlich, Red Kelly, Billy Harris, Eddie Litzenberger, Bob Nevin, Eddie Shack. Finally, there were the countless journeymen and referees who had formed the willing workers in an era when demotion to the minors was just a bad shift away.

Only the absence of Bobby Baun, the unselfish warrior of seven years earlier, made it an incomplete cast. Despite invitations and entreaties, Baun was sitting this one out. "I just couldn't handle it any more," he confesses. "I still get upset when I think of what happened earlier."

If Mark Zigler was in hockey heaven that night, Alan Eagleson was roasting somewhere south of the Pearly Gates. The prospect of so many former NHLPA members and clients turning him on the spit in his home town had him clearly rankled. To a power broker like Eagleson, being cut out of the action was almost as bad as being called nasty names by Bobby Hull and Ed Garvey. And so, as the meeting got underway, a courier appeared bearing a thick document from the executive director of the NHLPA to the retired players.

"Gentlemen," it began, "I understand that Messrs. Garvey and Winter have sent some material to you about me and the NHLPA."

The man who had shunned the retired players until this moment then spent twenty-one pages lashing out at Garvey and Winter, describing the NHLPA's part in the 1985 surplus distribution and the 1986 collective-bargaining process, condemning Garvey and Winter some more, conducting a quick course on international hockey and generally sounding put upon.

"There has been no negative result on retired players' pension [as a result of collective bargaining]," proclaimed Eagleson, adding an invitation to Larry Regan. "The NHLPA would be pleased to meet with you and your executive to discuss these matters further. Our membership is prepared to support you in discussions with NHL owners related to improved pension benefits for retired players."

Eagleson's eleventh-hour epistle was greeted with hoots of derision and sarcasm. This hasty show of concern about the pension—his first ever for the men whose rights he had taken for granted so often—meant they were on the right track. If Eagleson wrote, it meant the big boys were worried. This fumbled attempt at reconciliation gave Brewer, Foster and Winter a small sense of vindication.

Not that Brewer and Winter had finally become mainstream, accepted members of the conservative hockey fraternity as a result. Far from it; there were still plenty at the meeting that night who had reservations about Brewer's leadership of the cause.

"Carl just couldn't do it on his own," states Eddie Shack. "A lot of guys wouldn't listen to him."

"I knew Carl went his own way sometimes," says Bathgate. "I saw how he used to argue with Bob Baun. I wondered how we were going to get along if he couldn't get along with his old defense partner. I wanted to stay focused on the pension. I didn't want to get involved in a vendetta against Eagleson."

And some retirees were less than enamored of Winter, whose public image up till that point had been shaped by Eagleson-influenced media types. They thought he was simply using the retired players to take control of the present players.

The remarkable turnout for the meeting was attributable to the old pecking order that had existed when these men still played. "Well, if Gordie and Bobby think it's worth getting behind ..." and "If Orr and the Big M are going, then so am I ..." Marquee names on the pension lawsuit would be as crucial to success in court as Howe, Hull, Mahovlich and Orr on the ice had been to the success of the NHL in the old days.

The real magnet that night, however, was simply the NHL pension plan itself. It was the common cross borne by the men and women in the room, the last piece of their hide still owned—and controlled—by the NHL. It cut across old animosities and united former adversaries for the first and—in some cases—last time.

After years of rumors and deceptions, they wanted the truth. "It was quite remarkable," recalls Zigler, "to have all those people—virtually every hockey player who was worth anything in the '50s and '60s—

all of them sitting in a room, staring at you, actually paying attention to you ..."

For a time, the meeting took on a life of its own, going from a strategy session on planning a lawsuit to a hockey Gestalt session. Players like Hull and wives like Colleen Howe testified to the cold, indifferent manner in which the NHL and Eagleson had treated them, the true heroes of the game, after they retired. For many lesser lights, it had been worse, much worse.

"That meeting was as much to talk about Alan Eagleson as it was about the pension plan," remembers Norma Shack. "The conclusion was that [Eagleson] would be a tough one to get the guys together on. What the older players wanted was to find out if they were right in thinking their pensions were not where they should be."

In the course of the evening, the pent-up resentments and humiliations of two generations of hockey stars spilled over as Mark Zigler broke the news that in his opinion they had been ripped off for $25 million by the NHL on their pensions. Heads shook and shoulders sagged when Ed Garvey told them how their own former employee, the executive director of the NHLPA, had negotiated a succession of one-sided "sweetheart" agreements with the NHL. Even the most tentative, such as Frank Mahovlich, had to admit the time was ripe to act.

Ed Garvey likes to quote the old Irish joke: "Is this a private fight or can anybody join?" But the former head of the NFL Players' Association was a good man to have in the retired players' corner when the punches began to fly. He had gone toe-to-toe with the NFL, considered the most powerful and politically connected of all the pro sports leagues in North America. He had cowed and nearly beaten Eagleson eighteen months before, and he felt that the treatment of the players by Eagleson was "unconscionable."

As he faced the retired players and their wives that night in Toronto, Garvey joked that it was probably their first hockey meeting without "someone yelling at them for being stupid." That brought a laugh and relieved some of the suspicion of the high-powered American lawyer. Having won their trust, Garvey then urged the men and women present to give a voice to their protest. He joined Zigler in urging them to start a lawsuit, adding that they should also attempt to enlist the support of the current players in their fight.

A steering committee of fourteen—including Brewer, Bathgate, Howe, Hull and Stanley—was formed to represent the NHL Alumni

Association as its executive. They set to work that night outlining a course of action that would culminate in a lawsuit if the NHL and the Pension Society wouldn't compromise.

As the meeting reached midnight, the issue of the cost of the lawsuit was addressed. It was the pivotal moment of the night. Talk has always come cheap for the retired players, but now Brewer was assessing the cost of the suit as anywhere between $75,000 and $150,000. The money was a bracing slap for the men and women in the room, many of whom operate on very modest budgets as a result of the NHL's pension plan.

A trust account had been set up to handle donations, Brewer told the executive. If the lawsuit was to succeed, they'd have to keep it replenished. If they lost the suit and had to pay the NHL's court costs, the amount could be upwards of $1 million to meet the bill.

A fund-raising committee under Norma Shack and Keith McCreary was formed to organize events such as golf days and alumni gatherings. As well, the committee knew that the NHL had signed a $2.5-million deal with Coca-Cola to stage an old-timers' hockey game at the 1991 All-Star Game in Chicago. The retired players decided to ask for $50,000 from the game, or alumni members such as Hull would boycott.

As they wearily trooped out of the Ramada, the retired players knew the meeting had been a cathartic moment. What they didn't know was how long or how hard they would push to get their money back. That was all that tempered the euphoria of the meeting.

They also knew they'd been closely watched that evening by the very men they had set their sights on. Lawyer Shayne Kukulowicz (son of long-time Eagleson friend and former New York Ranger Aggie Kukulowicz) had attended the meeting, ostensibly representing his father. The next day Kukulowicz filed a four-page "personal and confidential" memo to Eagleson. The report spelled the name of Andy Bathgate "Backgate" and gushed, "apparently, quite a few of the attendees came from out of town specifically for this meeting."

While Kukulowicz had identified himself on the list of attendees at the meeting, he had failed to state that he was representing Eagleson at the meeting.

19

BATHGATE
ET AL

Mark Zigler's practice specializes in employee benefit law, representing working men and women in pension disputes with their employers. Perhaps because of his own family's experience fleeing Europe and the Nazis for Cuba in the 1930s, Zigler has a certain empathy for the underdog—although underdog is hardly the word most people would use to describe former hockey stars like Gordie Howe, Bobby Hull, Andy Bathgate and Carl Brewer, men whose fame and notoriety were built upon their status as favorites, winners when the chips were down.

Zigler has come to appreciate that retired hockey players—no matter how celebrated or accomplished their public deeds—are something less than conquering heroes in their personal lives. "Having been public personalities, they're still the most modest, self-effacing people," he says. "There's a certain civility and politeness about them that you don't expect from athletes now. For what he's done, Gordie Howe is the most incredibly modest man.

"Howe and Brewer were at the opposite ends of the spectrum on some issues, yet both of them were imbued with a very common, everyday approach."

In many respects, those qualities of civility and decency away from the rink were exactly what allowed the stars of the 1940s and '50s to be exploited by Conn Smythe and his peers. Their trust that the "right thing would be done" had left them at the mercy of the NHL Pension Society in December 1990. While they had learned from Conn Smythe how to fight on the ice, few among them other than Brewer had ever learned how to fight in the alley.

That changed after the meeting at the Ramada; a spirit of mission and purpose infused the participants of the "Toronto Tea Party." David Forbes, the wiry former Boston and Washington forward, fired the first shots on a guerilla mission of his own to NHLPA headquarters in Toronto. He decided to visit Alan Eagleson three days after the Ramada meeting to take Eagleson up on his statement that the "financial statements of the NHLPA have been available for more than twenty years."

Forbes was met by Eagleson, who by now had had time to digest the report prepared for him by Shayne Kukulowicz. After expressing his dismay that such a right-thinking fellow as Forbes could have fallen in with Brewer and Winter, Eagleson informed him that Mark Zigler had been wrong in asserting that surpluses in the pension fund belonged to the players. NHLPA counsel had informed him that the surplus was probably the owners' money.

According to Forbes, Eagleson offered that a lawsuit might go a long way to clearing up the question, so Forbes asked if the NHLPA's executive director might launch such a suit. Eagleson quickly demurred. Forbes then asked him if he knew that pension-plan regulations stated that all surpluses belonged to the players. Eagleson said no, he didn't. Would that change his mind, asked Forbes? No, replied the NHLPA's executive director.

Forbes's next gambit was to ask to see the Hockey Canada financial statements to ascertain whether the players had received their fair share of the profits of Canada Cups over the years. Eagleson said the financial statements were none of Forbes's business, and that he [Eagleson] was acting in his capacity of Chief International Negotiator for Hockey Canada when he organized events such as the Canada Cup. Having witnessed the hockey chameleon transmogrify before his very eyes, Forbes left the NHLPA offices, believing that Alan Eagleson's interest in the retired players and the pension plan was as close to nil as could be measured by modern instrumentation.

Carl Brewer was next off the firing line. Within a week of the meeting at the Ramada, Brewer wrote to NHL president John Ziegler on behalf of the Alumni executive to request a meeting at the upcoming All-Star Game and that $50,000 from the "Heroes of Hockey" old-timers' game be turned over to the newly formed NHL Alumni Association for research and education about the NHL Pension Society. Brewer added that "the game is in jeopardy if no arrangement can be made."

"We are representing the sentiments of hundreds of former players who believe they have been short-changed in their pensions," Brewer wrote. "We are extremely upset to learn that there were unilateral changes made in our pension plan without notice to us or input from us. All surplus money was to go for plan participants.

"Now we learn that the plan was altered to attempt to take that money for the club owners. That is unconscionable. That money belongs to the widows of former players, disabled players and those who built the game."

Just in case Brewer's letter got lost in the mail, Forbes phoned Ziegler to personally deliver the message and request a meeting for the newly minted NHL Alumni. The gauntlet had been cast down by the retired players. In keeping with NHL tradition, Ziegler ignored the gauntlet, writing Forbes instead to say he was much too busy to meet with the retired players during the All-Star Game festivities, but that he might be able to squeeze them in *if* there was "an appropriate time and place" after the game in Chicago.

"I trust that you are aware of the various inaccuracies in Mr. Brewer's letter," he added. "However, I do not believe we need concern ourselves with same at this moment."

"I don't understand why you would assume an adversarial position," Forbes replied to Ziegler six days later. "I was interested to see the term 'inaccuracies' in your letter, referring to 'Mr. Brewer's letter.' I don't believe there are inaccuracies, but even if there are it shouldn't surprise you, should it?

"... You, the NHLPS [Pension Society], Hockey Canada and the NHLPA have all the information. The players have none. The players ask you for it and you don't give it to them.... How can you expect 100% accuracy when the only source of information refuses to tell us what is going on.... If this is some game we're playing, please, at least tell us what the rules are."

Forbes and the NHL Alumni Association learned first-hand the rules of playing with the NHL when its executive travelled to Chicago for the All-Star Game. The first rule in this sort of warfare is to keep a united front, but by All-Star time, six of the players who'd said they'd boycott the "Heroes of Hockey" game—including Bobby Hull—had had second thoughts and were going to play. Only Gordie

Howe remained on the sidelines while the NHL raked in an estimated $2.2 million from the game—a format Howe himself had earlier presented to the NHL only to see it rejected as unworkable.

This backtracking by the retired players, and Ziegler's refusal to meet them, took much of the sting out of the NHL Alumni's demand for $50,000 from the contest. In its first battle with the NHL, the retired players' executive had been badly outflanked.

They had one more hope, however: to meet with the NHLPA representatives, who were holding their semi-annual meeting at All-Star time. Representations had already been made to Bob Goodenow, the new deputy director of the Players' Association, prior to coming to Chicago. David Forbes had prepared a four-page introduction of the NHL Alumni for delivery to the players association. There was hope of going over Eagleson's head to join in a common cause on the pension.

But the NHLPA was still an Eagleson-controlled organization in January 1991, and the player reps had been cautioned that the retired players—led by Winter and Garvey—were out to steal their $250,000 "Estate Security Plan."

"Mr. Winter is at it again," Eagleson warned his membership in December 1990. His allegations were "filled with rumor, deceit, half-truths, innuendo and few, if any, facts." He then intimated that Winter and Garvey were only using the cause of the retired players to get revenge on the NHLPA for not ousting Eagleson in Florida in 1989.

When the retired players and their executive tried to enter the NHLPA meeting room at the Marriott Chicago on January 18, they were ingloriously expelled by Goodenow until a vote could be taken. In this atmosphere of misapprehension, the executive of the Alumni waited outside the doors of the NHLPA meeting room, trying for all the world not to look like a convention of welding salesmen from Ohio hoping to catch a glimpse of the rich and famous young players behind the doors.

They knew that an agreement with the NHLPA that it shared the goals and aspirations of its predecessors would be the springboard that could finally wedge open the doors at the NHL Pension Society in Montreal, perhaps avoiding a lawsuit. A marriage of the two groups would finally put the players in the place of control they deserved. But a sheepish Goodenow soon emerged from the hotel conference room to tell Brewer, Forbes, Hull, Ted Lindsay and the other members of the Alumni group who'd assembled in Chicago that "by a hand vote" the players had said they didn't have time to see the retired players at this meeting. They were too busy.

"We've been kicked out of better places," cracked Hull, trying to mask the pain felt by one more slight from Eagleson. There were brave smiles all around at the NHL Alumni press conference the next day, as Brewer said he was encouraged that Goodenow had invited them to address the June meeting of the NHLPA. But Forbes summed up the prevailing mood: "If the retired players and the current players had gotten together, it would have been one of the greatest meetings in the history of the game," he sighed.

There were encouraging hints off the record from some NHL executives that the pension problems of the greats of the game would be resolved in due course. But it was still a long way to come to have the door slammed in your face, and it hurt.

Some of the current players tried to empathize. "Gordie Howe had told me that we all have one thing in common, and that is we will all be retired," said Wayne Gretzky, who had made no secret about his devotion to Howe and his legend in the past. "We are going to get it done. Nothing will be swept under the table. It is going to be taken care of."

And Goodenow, who was emerging as a very different type of leader for the NHLPA than Eagleson, made every attempt to prove that the Alumni would get the time they needed at the next NHLPA meetings. But for all the equivocating, the euphoria of the Toronto meeting in December had run smack-dab into reality. The biting wind off Lake Michigan was there to remind the retired players—if they needed reminding—that it was a cold, cold world outside hockey's privileged bosom.

The NHL's war strategy had not changed in the thirty-three years since the League crushed the first Players' Association. It was going to ignore the new retired players' association, its ninety-day ultimatum for a response before commencing a lawsuit, and the problems they represented. Any victories for the retired players would have to come in court and at great time and expense—two commodities the NHL could more easily afford than could the ageing hockey stars.

There were more icy blasts from the other side after the ill-fated All-Star weekend, which many in the League felt had been tainted by the retired players' lobbying. One came from an imperious John Ziegler in reply to David Forbes's "if-this-is-some-game-we're-playing" letter. "I am not knowledgeable as to whom you refer to as *we*," harrumphed Ziegler. "The Pension Society has no information on file which suggests you are authorized to represent anyone as to his pension other than yourself."

Ziegler, whose "*après moi, la deluge*" public relations style borrowed heavily from Charles de Gaulle, accused Forbes of publishing "inaccuracies and misstatements" and then concluded, "Regrettably, you and your colleagues have chosen the road of threats and boycotts first, rather than that of discussion. Since litigation has been threatened, any further communication will have to come from League counsel."

The other half of the Eagleson-Ziegler axis chimed in ten days later. "You continue to attribute comments to me that are untrue," Eagleson scolded Forbes. "The NHLPA has always acted in the best interests of its members."

Forbes, however, is a mean letter-writer in his own right, and he replied to Eagleson's memo with one of his own on February 12, 1991: "So here we are. $24 M[illion] has apparently been taken from the players. You either knew about it or you didn't. If you did know, you showed no loyalty whatsoever to the players' interests in the last CBA [collective-bargaining agreement]. And if you didn't know, why didn't you? Which is it? And why aren't you upset? And why aren't you helping?"

Forbes—who had been refused help by union leader Eagleson when he was charged by police for an on-ice incident with Henry Boucha of Minnesota in the 1970s—then took his former executive director to task for his conflicts of interest, his confused loyalties and his coziness with management.

"It appears at some point, Alan, you're going to have to make up your mind and decide who's [*sic*] side you're on and who it is you represent. If you decide to side with the players and participate with us in our efforts to recapture the surplus for retired players and many NHLPA members we would welcome your support."

For Eagleson, who'd spent his entire professional career playing the two sides off against the middle, choosing sides at this point was as likely as reconciling with Bobby Orr. Instead, he attacked Forbes and the leader of the retired players: "The frustration is that these complaints come from a group of losers, a bunch of moaners ... most of the ones doing the complaining haven't worked for the past 10-15 years," he complained to CBC TV.

It was a clear shot at Brewer, of course, whom Eagleson would never deal with. Eagleson and the NHL preferred to deal with the accommodating Larry Regan and his National Hockey Alumni in Ottawa, who could be more easily influenced to see things their way. (Regan explained he was like a conduit with the NHL for widows and orphans: "That's why we didn't get deeply involved in the lawsuit.")

But while Brewer's leadership would later become an issue amongst the retired players, in the late winter of 1991 he and the other members of the executive were more or less united in organizing the prospective lawsuit. "For fifty years, they've been able to dodge questions from their dumb players," deadpanned Brewer. "But this is one group, folks, who won't go away."

Letters had gone out to Ontario's NDP government, which had been elected, in part, on a pension-reform slate in 1990. The Rae government had promised to rule on ownership of pension surpluses, among other things, and to firm up existing legislation. In addition to lost monies, the players also sought to regain their places on the board of the Pension Society under the Ontario Pension Law Reforms of 1987—the laws Eagleson had helped the NHL avoid in 1989. This process was set back immediately when Premier Rae demoted Peter Kormos, the minister responsible for pensions. It was nine months before a meeting could be arranged with the new minister, Brian Charlton. Charlton could only offer vague promises. It took two full years before the players were restored to the Board by Finance Minister Floyd Laughren.

Meanwhile, the NHL Alumni Association's fund-raising efforts were sporadic but encouraging. A dinner in March 1991 featuring the great stars of the past fizzled out when Gordie Howe would not attend, but then a trading-card deal featuring retired players—a deal expedited in part by Bob Baun—breathed new life into the Alumni's finances. The retired players hoped to make almost $325,000 from the deal with Smokey's of Las Vegas for a "Stars of the Past" card set.

Meanwhile, Mark Zigler was crafting a combination of players from different generations in the NHL so as to have representation from the entire history of the plan in the lawsuit. Seven men had agreed to put their names forward in a lawsuit. "You've heard of the G7?" says Stanley. "Well, hockey now had its G7."

Brewer, Stanley, Hull, Howe, Shack, Bathgate and Leo Reise eventually committed their names to the process. "Only five of us put money directly into the lawsuit," says Stanley. Four—Brewer, Stanley, Shack and Bathgate—were named in the suit (which became

Bathgate et al. v. the NHL Pension Society et al.) and put in $5,000 each. The fifth contributor to the defense fund was Bobby Orr, who politely declined to have his name included in the suit. "He put money in in the first place, to get the thing going," explained Stanley.

The process of gathering information from the League and the Pension Society continued as well. Ken Sawyer and John Ziegler were kept busy answering inquiries from Forbes and Gordie Howe about their pensions. Forbes wrote to ask how the Society had amassed administrative expenses of $1,328,375 from 1986-90 while operating a basic "defined contribution" scheme, supposedly the method that involves the least actuarial work.

Gordie Howe wrote to ask for the financial statements of the past five years. Sawyer grudgingly offered up the most cursory documents, "even though we are not required to do so by applicable law. The photocopy costs for the enclosed financial statements are CDN $10.50. Please send me your cheque in payment to the order of the National Hockey League Pension Society."

The irony of hitting up Gordie Howe for ten bucks after his monumental contributions to the NHL was evidently lost on Sawyer.

It was clear that the NHL was on a war footing, and immortals like Howe were to be treated as confused, misled naifs. John Ziegler, who was once Gordie Howe's personal lawyer in Detroit, expressed the League's withering contempt for Howe publicly. When asked why the Pension Society avoided answering Howe's questions about changes in Ontario pension law, Ziegler adopted his best condescending tone. "He's been informed about absolutely everything that's taken place ... Gordie may not have *understood* it, but every letter has been answered."

J. D. Ford, the Society's first auditor, was more blunt. "I don't think hockey players are much different than anybody else," he stated. "They don't give a damn much about anything but themselves."

Despite such talk, many retired players were still secretly hoping for an amicable compromise with the NHL in the first half of 1991, a way for the League to retreat with dignity from its intransigence. In their heart of hearts, these men wanted to remain a part of the hockey fraternity if at all possible. It was why they had gone back to play in the "Heroes of Hockey" game for expenses plus a pat on the back. While the NHL could live without them, they could not bear to part from the NHL.

But the League snuffed out any romantic dreams of reconciliation. Procrastination and obstruction—the same weapons Conn Smythe and Clarence Campbell had used so successfully to crush the Players' Association back in 1957—eventually pushed even the moderates among the retired players to the wall in 1991.

The futility of trying to level the playing field with the NHL made rebels out of amenable fellows like Allan Stanley, who had managed to remain loyal to Punch Imlach even when many around him were abandoning ship. "I was always for the rules," he explains when asked what prompted him to risk his retirement savings to fight the NHL in court. "My personal opinion is that the NHL stepped out of line and went *against* the rules. It's something that should've been done years ago except we never knew who was going to do it."

The last door of compromise slammed shut in Toronto on April 26, 1991, when seven former NHL stars, led by their thirty-six-year-old attorney, Mark Zigler, filed suit in the Ontario Court of Justice to recover the surplus pension monies lost from the plan that had been administered for them by the NHL Pension Society. Named as respondents in the case were the League, its twenty-one clubs, the Pension Society, John Ziegler and the Manufacturers Life Insurance Company. (By order of the court, Ziegler and Manufacturers Life were later dropped from the complaint.)

Absent from the list were Alan Eagleson and the NHL Players' Association. Never one to miss a chance to claim even a tainted victory, Eagleson interpreted this as cleansing his good name. "In all the lawsuits, there has been no mention of Alan Eagleson or the Players' Association," he said. "We took our advice from legal counsel and actuarial experts. We think we did the right thing."

In fact, the *NHL* had wanted the NHLPA to be named in the suit, but the retired players had decided not to include it. Whatever sins its executive director might have been guilty of for not protecting the retired players' interests in collective bargaining, the NHLPA had not been the administrator of the pension plan. Further, the idea of the retired players suing the very organization with which they wanted to cooperate did not send out the right message for the players.

Almost thirty years earlier, the Toronto Maple Leafs had stood proudly on the steps of Toronto's City Hall to accept the cheers of their fans for winning the first Stanley Cup for that city in over a decade. Now, Carl Brewer, Eddie Shack and Allan Stanley stood in the spotlight again, joined by Hull, Howe, Reise and Andy Bathgate.

"Red Kelly had advised us, 'If you go into this, you've got to stick with it,'" says Norma Shack. "'Never settle. Take it right to the end.'"

Brewer confidently told reporters that day that the figure they were looking for could be as much as $40-$50 million with interest, and hinted there were other money pools elsewhere that were still unaccounted for. But for Bathgate and Stanley, who were not as experienced in the legal arena as Brewer, the reward on that day was the simple dignity of standing up as men for their fellow retired players.

Their stand had not gone unnoticed at NHL headquarters in New York. Clarence Campbell had understood forty-five years earlier what a pension plan organized by players might lead to and had acted accordingly. His successor, John Ziegler, now recognized exactly what the retired players going to court meant to *his* employers. It was more than a legal challenge; it was defiance that couldn't go unanswered. Having no experience with impertinence of this magnitude (and not having the benefit of Conn Smythe's counsel), John Ziegler wheeled out the NHL's big cannons.

In May, the former club lawyer for the Detroit Red Wings filed notice of libel in Ontario against the greatest Red Wing of them all, Gordie Howe, and against the man who personified the Boston Bruins, Bobby Orr, for comments attributed to them in *The National*, a now-defunct U.S. sports newspaper.

"The NHL has traditionally practised restraint in dealing with public criticism," Ziegler wrote to the players, referring to a tradition of restraint that stretched back about fifteen minutes. "However, the untrue accusations that the NHL is failing to honor its obligations to former players cannot go unanswered.

"We have directed that action be taken by outside counsel against those spreading these untruths."

This attacking-a-flea-with-a-sledgehammer approach stunned not only hockey fans; people who had followed pro sports for a half-century could not remember a sports league ever threatening to sue two of the greatest players ever to play its game for libel. But then, Ziegler and the NHL owners hadn't been challenged in fifty years, so they obviously had some catching up to do.

If the retired players were meant to run for cover as a result of Ziegler's libel threat, the tactic failed. "Perhaps your recent tactics of filing this notice and distributing it widely to all hockey players is seen by you as a worthwhile intimidation and scare tactic," wrote

Brewer, Stanley, Shack and Keith McCreary days later. "We believe that you will find this effort on your part to discredit the two players in question will succeed, instead, in rallying tremendous support for the players being maligned by you."

Indeed, Ziegler's tactic closed off for good any chance of a reconciliation or out-of-court settlement that the players might have made down the road. In early May, the Professional Hockey Pensioners Association (PHPA) was incorporated as a non-profit organization, with Carl Brewer at its head, to "promote, support and encourage the rights, interests and welfare of retired professional hockey players, referees and linesmen." The PHPA indemnified the seven players in the lawsuit from bearing the cost of losing the suit, and it set about raising the money to pay for the legal and actuarial fees needed to keep it going.

The NHL had plenty of money to fight the lawsuit. Having alienated the players to the point where a settlement was now out of the question, however, its range of options with which to fight the legal action was rapidly diminishing. In the near future, the NHL was finally going to have to rely on its weakest ally: the facts.

Those facts revealed that it had clearly not honored its irrevocable trust to the players as expressed by Clarence Campbell back in 1947. "The Plan is so calculated and designed to provide for the participants the maximum possible benefits and protection from the resources available," the NHL president had assured players upon commencement of the plan.

The "maximum possible benefits" had not been gained from the "resources available"—not by a long shot (see Appendix A). The contributions of the players and the NHL had not been directed to even remotely protecting players' pensions, and it had left the players embarrassed and humiliated when they talked with their peers from other sports.

20

BELLING
THE CAT

In late 1991, fifty-seven of the top NHL stars from the 1950s, '60s and '70s assembled at Chesswood Arena in Toronto. Bobby Hull, Allan Stanley, Eddie Shack and dozens more—their hair greying or gone, their bodies full and fleshy—descended on a modest arena more commonly associated with industrial and house-league hockey than with stars of this magnitude. The men were there for a special photo session. After years of being neglected and ignored, they were to become special again. Their pictures were going to be featured on a series of "Hockey Heroes of the Past" trading cards.

The money earned from the card deal would help fund the retired players' lawsuit against the trustees of their pension plan, the NHL Pension Society. But the get-together had a therapeutic as well as a financial purpose. "Some of the guys hadn't seen each other in twenty-five years," recalls Norma Shack. "It was a joy to see them. All they had to do was to get their picture taken in uniform. Some hadn't been on skates in years. It was so happy, so nice."

Players who'd exchanged punches and elbows during their playing days suddenly discovered a communal purpose as they frolicked like young pups, waiting their turn before the lens. They discussed the good times when the tide was with them, but they also shared less joyful experiences, like their transition from playing days to retired life. From a superannuated boyhood fantasy to a premature middle age—these men practised a hockey communion that day.

"While he was always older than he seemed, he is suddenly younger than he feels," Ken Dryden wrote of the retired player. "He feels old. His illusions about himself, fuelled by a public life, sent soaring then crashing, have disappeared just as those of his contemporaries have come to full bloom. He is left bitter, or jealous; or perhaps he just knows too much. It is a life lived in one-quarter time."

The emotional demons were not the only thing confronted by the players; they also came face-to-face with a more concrete foe: the NHL. Long-simmering resentment of the snubs and paltry pensions had found its voice in the lawsuit launched that spring in Toronto, and it echoed through the halls and dressing rooms of Chesswood Arena.

The photo shoot was an occasion to educate players first-hand about the issues in the lawsuit. A CBC TV series documenting their plight was shown to the players. "I'll tell you one thing that helped immensely at the photo shoot," says Allan Stanley. "In the hospitality suite, the tape was playing on the TV. There wasn't anybody who came into the room who didn't watch. It was all so interesting."

"Sid Abel sat there, shushing everybody to be quiet," says Norma Shack. "Guys came back two or three times to see it."

For these men, out of hockey and in the September of their lives, justice couldn't come soon enough. But it took more than a year for the retired players to get to court from the day they filed their lawsuit in April 1991, and eighteen months from filing to get a decision from Judge George Adams.

The public sniping between the players and the NHL ceased when the legal process took over; the issue that had stirred the passions of so many in hockey was swallowed up by months of affidavits, examinations, cross-examinations, motions, undertakings and files. (The assembled documents would fill several legal file boxes with their contents.)

With Mark Zigler forbidding them to shoot at anyone on the NHL side, the players turned their sights inward. By the summer of 1991, Ed Garvey had removed himself from active duty over disagreements in tactics. Garvey's limited role and the scope of the lawsuit—which ignored Alan Eagleson's role with the NHLPA—frustrated him when he wanted reform and action on an industry-wide scale. "Ed Garvey is a brilliant man," says Brewer. "But things got out of his control." A burned-out David Forbes, often the most cogent and effective voice among the ex-players, followed Garvey's lead, resuming his investment-consulting career in California, far from hockey's madding crowd.

With Garvey gone, the retired players needed one of their own to emerge as the group spokesman. But as Bob Baun had discovered, when it fell to players to decide, everyone wanted to be "boss cow." Brewer felt his instigation of the action entitled him to lead; others felt they were best suited to the job. Within months, the unanimity forged at the Ramada Hotel in December 1990 had splintered.

The first skirmish over who would lead started innocently enough when a group of retired players in the U.S. offered to join the battle. Word of the activities of the "G7" the previous year had reached many former NHL players in the United States through their various team alumni groups. In Philadelphia, former Flyers and Canucks defenseman Bob Dailey felt the same outrage as the Canadian players when he saw his modest $8,600 annual pension.

"You come out of it and say, 'I played ten years and this is all I'm getting?'" says Dailey. "All that time spent, all those things done ... we think it's a miscarriage of justice." Dailey and former teammate Reggie Leach discussed their case with American lawyer Ed Ferren in late 1990. They described how Alan Eagleson had said millions were going into the pension plan from international hockey. Then they showed Ferren their pension benefits. Ferren (who could pass for Jimmy Carter's former adviser Zbigniew Brzezinski) was as stunned as Dailey and Leach that their pensions were so low after many years of lucrative international hockey tournaments and high interest rates.

As Lorraine Mahoney had been ten years earlier, Ferren was at a loss to explain the discrepancies between large revenues and small payouts, particularly under the stringent Employee Retirement Income Security Act (ERISA) in the United States. Under ERISA, full disclosure of the plan assets and investments is a right of the participants, so Ferren contacted the Pension Society on behalf of Dailey and Leach with a list of questions. Who are the members of the Board of the Society? What are the investments? Where is the money from Canada Cup play and All-Star Games? he demanded. Like everyone else who made these inquiries, he was told he would get the pension entitlement pertaining only to the player he represented, no more.

Ferren next got in touch with Gordie and Colleen Howe to ask for their assistance in learning about the Canadian lawsuit. As a result, Carl Brewer, Sue Foster, Keith McCreary and Allan Dick, Brewer's lawyer, travelled to Philadelphia in May 1991 to meet him. They supplied Ferren with Mark Zigler's research and brought him up to date on the lawsuit in Ontario.

Though the NDP government in Ontario had announced that a ruling on ownership of pension surpluses would be one of the mandates of its term in office, no policy had emerged. This lack of legislation in Ontario was crucial, in fact, to the NHL's interpretation of pension law in the Canadian action brought by the "G7."

After viewing the limited documentation supplied by the NHL Pension Society, Ferren felt the chances of the U.S. action were better than those of the Canadian suit. Under American law, he felt, there is greater opportunity for disclosure and examination. As well, the ERISA legislation clearly spells out the rights of participants in pension plans to full disclosure of the investments, officers and details of their plan. They are also mandated to have representation on the board of directors or trustees of any plan. In Canada, where pensions are a provincial jurisdiction, the law is far less comprehensive or consistent than in the United States.

Ferren, Dailey and Leach decided there were sufficient grounds to launch a second court action, this one under U.S. law. In June 1991— eight weeks after the "G7" suit in Ontario—Bob Dailey and Reggie Leach filed suit on behalf of themselves "and all others similarly situated" in U.S. District Court in New Jersey, seeking the return of pension monies misallocated by their trustee, the Pension Society.

Carl Brewer quickly sized up the opportunity presented by Ferren's suit. Brewer, like Garvey, had openly criticized the restricted nature of the Canadian lawsuit that ignored the rumors of millions lost to the plan from international hockey. By the end of the summer of 1991, he and Foster were actively advocating a go-slow in Canada so that the more promising U.S. action could move ahead and set the precedent.

This brought him into conflict with fellow "G7" members Andy Bathgate, Allan Stanley, Leo Reise and Eddie Shack, who were supported by Norma Shack and Keith McCreary, the principal fund-raisers for the Canadian lawsuit. It was clear that McCreary, a journeyman NHL player, was gradually assuming the leadership of the alumni support group and was philosophically opposed to Brewer's crusading style. A conflict was inevitable.

While going to court was as normal for Brewer as changing his socks, McCreary and his supporters were less familiar with the process. They considered the legal action a very serious risk and feared Brewer would somehow derail the lawsuit in his zeal to get Eagleson. Brewer did little to reassure them. "The lawsuit on the pension has a limited interest for me," explained Brewer. "I was more interested in what it meant in providing an avenue for cleansing hockey, and that meant getting rid of Eagleson."

McCreary's faction rebuked Brewer for not having faith in the Canadian action; they informed him that they wished to pursue the pension issue, not a wide-ranging vendetta against Eagleson. And they had no intention of taking a back seat to the American legal action. But Brewer had no intention of being muzzled. Along with Sue Foster and Rich Winter, he widened his net to include issues beyond the pension plan. The trio tried to draw public attention to the distribution of profits from the upcoming September 1991 Canada Cup tournament in Toronto. When Team Canada coach Mike Keenan, a client of Eagleson's, was quoted in *The Toronto Star* as saying that players were helping their pensions by participating in the 1991 Cup, Brewer conducted a lively letter-writing campaign with Keenan and Eagleson, alleging misappropriation of international hockey funds, secret commissions and breach of trust.

While Eagleson boasted that "$18 million had been plowed back into players' pensions from international hockey since 1975," Brewer, Foster and Winter pointed out that much of the money had gone towards decreasing the owners' obligations to the plan during those years, not increasing the pensions of players. They also suspected that the players' share would have been much higher had expenses for international hockey not been so high. Eighteen million dollars of the $24 million generated by the Eagleson-organized Canada Cups of 1981, 1984 and 1987 had disappeared in expenses. Players and officials alike told of the extravagance and waste when Team Canada travelled abroad—often with a coterie of Eagleson's business pals in tow.

"Al would do things, and he'd do things the way he wanted to do them," remembers Derek Holmes, who managed Team Canada for Eagleson back in the late 1970s. "No one would challenge him at the board [of Hockey Canada]. It got to where I had less respect for those people because they wouldn't stand up and say, 'Enough of this B.S.'"

On one such trip to Europe in 1977, Team Canada had forty-five to fifty players and their wives on the trip, even though they could register only twenty-one. The extra personnel were eventually sent to Rome for eight or ten days on a holiday by Eagleson, a holiday that was paid for by Hockey Canada. Other stories told of elaborate dinners, first-class travel and expensive gifts—all of which were paid for by Team Canada. Eagleson subsequently reported a $12,000 net loss on the 1977 world championship to Hockey Canada.

Derek Holmes says that players were not to blame for the high expenses. "The players weren't paid a lot of money," he recalls. "They didn't take big salaries at all." In fact, players in the 1991 Canada Cup were told that, due to lower revenues, they would have to purchase their own disability insurance for the tournament. At the same time, some board members of Hockey Canada—who were supposed to be volunteers—were getting paid handsomely by Hockey Canada. Eagleson and treasurer Chris Lang were among those paid $267,000 in 1990-91 and $213,000 in 1991-92 for consulting, management, secretarial or other office services relating to the 1991 Canada Cup.

Eagleson, meanwhile, claimed innocence. He had vowed to the players in a March 13, 1989, letter that "Neither I nor any member of my family nor any company with which I am associated with has ever received money directly or indirectly from any international hockey event ... the suggestion of impropriety is without foundation and is insulting." Yet the numbers appeared to tell a different tale. By 1991, Eagleson had backtracked, admitting that he had received most of the $414,772 for office expenses in the Canada Cups of the 1980s (this in addition to generous office expenses he received from Hockey Canada and the NHLPA).

Eagleson also had a clause in his NHLPA contract that guaranteed him a $25,000 bonus if international hockey made more that $600,000 profit in a year. The tournament was very much a one-man show for the "unpaid volunteer" Eagleson, and yet more than $1.5 million in the Canada Cups of the 1980s went for unspecified "management services." Some details of these services emerged. Eagleson's son Allen, for instance, was paid $95,000 to work on the 1991 Cup. Former employees stated that they, too, had had their salaries paid by Hockey Canada or the Canada Cup while getting no compensation for their considerable work in Eagleson's law and sports-management firm.

Despite Eagleson's claim that these contracts had been approved by Hockey Canada, neither he nor Hockey Canada would release details to the players who participated in the Cups. "The NHLPA has no access to Hockey Canada statements," Eagleson wrote to players in December 1990.

To Brewer, Foster and Winter, this abstruse logic sounded like a statement from the Queen of Hearts in *Alice In Wonderland*, not the executive director of a powerful sports union. The NHLPA executive director was also the international hockey negotiator for Hockey Canada, yet he had no access to the financial statements he'd submitted when players requested them? Who else was getting money from the players' participation in international hockey? they asked, and how much went to Eagleson? The key, as always, was access to financial records, where the secrets were hidden.

As David Forbes learned, attempts to extract any detailed financial records from Hockey Canada, the sponsors of the tournament, were met with "The books are audited, it's none of your business" from Eagleson, and "You'll have to ask Al" from Hockey Canada chairman Ian McDonald. Hockey Canada was a federally funded agency, and the past and present players who'd participated in the events had a vested interest in the profit; this stonewalling on producing the detailed financial records reeked of collusion.

"If we are partners in international hockey as Mr. Ziegler says," stated goalie Andy Moog, an NHLPA vice president unafraid to buck Eagleson's influence, "it would only be fair to show current, full statements of financial endeavors we jointly participate in. That's common practice anywhere, and that's what we'd like to receive."*

But common practice and fair disclosure would not get access to the full and detailed financial statements for Moog or Brewer or members of Parliament when they requested them. In hockey's tribal society, only one man on the players' side had the clout to demand and receive those books from Alan Eagleson, the player known as "The Great One."

Coincidentally, Wayne Gretzky was also the one man who could make or break the 1991 Canada Cup for Eagleson with his participation. Not only would Gretzky's refusal to play remove the tournament's top attraction, but if he failed to show, other stars, like Mark Messier, would likely follow suit, decimating the tournament rosters.

Gretzky had been emphatic in January about helping Gordie Howe get answers and action on his NHL pension. He had become like a son to Howe in the minds of hockey fans, performing and appearing

---

* Hockey Canada released limited financial statements to the media and players in early 1993.

together with Howe at countless events. Gretzky had made sure Howe was in the stands when he finally broke Howe's NHL record for total career points. It warmed the hearts of romantics everywhere to see Number 9's record broken by the solicitous and likeable Number 99, the skinny kid from Brantford, Ontario. But since his pronouncements in Chicago at the All-Star Game, Gretzky had gone quiet on the pension issue.

Gretzky has been an ambassador for the sport, especially in the United States, speaking out against fighting and urging better marketing of the sport to attract American TV interest. He has made himself available for a range of charitable and community events during the off-season when he'd rather be healing his battered physique from the rigors of an NHL season.

The lucrative perks that come with being the number-one attraction in the sport have also made Gretzky a rich and powerful man. A reluctant public figure at first, he sees his face now plastered on commercial endorsements of every description, from shaving cream to his own cartoon show. Yet the League's number-one star and attraction has consistently shied away from his obligations to his fellow players on issues like the pension and reforming the NHLPA. It is a burden he shares with Michael Jordan and few others in sport, a burden that Gretzky dislikes. It is nonetheless a burden he must accept.

As Eric Lindros demonstrated in 1991-92 when he bucked the draft system and forced his trade from Quebec to Philadelphia, some players *are* bigger than the game and can force changes to benefit all the journeymen below them in the pecking order. But Gretzky has played it both ways—the star-of-stars financially, but one of the "grunts" politically. And while he talked about reform in private, he never made it a public issue when facing Eagleson or Ziegler.

In Gretzky's defense, it can be said that Howe, his reported idol, performed no better when it came to leading players in the direction of increased salaries and improved benefits when he was the top player in the NHL. But Howe—who played in hockey's Dark Ages—can at least plead ignorance.

Gretzky, with his close friendship with Kings owner Bruce McNall and his corporate connections, has had the implications of his role clearly spelled out, yet he has chosen to sidestep the opportunity of belling the cat named Alan Eagleson. The vacuum at the top of the players' ladder allowed Eagleson to survive and prosper at the expense of players for the almost dozen years that Gretzky has been the number-one player in hockey.

While he was apparently very bullish on reform of the NHLPA in private, Gretzky was a no-show at the NHLPA's West Palm Beach showdown over Alan Eagleson in June 1989, and he scrupulously tried to hide which side he supported.* If either side had been able to publicly claim his vote one way or the other at the meeting, it would have been a back-breaker. But Eagleson emerged from West Palm Beach with his job, while Gretzky stayed away and kept his opinions to himself.

The 1991 Canada Cup offered Gretzky another chance to take a leadership role, this time in helping Howe and the retired players find out where the money from international hockey was going. In the nine months leading up to the tournament, Rich Winter had sent Gretzky detailed letters outlining the many areas of concern he had about Eagleson profiting from international hockey, culminating in a July 30, 1991, correspondence on the eve of training camp for the Canada Cup.

In that letter, Winter reminded Gretzky of his influence over other players who might be considering whether or not to play in the 1991 Cup. He cited areas where Eagleson's claim that neither he nor his family received money from international hockey was patently false, and he asked Gretzky to demand a full, audited disclosure of the books of the Canada Cup and Hockey Canada before agreeing to play in the 1991 tournament.

"Should you pursue and receive full disclosure," wrote Winter, "you may just create a greater legacy for hockey players than you could have imagined."

But Gretzky wanted no part of the job. His agent, Michael Barnett, replied to Winter on August 2, 1991: "Wayne Gretzky would like to make it very clear, Rich, that he has not encouraged nor attempted to influence other players to participate in the upcoming Canada Cup ... he has always accepted the Canada Cup invitations solely on the basis of the opportunity they provided him to represent his country....

---

* Eagleson apparently thought he had Gretzky's vote. In a May 1989 memo to John Sopinka, he includes Gretzky's name as one of the executive board who are "behind me 100%."

Wayne does not want to investigate personally any of the matters mentioned in your July 30th letter."*

Gretzky suggested, instead, that Winter take his case before the executive board of the NHLPA, the same board whose votes had been the measure of survival for Eagleson in West Palm Beach in 1989. While Gretzky was ducking Winter's allegations, however, other players were more assertive. Andy Moog had passed up an opportunity to play in the 1991 tournament, in part because of the refusal by Eagleson and Hockey Canada to share financial information.

Winter was not the only one to buttonhole Gretzky. Both Gordie and Colleen Howe personally appealed to Gretzky and his father Walter, urging Wayne to demand a look at the detailed financial records in an effort to help out the retired players he professed to admire and respect.

When Gretzky finally arrived in Toronto in August 1991 to play in the tournament, he began making noises again about helping out the retired players if possible. While Eagleson had written that he did "not intend to bring the work of the NHLPA to a halt in an effort to answer Mr. Winter's demands," he quickly granted Gretzky an audience at NHLPA headquarters. (Of course, Eagleson would have spit green nickels had "The Great One" made it a prerequisite of playing in the tournament.)

Gretzky emerged from the tête-a-tête with Eagleson none the wiser for the experience. If he'd seen the detailed financial books for the Canada Cup, he didn't let on to the world. "As Wayne Gretzky said so well," Eagleson crowed after the meeting, "'Sure, I feel bad for Gordie Howe and the others who aren't getting the type of pension I'm getting. But I'll feel badly for myself because I won't have near the pension that Eric Lindros will have. That's part of life.'"

Eagleson then related how his own father, James Allen Eagleson, had worked twenty-five years at Goodyear Tire and his pension was only $80 a month. "It was great at the time, but now ... well, that's part of life," he declared. Eagleson neglected to mention that his guaranteed

---

* He did have the time, however, to try to influence the young Eric Lindros to drop his agent, Rick Curran, and move to Barnett's International Management Group. His recruiting ceased when a former teammate barked, "Will you leave the kid alone and let him play hockey?"

$50,000 (US) a year pension from the NHLPA was a part of life, as well—presumably because it wasn't part of any retired hockey players' life. A grateful Eagleson then issued the understatement of the year: "This Canada Cup owes a huge debt to Wayne Gretzky."

While Gretzky shadowboxed in September, the infighting among Brewer and the other members of the lawsuit escalated through the fall and into winter. Brewer's public advocacy on the Canada Cup brought him the censure of all the members except Gordie and Colleen Howe. Meetings of the group became more acrimonious, with the McCreary faction complaining that Brewer was making unilateral decisions for the group and ignoring fund-raising.

"Who's going to hustle the money we need?" asked Shack. "It sure won't be Carl. It's me that has to press on *my* friends for money."

Brewer, meanwhile, accused the others of fiscal irresponsibility and going behind *his* back in financial matters. He also wanted compensation for his considerable out-of-pocket expenses. "Any information being distributed publicly should be accurate, correct and professional in both content and appearance," he wrote McCreary and Norma Shack. "We very much have the eyes and ears of many interested parties, not all of whom are friendly."

Both sides claimed they were misunderstood. Brewer resigned as a director of the PHPA and, for a time, considered signing off the lawsuit to join the U.S. action in Philadelphia with Bob Dailey and Reggie Leach. The Howes seemed ready to join Brewer, too, after a raucous meeting of the "G7" in which Colleen Howe and Carl Brewer were ostracized for their actions.

The two sides stopped fighting only when reminded by lawyer Allan Dick that the NHL would love nothing more than to see discord within the group as an excuse to stall the lawsuit even further. A shaky truce was drawn up, and Brewer reluctantly handed over the symbolic leadership of his "sacred mission" to McCreary.

In short, it seemed like the old days to Bobby Baun. "I guess I'm still disappointed that we can't stick together," he says. "I think the time is right now to bring back some of the class of the late '50s and '60s. Most of that group were classy guys ... Timmy [Horton] would've boosted everybody had he lived. I think he would have shared his good fortune in more ways than just money."

While Mark Zigler proceeded with the lawsuit through the winter of 1991-92, the hockey world was turned upside down. The 1991

Canada Cup, which Canada had won in convincing style over the Americans, was Alan Eagleson's last grand, public gesture as the unassailable czar of hockey before an adoring public and media. Never again would he dominate the players and hockey as he had that September.

Later that month, Eagleson and the NHL were the subject of two unprecedented media thrashings that were both comprehensive and unflinching in describing the damage Eagleson and the NHL had wrought on the players, their pensions and the League that was celebrating its seventy-fifth anniversary in 1991-92.

First to emerge was the long-awaited *Net Worth*, by David Cruise and Alison Griffiths, two business writers based in Victoria, British Columbia. Perhaps the only Canadian sports book that can rival Ken Dryden's *The Game*, it promised to "explode the myths of pro hockey," and it delivered. The biggest myth it exploded was that of Eagleson as the benevolent "czar" of hockey. *Net Worth* said his handling of the pension plan was "the biggest sucker play in the history of sports."

Eagleson had always managed to exploit the press because it rarely bothered to check its own files on Eagleson's bold pronouncements over the years. Had they done so, they'd have seen a line that danced like a seismograph on the San Andreas Fault.

The NHL, too, was savaged as a short-sighted enterprise that had only succeeded due to its total domination of the players. Conn Smythe was portrayed as a union-busting anti-Semite, Clarence Campbell as an officious toady, Jim Norris as a mob-influenced bully and his brother Bruce Norris as a hopeless lush who'd nearly destroyed the Detroit Red Wings with the help of a young Detroit lawyer named John Ziegler.

The NHL levelled its crudest counter-offensive on *Net Worth*, always a sign that the attack had hit the mark. Through loyal media sources, John Ziegler admitted that while he hadn't read the book, his crack NHL research staff had counted eighty errors in the first 200 pages. Later, a confidential NHL memo could cite just twenty errors in the 394-page book, with only two bearing any importance.

Eagleson upped the ante in his criticism. "I call it 'Net Worst,'" he told a CBC TV interview in November 1991, "because it's the worst example of editing and research one could imagine. They are not telling the truth on several items ... their errors exceed two hundred. You can't give any credibility to something that is so far off on so many areas." Eagleson's "research staff" never documented the two hundred errors, but it was a claim he repeated constantly that fall to friendly media outlets.*

Another repeated boast of Eagleson's was that he never backed down from a fight. But he consistently refused to appear on TV and radio shows with Cruise and Griffiths to rebut any of the "two hundred errors" they had made in their book. Bob Goodenow, NHLPA deputy executive director, meanwhile, quietly bought copies of the book to distribute to players while he waited for Eagleson's departure as executive director.

The next media salvo for the Eagle and the NHL came from a small, Pulitzer-Prize-winning newspaper in Massachusetts, *The Lawrence Eagle-Tribune*. In a week of articles, *The Eagle-Tribune*'s sports editor, Russ Conway, took major slices from the hide of Eagleson and NHL president John Ziegler in a series entitled "Cracking the Ice: Intrigue and Conflict in the World of Big-time Hockey." Where *Net Worth* gave an overview of seventy-five years of NHL exploitation of players, Conway went into greater depth on the current state of the League. In painstaking detail, Conway sought to show Eagleson's hand in every phase of the hockey business: disability insurance, NHLPA mortgages to friends, partners and business associates, the mishandling of his client Rick Middleton's finances, his acrimonious split with Bobby Orr. The list of subjects covered by Conway was overwhelming and damning. The series came within a whisker of winning him a Pulitzer Prize.

Eagleson lamely scoffed that Conway was rehashing the old accusations of Garvey/Salcer/Winter from 1989. "Hey, it goes with the territory," he said at his NHLPA retirement luncheon on January 6, 1992. "People say it must be tough, but I'm a big boy."

But no one before Conway had ever unwound what Ken Dryden described as Eagleson's "immense web of hockey, political and business connections" to expose the inner workings of his empire. And rather than rely on hearsay and innuendo that Eagleson could rebut or obfuscate, Conway backed up his claims with documentation, leaving

---

* Eagleson's own book, *Power Play*, was considered a major disaster for its publisher McClelland and Stewart, which had to apologize to Rich Winter for certain statements made in the book.

Eagleson and the NHL—which rarely had encountered this type of thoroughness—with only half-hearted rebuttals in reply.

Evidently, someone else was impressed with Conway's series. On December 27, 1991, the FBI conducted a series of surprise visits to the NHL headquarters in New York and the offices of the fifteen U.S.-based clubs. They took away boxloads of documents on the NHL's relationship with the NHL Players' Association. FBI spokesmen said they were conducting an investigation into the affairs of Alan Eagleson and the NHLPA. Conway's material was subpoenaed as well.

Shortly thereafter, the RCMP said it was assisting the FBI by collecting documentation from the Canadian-based NHL clubs and was conducting a preliminary investigation of its own into the affairs of the NHLPA in Canada. (In truth, the RCMP sat on the case for another full year before questions asked in the House of Commons by Liberal House Leader David Dingwall finally sent the Ottawa establishment scurrying.)

While the RCMP conducted its half-hearted investigation into one of the most influential men in Canada, the U.S. Justice Department decided in the spring of 1992 that there was enough evidence to convene a grand jury hearing into Eagleson's running of the NHLPA. "Everything I did in representing the players and the union was well-known, accepted, confirmed and not unethical," Eagleson said at a rambling press conference following his retirement as NHLPA director. "In the old days, they used to investigate and find out if anything's wrong, and then act. Now, they announce they're having an investigation. You can't win. I've got a wife, family, reputation ... I don't want those things sullied at this stage of my career. I'll tell you this, it beats getting hit over the head with a bludgeon and getting killed.... Maybe that's what they're trying to do to me indirectly."

The winter of 1991-92 was no easier on Eagleson's old axis partner, John Ziegler. After the announcement of the two lawsuits against the NHL's pension plan, the flubbed expansion to Ottawa and Tampa Bay and the threatened libel suits against Howe and Orr, Ziegler and the owners came face-to-face in September with Eagleson's successor as NHLPA executive director, Bob Goodenow, in negotiations for a new collective-bargaining agreement.

Typically, Eagleson was deeply immersed in his "other" duties at this crucial moment for his membership. While he complained that Rich Winter "is doing his best to drag the NHLPA back from this important business," he was too busy running the Canada Cup to participate in "this important business" himself. He left Goodenow solely responsible for negotiating the new collective-bargaining agreement with the League. Goodenow gave his counterparts early warning in the legal jockeying before the bargaining that negotiating with the NHLPA would be very different with Eagleson out of the picture.

Ziegler and the NHL Board of Governors chose to ignore the early warnings from the players and their rookie leader—just as they had done with Brewer and the retired players. It was a move that proved fatal to Ziegler's presidency.

Unlike Eagleson—the Canadian patriot and media darling—Goodenow was an inscrutable, media-shy American lawyer and former player agent for stars such as Brett Hull. Rather than conduct negotiations through the pages of the newspapers, Goodenow kept his own counsel strictly with the players. He told them he had every intention of using the NHLPA's long-dormant strike threat to achieve some real progress for the players in the new agreement. The best opportunity to get action, he told them, was at playoff time, when the owners made their greatest profits and when players had already been paid their full season's wages. For the Stanley Cup winners, the most they would lose if the playoffs were cancelled by a strike was $25,000, a relatively minor amount if the price was breaking the League's stranglehold on its players. For the six teams that missed the playoffs, striking at post-season play meant no income loss at all.

After getting their first taste of Goodenow and the new NHLPA in the summer of 1991, a few concerned owners urged a lockout of the players in training camp or the early season to take the initiative away from them. But as the previous agreement expired on September 15, 1991, Ziegler blithely promised the NHL Board of Governors that, with a little pressure in the right places, Goodenow and the players would soon collapse.

And so the NHL's seventy-fifth anniversary season rolled on, oblivious to the impending threat of a first-ever League-wide strike by players. By All-Star time, Goodenow had had five months to build up a strike fund and hire a team of specialists in the areas of pensions and anti-trust. He'd also had time to deliver a crash course in labor-management relations to his players, who'd been left uneducated and vulnerable by Eagleson. Better yet, with the playoff deadline drawing ever nearer, time was on his side.

John Ziegler professed to be unconcerned as the League celebrated its seventy-fifth birthday in Philadelphia in January, describing the NHL's lawsuits and labor deadlines as "common business problems ... people say you're in troubled times because the CBA [collective-bargaining agreement] expired. If that's your definition of troubled times, then every company that has a union has troubled times."

John Ziegler wasn't offering up his own definitions of troubled times, but the first week of April 1992 probably fit the bill. Despite frantic last-minute bargaining with the players—and the obligatory bludgeoning of the players in the media—the NHL was handed its hat by Goodenow and the players. By a vote of 560-4, the NHLPA voted for its first-ever strike on April 1, an April Fool's gift to Ziegler.

The next day the players walked out, leaving twenty-seven regular-season games and the playoffs hanging in the balance. A reported $75-million contract with CBC TV also weighed heavily on the owners. For the players, it was a bittersweet moment, a display of independence and power that players like Carl Brewer and Bob Baun and Allan Stanley had never known, but also a venture into the unknown for many young men with little education or job skills.

While the players feared the consequences their strike would have on John Ziegler's "$450-million business," they also felt the sense of self-respect and purpose that comes from finally shaking off a bully. For ten days, they withstood a high-powered public-relations campaign from Ziegler that was larded with questionable statistics and crocodile tears for the cameras.* On an almost daily basis, Ziegler or his advisers produced flow charts, pie graphs and ersatz emotion for the TV cameras, all meant to prove that if players didn't reduce their demands, the NHL would be $150 million in the red within two years.

What was never explained to the assembled media was how a business that Ziegler had extolled as lucrative in his 1990 prospectus to expansion applicants had suddenly found itself on death's door just eighteen months later. Explaining that the NHL had sold 87 percent of all its available seats in 1988-89, Ziegler had bragged in 1989, "I don't think there is another live entertainment business in the

---

* Ziegler's lament for "Hockey Night in Canada" was a particularly cherished piece of theater among reporters who could not recall having seen Ziegler at a hockey game in the previous three months.

world that does that good [*sic*]. Now, if I sound like I'm a little proud of that, you bet your bippy I'm proud."

All that was noted was that Ziegler's press conferences were a lot niftier than Goodenow's informal press briefings. More troubling to players than style points in the press were the ten days of abuse and criticism from fans who saw players as overpaid prima donnas who were out to wreck the sport for their own benefit.

Wayne Gretzky made a contribution, too, late in the strike. Along with several players and agents, Gretzky tried to force Goodenow into a truce "for the good of hockey." (However, his close friendship with Bruce McNall made many wonder how Gretzky could act impartially on behalf of anyone.) Nonetheless, Goodenow recognized that no rookie leader of the Players' Association could win a public power struggle for control of the NHLPA with Wayne Gretzky, "The Great One." And so he took the best offer available from the now-desperate owners and chose to fight another day—perhaps when Gretzky had been supplanted as the number-one player in the NHL by the more politicized Eric Lindros.

When the two sides finally settled on April 12, 1992, it could truly be said that professional hockey had changed forever. While the players realized only modest concessions in the collective-bargaining agreement, they had finally called the owners' bluff, winning credibility and their rightful place in the industry as the game's ultimate asset. A strong, autonomous players' association would be good for hockey as it sought to overcome decades of "short-term gain, long-term pain" management strategy.

Better yet, the players had broken the Eagleson-Ziegler axis, which had held them back for so long. Eagleson was too busy scrambling to line up friends and allies to fight the U.S. Justice Department to have any time to sabotage the negotiations. Former Prime Minister John Turner and close friend John Sopinka of the Canadian Supreme Court were reported to be standing by, ready to advise him.

Three weeks after the playoffs belatedly ended, the NHL owners made Ziegler the sacrificial lamb, cashiering him and his spin doctors for their strike strategy. Just so that no hard feelings would emerge—along with any public revelations about the inner workings of the NHL—the NHL Board of Governors awarded Ziegler a reported $1-million "golden handshake" to smooth his transition to civilian life. And Red Wings owner Mike Ilitch found a place for Ziegler with his Detroit Tigers baseball team—in case he felt the need to reminisce about the good old days.

Ziegler was replaced as president on a *pro tem* basis by League counsel Gil Stein, a cheerful Philadelphia lawyer who promptly assured everyone that he had had nothing to do with any unpopular or unsuccessful policy adopted by the NHL in the past fifteen years. Despite his own presence on the NHL Pension Society's board of directors, for instance, Stein claimed the responsibility for legal decisions lay with outside counsel. Stein similarly laid the blame for fighting, expansion and the metric system on Ziegler loyalists like NHL vice president Bryan O'Neill, who was shown the finely crafted oak door.

Stein's greatest accomplishment as president was arranging his own induction into the Hockey Hall of Fame as a "builder" in return for stepping aside to allow Gary Bettman to succeed him and become the NHL's first commissioner in 1992.

The firing of John Ziegler occurred on Day Three of *Bathgate et al. v. the National Hockey League Pension Society et al.* The fireworks elsewhere in hockey had driven the retired players' lawsuit out of the public spotlight, and with it, the issues so central to the lives of hundreds of retired NHL players and referees. After the dramatic press conferences, the last-minute brinksmanship and the intrigues of the strike, the five-day trial could add little glamour to the issues and characters in the lawsuit for the media. With only the submissions of their clients' arguments by the lawyers, the proceedings had a distinct shortage of headline-grabbing revelations.

Luckily for the retired players, the drama elsewhere had drawn the NHL's attention away from the growing rift within their numbers. It was a rift that was growing larger by the day, and one the NHL might have exploited had it not been so involved with the strike.

For Brewer and Stanley—the Maple Leafs players present—and the other retired stars who gathered each day to hear Mark Zigler and then NHL counsel Earl Cherniak present their respective cases, the trial was the product of seeds sown long ago. The retired players had shown the current hockey stars the way by standing together long enough to sue the NHL. Now they hoped to reap the harvest of so much hard work.

21

VINDICATION

When Earl Cherniak, Q.C., rose in the Provincial Courthouse on June 11, 1992, to present the NHL's 162–page defense in *Bathgate et al. v. the NHL Pension Society*, he was considered among the most respected and successful lawyers in Canada. A senior partner in the Toronto firm of Lerner and Associates, Cherniak had made his reputation in the field of personal-damage suits in his native London, Ontario, winning huge awards for his clients.* Now, he was the legal version of a power-play specialist, brought in when a big score was needed in the high-pressure atmosphere of the courtroom.

The hawk-faced Cherniak had had to overcome a serious stutter to become an effective courtroom lawyer; ever resourceful, he had learned to use the pauses needed to control his stutter as an effective speaking device when addressing a judge. "Mr. Cherniak is very much at home in a courtroom," says a fellow lawyer, with a trace of awe.

The Windsor-born Cherniak would need all his practised skills in defending the NHL's case. Before the trial had even started, the League had been forced to concede that the Pension Society had erred in calculating the surplus divisions in 1982 and 1985. The NHL had said that all contributions to the plan had been split fifty-fifty between players and owners until 1969. In fact, the owners had paid at least $300 a year less than players until 1957. The Pension Society had to promise to

---

* Ironically, Cherniak also successfully defended Ron Joyce and Tim Horton Donuts against Lori Horton when she sued in 1992 to regain the company shares she'd sold in 1975. Horton claimed she wasn't mentally competent at the time of the sale due to drug abuse, but the court denied her claim.

rectify the mistake and credit the players' pension accordingly. It was not a major problem, but hardly an encouraging start to the trial for the League.

When it came to evaluating the League's chances of winning, Justice George Adams had to be taken into account as well. He had a reputation as an expert in labor cases dating back to his chairmanship of the Ontario Labour Relations Board in the early 1980s. Some felt his record showed a tendency to find for the labor side in such cases.

"Some judges will let you know quite candidly right away how they're inclined," says Zigler. "They want to hear from counsel why they shouldn't do something. Others are more poker-faced." Adams maintained an "inside-straight" demeanor throughout the trial.

While Justice Adams could look out at almost two dozen former NHL stars in attendance during the trial, none of the NHL executives in question—including John Ziegler and Ken Sawyer—were to make an appearance. The modest show of player solidarity was important in boosting the morale of the players; conversely, Cherniak was probably aided by *not* having the perpetually tanned Ziegler exuding wealth and power in an expensive Italian suit behind him in the seats.

Cherniak also had to counter the natural public sympathy for the ageing hockey heroes as they took on the trustee of their own pension plan. Being a lawyer is by definition an adversarial occupation, where one checks one's feelings at the courtroom door. But the prospect of branding legends such as Bobby Hull, Gordie Howe, Carl Brewer, Andy Bathgate, Allan Stanley and Leo Reise as chisellers or malcontents was unlikely to win Cherniak any friends in hockey-crazy Canada.

Cherniak and the NHL had decided not to dwell on whether the players' pensions were sufficient compensation for their many years in the League. Despite claims from the NHL and Eagleson that players were reducing their payouts by taking their pensions too early, at age forty-five, the NHL never tried to make the argument that the players' modest benefits were adequate. It was a public-relations fight Cherniak could never win.

For instance, to guarantee fifty-four-year-old Carl Brewer almost $18,000 a year pension for life in 1992, the NHL would have had to invest approximately $23,000 at 10 percent interest in 1970, Brewer's last full year in the NHL.* Brewer and the NHL, however, had already contributed $28,500 in *principal* alone by 1970. It was as if Brewer's 1992 pension benefit didn't even reflect his principal contributions, let alone the interest he had earned on that principal while he played. There were many such stories, especially from the players of the 1950s and '60s.

But what the players might have earned in other circumstances was not the issue at law for the NHL. Cherniak was to argue that the NHL's pension plan had been a "defined benefit" scheme until 1986, and that the Pension Society had delivered exactly the benefits it had promised to the players as described in the regulations and collective-bargaining agreements. How they arrived at those "defined benefits" was their business. So long as the plan was fully funded, that would fulfil the trustees' obligations to the players.

As well, Cherniak intended to show that the member clubs had reserved the right in the original regulations to amend the NHL Club Pension Plan and Trust at any time without notification to the players. As a result, they were justified in rewriting the amendments in 1983 and claiming the lion's share of the surpluses in 1982 and 1985. Simply because the Pension Society as trustee had seen fit to distribute surpluses generated by the Manulife group-annuity plan to the players on seven occasions in the past did not imply that the Pension Society felt the surplus permanently belonged to the players. Nor did it disqualify the Pension Society and the NHL from deciding to change the practice in the future.

Finally, Cherniak was to assert that the players had come up with a "tortured interpretation" of the facts concerning the 1969 Owner/Player Council agreement that called for removal of the players from the board of the Pension Society. "In hindsight, they wished they'd made a different deal in 1969," he told the court. "So now they've come up with this tortured interpretation of the documents."

The NHL was sticking by the deal it believed it had made with Alan Eagleson in 1969, as described in Clarence Campbell's letter to the players that year. Campbell had written that the players had given up their right to all surpluses in the future, and the NHLPA

---

* Interest rates averaged 10.12 percent on federal bonds between 1970 and 1991. The Federal Bond Rate is a conservative, long-term security. Among other securities, mortgages, corporate bonds and five-year GICs all performed even better during the period.

under Eagleson had never chosen to dispute that statement. Nor had the retired players turned up one witness to support their interpretation of what happened, added the League.

The NHL was looking for a complete dismissal of the application by *Bathgate et al.*, with the NHL's legal costs paid on a "solicitor and client" basis by the applicants.

The legal arguments for the retired players had been spelled out during the previous two days by Mark Zigler from his seventy-one-page brief for the applicants (the players and referees covered by the NHL's pension plan). Zigler's task had been to translate into cold, legal arguments the heated passions expressed by the retirees about their pensions at the Toronto meeting of 1990.

Zigler's case for the players had four principal arguments. According to the retired players, the regulations of the original plan in 1947 and articles in the subsequent trust agreements stated that the plan was an irrevocable trust—that is, all the monies contributed to the plan in the names of the players *and* the surpluses generated by those contributions belonged to the players, not to the NHL member clubs who set up the Pension Society. Further, the NHL had no right later to amend the plan to retroactively claim an interest in those contributions after they'd been made.

Second, Zigler contended that the pension plan had always been a "defined contribution" scheme, not a "defined benefit" scheme. Under the former, surpluses accrued to the plan participants (the players and referees) because they—not the NHL—bore the risk of losses due to inflation and lower-than-expected interest rates. Had the pension plan been a true "defined benefit" scheme, the owners would have been responsible to make up any shortfalls in the plan during bad economic conditions—which they never did. According to Zigler, the NHL could not claim a share of the surpluses in the plan if it was not prepared to similarly share in any losses.

While the NHL pension plan had described the annual benefits a player was to receive, it also explicitly spelled out the annual *contributions* by both participants and the NHL. Furthermore, those contributions had always been defined in the plan's regulations and articles or in the collective-bargaining agreements between the League and the Players' Association.

Third, Zigler stated that as trustee for the players, the Pension Society had both a fiduciary and a moral obligation to protect the pensions of those players from the impact of inflation. The distribution of surpluses in the form of experience-rate credits was the method the Society should have employed to fulfil its obligation. Further, the Pension Society had ignored its responsibilities to the players when it failed to seek the opinion of the courts over the question of who owned the surpluses, and when it failed to notify them of the circumstances surrounding the 1982 and 1985 surplus decisions.

Fourth, the players asserted that the NHL Players' Association had no mandate to negotiate for them on pension matters in collective bargaining. Any agreements reached between the NHL and Alan Eagleson's NHLPA concerning pensions were made without their consent, and were therefore null and void.

The players asked the court to declare that all plan surpluses were for the exclusive benefit of the participants, and that the Pension Society had no right to allocate surplus monies to anyone other than the participants. In addition, any subsequent amendments permitting allocation to the clubs should be invalidated.

They also requested an order to reimburse all surplus monies unlawfully allocated to the clubs (approximately $40 million including interest) for the purchase of pension benefits, to be distributed evenly among the participants. Further, they asked the judge to replace the Pension Society as trustee of the plan and requested that a new trustee be appointed. Finally, the players asked that their legal and court costs be paid by the NHL.

The trial lasted five days. When Earl Cherniak concluded his final remarks on June 29, the fifth and final day of the trial, he joked to bystanders, "See you in appeals court."* It had at last fallen to a judge to resolve a dispute that had its roots thirty-five years earlier in the still-born Players' Association of 1957, a dispute prolonged and exacerbated by the refusal of Conn Smythe, Clarence Campbell and the NHL to distance themselves from the plan's administration by appointing independent trustees, a simple move that would have removed the manipulative hand of the employer from their employees' financial future.

As Justice Adams strode from the court, the players present could only reflect on how avoidable the whole costly process had been.

---

* Cherniak was not around to fight the appeal, however. He was replaced by Neil Finkelstein of Blake, Cassels & Graydon in Toronto for the appeal scheduled for September 1993.

Carl Brewer and Allan Stanley, teammates with philosophies on life as different as chalk and cheese, might never have travelled this road together had the NHL met the most basic requirements for disclosure of investments, had it performed the simplest procedures to protect their pensions from the ravages of inflation, had it cared.

Similarly, had Alan Eagleson, the man hired to represent the players—to prevent exactly this kind of one-sided scenario—honored his moral obligation to fight for them and to give due diligence to the players' concerns about their pensions, then Andy Bathgate and Eddie Shack might be golfing this lovely early summer day, not risking their financial futures on the outcome of a lawsuit. "If you have someone looking after your interests, he has to be loyal," said Bobby Hull. "We never had anyone loyal to the players."

"I think the first time I heard no one represents us [in collective bargaining] was in Russ Conway's article," says Stanley, referring to the Eagleson series in *The Lawrence Eagle-Tribune*. "I had always thought that ... I always *knew* we weren't being represented ... but I thought they at least had an obligation. Hell, they do have an obligation!"

The applicants in the suit, though satisfied, took no joy in discovering during the course of the lawsuit how the greatest names had been treated as chattel by the men they had made rich. "It's sad," says Norma Shack, "because hockey's a great game. But the pension dispute has given the NHL a dirty name."

"I'm not bitter," Gordie Howe wrote in *The New York Times*, "but I am disappointed that it had to come to us suing the people who control the game we love so much. Who needs the black eye?"

The NHL—with $150 million in expansion fees in its pocket—would have no trouble finding the money in the event the players won the suit. But the seven men who'd brought the suit and their supporters would have to dig very deeply to come up with the many hundreds of thousands of dollars a lost decision would cost.

Unlike their counterparts in the United States, who were able to hire on a contingency basis, the Canadian applicants were constantly trying to raise money. "I remember sitting in Mark Zigler's office with Ed Ferren and Allan Stanley and Carl [Brewer] and Andy Bathgate when we started the suit," recalls Norma Shack. "Mark said, 'You'll have to come up with $15,000 a month to keep the suit going,' and everybody said, 'Oh, sure, no problem.' But I said, 'My God ... actuarial costs alone were running $450 an hour.'

"I probably wouldn't have done it if I'd known what was involved. It always falls on a couple of people to raise money. That's not an easy thing, and it still gets me down sometimes."

In the sixteen weeks between the end of the trial and October 21, the day Judge Adams's decision was announced, the tumultuous NHL seventy-fifth anniversary season staggered to a merciful conclusion. On every front, the NHL's previously invincible management wall lay in pieces, smashed by the strike, the lawsuit and Eric Lindros's brazen challenge to the draft.

By early summer, Bob Goodenow had begun the work of cleaning up the toxic waste dump left by his predecessor as executive director of the NHLPA. Having finally established an autonomous, viable bargaining agent for players during the strike, Goodenow was faced with the FBI investigation, a new collective-bargaining agreement to negotiate in eighteen months, a lawsuit with the firm that had handled the Association's marketing and the process of building an experienced, capable support staff at the new NHLPA head offices in Toronto.

For his part, Eagleson was fighting a desperate rear-guard action to save his power and reputation, and auditioning lawyers to help him fight the FBI probe. He was also putting assets, such as his Collingwood farm and his cottage on Georgian Bay, up for sale. Hockey Canada, meanwhile, was barraged by demands that Eagleson be asked to step down until the FBI was through its inquiry. Hockey Canada eventually called a press conference just to say that Eagleson would not be asked to step aside; Ian McDonald, the chairman of Hockey Canada, said he was entitled to due process. McDonald, who for years had stonewalled players' attempts to get information on international hockey denied to them by Eagleson, also declared that since people were *suddenly* so hot and bothered about how they did business, the Hockey Canada board of directors had decided to conduct an internal audit and to release some of its financial statements.

This desperate scramble for survival was a dramatic comedown for the bold "hockey czar" who just months before had made a job application to replace Gunther Sabetski as president of the International Ice Hockey Federation (IIHF). "If he decides to step down, and I think I can contribute," Eagleson wrote hopefully in *Power Play*, "then I would consider running for the job he has done so well." But by September 1992, Eagleson was a spent force in the hockey world, just one year after he and Gretzky had led Canada to triumph in the 1991 Canada Cup. Hockey insiders joked that he couldn't get elected to run a Zamboni machine, let alone to the presidency of the IIHF.

Coincidentally, a depressed Wayne Gretzky was said to be contemplating retirement in the fall of 1992 over a serious disc problem in his back that was to sideline the NHL's top attraction for almost four months. His likely successor, meanwhile, was busy trying on Gretzky's crown. At the NHL draft in June 1992, Eric Lindros had finally forced a trade to the Philadelphia Flyers from the Quebec Nordiques, the team that had drafted his rights in June 1991 and for whom he had refused to play.* In so doing, he had defied a monopoly over player talent that had existed for twenty-five years. In the process, Lindros suffered eighteen months of bluster and bitterness from the Nordiques' president Marcel Aubut, Quebec hockey fans and the many NHL apologists in the media. Even Prime Minister Brian Mulroney had weighed in on the side of Lindros reporting to the Nordiques.

Rather than go to Quebec, Lindros played Olympic hockey, world junior hockey and in the Ontario Hockey League in 1991-92. He was unique in the modern hockey world and he knew it; he was willing to pay the price of exile for two years to determine his own fate. Whatever his destiny as a hockey player, Lindros's successful power play shattered the NHL myth that the players—even ones as talented as Lindros or Wayne Gretzky—are disposable, interchangeable pawns. The NHL clearly needs them as much—if not more—than they need the NHL. In an age where the NHL cared only for itself, Lindros returned the affection.

Carl Brewer could have explained that to Lindros before he was drafted, of course. The retired players had learned the hard way that it was foolhardy to expect sentiment from the NHL. Franchise player or journeyman, the pension lawsuit had taught them all that hockey's window of opportunity stays open but a brief time. Not even the superstars get a second chance once that window slams shut.

---

* Having botched the Lindros case from the first, Nordiques owner Marcel Aubut capped his folly by trying to trade Lindros to the Flyers *and* the Rangers on the same day. It took an arbitrator to decide that Philadelphia had obtained his rights.

For that reason, Judge Adams's decision would transcend the money issue for both sides. For the players, a positive decision would be a reprieve, that rare chance to reach back and correct the past. For the NHL, a successful defense of the charges would be the positive punctuation on its star-crossed anniversary season, the final chance for redemption in an otherwise miserable year for the world's most famous hockey league.

Thursday, October 22, 1992, is probably best remembered for Game Five of the first World Series ever played on Canadian soil. TV, radio and newspaper attention was glued on Toronto's SkyDome, where the Jays were playing the Atlanta Braves with a three-games-to-one lead. People seemed to think or talk of nothing else but their beloved baseball team on that sunny, pleasant fall afternoon. Lost amid Toronto's giddy anticipation was the news crossing the Canadian Press wire that Justice George Adams had finally rendered his decision in the case of *Bathgate et al. v. the National Hockey League Pension Society* the day before.

It was two months shy of four years since Carl Brewer had opened his mail to find out about his pension Christmas present from Alan Eagleson and John Ziegler. It should have been a moment to savor, to stand with Sue Foster in the lights of the TV cameras and be recognized for a monumental feat of endurance and skill. Yet Brewer missed the announcement. Having grown tired of waiting for Judge Adams's decision, Brewer and Foster were on holiday in Switzerland on October 22, and they would have to find out the good news from her son via the telephone.

Allan Stanley, meanwhile, was tinkering with his boat on Pigeon Lake near Bobcaygeon, getting it ready for the winter; Gordie Howe, Andy Bathgate and Bobby Hull were on business in the United States; Eddie Shack was at his golf course in Toronto, hooting and hollering as always; Leo Reise was finishing up work for the day at his office.

Mark Zigler was just leaving a meeting at his eighth-floor office at Koskie and Minsky in Toronto. "I was walking down the hall, coming out of a meeting, when I heard a scream down at the other end of the office, people cheering ... somebody told me, 'You've won the NHL case.' It was a wonderful day."

Zigler was anxious to read the decision immediately, but fate intervened. When the 150-page decision was delivered from Judge

Adams's office to Koskie and Minsky, only one side of the page had been copied; Zigler had just half the decision. "I knew we'd won, but I couldn't tell why till much later that day," he says with a laugh.

The players had scored a near-unanimous decision over the NHL, winning on all their claims except the removal of the Pension Society as their trustee. The NHL was being ordered to return the surpluses to the retired players' pensions with interest, a figure estimated at $35-$40 million. And the NHL was ordered to pay the players' legal costs from their own pockets, not out of the assets of the Pension Society.

Zigler phoned as many of the members of the lawsuit as he could find. Colleen Howe was the most animated upon hearing the news. "She was terribly excited," remembers Zigler. Calls were also flooding in from well-wishers and media outlets looking to cover the story. In the process of getting out the news, the complete version of Judge Adams's decision arrived—this time photocopied on both sides of the page.

To escape the din and the phone calls, Zigler eventually had to retreat home to read the full decision. After stopping off briefly for a celebratory drink at Eddie and Norma Shack's home in midtown Toronto, Zigler—like everyone else in Canada that night—settled in to watch Game Five of the World Series. Lonnie Smith of the Atlanta Braves hit a grand slam off Jack Morris in the fifth inning to beat the Jays 7-2, breaking hearts around the country. (The Jays, of course, beat the Braves 3-2 two nights later in Atlanta to become the first Canadian-based baseball team to win the World Series.)

Zigler was not among the crestfallen that night, however. "While I watched the Blue Jays getting bombed on TV, I was reading the 150-page decision," he recalls, adding that he always starts at the back first ... where the decision is printed in legal judgments. "Professionally speaking, this is a very big decision, and it's for a bunch of people I really like."

Justice Adams had decided that in lieu of any prevailing pension legislation in Ontario governing the disposition of surpluses, he would place a great deal of emphasis on the NHL's early undertakings to the players, "made early in the life of the Plan when memories and understandings were fresh." Basing his decision on the Society's non-profit status, the distributions of surplus to players exclusively between 1957-70 and the language of the plan that stated categorically that "the players are the only participants entitled to share in said surplus," Adams rejected the NHL's claim to ownership or control of any surplus monies built up in the NHL pension plan.

"Both the language of the Regulations and the cumulative effect of all the intrinsic evidence clearly establish an exclusive and irrevocable entitlement to all 'excess' funds in the original Plan regardless of source," he wrote.

As well, those original plan regulations did not grant the NHL "a sufficiently express power of revocation of the beneficial interest of the participant players in the fund." In other words, once the work was done by players to earn the money, that money belonged to the players forever. Nothing in the language of either the plan or the trust agreement gave the NHL the right to retroactively amend the rules and reach back to claim surplus monies.

Similarly, under the terms of the NHL Club Pension Plan and Trust created in 1966, Adams found that it qualified as a "defined contribution" scheme, not a "defined benefit" scheme. As such, the players were entitled to whatever pensions could be generated by the annual contributions to the plan, not to fixed benefits at retirement.

The NHL had felt it had a strong case regarding its claim to surpluses after 1969. The linchpin in that conviction had been the letter from Clarence Campbell to the players in which he claimed that, as a result of bargained "deal" with the NHLPA, no surplus funds would be available in the future to supplement pensions. It was this agreement that Cherniak had described as the "bad deal" the retired players wanted to change twenty years later through their "tortured interpretations" of the documents.

Earl Cherniak had argued that the applicants in the suit couldn't produce one NHLPA witness to support their interpretation of the 1969 "deal" between the League and the Players' Association. "But neither did the Respondents [the NHL]," wrote Judge Adams. "The Applicants are not the NHLPA, and it is the Respondents who are asserting a fundamental change was negotiated with the NHLPA despite the absence of any contemporaneous written agreement recording such a crucial accord and affecting so many."

Adams also ruled that Clarence Campbell's controversial letter to the players in 1969 was, at best, one piece of evidence in a confused, contradictory record from that time, a record made more confusing by the lack of pension expertise on Campbell's part and the slapdash nature of bargaining between the NHL and the NHLPA. Justice Adams ruled that the "surplus" referred to in Campbell's letter concerned only those surpluses produced from "premium rate" discounts. Thus, the players were entitled to all the huge surpluses released in 1982 and 1985 that were earned by experience-rate credits.

Further, reasoned Adams, if the NHLPA had agreed to forgo any future surpluses, why had it been allowed to share in the approximately $10 million in 1986 that went to fund the NHL's "Estate Security Plan" for players with four hundred or more games experience?

"Why was the NHLPA not reminded about the 'bad' deal it made in 1969 when it claimed such a sizeable share?" Adams asked tartly. "It seems the Respondents only wish to remind the Applicants of the alleged 'bad' deal."

Adams turned up his tone a notch in describing how the NHL and the NHLPA had negotiated away the rights of the retired players in 1986 when neither side represented them. "Monies to which they were exclusively entitled were used by the NHL and the NHLPA to fund a benefit of little or no value to these former players," he scolded. "The Pension Society had trust, contractual and fiduciary duties to ensure that the beneficial interest of former players in these funds was protected. Obviously, no one else was concerned about these people."

Adams then turned his sights on Alan Eagleson: "Had the NHLPA been representing the Applicants and had it been a trade union subject to duty of fair representation under the Ontario Labour Relations Act, I fail to see how it would have honored its duty in the circumstances. However, the apparent moral shortcomings in the NHLPA's conduct captured by its participation in the November 1988 'Merry Christmas' letter to former players, should not be confused with the Association's then-limited mandate. Moreover, the NHLPA was not a party to these proceedings and, accordingly, it is not appropriate to say more."

The fashion in which the Pension Society fulfilled its trust obligations to the players on the surpluses also drew the ire of Adams. "I am very concerned that the Respondents did not apply for directions beginning some ten years ago," he wrote. "The approval of the PCO [Pension Commission of Ontario] on an application without notice to the Applicants in no way responds to this concern. The Applicants are beneficiaries who have been put to great expense and effort in pursuing this matter against 'their' trustee."

While not removing the NHL Pension Society as trustee, Adams awarded legal and court costs to be taken from the NHL, not the pension plan itself. The surplus payments that he ordered returned to the players' pensions, meanwhile, might double, triple, maybe even quadruple the benefits of some retirees. It was a cause for celebration amongst the retired players and people who love the underdog.

"It's now all worth it," said Norma Shack of the decision she had worked so hard to see. "What a decision ... just a great decision."

"It's a unique decision," Mark Zigler offered. "It's the first time a group of retirees only has won this sort of case. It should send a warning outside of hockey, too."

Carl Brewer, while pleased, was looking at the bigger picture. "It's just the first step," he promised.

The media reaction to Adams's decision was emphatic. "NHL Acted Reprehensibly Toward Former Players," announced *The Toronto Star*. "A court decision that says the NHL knowingly deprived its retired players of millions of dollars which rightfully belonged to them?" asked *Star* columnist Bob McKenzie. "It's the pits, man. And it doesn't really get any lower than this.

"How in heaven's name do you rationalize ex-players, from no-name journeymen to Mr. Hockey himself, having to sue the League to get what belonged to them?... It's sad, really. It typifies everything that is wrong with the sport."

The NHL immediately announced it would appeal the ruling, but it took almost a month before the appeal was placed with the Ontario Court of Appeal. In its appeal, the League requested that Judge Adams's decision be set aside because he erred in his interpretations of the original plan documents and the Pension Plan and Trust documents, allowing the players to claim the surplus funds produced.

Most observers felt that, considering the chaos in the front office of the NHL, the appeal was a maneuver to gain time. With the selection of the first commissioner of the NHL still up in the air,* the League could use the appeal time of up to two years to fight the Bob Dailey/Reggie Leach suit in the United States and to wait out the retired players in Canada. With a number of elderly and sick retired

---

* Former NBA vice president and counsel Gary Bettman was selected in December 1992 in West Palm Beach, Florida, at the NHL Board of Governors meeting.

players needing their pensions immediately, the NHL might produce a settlement by stalling in Appeals Court.

As well, the coalition of players in the "G7" and its supporting groups might finally come apart, allowing the NHL to exploit the rift for a quick and easy settlement. If that's what the NHL was hoping for, it soon got its wish. Rather than fulfil Bob Baun's dream of bringing together players in a joint organization that would help the needy and foster a new awareness of their common concerns, the decision in the lawsuit seemed to leave them as divided as ever. While fundraising events continued for the Professional Hockey Pensioners Association, no one group emerged that could represent itself to the NHL or the NHLPA as the legitimate voice of retired players.

What was needed, suggested some, was a business person other than a retired hockey player, a person with no previous ties to one group or the other, to be appointed the executive director of the PHPA. Only when the retired players set up their own organization with the same businesslike thoroughness as the League and the Players' Association could they operate on an even basis in negotiating a place for retired players in the hockey power structure.

Accelerating the need for such an organization were the strides being made for retired players in the wake of the pension decision. After eighteen months, the retired players finally got the support they'd been looking for from the Ontario government, by being restored to the Board of their pension plan. Treasurer Floyd Laughren, who had assumed responsibility for pensions in Ontario, had written to the NHL Pension Society on behalf of the players. Stating that it no longer seemed in the best interests to continue the NHL's exemption to Ontario law, Laughren asked the Pension Society to ask the participant players whether they wanted to regain their seats on the board of their Pension Society.

When the NHL's response failed to satisfy Laughren, he removed the NHL's exemption. After twenty-five years, players once again were parties to the investment decisions and administration of their pension, however late and after the fact it might be. But from where and from whom would these representatives be drawn?

Events in the United States also dictated that the retired players get organized as soon as possible. After a favorable start, the lawsuit launched in New Jersey by Bob Dailey and Reggie Leach had hit a major roadblock. Appeals Court in that state ruled in favor of the

NHL's motion to dismiss the action; the NHL said that because a decision was to be rendered in Canada on the same grounds, the American action was unnecessary.

Dailey and Leach and Ed Ferren vowed to fight on and considered starting a class action suit. This time, they would be supported by Bob Goodenow and the NHLPA. Until then, however, it meant that if all the money owed to the players' pension was to be returned—including monies not requested in Mark Zigler's suit but listed in Ferren's action—then the organization and research would have to come from the Canadian alumni. It was a tall order for an organization that was bogged down in confusion and disagreements.

To Carl Brewer and Sue Foster, it appeared that there might be plenty more than the approximately $40-million award at stake as well. In the decision, Judge Adams had ruled that the NHL pension plan was a "defined contribution" scheme and that players were entitled to *all* the contributions made on their behalf. Brewer and Foster felt that must also include the monies the NHL had promised to contribute from international hockey. "All of the profits [from international hockey] go into the players' pensions," John Ziegler had said in 1989. "Not only regular pensions but supplementary pensions."

Yet Ken Sawyer, who was quietly bumped from his job as the Pension Society's treasurer and an NHL vice president in the summer of 1993, had admitted in his cross-examination that the NHL did *not* automatically put all its share of that money to the pension plan—a share that totalled more than $7.5 million in 1988. No one knew just how much had been diverted from that purpose, and Mark Zigler had not included the NHL's missing international-hockey contributions as part of the damages. Brewer and Foster wanted the NHL held to the undertaking made by its president.

In the plan's early documents, the NHL had also undertaken to pay for the administrative costs of the pension plan out of the revenues of the All-Star Games. Yet to Brewer and Foster, annual statements from the Pension Society appear to indicate that the League had the used plan's assets to pay the administrative costs of running the Pension Society. And where were the financial statements from the All-Star Game, the profitable event that owners had said would fund the pension plan? Had the All-Star monies been contributed as promised? Brewer and Foster asked. The amounts reached into the millions as well.

There were also the millions from international hockey profits that had not been needed for the NHL Pension Society and had instead been squirrelled away into the NHLPA "Bonus Pension Pool." Despite its name, this so-called pension fund was never certified as a true pension plan by the Ontario Pension Commission and instead functioned as an escrow or trust fund administered by Alan Eagleson and the NHLPA.

It was from these funds that Eagleson had made mortgage loans to his law partner, friends and business associates without the approval of the NHLPA board. (Hamilton lawyer Bill Dermody had examined only some of these loans at the West Palm Beach showdown in 1989.) Shocked players learned in 1993 from *The Lawrence Eagle-Tribune* in Massachusetts and CBC TV in Toronto that Eagleson had made more mortgage loans from these funds, funds set aside "for retirement benefits," according to Eagleson. These additional loans were also to close personal and business contacts, but the players' money had been jeopardized when one mortgage went power of sale and another had needed five years and numerous extensions to pay off the investment.

The mortgages reviewed by Dermody were awarded without proper searches of the investors, credit histories, certified appraisals and environmental studies. Banking and investment experts called them imprudent and extremely risky. Brewer and Foster sought a ruling from the Pension Commission of Ontario on whether this escrow fund described as a supplementary pension by Ziegler and Eagleson constituted a true pension fund. Should the "Bonus Pension Pool" be ruled a true pension plan, then Eagleson's investment of and administration of the funds was in violation of the Ontario Pension Reform Act of 1982 and 1987, and players might be entitled to seek compensation for its handling in a civil suit.

Finally, Brewer and Foster wanted to know what had happened to the contributions lost in 1969 when the NHL took over financing of the pension plan. The estimates were that contributions per man dropped by about $1,200 a year after 1969. And yet, the players had all been led to believe that there had been no decrease in the money put aside each year for their pensions. If Justice Adams was right, and the players were entitled to *all* contributions made on their behalf, then these lost revenues would amount to many more millions for players. It was a daunting thought.

While Brewer and Foster pursued their quest, the Toronto Maple Leafs' gallant—but futile—attempt at their first Stanley Cup in 26 years dominated the hockey headlines in Toronto in the winter and spring of 1993. Not since Tim Horton, Allan Stanley, Bob Baun and their teammates had shocked Montreal in 1967 had a Maple Leaf team come so close to winning the Cup. Before their run ended, the 1993 Leafs played later into a season than any club in Toronto team history. And while the Leafs playing past Victoria Day owed more to the NHL's endless playoff schedule than to the team's proficiency, coach Pat Burns' workmanlike team reminded many of Punch Imlach's blue-collar boys of the 1960s.

The nostalgia and longing created by that comparison to Imlach's clubs created a time warp in Toronto, one lovingly embraced by those elements of the city immune to Blue Jays fever, and thus unfulfilled for over a quarter century. Bumper stickers and silly newspaper campaigns whipped up the city with entreaties to glories past. Stanley, Johnny Bower and Mike Walton fronted newspaper columns devoted to playoff efforts of the Leafs' defense, goaltending and forwards. Twice, the city erupted in enthusiastic parties when the Leafs won playoff series in the seventh game. Blue and white was everywhere; it was all right to be a Maple Leaf fan again.

Critics insisted that the fervor and excitement created by the 1993 Leafs proved that Toronto was still a hockey town at heart. In fact, the 1993 success of the Maple Leafs revealed a deeper truth about Hogtown, a schism in the municipal mosaic. The Blue Jay and Maple Leaf audiences had become very separate communities, tribes living parallel lives within the same city.

Media types puzzled over the fact that while the Maple Leafs were playing uptown to a full house at the Gardens, down by the lake the SkyDome was packed on the same night for the Blue Jays. Toronto sports fans were a homogeneous, heterosexual monolith, were they not? No one in the Toronto press corps—which microscopically studied every other aspect of Leaf mania—ever realized that there were now different audiences within the sports crowd in Toronto, much as there are within movie audiences.

The Blue Jays crowd was arriviste, corporate, impeccably attired and to a considerable extent female. They were docile and prone to attention lapses unless the scoreboard exploded with fireworks or the pathetic mascot B. J. Bird essayed one of his lame routines. The Leafs crowd, by comparison, was blue-collar, old Toronto, very male and very receptive to the racist, paranoid blandishments of Don Cherry on TV. In the beer business, these Leafs fans are called "sweats."

The Leafs' progress through the playoffs would have gladdened Conn Smythe's heart. Toronto first dispatched a more powerful and talented Detroit team by observing hockey tenets Smythe had established over 60 years before. Burns outcoached a hapless Bryan Murray, Toronto got better goaltending and the Leafs simply outworked the talented but undisciplined Red Wings in seven games. (The tying goal in Game Seven came with less than two minutes to play, and the winner in overtime on Detroit ice, a poetic finish.)

The Leafs reprised the formula against a gritty St. Louis club, winning at home in Game Seven. Then, with their first berth in a Stanley Cup final in 26 years beckoning, the Leafs failed in two attempts to eliminate a revived Wayne Gretzky and the Los Angeles Kings. After six gruelling, often brutal games with Toronto, Gretzky put his team into its first final series ever by scoring a hat trick in a dramatic 5-4 win in Toronto. The tank had run empty for the plucky, determined Leafs, an ageing team that would need to retool before scaling such a height again. They had fallen short of the Maple Leafs' twelfth Cup, but they had given hockey a renaissance in Toronto.

There was no renaissance for Alan Eagleson. While the four-year FBI probe and the Grand Jury investigation by the U.S. Justice Department wound up its work, Carl Brewer could only lament what might have been. "Alan Eagleson is a brilliant man," reflected Brewer. "Would that he had directed his full talents towards improving the welfare of the players he represented and fighting for their rights ..."

American investigations were due to wind up in the fall of 1993; the RCMP, which claimed to be conducting its own investigation, said it was not yet prepared to report on its findings. And as the summer of 1993 drew to a close, there was also no word from the Law Society of Upper Canada on when it would conclude its investigation, which had begun in January of 1990.

For Carl Brewer and Sue Foster and Rich Winter, these investigations—whatever their result—were a vindication of years spent in the hockey wilderness. Their suspicions and research had produced a search for truth in the hockey business that equalled any Stanley Cup triumph. And while their accomplishments might not win them a place in the Hockey Hall of Fame with such revered figures as Alan Eagleson and John Ziegler, their place in hockey's history was assured.

LEST WE FORGET

George Gross
The Toronto Telegram

Toronto, Monday April 27, 1964; Four crippled Maple Leafs beat off pain and the Red Wings to help bring the Stanley Cup to Toronto for the third year in a row.

A hard-skating Leaf team whitewashed Detroit 4-0 before 14,561 emotional fans at Maple Leaf Gardens Saturday night to earn a bonus of $4,000 per player.

–George Armstrong played with a frozen shoulder injury

–Red Kelly with damaged knee ligaments

–Bobby Baun with a fractured fibula

–Carl Brewer with separated ribs

Armstrong's injury was the best kept secret. The Leaf captain explained it this way: "I played with a bad shoulder against the Canadiens in the semifinal and had to have it strapped. I took the straps off for the Red Wing series but in the fifth game, Marcel Pronovost hit me pretty good.

"Tonight in the shooting warm-up, it felt alright on the forehand, but it was painful when I tried backhand shots. So I asked the doctor to freeze it."

Red Kelly, who could barely limp into the car before being driven to the Gardens, had his knee frozen. He came up with a solid performance and added to scoring a goal, he successfully shadowed Wings' Gordie Howe.

Baun received three needles before and during the game to deaden the pain in his lower right leg. Doctors are convinced he has a broken fibula, but Baun still refuses to have it X–rayed until today. "I didn't want to miss Mr. Smythe's victory party last night."

FROZEN RIBS

Brewer, who played the finals with separated ribs and received as many as 20 injections in each game to freeze his side, said after the victory, "This was an easy night. I only needed eight needles."

The hurt clutch-players' desire to win the Cup defeated adversity and shot esprit de corps through the team.

From Johnny Bower in goal to bouncing Billy Harris, the whole club's effort was indeed dedicated. "The veterans won it for us," said a jubilant Harris after the game. "The Red Wings used their young- sters who gave it all they had. Our veterans like Bower, Kelly, Stan- ley, Horton, Armstrong gave all they had too. The fact they matched the youngsters and had the edge in experience won the game for us."

Andy Bathgate, playing in his first Stanley Cup final, started the victory tide rolling for the Leafs. He picked up the puck that bounced off Albert Langlois, darted in and beat Terry Sawchuk and scored at 3.04 of the first period.

Leafs had several other scoring opportunities but Sawchuk was great again. He foiled Dave Keon, Kelly, Ron Stewart, Gerry Ehman with remarkable saves and kept Wings in the game for two periods.

But Johnny Bower was brilliant. He made the key save in the game early in the third period, when he turned away a searing drive hot off the stick of Alex Delvecchio.

On the next move Harris passed the puck to Keon and the Leaf centre made it 2-0 with a slapshot to the far corner.

A pale Red Kelly increased the lead to 3-0, 87 seconds later with a backhander on a pass from Frank Mahovlich. The Big M also set up Armstrong's goal at 15.26.

BEST GAME

There were few weak links in the Leafs machinery. Mahovlich played his finest game of the series and came close to scoring a couple of goals. Gerry Ehman did a working-man's job on the line with Pulford and Stewart. So did Harris and Eddie Shack.

But the Red Wings never gave up. They hustled until the final whistle—tired, sore but inspired. Their skating wasn't as effective as in previous games—playoff pressure seemed to wear down their scoring punch.

Howe, who averaged over 30 minutes per game throughout the series, was showing fatigue. So were Normie Ullman and Bill Gadsby. The younger ones were trying but couldn't cope with experience.

The Cinderella club lost to a better team on the night's performance. But the Wings are strong. They'll probably be around next year come Stanley Cup time.

SLAPSHOTS

It was Eddie Litzenberger's fourth consecutive Stanley Cup, one with Chicago and the last three with Leafs ... It was a first for Gerry Ehman, Andy Bathgate and Don McKenney.... Eddie Shack was cut on the side of the head by a puck, and Billy Harris was nicked for three stitches on the bridge of his nose.... Allan Stanley insists he'll be back at training camp next fall, but if he gets lucky with 36 claims he staked last summer in the Timmins boom area, he might contemplate hanging up the runners.... Seven of the Red Wings wore good luck charms in their uniforms.... Prime Minister Lester Pearson won a 25-cent bet from a Montreal writer who challenged him to pick the winner.

A

COMPARATIVE PENSIONS

In a comparative study of the NHL Pension Plan's "defined benefit" scheme versus a money-purchase plan begun the same year and using the same contributions from players and the NHL,* the results prove shocking. Sample players who began either ten- or fifteen-year careers in 1947, 1952 and 1957 at the age of twenty-one would have improved the annual pensions they have now by anywhere from three times up to nine times as much.

Two conservative methods of investment were used in the study. One method used five-year Guaranteed Investment Certificates as investments for the contributions made on behalf of players. The other proposed a fixed-income strategy consisting of 50 percent federal long bonds, 25 percent conventional mortgages and 25 percent equities. The investment return statistics were based on figures from 1947 to 1991 issued by the Canadian Institute of Actuaries.

BASED ON YEARLY AMOUNTS

10-year career starts:	1947	1952	1957
NHL Plan at 45	$900	$1,350	$2,160
GIC Plan at 45	$2,960	$4,449	$10,325
Fixed Income at 45	$3,517	$4,649	$9,946
NHL Plan at 55	$1,575	$2,363	$3,780
GIC Plan at 55	$10,276	$14,823	$26,520
Fixed Income at 55	$11,650	$18,259	$28,546

15-year career starts:	1947	1952	1957
NHL Plan at 45	$1,800	$2,610	$3,660
GIC Plan at 45	$4,465	$6,959	$12,577
Fixed Income at 45	$5,113	$6,929	$12,053
NHL Plan at 55	$3,150	$4,568	$6,405
GIC Plan at 55	$15,499	$23,184	$32,304
Fixed Income at 55	$16,937	$27,214	$34,592

---

* While the results have a margin of error of five percent, the ratio of the figures for the NHL's "real" pensions versus what they might have gained in even a modestly invested plan show that the NHL Pension Society was hardly the "great boon to the players of the League for many years to come," as Clarence Campbell described it. It was closer to a swindle.

B

NHL'S ESTATE SECURITY PLAN

This study reflects the real value of the NHL's Estate Security Plan negotiated in the 1986 collective-bargaining agreement for players who play 400 or more NHL games. This plan promised to provide $250,000 in pension benefits at age fifty-five; many players mistakenly believed that the benefits would be paid in a lump sum. But the Estate Security Plan is to be paid in monthly amounts to the player via an annuity. And the $250,000 figure is not guaranteed.

The study shows the monthly return at age fifty-five for a player who reached the 400-game mark between twenty-seven and thirty years of age, the average age players qualify for that service. The NHL Estate Security Plan assumes a ten percent rate of interest when it promised the $250,000 figure, although interest rates have been well below that figure since the end of the 1980s.

The study also shows the effects of inflation on this bonus before these players reach fifty-five years of age. There are no provisions in the NHL Estate Security Plan for inflation or cost of living. While inflation averaged 6.36 percent between 1967 and 1991, we are using more conservative rates of 4 and 5 percent. The terms given are for a Life Policy with a ten-year guarantee, the same as the NHL Pension Plan and Trust.

	Monthly Amount at Age 55 from $250,000	Real Amount 4% Inflation	Real Amount 5% Inflation
Age 27	$1,953.16	$651.34	$498.23
Age 28	$1,953.16	$712.55	$523.15
Age 29	$1,953.16	$704.48	$549.31
Age 30	$1,953.16	$732.67	$576.77

C

NHL PLAYERS' PENSIONS

(AS OF JANUARY 1, 1992)

This chart was prepared by the *Lawrence Eagle-Tribune* of Lawrence, Massachusetts. It lists annual pensions for former NHL players; the figures were supplied by the players. (The NHL would not supply pension figures.) They indicate how much they were collecting, or in the case of players who had yet to take their pensions, how much they were entitled to at age forty-five. Pensions are paid in Canadian dollars, except for some seasons prior to 1957.

	Years	Games	Annual Pension
Lou Angotti	10	718	$ 6,000
Don Awrey	16	1,050	$13,983
Ralph Backstrom	17	1,148	$10,800
Andy Bathgate*	18	1,111	$10,400
Jean Béliveau*	20	1,287	$12,000
Red Berenson	17	1,062	$ 7,500
Carl Brewer	12	676	$13,000
John Bucyk*	23	1,664	$13,200
Wayne Cashman	17	1,712	$13,200
Yvan Cournoyer*	16	1,115	$11,000
Gary Doak	16	867	$13,000

	Years	Games	Annual Pension
Jim Dorey	4	243	$ 5,400
Phil Esposito*	18	1,412	$10,800
Fern Flaman*	17	973	$ 5,200
Dave Forbes	6	408	$10,800
Phil Goyette	16	1,035	$ 9,500
Billy Harris	12	820	$ 8,300
Dennis Hextall	12	706	$ 6,800
Ken Hodge	13	978	$10,000
Réjean Houle	11	725	$ 9,800
Gordie Howe*	26	1,924	$13,000
Bobby Hull*	16	1,182	$10,500
Don Marcotte	15	1,000	$11,000
Johnny McKenzie	13	760	$10,000
Bobby Miller	6	440	$ 4,800
Doug Mohns	22	1,484	$12,000
Dickie Moore*	14	854	$ 6,000
Bobby Orr*	12	731˙	$ 8,400
Brad Park*	17	1,274	$13,000
Jean Ratelle*	21	1,404	$12,924
Rocket Richard*	18	1,111	$ 7,200
Milt Schmidt*	16	864	$ 5,800
Eddie Shack	17	1,121	$ 9,000
Tod Sloan	13	892	$ 4,716
Dallas Smith	16	976	$ 7,574
Rick Smith	10	764	$ 9,742
Allan Stanley *	21	1,353	$12,000
Marc Tardif	8	579	$ 8,400
Harry Watson*	14	871	$ 4,800

* Hall of Fame member

D

ALAN EAGLESON'S EXPENSES

A joint examination by CBC TV and the *Lawrence Eagle-Tribune* in 1993, revealed the full picture of Eagleson's expenses and salary during the fiscal years 1987, 1988 and 1989. Because Eagleson had previously refused to release such information on the advice of his counsel, it was the first time that anyone—including the NHLPA membership—had seen such a detailed study of how NHLPA funds were spent.

Eagleson told CBC TV in 1991, "Everybody who knows me knows I'm careful with not only my own money but my clients' money and association money. I'm not a spendthrift, and that accusation bothered me as much as anything else ..." But when Ed Garvey sought to examine Eagleson's spending in 1989, he noted, "Any player who has seen Alan at international events can confirm that Alan does, indeed, go first class ... There are no limits on his travel expenses and he has refused to allow us to examine his expense record."

But few players saw the draft Price Waterhouse report that was produced in 1989 as a result of Garvey's challenge. Its contents only received a full airing almost four years later. That report and other NHLPA documents revealed that while the NHLPA revenue from dues, licensing and interest in the years 1987–89 totalled $4.011 million, $1.85 million of that figure was attributable to Eagleson's fees as executive director and spending attributable to him. The following are some details of the 1987–89 spending:

PAYMENTS TO EAGLESON FIRMS:

$730,384   to Eagleson, Ungerman in fees for Eagleson's services as NHLPA executive director

$ 24,000   to Jailson Holdings, an Eagleson family company, for NHLPA office rental

$ 15,000   to Rae-Con, whose president is Mrs. Alan Eagleson, for renovation and moving expenses

REIMBURSEMENTS TO EAGLESON:

$ 52,342   for promotions, gifts, awards

$ 30,778   for special meetings

$ 24,584   for international hockey expenses

$ 32,648   for automobile lease payments

OTHER EXPENSES:

$238,940   for airline tickets on NHLPA business

$ 60,104   in charitable donations

$ 36,917   in gifts

$ 21,404   for social, golf and tennis club memberships

$183,664   for hotels

$ 24,000   for an apartment in London, England

$ 43,370   for the promotion of the Rendezvous '87 series between NHL and USSR teams

BIBLIOGRAPHY

I had access to a number of helpful sources and published works in writing this book. In particular, I wish to thank Lori Horton for supplying a wealth of programs, newspapers and materials that made the era come alive. As well, the staff at the Government of Ontario Archives was invaluable. Mark Zigler of Koskie and Minsky kindly made the trial transcripts and documents available, as well as Judge Adams' judgement. Russ Conway shared his extensive and valuable research with me, as did David Cruise and Alison Griffiths. Rich Winter offered his heroic volumes of correspondence and documents of the period from 1986 to the present. And Hockey Canada supplied me with their financial statements for the Canada Cup and Team Canada.

Among the books consulted or used in research for this project were the following:

Clayton, Deidra. *"Eagle": The Life and Times of R. Alan Eagleson.* Toronto: Lester & Orpen Dennys, 1982.

Cruise, David, and Alison Griffiths. *Net Worth.* Toronto: Viking, 1991.

Diamond, Dan, ed. *The Official National Hockey League Stanley Cup Centennial Book.* Toronto: McClelland & Stewart, 1992.

Diamond, Dan, and Charles Wilkins. *Hockey, The Illustrated History.* Revised ed. Toronto: Doubleday, 1989.

Dryden, Ken. *The Game*. Toronto: Macmillan of Canada, 1983.

Eagleson, R. Alan, with Scott Young. *Power Play*. Toronto: McClelland & Stewart, 1991.

Fischler, Stan, and George Hall (research ed.). *Hockey's 100: A Personal Ranking of the Best Players in Hockey History*. Toronto: Stoddart, 1984.

Henderson, Paul, with Mike Leone. *Shooting for Glory*. Toronto: Stoddart, 1992.

Houston, William. *Maple Leaf Blues*. Toronto: McClelland & Stewart, 1990.

Howe, Colleen and Gordie, and Charles Wilkins. *After the Applause*. Toronto: McClelland & Stewart, 1989.

Imlach, Punch, with Scott Young. *Hockey Is A Battle*. Toronto: Macmillan, 1969.

Imlach, Punch, with Scott Young. *Heaven and Hell In the NHL*. Toronto: McClelland & Stewart, 1982.

Irvin, Dick. *The Habs: An Oral History of the Montreal Canadiens. 1940–1980*. Toronto: McClelland & Stewart, 1992.

Jenish, D'Arcy. *The Stanley Cup: A Hundred Years of Hockey at Its Best*. Toronto: McClelland & Stewart, 1992.

Miller, Marvin. *A Whole Different Ball Game*. New York: Birch Lane Press, 1991.

Smythe, Conn, with Scott Young. *If You Can't Beat 'Em In The Alley*. Toronto: McClelland & Stewart, 1981.

Young, Scott. *The Leafs I Knew*. Toronto: Ryerson Press, 1966.

INDEX